RUSSIAN POPULISM

THE BLOOMSBURY HISTORY OF MODERN RUSSIA SERIES

Series Editors: Jonathan D. Smele (Queen Mary, University of London, UK) and Michael Melancon (Auburn University, USA)

This ambitious and unique series offers readers the latest views on aspects of the modern history of what has been and remains one of the most powerful and important countries in the world. In a series of books aimed at students, leading academics and experts from across the world portray, in a thematic manner, a broad variety of aspects of the Russian experience, over extended periods of time, from the reign of Peter the Great in the early eighteenth century to the Putin era at the beginning of the twenty-first.

Published:

PEASANTS IN RUSSIA FROM SERFDOM TO STALIN:
ACCOMMODATION, SURVIVAL, RESISTANCE
by Boris B. Gorshkov (2018)

CRIME AND PUNISHMENT IN RUSSIA: A COMPARATIVE HISTORY
FROM PETER THE GREAT TO VLADIMIR PUTIN
by Jonathan Daly (2018)

MARX AND RUSSIA: THE FATE OF A DOCTRINE
by James D. White (2018)

A MODERN HISTORY OF RUSSIAN CHILDHOOD
by Elizabeth White (2020)

MARRIAGE, HOUSEHOLD AND HOME IN MODERN RUSSIA:
FROM PETER THE GREAT TO VLADIMIR PUTIN
by Barbara Alpern Engel (2021)

A HISTORY OF EDUCATION IN MODERN RUSSIA
by Wayne Dowler (2021)

RUSSIAN POPULISM: A HISTORY
by Christopher Ely (2022)

Forthcoming:

THE RUSSIAN INTELLIGENTSIA
by Christopher Read (2022)

THE HISTORY OF THE RUSSIAN WORKER: LIFE AND CHANGE
FROM PETER THE GREAT TO VLADIMIR PUTIN
by Alice Pate (2022)

THE RUSSIAN MILITARY AND THE CREATION OF EMPIRE
by John Steinberg (2022)

GENDER IN MODERN RUSSIA
by Aaron B. Retish (2022)

RUSSIAN POPULISM

A HISTORY

Christopher Ely

BLOOMSBURY ACADEMIC

LONDON • NEW YORK • OXFORD • NEW DELHI • SYDNEY

BLOOMSBURY ACADEMIC
Bloomsbury Publishing Plc
50 Bedford Square, London, WC1B 3DP, UK
1385 Broadway, New York, NY 10018, USA
29 Earlsfort Terrace, Dublin 2, Ireland

BLOOMSBURY, BLOOMSBURY ACADEMIC and the Diana logo are
trademarks of Bloomsbury Publishing Plc

First published in Great Britain 2022

Series design by Sandra Friesen
Cover image © Life Pictures/Getty Images

A catalogue record for this book is available from the British Library.

Library of Congress Cataloging-in-Publication Data
Names: Ely, Christopher David, 1963– author.
Title: Russian populism : a history / Christopher Ely.
Description: London ; New York : Bloomsbury Academic, 2022. | Series: The Bloomsbury history
of modern Russia series | Includes bibliographical references and index.|
Identifiers: LCCN 2021036295 (print) | LCCN 2021036296 (ebook) |
ISBN 9781350095540 (paperback) | ISBN 9781350095533 (hardback) |
ISBN 9781350095557 (pdf) | ISBN 9781350095564 (ebook)
Subjects: LCSH: Russia–Intellectual life–1801–1917. | Russia–Politics and government–1894-1917. |
Populism–Russia–History–19th century. | Radicalism–Russia–History–19th century. |
Peasants–Russia–History–19th century. | Populism in literature.
Classification: LCC DK189.2 .E46 2022 (print) | LCC DK189.2 (ebook) | DDC 947/.07—dc23
LC record available at https://lccn.loc.gov/2021036295
LC ebook record available at https://lccn.loc.gov/2021036296.

ISBN: HB: 978-1-3500-9553-3
        PB: 978-1-3500-9554-0
        ePDF: 978-1-3500-9555-7
        eBook: 978-1-3500-9556-4

Typeset by RefineCatch Limited, Bungay, Suffolk
Printed and bound in Great Britain

To find out more about our authors and books visit www.bloomsbury.com
and sign up for our newsletters.

CONTENTS

Contents

ILLUSTRATIONS

PREFACE

In the late 1960s Richard Wortman described Russian populism as a familiar topic often covered by historians of Russia. For a variety of reasons that is no longer the case. The generation of historians of Imperial Russia who came of age around the time that the Soviet Union was drawing to an end felt intellectually hemmed in by what they considered the previous generations' fascination with revolutionary politics and ideology to the exclusion of other important topics. They struck out boldly in many new directions. As a result, at the same time the opening of archives was expanding our knowledge of the Soviet period, a wealth of new interests and perspectives was transforming the history of Muscovite and Imperial Russia, opening up a broader and deeper understanding of the time before the Revolution.

But a change in what historians choose to write about cannot, of course, alter what happened in the past. That radicalism which led to the Revolution in 1917 was not an anomaly; it was very much intertwined with the whole history of late-Imperial Russia. In particular it was part of that great struggle to bring the Russian Empire one way or another into alignment with the wealthier, more technologically advanced, and more democratic parts of Europe. The abolition of serfdom raised the most fundamental questions of all. Now that the peasants—the vast majority of the Russian population—had become fellow citizens: Who were they? How would they join together with the rest of society? What would that society look like once some kind of merger had taken place? These concerns played a central role in the journalism, the ideological debates, the political activism, and even the literature and art of late-Imperial Russia. This book takes a fresh look at these questions, less with an interest in how they stimulated revolution and more for what they meant to the people who took them up in their own prerevolutionary context.

My purpose here is a pedagogical one. Having taught the history of Imperial Russia now for more than a quarter century, I have come to recognize just how alien that history can be to my contemporaries. To accurately grasp the nature of Imperial Russia's social structures, economics, politics, culture, and ideas requires a great deal of background preparation and assumption-breaking. I have found certain texts particularly useful as teaching tools to help students expand their understanding, but I have long hoped to find a general and broad introduction to the history and thought of Russian populism. A great wealth of material on Russian populism exists on library bookshelves, and indeed on the shelves of my own office, but for undergraduates some of it is lengthy, some out of print, some overly technical or specialized. Not having found a relatively brief but comprehensive introduction to the topic, that is what I have tried to provide here. Whatever the strengths and weaknesses of the book, my sole aim in writing it has been to produce an accessible overview for the use of students and those unfamiliar with the history of Imperial Russia. This book defines Russian populism in very broad terms. It goes back as far as the late eighteenth century and extends into the first half of the twentieth century, and it runs roughshod over any narrow definition of *narodnichestvo* [populism], accepting populism as a broad enough phenomenon to include room for all those members of the intelligentsia fascinated by the *narod* [people], from conservative Slavophiles to radical socialists.

Not only is the basic structure of Russian history opaque to the uninitiated, but even the language causes difficulty. It is the rare American student who can remember Russian names, much less pronounce them correctly. For this reason I have done what I could to make the text as accessible as possible. In transliterating names I've freely accepted Anglicisms that did not seem egregious, I have only used Russian words when they seem entirely unavoidable, but those that are untranslated are defined in the text and can be found in the glossary at the end of the book. I have kept the footnotes to a minimum, and I have added illustrations as well as longer quotes in boxes as a sort of "verbal illustration" of the book's arguments. Many of these quotes have been taken from previous English translations, not for the sake of ease but as a nod of gratitude to those who have done much of the (English language) research on which the book rests. I have also included suggestions for further reading in English, which, again, can be found at the back of the book. This book does not seek to break any new ground in our understanding of Russian populism. If anything it is an attempt to convey to undergraduate readers the fascination I myself developed about the populist movement as a student. If it accomplishes that goal to any extent, it will have hit the mark I've aimed at. Unfortunately, writing a textbook is, as one textbook writer recently put it, "an exercise in gross over-simplification." The abundance and complexity of the materials I have tried to distill into accessible form here necessitates a great loss of subtlety, not to mention a great opportunity for mistakes and inaccuracies. For those that occur, I take full responsibility. For helping me to minimize them as far as I could, I would like to acknowledge the invaluable support of Cinda Ely, Steven Frank, Rebecca Friedman, Andrew Gentes, Rachel Luria, Susan McCaffrey, John Randolph, Andreas Schonle, Christopher Strain, and Marc Viscovi. For editorial assistance my thanks go to Rhodri Mogford, Laura Reeves, and Sue Littleford. I am indebted to Michael Melancon for welcoming me to this project and helping me shape it, and my biggest debt of thanks goes to Madeleine Ely for sharing all my ups and downs in the process of research and writing.

CHAPTER 1
INTRODUCTION: TOWARD A DEFINITION OF RUSSIAN POPULISM

In the summer of 1907, Lev Zilberberg awaited execution at the Peter and Paul Fortress in Imperial Russia's capital city, Saint Petersburg. Zilberberg had been sentenced to death for taking part in the assassination of a high-ranking official in the government of Tsar Nicholas II. The 26-year-old prisoner, from a middle-class Jewish family, was married with a young daughter, and the letters he wrote home to his mother show his anguished concern for the loved ones he would be leaving behind. Zilberberg had been studying math and physics at Moscow University until 1902 when he was expelled and sentenced to Siberian exile for participating in a student demonstration. Not long after his return, he joined the "combat organization" of the Socialist Revolutionary Party. Together with other members of this underground terrorist squad, he took part in violent acts, including assassination attempts, in the hope of inciting a revolution that would overthrow the Tsarist autocracy. Sharing stories with his fellow inmates, as one of them recalled, Zilberberg described one of the happiest moments he had experienced during his two years underground:

> with childlike delight he told the story of a cab driver he worked with at the livery stable . . . "I look at you from afar," said the cabbie, "and it seems you are a gentleman, but then when I speak to you and look in your eyes I see that you are one of our own." He was deeply touched by the peasant's recognition of him as a brother.[1]

Alongside his family, his studies and his terrorist activities, one of the most indelible impressions Zilberberg retained on the eve of his execution was this peasant driver's appreciation of him as an equal member of the working class.

Why did Zilberberg find the cab driver's recognition so gratifying? The answer to this question is inseparable from the very reasons Zilberberg became an assassin in the first place. Both his engagement in political violence and his longing for the respect and camaraderie of the lower classes had their roots in the social and economic history of Imperial Russia. Although serfdom had been abolished in 1861, its impact on Russian society still remained palpable in 1907. Tantamount to slavery, the institution of serfdom had helped transform large parts of the Russian Empire into a starkly divided society, split between a majority population of poor rural laborers (some 80–90 percent of the population, more than half of them bonded serfs before 1861) and a small, wealthy, and educated noble elite, augmented by increasing numbers of educated urbanites from other social classes. Even by the early twentieth century the peasantry was still mostly illiterate, with few prospects for economic advancement, while the privileged and educated classes inhabited a largely separate realm, a multiethnic, cosmopolitan, Europeanized culture centered in Russia's large cities, and performing much of the work that held together the geographically enormous and ethnically diverse Russian Empire. Because of the way the state parceled out land and "souls" (serfs) as gentry property, landowners quite often had little personal connection to the region and to the people they owned. Though they lived in the same country, the educated elite and the working poor remained distant enough that each had difficulty comprehending the needs, desires, and worldviews of the other. The abolition of serfdom ended direct gentry control of estate peasants. It did not immediately alter conditions of social and cultural difference, but it began the process of renegotiation that is a central concern of this book.

If by 1907 Imperial Russia's socioeconomic landscape had grown increasingly layered and complex, awareness of the profound separations and built-in inequalities in Russian society was still strong enough among the educated classes to inspire many of them to find a way to "right the wrongs of history" in an effort to make life more just and equitable for all Russians. Zilberberg's satisfaction that a man from a peasant family could see him as a brother arose from a characteristically desperate desire to knit back together Russia's deep social divisions. It was that same impassioned wish that encouraged many Russians from the educated classes to believe their only hope lay in a revolutionary transformation of their country. Under the influence of these revolutionary aspirations, an act as terrible as murder could be carried out by a well-meaning father, husband, and son like Zilberberg. Violent acts, and literal self-sacrifice, on the part of someone like Zilberberg are a good place to begin this inquiry into Russian populism, for Zilberberg's longing to make Russia more united and equal was shared by all those who contributed to the populist movement.

What was Russian populism? Unfortunately no simple definition—no matter how nuanced and multifaceted—could capture the rich, variegated, long-lasting, self-contradictory, and endlessly disputed nature of this phenomenon, a phenomenon that manifested itself at times as a political movement, at times as an articulated ideology, at times as a form of artistic expression, and at times as little more than a cast of thought. That complexity did not, however, prevent populist values and ideas from exerting a profound influence on Russia's educated classes from the mid-nineteenth century to the 1917 Revolution and beyond. Since the aim of this book is to provide a basic introduction to Russian populism, even for those who are entirely unfamiliar with the concept, we will start with the fundamentals and build up a more complete picture in everything that follows. To begin with, all words translated from Russian as "populism" or "populist" contain the root word *narod*. *Narod* means "people." It can refer to any nationality or ethnicity as a whole, i.e., "a people," but by the middle of the nineteenth century it carried the strong implication of "the common people" or "ordinary folk," as opposed to social elites. The contrasting term for these elites was *obshchestvo*, meaning "educated society" or "polite society." Since neither *narod* nor *obshchestvo* has a direct English counterpart, this book will usually refer to them in the original Russian. A member of the *narod* could, like Zilberberg's fellow cab driver, live in the city, but the majority of the *narod* consisted of (mostly) poor, (mostly) illiterate rural farmers, most of whom were legally designated as members of the peasant estate.

By and large, historians would agree on some basic specifics about the populist movement. That populism reached its first full flowering in the latter half of the nineteenth century, for instance, is not a matter of dispute. Most historians would also agree that populism reached the apogee of its influence during the reign of Alexander II (1855–81), even though that influence continued for decades afterwards. It is also fully accepted that while Russian populism focused its interest on the *narod*, it was almost entirely a product and practice of *obshchestvo*. In the widest sense of the term, populism refers to the specific worldview espoused by members of *obshchestvo* that encapsulates respect for and devotion to the *narod*, and that devotion included a variety of hopes and expectations for the positive impact the *narod* would exert on Russia's future development. For the populists, the prototypical Russian, the self-evident embodiment of Russian identity, was the *muzhik*—a word for peasant literally meaning "small man"—who had retained the genuine Russian characteristics they had lost as *obshchestvo* adopted European ways, especially since the early eighteenth century.

After these essential points we find less consensus for the simple reason that, as Oliver Radkey has remarked, "populism was less an ideology than a state of mind."[2] As such it can't be explained as either a consistent set of principles or a coherent movement. The nouns *narodnichestvo* [populism] and *narodnik* [populist] are usually used to designate a collection of revolutionary ideologies and activism that lasted into the early Soviet period. However, while these terms originally applied to certain groups of radical socialists in the late nineteenth century, it has become common practice to use the term "populist" to describe a more general phenomenon of elite esteem for the peasantry in expressions like "populist art" or "the populist age." Throughout this book I intentionally use the term "populism" broadly, not as a name for any special doctrine or principle but as a means of encapsulating a general pattern of hopes and ideas that characterized the interests as well as anxieties of much of late-Imperial Russian educated society.[3]

In passing we should note that there is a profound discrepancy between today's definition of the word "populism," so familiar in the contemporary press, and the nineteenth-century Russian version. In the Russian language, the two phenomena have different names. For modern populism—the kind that Vladimir Putin often practices—Russian draws its word from the same Latin root that we do: literally *populizm* in Cyrillic letters. This version of "populism," in Russian and other languages, refers primarily to the political practice of demagogic politicians who show disdain for establishment elites and claim to represent the voice of the people as a whole.[4] Historically, however, global manifestations of populism have been extremely varied. Populism has referred to grassroots movements that come from among the people themselves, it has been connected to race-baiting forms of fascism, it has been used by crony capitalists invoking the popular will as a means of retaining power, and it has served as a basis on which socialist parties have attempted to fuse the policies of left-wing activists with the concerns of the masses. Russian populism was closest to this latter category, but emerging from the special set of circumstances that arose in nineteenth-century Russia it was unique in its form and its political and cultural importance.

Among the most important reasons for the special nature of Russian populism were the aforementioned socioeconomic and geographical segregations that characterized Imperial

Russia. All European countries in the nineteenth century struggled with the effects of steep gradations in social class, but few of them can be compared to Russia in the degree to which those classes, or rather legally differentiated social estates, formed distinct worlds and separate cultures. The language, habits, aims, and expectations of the minority of educated Russians had, at least since Russia's initial Westernization under Peter the Great (r. 1689–1725), grown almost entirely distinct from those of the peasant majority. As late as 1908, the poet Alexander Blok gave a speech in which he marveled that such a deep fissure could actually characterize Russian society. "Does the terrible gulf exist only in our imagination," he wondered, "Sometimes one doubts that it can be true, but apparently it is—in other words, there actually exist not merely the two concepts but two realities: the people and the intelligentsia: a hundred and fifty million on the one hand, and a few thousand on the other, unable to understand each other in the most fundamental things."[5]

Because of this deep cultural separation, Russian populism could not come together as a joint production of different social classes. Unlike the populist movement that emerged in the United States in the 1890s, a movement with deep roots in the farming communities themselves, populism in Russia thrived almost exclusively in the minds of those privileged with a higher education, most of whom lived their lives in urban centers or on country estates, separated from the small villages where the people and cultural values populism admired were to be found. When Russian ethnographers from the intelligentsia went out to study folk cultures, for example, they applied the same methods to studying Russians and Ukrainians as they used for the study of people from other lands. For all the profound thought, incisive polemics, and powerful art the populist intelligentsia produced, it must be stated bluntly that much of that creativity and energy was grounded in fantasy: the unrealized, and almost certainly unrealizable, aspiration to heal the wounds that Russian history had inflicted upon itself.[6]

Since nineteenth-century Russian populism was, as one scholar put it, "a pure product of the intelligentsia . . . an expression of its alienation from the *narod*," the varied forms it took were all closely connected to that intelligentsia.[7] Again indicative of the special circumstances under which populism arose, the word "intelligentsia" was a mid-nineteenth century Russian coinage. It referred to the intellectually and politically engaged members of *obshchestvo*. The members of this intelligentsia had a strong tendency to believe the peasants retained a native Russian authenticity they themselves had lost in their Europeanized upbringing and social milieu. They grew convinced that, separate and distinct from *obshchestvo*, the *narod* comprised the essence and the strength of Russian society. In this respect, populism was rooted in a rarely articulated but unmistakable defense of national pride. Indeed, it was a national pride and a project to envision a Russian nation that constructed itself in opposition to the imperial project of the Romanov Dynasty. That imperial project drew on the services of both Russian and non-Russian elites to bind together, through such methods as government service and land ownership, all the separate and distinct classes, ethnicities, languages, and religions inhabiting an Empire that stretched from Eastern Europe to the Pacific Ocean.

Populists tended to envision the special nature of peasant culture and institutions as the source of Russia's future, a future that, they believed, might well prove instructive to the rest of the world. Some populists were convinced that the peasantry possessed a deep-seated communal and revolutionary instinct which, once activated, would enable them to overthrow the old regime and institute a new socialist order in Russia. Others were more interested in finding a way to learn from and merge with the peasantry in order to remake themselves and Russian culture as a whole. Perhaps the most original aspect of Russian populism was the aura of self-abnegation surrounding its adherents. Unlike other movements of national rejuvenation, where the cause involved uniting all members of society into a single community, in Russia the populist intelligentsia, to varying degrees, denigrated aspects of the European cultural and educational inheritance they had received in favor of exalting the culture of the *narod* as its superior counterpart. For this reason, the populist intelligentsia typically expected the merger of *narod* and *obshchestvo* to be accompanied by a positive, even utopian, transformation of Russia.

It would be difficult to imagine the breadth and depth of populist enthusiasm apart from the historical context of the 1861 emancipation of the serfs. It was a time when, as Fyodor Dostoevsky put it in 1860, "millions of Russians will enter into Russian life, will bring to it their fresh untapped strengths, and will utter their new word."[8] The struggle to re-envision Russia as a unified national community generated waves of alternating euphoria and trepidation. After all, this generation was confronting the most urgent of what it called Russia's "cursed questions." It was tasked with reimagining Russia as a country in which the roughly 85 percent of the population that had been little more than an alien class of laborers and servitors—slaves and rabble to earlier generations—would now become fellow citizens. These mostly poor and illiterate Russians were to constitute the great majority of Russian society. The internal and alien "other" was now somehow to become "us," while "we" (educated society) were to become "them." Whether this transformation was to be achieved through liberal reforms, revolution, or some kind of moral regeneration of society no one knew, but most developed strong opinions, and the emancipation unleashed an epoch of spiritual, psychological, and social crisis that did not fully abate until well into the Soviet period.

> I was struck most of all by the unhappy situation in which the so-called black people, the good Russian *muzhik* who is oppressed by everyone, now live. I felt greater sympathy for him than for the other classes, incomparably more than for the characterless and profligate Russian nobility. I based all hopes for a rebirth, all faith in the great future of Russia, on him. I saw in him freshness, an expansive soul, a lucid intelligence not infected by foreign corruption, and Russian strength. And I thought: what might these people be if they were given freedom and property, if they were taught to read and write! And I asked: Why does the present government—autocratic, armed with boundless power, not limited by statute or in fact by any outside law or any competing power—why does it not use its omnipotence for the liberation, elevation, and enlightenment of the Russian people?
>
> Mikhail Bakunin's "Confession" to Tsar Nicholas I, trans. Robert C. Howes

Having emphasized the gulf that separated the disconnected realms of Russian society, it is also necessary to point out that the emancipation not only unleashed the quest to reimagine Russia in the urban sphere among the intelligentsia. In ways that are more difficult to discern but that social historians have teased out from economic records, census data, and other sources, life in the peasant village was undergoing change in the post-emancipation era. Rising, if limited, literacy, migration to the cities, factory labor, rapid population growth, governmental and societal attempts to advance the interests of the peasantry, and improvements in agricultural techniques all had a cumulative effect on the apparently static and traditional world of the Russian (and non-Russian) peasants. The changes in rural life that did come about in the late nineteenth century were often bemoaned by those populists who celebrated peasant traditions, in particular their communal arrangements, but by the twentieth century such changes had to be accounted for, and we will observe in later chapters how the growing dynamism of the *narod* playing an increasingly significant role by the revolutionary period of the early twentieth century, a role to which the populists would have to learn to adjust.

With the caveat that there are many intermediate shadings between them, one can identify three essentially different analytical conceptions of populism that have been advanced over the years. The Marxist version, first expressed in the 1890s, equated populism (of the revolutionary type) with any kind of Russian agrarian socialism—i.e., socialism based on rural, peasant institutions—that pre-dated the late-nineteenth-century advent of Marxism in Russia. Marxian socialism fundamentally differed from agrarian socialism in that it was premised on the development of industrial capitalism. The Marxist equation of populism with agrarian socialism was later accepted implicitly by many non-Marxist scholars and became the most common way of thinking about populism.[9] The idea of populism as agrarian socialism has the advantage of providing historians with a clear target of analysis, but unfortunately it excludes all non-socialist expressions of populism (of the more general kind), and thereby distorts and minimizes populism's historical relevance.

A second conception is much more encompassing of Russian culture as a whole in the nineteenth and early twentieth centuries. This version conceives of populism as the general aspiration among educated Russians to understand and connect with the Russian peasantry. This desire was found among a wide variety of Russians across the political spectrum.[10] Perhaps the most extreme expression of this view was held by the historian, G.P. Fedotov, who not only included liberals and conservatives among Russian populists but claimed that even the final tsar of the Romanov Dynasty, Nicholas II, was himself a "*narodnik*."[11] While we will not take the argument quite that far here, this book accepts the legitimacy of Fedotov's "big tent" approach. As an introduction to Russian populism, it includes both of these ways to frame the topic, attempting to weave them together as parts of an interconnected whole.

A third, more recent, view emphasizes the intelligentsia's active "social construction" of the peasant as other. This conception of populism holds true for almost every aspect of the movement since Russian populists constantly imagined and reimagined the *narod* in ways that suited their own needs. And yet such construction was also an ontological necessity since the distance between the populist intelligentsia and the *narod* transcended the social and cultural. It was a geographical distance, in terms of the separate physical spaces they occupied, and in terms of diet, disease, physical exertion, and relative exposure to the elements, it was biological distance as well.[12] This difference also explains why the peasants themselves "constructed" the populists as "foreigners in their own country."[13]

Since Russian populism involved such a diffuse array of ideas and values, it is hardly surprising that for decades historians of Imperial Russia have disputed how to define it. As early as 1964 Richard Pipes pointed out that "there exists little agreement among the authorities not only on what actually constitutes *narodnichestvo* but also on what personalities and events come within its range."[14] Pipes convincingly argued that the Russian words populist and populism, which were used in a strictly limited way when they first appeared in the 1870s, had been co-opted and repurposed by Marxist polemicists in the 1890s, those who first defined populism as a misguided and naive form of agrarian socialism. These motivated critics of an opposing ideology missed the fact that strikingly populist views were sometimes espoused by liberals and even conservatives. Soviet historians would later get around the problem by positing two types of populism: liberal and revolutionary (the lines between which, however, were exceedingly blurry). To eradicate such inconsistencies, Pipes proposed that historians should limit their use of the term populism to the narrow and extremist original definition of the Russian word *narodnichestvo*. But such a move would so severely curtail our use of the term populism as to necessitate the invention of a new term. In coming to grips with the history of late-Imperial Russia, one cannot dispense with the syndrome of viewpoints and values—in ideology, politics, philosophy, and the arts—that we have come to call populism.

It is worth noting that since the demise of the Soviet Union historians have paid rather less attention to Russian populism, partly because its role in helping to bring about the Bolshevik Revolution had come to seem less consequential. Without entirely abandoning recognition of populism's importance, recent generations of scholars have shifted focus away from questions that foreground the populist ethos. The shift has been hugely beneficial to our understanding of the late-imperial era. By opening previously untapped areas of interest, historians have revealed a far more complex, nuanced, and multidimensional portrait of Imperial Russia. But for all we have gained, it does not change the fact that the period between the 1861 emancipation of the serfs and the Bolshevik Revolution in October 1917 witnessed the rise and proliferation of a revolutionary socialism that eventually triumphed in its Bolshevik permutation. Russian populism played a central role in that revolutionary story, and the sphere of its influence extended far beyond revolutionary politics as well. It cannot be passed over without losing an essential component of what Nikolai Berdiaev called "the Russian idea," a term he used mainly to encapsulate the cultural legacy of the Russian intelligentsia.[15]

Berdiaev's attempt at a definition of populism, listing many of Imperial Russia's most important figures and movements, suggests why a wide and inclusive definition of populism is warranted: "[Populism] had many manifestations. There was a conservative *narodnichestvo* and a revolutionary; there was a materialist form of it and a religious. The

Slavophiles and Herzen were *narodniks*, so were Dostoevskii and the revolutionaries of the 'seventies. But all the while at the root of it was a belief in the people as the guardian of truth and right."[16] Hans Rogger's description of educated society's obsession with the *narod* goes even further:

> The "Russian Peasant" was an essential element in nineteenth-century discussion of Russia's past or present, her destiny, her mission, and her character. Whether he bore the conservative features of Konstantin Leontiev's "bearded Orthodox muzhik," who would defend and extend Orthodox tsardom; or served as the Slavophiles' embodiment of the communal spirit; whether he was Herzen's motive force of history, regenerating an exhausted Europe; the object of admiration on the part of Populists; or Dostoevskii's God-bearing man, social and political thought was occupied with him to an extraordinary degree. Russians, insofar as they tried to arrive at a definition of the national character and its unique elements, had in one way or another to come to terms with the peasants as a phenomenon of Russian reality.[17]

While Rogger's list is long, he actually neglects to mention several other important peasant-centered movements and philosophies like those of Russian anarchists, the peasant Tolstoyans, and the Socialist Revolutionary Party.

These broad interpretations of Russian populism span many decades and throw together fierce political antagonists, but they still locate the mystique of the peasant at the center of numerous, if often incompatible, ideological perspectives. The stark disparity between these varied individuals and movements, juxtaposed against their mutually agreed upon insistence on the central importance of the peasantry, implies that some underlying unity was at play. What bound together all of these disparate figures and ideas was not the answers given but the questions asked. Who were the Russian people? How are we to join together with the peasant majority in a common cause? What is the future of the country when that unification has happened? Who will we ourselves become once that change has occurred? These questions produced a surprising unity across radical differences that forces us to examine how the various manifestations of populism were connected to, dependent upon, and compatible with one another, as well as the ways in which they were contradictory or irreconcilable. Such questions lie at the heart of the analysis offered in the following pages.

If Russia has been considered mysterious and impenetrable to outside observers, the influence of populism is one of the main reasons why. The nineteenth-century aspiration to overcome the disunity of Russian society, based on some form of integration between peasant culture and the rest of Russian society, informed much of the thought, activism, and productivity carried out by educated Russians from the middle of the nineteenth century to the Bolshevik Revolution. The dream of that integrated future Russia, as well as the profound difficulty of realizing it, informed multiple political ideologies from that of the conservative Slavophiles to far-left anarchism; it was instrumental in ushering terrorism into the modern world; it gave inspiration to many of Russia's world-famous

Figure 1.1 Peasant portrait, *Mina Moiseev* by Ivan Kramskoi, 1882 © Wikimedia Commons (public domain).

novelists, composers, and other artists in the nineteenth century; in the twentieth century it underlay the only revolutionary ideology in Russia to successfully compete with Marxism; and simultaneously it had a profound influence on the Leninist Marxism that took over and completed the Revolution. Therefore, in spite of the rather alien character of populist aspirations from a Western vantage point, the flood of creativity and political ambition it produced had a great deal to do with why Imperial Russia, as Steven Marks has argued, played a surprisingly large role in shaping the modern world.[18] Because of its broad and deep importance in a crucial period of Russian history, populism deserves to be better understood by a wider public.

Historians have had a hard time agreeing on any precise definition of populism, in part because it did not have a single origin as, say, Marxism had in the texts of Marx and Engels. As a reaction to the same basic problem of a divided society, it sprang up in different ways at different times—here as defined ideology, there as a work of art; here in a book review, there in an underground organization. All of these rippled and reverberated against one another. Attempting to reconcile these disparate manifestations, the story told here will proceed in a rough chronological order. For the moment, however, it may also assist readers in the effort to sort out all the overlapping complexities of Russian populism by considering the subject not as a temporal phenomenon, unfolding over time, but spatially, as a ring of concentric circles.

The small circle in the very center, the most dense and concentrated conception of populism, was the ideological position for which the word *narodnichestvo* was first invented. This view held that *obshchestvo* had no right to impose its aspirations on the *narod* and should instead simply listen, learn from, and follow the lead of the peasantry. Only the Russian people themselves could determine the path to the future, a path that would inevitably be collectivist and anarchist, and those on the right side of history, as good populists, must submit to the will of the people and accept the result, come what may. While this self-abnegating position was certainly a pure expression of populism, to limit our definition to this perspective would be to render populism incomprehensible, as it would exclude the outlook of almost all important populist thinkers, every one of whom believed it was the role of the intelligentsia not only to learn from the peasants but to use the advantage of their education to guide the *narod* and the rest of Russia forward into a better future.

Thus the second circle out would represent populism as the more widespread phenomenon of populist agrarian socialism in the period from the late 1860s through the early 1880s: the era that Andrzej Walicki has labeled "classical" populism.[19] The populists at this level hoped to use the benefits of peasant culture and institutions to bring socialism to Russia, believing that the communalism Russian peasants practiced, in sharing and redistributing land in their villages and working together in a collective known as an *artel'*, could serve as a basis on which to transform Russia into a socialist/anarchist federation through a popular uprising and sweeping social revolution. These populists, relying on the historical precedent of peasant rebellions that occurred from the sixteenth to the eighteenth centuries, felt confident that Russia's peasantry was innately revolutionary. They also believed that the peasants' revolutionary tendencies had to be brought to life through the exertions of the intelligentsia, which is why many of them went to live and work in peasant villages. At this level, however, there was a great deal of debate about the proper course of action, and the actions of the "classical" populists were in a constant state of flux as they cast about for an effective way to ignite a peasant-based revolution. These first two rings of populism comprised that which the Marxists later labeled agrarian socialism.

To identify these competing expressions of populism as the "classical" version presupposes that other related, though less perfect and complete, expressions of populism surrounded them. Here we come to the next ring out, which might be thought of as the layer of people who hoped for a peasant-centered revolution but did not share the same radical fanaticism about the immediate need to institute peasant-based communal socialism throughout Russia. This circle would include the founder of revolutionary populism, Alexander Herzen, who advocated what he called "Russian socialism" but was intent on maintaining the blessings of Western civilization and full personal liberty, while hoping that a bloody confrontation could be avoided. This level would also include members of the Socialist Revolutionary Party, like Viktor Chernov, who continued into the twentieth century to regard the *narod* as the essential *raison d'être* of their revolutionary activism but still supported such "liberal" institutions as electoral politics and representative government. These individuals and groups did not necessarily refer to themselves as populists [*narodniki*] (for some of them the word had yet to be invented), but it would be very difficult to see them as anything other than populist in orientation.

And indeed this populist orientation did not spring out of thin air. The fourth circle out can be thought of as the common propensity among the Russian intelligentsia to use the peasantry as a way to think about Russia's history and destiny. Herzen's original populist ideas were cobbled together from an admiration of the peasantry originally espoused by his Slavophile acquaintances. The Slavophiles engaged in a proto-populist adulation of the peasantry, if an absolutely non-revolutionary one, as did many other conservatives and liberals willing to celebrate that which they saw as the praiseworthy and characteristically Russian features of peasant culture. The intelligentsia's widespread admiration for the peasants, and the desire to premise some more or less explicitly ideological position on what the peasants purportedly stood for, reached back as far as the eighteenth century and had such deep roots in educated society that it continued to flower well into the twentieth century. The representatives of this circle, which would include familiar figures like the novelists Dostoevsky and Tolstoy, could be highly skeptical of the revolutionary fervor of the radical socialist populists, but they still believed the Russian peasantry was bound up with the destiny of the country as a whole.

All of the above expressions of populism bear an either explicitly or implicitly political character. For that reason we need to imagine yet one final ring of populist sentiment. This outer circle can be characterized as that broad Russian cultural affirmation of the peasant, the heartland, rural values, and the wisdom of the poor and downtrodden. It is highly visible because of its prominence on the world stage in the form of Russian novels, opera, painting, and poetry, and it can even, in a more remote sense, be found in rough-hewn wooden toys, or the present-day vogue among Russian city dwellers for living rustically in their country dachas. The cultural and artistic markers and memories that helped give Russia its sense of a national character based on the rural values of the *narod* also helped to fix and perpetuate the idea that the rescue and revitalization of Russia had to come from among the rural majority itself. This outermost form of populism was not articulated as an ideology; it was experienced by educated Russians as a feeling of sympathy for, and admiration of, the *narod*, its environment, its history, and its "unspoiled" Russian identity.

This metaphor of concentric circles reminds us that populism was also the expression of a long-standing condition that faced Russian elites when they considered how to unite their divided society but kept running up against the intractability of the preexisting divisions. Aspects of populism in Russia could be found in everything from well-articulated economic arguments about the inevitable communalism of the Russian people, to the act of taking up residence in a peasant hut, to the simple decision to grow a long beard to signal one's preferences and affiliations. In the broadest sense, populism was the intelligentsia's attempt to envision a Russia that could transcend the divisions that defined it. This book aspires to provide a panoramic view of the whole extent of populist thought, expression, and activity in an attempt to reveal how its apparently disconnected ideologies, actors, cultural products, and expressions of opinion were more broadly connected in their united desire to guide Russian culture and society into an improved position in the modern world.

While it may be helpful to envision Russian populism apart from its historical trajectory, populism did in fact have its narrative arc, its rise and fall. We will trace that trajectory over the following seven chapters. Chapter 2, on the origins of populist thinking, explores the roots of populism prior to the creation of any distinct populist ideology, focusing especially on how a proto-populist vision began to congeal among the Slavophiles in the 1840s. Chapter 3 describes the initial appearance of populism proper, including Herzen's concept of "Russian Socialism" and the ideals and explorations of other early populists in the 1850s and 1860s. Chapter 4 introduces the seminal theorists of classical populism, such as Petr Lavrov and Nikolai Mikhailovsky, and the views they espoused, while Chapter 5 describes the evolving ways in which radical activists attempted to effect a revolutionary transformation of Russia on the basis of populist ideas, a search for methods that culminated in terrorism and assassination. Chapter 6 examines the ways in which populist thought began to spread through Russian art and culture from the mid-nineteenth century. Chapter 7 concerns the disappointments and reorientations many populists experienced when their idealized peasantry did not materialize in the real world. Chapter 8 focuses on the early twentieth century revitalization of populism as "neo-populism" in the form of the Socialist Revolutionary Party and its contribution to revolutionary Russia. It is hoped that the reader will come away from the following chapters with a strong grasp of how and why populism had a resounding impact on nineteenth-century Russia, an impact that continues to echo in Russian culture and society to the present day.

CHAPTER 2
ORIGINS

Every clear thinking person saw the terrible result of the complete rupture between national Russia and Europeanized Russia. Every living link had been broken between these two parties and they had to be renewed, but how? That was the great question.

Alexander Herzen

The original source from which Russian populism arose was not the people themselves. The most immediate origins of populist thought are to be found in the growing crisis of identity experienced by the members of educated society during the first half of the nineteenth century. That crisis, made dramatically apparent in the Decembrist Revolt of 1825, reappeared in a different form in 1836 with the publication of a letter in the Moscow journal *Telescope*. Written by Petr (Pyotr) Chaadaev, the letter outraged the government and sent shock waves through Russian society. It so appalled government officials that they fired the censor who passed it, shut down the journal, and exiled its editor to northern Siberia. Chaadaev himself they declared insane and placed under house arrest with daily medical supervision. Any further mention of his letter was outlawed. How did one letter, no longer than a shortish book chapter, manage to hit such a nerve?

The document, blandly titled "First Philosophical Letter," bemoaned the condition of Russian society and forcefully contended that Russia was doomed to remain a nonentity in the pantheon of global civilizations. Chaadaev held that Russians themselves were capable of nothing but blind imitation of foreign cultures and lacked any meaningful historical past that might point the way toward a better future. Inspired primarily by romantic, conservative Catholicism to place high regard in the grand moral inheritance of Western civilization, Chaadaev believed Russians never had the chance to learn the lessons "of duty, of justice, of right, of order" from which the more fortunate Western Europeans had long profited.[1] Without any organically inherited sense of ethical purpose, Russians were "strangers in our families … nomads in our cities … children who have not been taught how to think for themselves." Worse, they were impervious to "all good, all evil, all truth, all deceit." Chaadaev's denunciation of Russian society was brutal and unrelieved by even a drop of countervailing hopefulness. Yet despite the swift and furious reaction of the state, not to mention universal condemnation in the press, Chaadaev's *cri de cœur* clearly expressed an anxiety shared by many others. After Russia's rout of Napoleon two decades earlier, the country had become a great military and diplomatic power in Europe, but to many it seemed to have nothing to recommend itself beyond raw force.

Alexander Herzen later called Chaadaev's letter "a shot that rang out in the night," awakening Russian society to its lack of independence and its tacit support for the twin evils of serfdom and autocracy. Chaadaev's lament resembled an intervention in the life of a troubled soul. It told harsh truths that could only be answered by continued denial or some kind of recognition and response. Chaadaev had thrown down the gauntlet, and if there was any substance behind his assertions, then the challenge to answer him had to be taken up. What was Russia's role in the world? By what path should it try to move forward? Should Russians imitate or reject Western models? What role did the public have to play? Did only *obshchestvo* matter? Was the *narod* relevant in Russian society as anything other than a source of labor? Chaadaev did not ask these questions directly, but his condemnation of Russian aimlessness and lack of potential was symptomatic of an urgently felt need to take stock of Russia's place in a rapidly evolving modern world.

In the wake of Chaadaev's letter there arose a churning mixture of responses to his challenge. Populism would eventually emerge as one of them. This chapter explores the tensions and anxieties that informed Russian populism as they gathered momentum beginning in the late eighteenth century, and that grew acute toward the middle of the nineteenth. The two underlying aims that would come to characterize Russian populism both emerged in this period and remained in dialectical tension—sometimes reinforcing and sometimes contradicting one another—throughout the remainder of the populist era. The first aim was the urge to improve, liberate, and unite with the *narod*, rendering the peasantry fully equal members of Russian society. The second aim involved a search to find the hidden resources of the *narod* that would, once discovered, provide a meaningful identity and proud destiny for Russia as a whole.

The *Narod*

Before turning to the origins of populism we must make a brief digression in order to better understand the object of the populists' interest: the people themselves, in particular the peasantry. The Russian word *narod* is notoriously complex. It can refer to an ethnic group, a national community, the Russian people as a whole, or the Russian laboring masses exclusively. At times it can be unclear which meaning is intended, and it is easy for writers to leave its meaning intentionally ambiguous when it suits their purposes. In the early part of the nineteenth century, use of the word with reference specifically to the laboring poor was not yet well established, and into the 1850s one usually finds the addition of the word "simple" [*prostoi*] as clarification. As the significance of the simple people [*prostoi narod*] gained traction within educated society, the modifying adjective mostly dropped away. When the term *narod* is used by populists and others in these pages it refers to those "simple people," meaning the unprivileged laboring majority of Russian society. In Russia's system of legally defined social estates, the word *narod* would generally be applied to two specific estates: the peasantry, constituting some 85 percent of the population, and the townsfolk, who made up around 10 percent. The word could even apply to a potentially wider category that might include poor, uneducated, and rural members of the clergy and merchantry, as well as members of non-Russian ethnicities (although that most typically meant non-Russian Slavs). Since *narod* was not a technical term, who exactly fell into the category lay in the eye of the beholder. Given all this ambiguity, the category *narod* is probably best thought of simply as the imagined lower-class counterpart to the small minority population of educated, urbanized elites. This latter group was dominated by the nobility, but over the course of the nineteenth century it would be joined by an increasing number of educated people from diverse backgrounds. All of elite society, even as late as the census of 1897, comprised little more than 2 percent of the population.

The designation "peasant" originally applied only to those who worked the land. As times changed, nominal peasants took on a variety of different occupations, but agriculture remained their primary form of labor. The townsfolk generally worked as artisans, shopkeepers, and various kinds of servitors. Over the centuries, as Russia modernized and occupational demand multiplied, massive complexity crept into these seemingly self-evident social categories. One thing that did not change, however, was the fact that the peasantry and townsfolk paid the taxes and undertook almost all the manual labor. Because the peasantry was by far the most populous social estate in Russia, and because Russia's economy was so firmly rooted in agriculture, the peasantry typified what *narod* meant to the members of educated society. Until 1861, around 50 percent of the peasantry lived and worked as serfs, and even after serfdom was abolished in that year, the terms of the settlement left peasant communities responsible for the next several decades to repay the state for the allotments of land they had received as part of the emancipation settlement. In its concern to ensure that these payments were not defaulted on, the state maintained the institution the peasantry had long made use of in order to more easily pay their taxes and dues to landowners: the peasant commune. It should be noted that in ways such as this the Romanov project of sustaining the Empire at all costs brought about and fed into the perpetuation of social difference.

The "village commune" served the needs of the peasantry by sharing out the harsh obligations under which they labored and which served as the main support of Russia's economy. These burdens often rendered peasant life risky and onerous, and communal integration of land use helped deflect threats like poverty and famine. As the reader will discover at length here, the commune would be lionized by Russian populists as the expression of inborn and age-old characteristics of the *narod*, and hence as a reflection of Russian identity as a whole. But it must be understood from the outset that the communal organization of peasant life arose as a pragmatic response to the circumstances in which the peasants found themselves. Nor was communalism particularly unique to Russia; variations of it had arisen in other parts of Europe as far back as the early Middle Ages. Since the village commune would become the centerpiece of the populist idealization of peasant life, it will be useful to begin with a brief overview of its function and purpose in the actual circumstances of peasant life.

The commune, typically referred to simply as the *mir*, the village itself, varied widely from place to place, and in some regions it was not in use at all. It was, however, by far the most common form of self-government in rural Russia. Just as peasants saw the commune as a means of limiting risk and enabling collective economic survival, the state and landowners also understood it as the most effective means of ensuring remuneration and therefore mostly favored its use. Peasants earned their livelihood, as well as paid their dues and taxes, primarily from the grain yields derived from farming the strips of land surrounding their villages. Through an assembly of elders, the commune periodically redistributed arable land so that, as circumstances changed, each family would take charge of a sufficient amount of land, and the village as a whole would be able to make its payments. The elders also made decisions about other village concerns like the recruitment of soldiers, punishment of transgression, and maintenance of the peace. Communal arrangements were familiar and comfortable enough for Russia's working classes that they were also often adapted for use as non-agricultural labor collectives called *arteli*. To what extent communal organization was a practical arrangement, and to what extent it rose to any sort of popular ethical principle has remained unclear, but the point was hotly disputed during the nineteenth century.

Contrary to the beliefs of some Slavophile and Populist intellectuals, Russian village communes did not adopt the practice of land redistribution on account of some innate idea of egalitarianism, but because they saw it as the best way to make the most effective use of their land and human resources in order to ensure that their village communities, and the households that comprised them, were able to meet their obligations and subsist.

David Moon, *The Russian Peasantry, 1600–1930*

As will become apparent, this snapshot of our contemporary understanding of the peasantry, an understanding arrived at through generations of study and debate among historians, radically differs from the view of the commune propounded by the left-wing populist intelligentsia in the nineteenth century. Where historians today tend to find that the peasantry differed from region to region and over the course of time, the populists emphasized communalism's deep roots of continuity and general uniformity across the Slavic parts of the Empire. Where historians interpret the commune as a practical, and familiarly human, response to difficult conditions, populists saw the commune as a representation of deep-seated peasant justice and egalitarianism, an especially Russian sensibility. The historical reality of peasant culture and the populist idealization of "the peasant," then, are two separate things that should never be confused with one another.

Discovering the Russian People

The Russian landowning classes prior to the 1861 emancipation of the peasantry treated their serfs, and the peasantry in general, in ways that varied from abusive and contemptuous to tolerant and paternalistic. Most commonly, perhaps, landowners evinced minimal interest as long as their income arrived in a timely fashion. Toward the end of the eighteenth century, however, we begin to detect increasing curiosity, even on occasion sympathy, for the peasants among the members of the landowning classes. Why at this time? Other than gradually intensifying exploitation, there was no particular change in the relationship between *narod* and *obshchestvo* in this period. To understand the increase in interest we must look not to changes in Russia but to the wider world. By the late eighteenth century, educated Russians were growing increasingly cosmopolitan, with their eyes focused almost exclusively on the glittering spectacle and intellectual treasure house of Western Europe. Catherine the Great (r. 1762–96), born in Germany and sympathetic to certain strands of Enlightenment thought, firmly avowed that "Russia is a European power." When she wrote these words in 1767, they probably seemed relatively innocuous—a mild wish for greater status and international recognition as well as an affirmation of her policy direction. After all, Peter the Great had already initiated the identification of Russia as European two generations earlier. As it turned out, defining Russia as European would prove fraught with consequences that Russia would reap for generations to come.

Russia's growing social, political, and economic proximity to Europe had the effect of exposing the differences between the two regions that had long remained isolated from one another. By the late eighteenth century, Western European states, though far from democratic, increasingly had to justify themselves in the court of public opinion, a problem Russian rulers would not really face for decades to come. Western European governments presented themselves as the leaders of integrated national communities, whose authority rested on the good of their subjects (or citizens) as one of their top priorities. Russia's tsars, rulers of a multinational empire premised on absolute loyalty to the autocratic state, with a majority of its population reduced to a brute labor force, could more easily avoid questions about universal justice and equality. In practice this meant that the subjects of the Tsar took directions from above: the rulers imposed their will, and their subjects responded to the degree to which they could be compelled. This state of affairs might well have continued indefinitely for the Crown and the populace, but three fundamental changes occurred during the eighteenth century that made autocratic absolutism more difficult for the educated classes to accept. First, Peter the Great had reconceptualized and repositioned Russia as a European country, a premise accepted by future generations. Second, Europe itself was a moving target. It had entered a phase of dynamism and radical change during the eighteenth century that only intensified in the nineteenth. Third, in the early nineteenth century Napoleon's invasion injected Russia into the heart of European affairs. By this time it had become impossible to ignore the question of what exactly the Russian Empire was when conceived of as one among other European nations.

The crux of the problem lay in the fact that Peter's Europeanization of Russian culture had been sweeping in one way but limited in another. Peter mandated that the court and nobility adopt European dress and manners and transferred state servitors to his new and ostentatiously European capital city of Saint Petersburg. He needed a noble class that could more easily understand and interact with the Western powers. Over the course of the eighteenth century, the external Westernization of the nobility gradually became internalized so that, with a European-style education, the adoption of Western languages, consumption of European products, appreciation of Western art and ideas, and increasing travel to Europe, Russian nobles could begin to see themselves as members of an international elite anchored in Western civilization. Yet however much Western customs and values became second nature to the wealthy minority in Russian society, the vast majority of the Russian population shared in virtually none of that transformation. Where Russian elites shaved their beards and wore powdered wigs and the latest Paris fashions, peasants wore the same homespun clothing and healthy beards to which they had long been accustomed. Merchants, priests, and members of other estates also remained mostly rooted in traditional Russian ways. On occasion people from humble backgrounds found opportunities to move into the sphere of educated society—the scientist and philologist Mikhail Lomonosov is a famous example—but the change required radical personal reinvention and remained rare.

The institution of serfdom, consolidated in the seventeenth century, compounded the growing disconnection between educated elites and the rest of society. In an effort to more firmly harness Russian society to the purposes of the imperial state, Peter the Great and his successors further strengthened the power of landowners over serfs while also placing heavier tax burdens on the serfs and other peasant communities. By the eighteenth century serfdom had acquired some aspects of chattel slavery, as serfs could be traded and sold on the open market as well as ruthlessly disciplined without recourse to legal protection. Among the nobility, the increasing secularization, bureaucratization, and urbanization of Russian elites continued the transformation of their world. The process of building and extending the Empire had the effect of harnessing both the elite and the masses to the system, but it did so according to entirely separate processes, and this duality only helped to widen the gap between landowning state servitors and those who worked the land that sustained the economy. As a result, the ruling class came to occupy a more and more separate sphere from the rural masses; they not only looked different but came to possess entirely different forms of knowledge. For many of them, for example, the French language became more comfortable than their native Russian.

Perhaps an even more significant factor leading to the alienation of noble Russia from peasant Russia involved the Russia Empire's particular conception of land ownership. Unlike in many parts of Western Europe where a "de" or a "von" in front of a place name indicated the patrimonial land inheritance of a given aristocrat, in Russia the only absolute patrimony was that of the Tsar who could, and often did, hand out parcels of land (before 1861 including the local serfs) to his noble servitors. As a consequence, many of the largest landowners held multiple plots in a variety of regions across rural Russia. Certainly, the local dominance of Western European nobles in their ancestral terrain was accompanied by its own set of problems, but in cases of difficulty landowners could make good on their right to reap rewards from agricultural labor based on personal control or beneficence. The local peasantry would know them by name, see them in church, and possibly turn to them when in need. Such local connections did exist in Russia, especially among less wealthy nobles, but some Russian grandees never even saw the peasant villages they owned, which were managed by a bailiff or overseer. In Russia the landowner might not share the same ethnic background as the peasants on his estates. He might not even speak the same language or practice the same faith.

As a result of these social and cultural bifurcations, while Russian society was highly differentiated and stratified in many ways, the most essential and glaring distinction became that between the serf-owning minority and the rural, and often enserfed, peasant majority. Elites reinforced the distinction early on as a mechanism for creating a distinct privileged culture with a keen awareness of its own superiority. An etiquette guide produced to train the nobility during Peter's reign encouraged nobles to perceive the lower classes as "by their nature uncivil, obstinate, shameless, and proud" for which reason "they should be restrained, subdued and humiliated."[2] Echoes of this disdain never died out among the educated classes. As late as the mid-nineteenth century Vasily Botkin haughtily referred to the Russian *narod* as "Eskimos, Hottentots!"[3] How were these two disconnected populations—not to mention the other distinct social estates of merchants, clergy, and townsfolk, or the plethora of non-Russian ethnic groups—to be envisaged as a single national unit?

In response to the social abyss that grew so stark in the eighteenth century, the autocracy liked to fancy itself the protector and the bridge between the distinct parts of Russian society. In fact, however, the gap between the ruling classes and the people very much included the autocracy itself. Alexander Herzen, in writing a preface to the memoirs of Catherine the Great, aptly likened the relationship between the autocracy and the *narod* to "a ship floating on the surface of the ocean without any real connection to the inhabitants of the deep, except for the habit of eating them."[4] One finds a clear example of that distance in Catherine the Great's *Nakaz* [instruction], a document that laid out her views on the purpose and administration of the state. The *Nakaz* pays scant attention to the peasantry, but when Catherine does mention this estate she demonstrates not only ignorance of their world but virtual helplessness with respect to improving it:

> The Peasants have generally 12 to 15 or 20 Children by one Marriage; but rarely does a fourth part of them attain the Age of Maturity. Wherefore there must certainly be some Evil, either in their Diet, or in their manner of Life, or in their Education, which is so destructive to this Hope of the State. How flourishing would the Situation of this Empire be, if it were possible by wise Institutions to avert or prevent this fatal Ruin.[5]

Recognizing the stark segregations that characterized Imperial Russia, we should also note that the separation was not absolute. Many landowners, especially those with fewer serfs, did live on their estates and engage in agricultural pursuits as managers. Some peasants managed to grow wealthy, gain merchant status, and thereby, eventually, access to the urban sphere. Even some important figures in government came from classes outside the nobility. Mikhail Speransky, for example, who contributed a great deal to the governments of both Alexander I (r. 1801–25) and Nicholas I (r. 1825–55), was the son of a village priest. Romances between peasants and wealthy landowners, even royalty, were also not unheard of. In the memoirs and recollections of members of the gentry one finds a pattern in which contact with the *narod* tended to be fleeting but memorable. The world of the Russian peasant remained opaque and mysterious to most educated Russians, but for that very reason it was often regarded as intriguing. The most common contact, repeated so often that it seems a cliché of the gentry memoir, involved warm and loving early childhood connections to peasant nannies, who would pass along stories and lore from "the other side" to their gentry charges. Memories of kindly house servants, or opportunities to play with serf children, were also recollected fondly.

Such memories notwithstanding, the main reason Russians began to train their interest on the *narod* in the latter part of the eighteenth century had little to do with their own past experiences. Strange as it may seem, interest in the Russian peasants mainly arrived from abroad. For in the same century when serfdom reached its apogee in Russia, influential Western Europeans, like Locke, Voltaire, and Rousseau, were busy developing theories to justify the social and/or political integration of the social classes. Somewhat later, others like Herder and the Grimm Brothers began to reimagine their ethnic inheritance as something rooted in popular culture. As much as all of this may have existed in theory more than practice, such new European attitudes left educated Russians in an awkward position. Their sense of superiority had been based in part on their mastery of European culture against its conspicuous absence among other classes. Now that same European culture they so admired was beginning to discover hidden importance within the very social classes over which their intellectual superiority had hitherto justified their literal ownership.

Equally important, starting in 1789 the great upheaval of the French Revolution and Napoleonic Wars began everywhere to erode the constancy of the pact of mutual assistance between Crown and nobility. Before the Revolution, ideas like popular justice and social equality, or the importance of public opinion in decision-making, still bore only minor relevance to European rulers. But by reconceiving of the public good as the exclusive reason for the existence of the state, as did the "Declaration of the Rights of Man and Citizen," revolutionary France propagated a new way of thinking about the body politic that would challenge all European governments over the ensuing century. Despite staunch resistance to change among the ruling classes and their conservative supporters, the constant fear, and occasional outbreak, of popular revolution, in tandem with the general desire to unlock the potential of a large educated and civically engaged populace, made appeals for popular participation and relative equality a central feature of Europe's political landscape. In Russia, at first such appeals had an extremely limited audience. Russia's absolute monarchy and dominant nobility understood their sizable powers as natural, foreordained, and beneficial to the rest of Russian society, while Russia's scattered, partially unfree, and largely illiterate population had little capacity to voice any kind of united protest. Still, as a "European power" Russia could not so easily claim full immunity from the tides of political change rolling out of the West, nor could it remain entirely aloof from the dramatic socioeconomic transformations which would soon begin to sweep across industrializing Europe.[6]

Because of the vast gulf between *narod* and *obshchestvo*, in order even to imagine a Russian version of inclusive national community, educated Russians had to set out on a voyage of discovery to find and learn about the poorly known peasant population in their midst. They did so, as was customary, in imitation of Western European models. In literature, plays about poor folk with noble and sentimental, if unrealistic, heroes had become popular in eighteenth century Europe, and Russian playwrights began, under Catherine, to imitate the genre. While many of these plays were nearly line-for-line imitations of European dramas on similar themes, they certainly helped to jumpstart a tradition of literature about the common folk, and over time that tradition would grow much closer to the actual lives and language of the *narod*. Pastoral stories, in a neoclassical or sentimentalist vein, about admirable and innocent members of the lower classes were sometimes used to point out the plight in which virtuous working people could find themselves. A much more gritty and damning story, probably written by the satirist Nikolai Novikov in 1772, described a visit to a decrepit village in the Russian countryside. Novikov agonizes over the miserable conditions in which he finds the village's inhabitants in an exposé of rural injustice. Even so, the peasants he portrays in this story remain nothing more than faceless victims.[7]

The earliest Russian searches for the world of the actual *narod* mimicked the European vogue for compiling collections of folk songs and tales.[8] By the end of the eighteenth century collectors of similar materials in Russia had begun to believe folklore and popular culture offered some access to that authentic Russian character and identity they felt they had lost. Nikolai Lvov, compiler of one of the more famous volumes of songs, wrote about his collection: "Philosophy will perceive . . . the tenderness and sensitivity of the Russian people and also that inclination of the soul to melancholy, which produces great people of every race."[9] In 1801 Andrei Turgenev claimed that "only in tales and songs do we find the remnants of Russian literature, in these precious remains . . . we find and still feel the character of our people." Yet at the same time he lamented that songs like this would never be able to serve as the basis for a revival of Russian *belles lettres*: "For that to happen, we would need to return to Russian originality, from which we grow more distant every day, in our customs, our way of life, and our character."[10] Already at the turn of the eighteenth century we find in Lvov and Turgenev the desire to discover and reveal the genuine Russian character hidden within the culture and traditions of the *narod*, and as yet untouched by the transformative influence of European culture.

One Russian writer working within the sentimentalist genre, Alexander Radishchev, clearly rose above mere imitation. Radishchev used the vogue for sentimentality to stage a frontal attack on the institution of serfdom in his travelogue-style novel *A Journey from St. Petersburg to Moscow* (1790). Appearing decades before the advent of populism, Radishchev's *Journey* for the first time raised directly and unflinchingly the theme of social injustice toward the lower classes. Radishchev published his book on his own printing press, and after the first limited printing it would remain officially banned all the way until 1905. So bold for its time was Radishchev's criticism of Russian society that the author was thrown in prison and condemned to death, although his original sentence was commuted to ten years of Siberian exile. Radishchev's book, published during the early years of the French Revolution, and far ahead of its time, demonstrates that a profound awareness of the inequalities built into Russian society was at least possible among the upper classes as early as the late eighteenth century, even though such views remained rare and usually went unspoken.

> Ravening beasts, insatiable leeches, what do we leave for the peasants? What we cannot take from them, the air. Yes, and nothing but the air. We frequently take from them not only the gifts of the earth, bread and water, but also the very light. The law forbids us to take their life—that is, to take it suddenly. But there are so many ways to take it from them by degrees! On one side there is almost unlimited power; on the other, helpless impotence. For the landlord is to the peasant at once legislator, judge, executor of his own judgments and, if he so desires, a plaintiff against whom the defendant dare say nothing. It is the lot of one cast into fetters, of one thrown into a dismal dungeon: the lot of the ox under the yoke.
>
> Alexander Radishchev, *A Journey from Saint Petersburg to Moscow*,
> trans. Leo Wiener

Radishchev's fictional travelogue voiced the first political plea of an educated Russian to his literate compatriots to fully recognize a common humanity between the members of *obshchestvo* and *narod*. It anticipates the populist theme of immoral elites living grandly on the proceeds of peasant labor, and Radishchev even predicts the likelihood of a peasant rebellion if such inequity is to continue. The *Journey* condemns the arbitrary rule of the gentry over their serfs, and even at times takes the autocracy itself to task for its resistance to recognizing all people as equal before the law. Radishchev again and again hammers on the theme of equality, either in simple declarations such as referring to the peasants as "equal fellow citizens," or in more elaborate ways, like the digression in which a friend of the narrator who almost drowns at sea literally comes to recognize that class differences have no meaning on a sinking ship.[11] Along the route of his journey, Radishchev's narrator unveils the Russian countryside as a realm of inhumanity and suffering, but he also represents it as a realm of innocent peasant morality by contrast to the corrupt urban sphere of the nobility. Following in the footsteps of Rousseau and other sentimentalist writers, Radishchev paints a picture of the lower classes as uncorrupted by the evils of civilization. In comparison to their social superiors, the peasants are genuine, not hypocritical, and not spoiled by the love of wealth and the upper-class need for physical comforts and pleasures. Since populism, too, would later attribute high moral standards to the *narod*, the twentieth century scholar Nikolai Berdiaev referred to Radishchev, with some exaggeration, as "one of the first narodniks."[12]

We must object to that description since, for all of Radishchev's anticipation of the populists, in one essential respect he remained fundamentally at odds with them. The most important task of his *Journey* was to demonstrate that the lower classes were, at bottom, no different from the elites who dominated over them. In standard Enlightenment discourse, which was at or near its apex of influence at the time when Radishchev published his book, the narrator seeks to persuade his readers that all Russians come from the same human family. Even if they find themselves either more or less fortunate in their birth and education, all are fully deserving of equal rights and opportunities. Unlike the later populists, Radishchev attributed no uniqueness, no world historical significance, and no ultimate superiority to the peasants he describes. In this respect, Radishchev can be thought of as a progenitor not of the populists, who emerged under different circumstances at a later date, but of a different approach to the *narod* that emphasized common humanity over laudable difference. This conception of Russian society is accurately termed the "liberal" view. A similar understanding of the peasantry would later be expressed by the Decembrists, and something akin to it is evident in the peasant-focused fiction of Ivan Turgenev, who generally refused to exalt the peasants about whom he wrote, even though he always treated them as deserving of full respect as distinct but equal human beings. These figures shared with later populists a sympathy and an aspiration to improve the lot of the *narod*, but they showed little of the interest that populists would later display in the Russian peasantry as the distinctive and defining element of Russian society.

Russia as a National Community?

Radishchev's defense of the peasantry in 1790 was a rarity, a quickly silenced howl of rage, but the attention of *obshchestvo* would again turn toward the *narod* in and around the year 1812 when Napoleon invaded Russia. Radishchev's rebellion against ingrained social inequality had been personal and intellectual. What happened in 1812 and the ensuing years resulted from the shock of external events. Napoleon invaded Russia with an army of more than 600,000, the largest army ever yet assembled on European soil. Russia had Europe's largest standing army but could only muster forces about two-thirds the size and famously had to engage in a series of strategic retreats. Not only did Russian forces predominantly consist of peasant recruits, but the French attack made it clear that all Russians, including the lower classes, were afflicted by the war. Those peasants in the path of Napoleon's army proved essential to repulsing the invasion. During the *Grand Armée*'s retreat from Russia in the winter of 1812–13, the Russian military worked hand in hand with bands of peasant partisans. The sources on peasant participation in the war effort come mostly from non-peasant observers and are not entirely reliable, so it is unclear whether peasant militias saw themselves as participating in a national cause or were merely furious at the foreign soldiers trying to requisition supplies from them. Either way, the army supplied the peasants with arms to conduct militia raids, and the peasantry supplied the Russian cause with fighting forces and a knowledge of the local terrain.[13]

Aware of these combined efforts, educated society began to portray the peasantry as a force of national restoration. The image of the peasant as the quintessential defender of Russia comes across clearly in political caricatures from the popular press during the war. Numerous etchings represent the fighting peasantry as powerful, heroic, self-sacrificing, and clever (Figure 2.1). Pictures of Russian peasants outsmarting and attacking French soldiers portrayed the *narod* not only as helpful to society, but even as

Figure 2.1 The Russian peasant became, for a short time, an embodiment of the war effort © The Picture Art Collection / Alamy Stock Photo.

a sort of John Bull–type distillation of the national character, a bold mascot that showed why Russia was worth fighting for. For the first time the image of the *narod* stood as the representation of Russian identity as a whole. Although he wrote his memoirs long after Napoleon's invasion, Sergei Glinka later claimed that as a result of the war he began to see the peasantry as "the wellspring of Russia's originality and strength."[14] He recalled that upon spending time with a group of soldiers, he felt ashamed that "before this, wandering through some unknown world, I did not know the spirit, nor the native forms of thought of the Russian people. In the clamor of high society, at balls and parties, there was none of this. But time used its great power to manifest the Russian spirit before our fatherland and Europe."[15]

Not long after Napoleon's defeat, government censorship intentionally clamped down on images glorifying warlike peasants for fear it might give them pretensions to freedom or new rights, but the idea of the *narod* as something more important than a brute labor force had now been unleashed. It would become increasingly difficult to ignore, even though the privileged classes had ample reason to prefer the status quo. The problem was compounded by the fact that the defeat of Napoleon, and the pursuit of his army back to Paris, entangled Russia in European affairs and Western culture to a greater extent than ever before. At this point Russia found itself on the verge of an intractable dilemma. Both the civic nationalism of the French Revolution and the ethnic nationalism associated with German Romanticism rooted themselves (in different ways) in a belief in the civic importance of the common people. With its new seat at the table of European nations, Russia had to ask itself where ordinary Russians fit in as a constituent part of the national polity. Already prior to the war, Tsar Alexander I, who had been tutored by the Swiss Enlightenment *philosophe* Frédéric-César de La Harpe, recognized the need for a change in Russia's socioeconomic structure. He was well aware of both the stigma and the economic immobility produced by serfdom, and he did manage to take a few small steps toward its eradication. But contemplation of the potential damage to the Russian Empire posed by uprooting serfdom—after all it was the cornerstone of the imperial economy— suggested to Alexander the need to proceed with great caution. When it had been necessary for social and economic purposes to represent the common people as debased and incapable of much beyond manual labor, to then turn around and promote that same people as prepared for freedom and full participation in society presented obvious difficulties. Even more concerning, to remove (human) property from the most powerful class in the state's support network seemed to risk outright gentry revolt. All the same, by continuing to rely on serfdom Russia risked criticism as an exotic, not to mention despotic, outlier among the European great powers.

The first serious answer to rethinking Russia as a national community arose in the aftermath of the war and relied on the familiar solution of liberal or republican revolution. After their adventures abroad during wartime, numerous army officers returned to Russia in the 1810s inspired by the democratic political ideas they had imbibed in France and elsewhere in Europe. Organizing themselves into secret societies, the officers encouraged each other first to imagine a democratic revolution in Russia and then to act to bring it about. The most influential groups among these conspirators hoped to end autocracy and establish a constitutional monarchy. After the death of Alexander in December of 1825, some three thousand participants staged an armed insurrection on Saint Petersburg's Senate Square, demanding the formation of a constitutional monarchy under Alexander's brother Konstantin. Konstantin, however, refused the throne, and without support in society both the Saint Petersburg rebellion and a joint rebellion in southern Russia were easily put down by soldiers loyal to the new tsar, Nicholas I (1825–55). Five leaders were executed and more than two hundred participants were exiled for life to Siberia. The Decembrists, named for the month of their rebellion, had opposed not only autocracy but serfdom as well. In addition to their democratic politics, they tried to solve the social problem of an ineradicably divided society using the blade of anti-autocratic revolution to slice through the Gordian knot of social disunity. As revolutionaries they failed miserably, but their failure did nothing to resolve the quandary in which Russia found itself. In fact, in certain ways their political prescriptions reflected those divisions. The more conservative among them favored property qualifications for voting and holding office, and they planned to retain the vast majority of their land in their own hands after abolishing serfdom.

Pavel Pestel, who led the southern rebellion, stood in contrast to the more conservative Decembrists. He was among the most far-sighted of the Decembrists and was more concerned about the welfare of the peasantry. Pestel wrote a treatise called *Russian Justice* in which he attacked the social problem directly. Ardently democratic, he held that "the people [*narod*] is the sum total of all the people [*liudi*, or persons] who belong to the same state and form a civil society, the aim of which, insofar as possible, is the welfare of each and all."[16] Accordingly, Pestel called for the abolition of the entire estate system: "Estates are so pernicious that they only exist because of the single bias that they give certain members of the nation [*narod*] that which others are groundlessly refused ... that for the greedy satisfaction of a few cruel people they render injustice to the vast majority." Together with abolishing social estates, Pestel condemned serfdom as "a shameful thing, against humanity, against the laws of nature, against the Christian faith," and demanded "freedom of the peasant from slavery." In many ways, Pestel's view of the *narod* resembled that of Radishchev. He interpreted the peasantry's central problem as lack of political equality and called for an end to the injustices perpetrated against them. But he did take one step farther than Radishchev had. Arguing that since many Russian peasants held their land in common in village communes, he predicted they would be better off economically if they continued to do so in the future. He proposed dividing the land into one half that would remain in the hands of the communes, while the other half would be privately owned. Recognizing the benefit of communal landholding under conditions of political freedom, in a sense he favored a degree of what was just beginning to be called "socialism" in the West. Pestel was executed after the uprising, and *Russian Justice* was not published until 1905, so Pestel's ideas had little influence on the future intelligentsia. Nevertheless, he sounded a new note that would go on to fascinate many educated Russians: the importance of the peasantry and its commune as an integral part of Russia's socioeconomic system.

The state itself was not unaware it needed an answer to the dilemma of Russian nationality. The solution arrived at under Alexander's successor, Nicholas I, came to be called "Official Nationality." In contrast to the French Revolutionary slogan of liberty, equality, and fraternity, in 1833 Nicholas's minister of education, Sergei Uvarov, proposed an alternate Russian triad—Orthodoxy, Autocracy, and Nationality [*Narodnost'*]—intended to sum up the core values Russia stood for and the patriotic ideals Russians should adhere to. Of particular interest about Official Nationality is the simple fact that the autocracy felt the need to promote it. Prior to this time the Orthodox religion and autocratic rule could be taken for granted. To publicize them amounted to the recognition that alternative religious and political views were available elsewhere, even that public opinion existed in Russia. The third term of the triad, *narodnost'*, is accurately translated as "nationality" since it did not yet necessarily imply "the common people" or "folk culture," even if by the 1830s that association was becoming more difficult to avoid. One adherent of Official Nationality explained that in the context of the full slogan, the term *narodnost'* served as a reminder of the Russian people's "unqualified submission to the Church, and the same devotion and obedience to the Empire."[17] Exponents of Official Nationality juxtaposed what they considered the admirable and abiding Russian love for authority against the hatred for authority they saw emanating out of the liberal West. Yet despite their insistence on the submissiveness of Russian society, inclusion of the term *narodnost'* seemed to offer a degree of recognition that the (Russian) subjects of the tsar at least counted for something consequential within the Empire. Even this vague concession sounded a new note. The *narod* (here meaning the entire nation) was now presumed, even by the autocrat, to have some kind of as yet unspecified but significant role in his dominions.

Returning once again to Chaadaev, he had written his famous letter in 1829 prior to the dissemination of Official Nationality. The importance Nicholas's government placed on Official Nationality helps us understand its indignation when the letter was published in 1836. Chaadaev's characterization of Russia can be read as a direct refutation of the official position, a sort of inverse mirror image of Official Nationality. If Uvarov had wanted to endow Russia with a sense of collective identity, then clearly he recognized that Russia lacked a unified conception of itself as a whole. If Chaadaev despaired that Russia lacked any rooted identity at all, he also desperately hoped to endow it with one. Both figures were caught up in the overarching problem of imagining the Russian Empire as a part of Western civilization, a national (or rather supranational) community beneficial to the people as a whole. Official Nationality's imposition of a submissive identity, faithfully propagated by loyal stooges, and Chaadaev's despair that Russia's culture and history were devoid of intrinsic worth both represented attempts to find meaning and purpose in Russian life that went beyond military victories or the august power of the tsar. As suggested by the Decembrist Revolt a decade before its publication, Chaadaev's letter spoke to a society anxious about its position in the world and in search of a way forward. It said aloud what some felt but could not express.

The first significant answer to the letter came from the pen of Chaadaev himself. In his wryly titled "Apology of a Madman" (1837) Chaadaev reversed his former position to argue that Russian society had made huge gains in the wake of Westernization by being humble enough to reject its own cultural inheritance in order to recognize and take for its own the achievements of the West: "Never was a people less self-infatuated than the Russian people," he wrote, and as a result of Russia's humility "by abdicating its power in favor of its masters . . . the Russian nation gave evidence of profound wisdom."[18] Chaadaev now contended that lacking its own moral and intellectual foundations, Russian history had been a "blank page" that could easily adopt European traditions, accepting the best of them and rejecting those that were faulty or destined for failure. Chaadaev even argued that the very absence of cultural foundations might enable Russia to leap beyond Western civilization: "if we have made our way after others, it was to do better than others, not to fall into their superstitions, their delusions, their infatuations . . . it is a great privilege to be able to contemplate and judge the world from a level of thought unencumbered by unrestrained passions, the paltry prejudices that invade men's minds." Although "Apology of a Madman" was not published in his lifetime, Chaadaev's contention that Russia's historical insignificance may well be its greatest blessing—a version of the so-called "advantages of backwardness" argument—would later become a common contention among the Russian populists.

The Slavophile Contribution

The notion that glorious benefits may result from strategic imitation did not, however, appeal to all Russian thinkers. While deference to European cultural and intellectual superiority had been the norm in the eighteenth century, Russia was now one of the dominant powers in Europe. Not only the state and the publicists of Official Nationality, but many members of educated society as well had begun to consider habitual deference to Europe an unnecessary relinquishment of Russia's own distinctive virtues. Most notably, the group that would acquire the collective name "Slavophile" looked to Russian history and home-grown institutions to discover a meaningful counterweight to what they believed to be the West's baneful influence on Russia. If, as Chaadaev held, Russians were homeless imitators lacking inherited traditions, the Slavophiles countered that such a condition had only come about as a result of abandoning their own native traditions under Peter the Great. The key figure to pioneer the Slavophile worldview was the erudite gentry conservative, Ivan Kireevsky. Whereas the difference between Russian and Western culture in the eighteenth century had been considered a matter of degree rather than kind, Kireevsky followed Chaadaev to the extent that he accepted the difference amounted to two entirely distinct "principles of civilization." In absolute opposition to Chaadaev, however, Kireevsky understood the Russian principle as fundamentally superior to its Western counterpart. The problem, Kireevsky acknowledged, was that the virtues of Russian culture lay in the shadows and had to be teased out since they "have not manifested themselves as clearly as have the principles of Western culture in its history."[19]

In spite of the profound differences between the Slavophiles and later populists, it was the Slavophiles who originated some of the essential ideas the populists were later to adopt, including the exaltation of peasant culture and the celebration of the village commune. Martin Malia gave credit to the Slavophiles as the first Russians to commit "an act of faith that there was *something* in the Russian people that made it worthwhile for their enormous but enslaved country to exist."[20] Since the Slavophile worldview was unique and complex, we must familiarize ourselves with their thinking in order to come to an understanding of how they developed certain ideals later taken up by the populists. The primary Slavophile thinkers and writers gathered mainly in Moscow and included the Kireevsky brothers, Ivan and Petr, A.S. Khomiakov, the Aksakov family, Sergei (father) and Konstantin and Ivan (sons), and Iu.F. Samarin. Though they grudgingly accepted the designation "Slavophile," the word is a misnomer since the Slavophiles mainly sang the praises of Russia and took less interest in Slavs as a whole. The salons and intellectual circles attended by the Slavophiles and other members of the emerging intelligentsia in the 1830s and 1840s were steeped in the influence of European philosophers, particularly German idealists like Hegel and Schelling. As we explore the Slavophiles' fevered search for Russian uniqueness and superiority over the West, one should keep in mind that their arguments arose on the basis of Western European thought. The very notion that Russia needed to have its own national path and its own folk culture sprang from the philosophies of European romantic thinkers about their own native lands. Kireevsky liberally borrowed from German idealist philosophy and graciously acknowledged the value of Western civilization in its own context, but he repudiated it as a model for Russia.

Despite their dependence on European thought, one key Slavophile innovation was unequivocal disdain for Western civilization. Contempt for Europe and its history can almost be considered a necessary component of Slavophilism since, for generations,

Russian intellectuals had professed a rarely questioned admiration for the West. The cosmopolitan arena of Western philosophy, literature, and art was the temple in which Russian intellectuals had long studied as acolytes, so in order to erect their own monument to Russian glory the Slavophiles needed to tear down the European monolith that stood in their way. As early as 1839 Kireevsky had begun to condemn the Western traditions Chaadaev had praised. In particular, he held European individualism in contempt. "The entire private and social life of the West is based on the idea of individual, separate independence, and presumes individual isolation," wrote Kireevsky, "The first step of each individual in [Western] society is to build a fortress around himself from within which he enters into agreements with other independent powers."[21] For the Slavophiles, Western individualism isolated people from one another, leaving them abandoned in self-centered and impersonal relationships and therefore beholden to formal structures like contracts and legal codes.

Western Europeans, ran the Slavophile argument, had lost the ability even to recognize warm and genuine interpersonal relations. They understood the letter of the law but not the spirit of the situation, losing the capacity to trust one another and unite for the common good. The Slavophiles were horrified by formal institutions such as a legal system in which attorneys could adamantly defend their clients while fully aware of their guilt, putting faith in the system rather than in their own personal knowledge of the truth. To elevate abstract reason and institutions above ordinary human ethics led Khomiakov, for example, to the conclusion that the West was "one-sided, deceptive, corrupting and treacherous."[22] What may have looked like unending scientific and economic progress in Western civilization underneath was little more than the soulless pursuit of status and wealth.

One senses that the Slavophile rejection of Russia had less to do with the West itself than it did with their dismay that their fellow Russians had, at least on the surface, rejected all visible traces of uniquely Russian traditions and, in everything from language and dress to art and philosophy, had accepted the European inheritance as their own. But the Slavophiles argued that Russia had none of Europe's outward glory to display before the world for the simple reason that Russians had never been caught in the trap of raising external accomplishment above inner morality and interpersonal connection. Where European culture had long been atomizing into autonomous individuality, the world of Slavic Orthodoxy had managed to retain intact the truly Christian principles of human dignity, brotherhood, and social unity, characteristics apparent in the Orthodox Church and still evident in peasant communalism. Russians had managed to avoid becoming crassly bourgeois and materialistic like Europeans because the institutions of the Church and the commune enabled them to retain the value of community, the genuine freedom an individual experiences when realizing that freedom within the larger collective whole.

For evidence of Russia's moral and spiritual superiority the Slavophiles turned mainly to Russian history prior to the reign of Peter the Great. Their examination of history led them to conclude that Russian life before Peter had been integrated and harmonious. Pre-Petrine harmony and integration continued to permeate the life of the *narod*, but it had been cruelly torn away from the nobility by Peter's forcible Westernization. In this way, the Slavophiles created a neat dichotomy between the authentic Russia of earlier times and the distorted and confused Russia of modern times. The true Russia—"healthy, powerful, original"—lived on among the "unspoiled" peasants, as well as Orthodox Christians, while *obshchestvo* continued to suffer from the European excrescence falsely grafted on to the culture of educated elites. One of the most frequently met words in the Slavophile vocabulary is *poltorasta* [one hundred and fifty years] for the simple reason that they constantly referred back to that fateful disjuncture of Peter's reign around a century and a half earlier. Under Peter, they believed, *obshchestvo* had lost its way. In contemporary Russia only the *narod* had retained the spirit of the past. When Peter forced a cleavage between the two halves of Russia, the formerly united and harmonious Russian civilization fell into disarray. As a result, in Khomiakov's words, "having become separated from the people the enlightened classes lost their immediate sense of the latter's historical significance."[23]

Unlike Chaadaev, who merely commented on Russian missteps and future potential, the Slavophiles actively sought to rectify Russia's mistakes and turn the country back onto the proper path to future greatness. They wanted to reunite Russian society in the form they believed it once possessed. One all-important cornerstone of that reunification was the Russian Orthodox Church. The Slavophiles imagined the Russian past as deeply, even physically, enmeshed in the true and righteous Christianity of Russian Orthodoxy. They conceived of pre-Petrine Russia as covered in churches and monasteries throughout its great expanse, a sort of second Holy Land in which Christianity flourished and informed all the functions of everyday life. Because Russia had managed to stay aloof from the West, which suffered from the twin evils of corrupt Catholicism and creeping secularity, only in Russia and certain other Orthodox lands had it been possible to sustain authentic Christian values.

Russia's thorough infusion of Orthodoxy nurtured a spirit of unification and collectivity: "man achieves his moral fulfillment only in a society in which the strength of the individual belongs to everyone, and the strength of everyone belongs to the individual."[24] The Slavophiles dubbed this Orthodox unity *sobornost'*, an untranslatable term roughly meaning "unity within the spiritual community," or as Khomiakov liked to put it more generally "unity within plurality." The word is perhaps most closely related to English terms like "communion" and "brotherhood," but it could also apply to unity within the peasant commune, and could even be used, optimistically, to describe the national spirit in general. A community based on *sobornost'* had no need for external systems like contracts, constitutions, elections, or political representation. It favored local and direct personal connections, a spirit of cooperation, and a striving for unanimity. Unlike Westerners, who had the unfortunate capacity to compartmentalize their lives, Slavic *sobornost'* released Russians from that burden. In Europe, according to Kireevsky, "one corner of the heart shelters the western person's religious feeling; another, quite separate, harbors the faculties of reason and the capacity for worldly activity."[25] In Russia, by contrast, individuals within *sobornost'* are complete because the community as a whole can encompass and share in common the separate realms of human existence. Khomiakov, in an 1849 essay, gave an example he claimed to have witnessed of a family dispute settled at a communal meeting in which the community forced the offending family member, an uncle, to pay damages to his nephew. When the uncle asks upon whose authority the commune is acting, a commune member replies: "If I am right, then I am master."[26] The commune here ensures that the entire community will act honestly. The Slavophiles, in other words, believed genuine morality could only be achieved within the context of a well-integrated community.

The Slavophile view of the proper use of political power also grew out of their reading of the distant past. They accepted as historical fact that the original Russian (*Rus'*) state had been established by Scandinavian conquerors, and they considered the Russian willingness to yield to their Scandinavian overlords a primal moment in the formation of the Russian political consciousness. For the Slavophiles the act of ceding control to external rulers constituted nothing less than a Christ-like renunciation of the superficial satisfactions of this world, such as political power and material gain, in order to make room for the higher realms of ethics and spirituality. Peaceful acquiescence to foreign rule revealed Russians as a virtuous people, all the more able to thrive in spirit because the burden of rule had been handed over to outsiders in authority. Unlike in the West, where the Church had sullied itself by getting involved in the world of politics, in Russia the Orthodox Church had pride of place. Ceding plenary power to the state released the people as a whole to profit from the spiritual and ethical independence that concession offered them. Westerners, meanwhile, remained in thrall to their fruitless struggle for advancement in the material world of wealth and power.

Thus the Slavophiles saw the state not as an entity domineering over Russian society so much as a defensive rampart put up by the will of the Russian people to keep them free from outside influence. Russians had managed to remain freer than other peoples because they had liberated themselves from political power. For this reason the ideal political institution was an absolute monarchy that could serve as the most effective defense against any incursion upon their communities. As a result of their political perspective, when Russian officials feared the possibility of a revolutionary outbreak among the people, the Slavophiles believed they were "seeing western ghosts."[27] The *narod* wished only to remain aloof from politics. Only the deviant world of post-Petrine *obshchestvo* had been sufficiently Westernized to take an interest in politics, and thankfully the number of educated elites was relatively minute. It had been one of Peter the Great's most fundamental errors that by further binding gentry elites to state service he forced them to engage in the political realm, thereby severing Russia into a politically inclined *obshchestvo* and a non-political *narod*. At that point, the gentry stopped being part of the people and, harnessed into imperial service, became something alien and apart from the true Russia of the Church and the people.

Objections to Slavophile arguments would reasonably begin with the fact that they themselves were not only members of *obshchestvo* but gentry landowners largely disconnected from the peasants whose labor they profited from. Their answer was that a drastic reorientation of Russian life had to occur, and they could only begin by attempting to persuade their contemporaries of the accuracy of their views. However, to say that the Slavophiles' understanding of history was biased and inaccurate would be a considerable understatement. They idealized a dimly understood past as a way to promote a sweeping glorification of abstract ideas like "the people" and "the Church." Such abstractions enabled them to envision a glorious future based on some unspecified revivification of the historical utopia they had dreamt up in the first place. Even though they purported to be arguing from history, their arguments were steeped in a prophetic view of the Russian destiny they wished to bring about. They did claim to recognize that they could not fully return to the past, but by and large their vision of the past was all they had to offer. They tried to use the bricks and mortar of a bygone age to build Russia's future, and something of the doomed romanticism of Miss Havisham's boudoir hangs over their entire enterprise. That said, the Slavophile interpretation of Russian history did contain a crucial diagnosis. *Narod* and *obshchestvo* were indeed almost entirely disconnected from one another even as they shared the same religion, the same soil, and the same government. Deeply conservative in certain respects, the Slavophiles were not so dissimilar from Radishchev and the Decembrists in their desire to incorporate the *narod*, not as Russian helots but as an independent constituent element of society as a whole.

This brief summary of Slavophile thought has been necessary if we are to grasp the Slavophiles' reinterpretation of the role of the *narod* in Russian society. When Slavophile ideology began to coalesce in the late 1830s, at first they had little concrete to say about the *narod*, and they continued to refer to the lower classes as "simple people" [*prostonarod'e*]. With time, however, the significance of the peasantry gained greater traction in their thinking, largely because they came to rely on the example of peasant communalism as a familiar and recognizable demonstration of Russian social integration. The deep irony of the Slavophile appeal to the peasantry was not lost on their opponents. Critics of the Slavophiles pointed out that it was impossible to separate the Christian resignation the Slavophiles praised in the peasantry from the social oppression they themselves helped inflict as owners of serfs. Similarly, how would it be possible to differentiate the purportedly ethical disinterest in politics of the *narod* from simple illiteracy and ignorance? And how would one discern whether communalism was an expression of *sobornost'* or a form of economic expediency under impoverished conditions? The Slavophile philosophy, rooted in Romanticism, did not have convincing answers for such questions. They were not oppressors in the sense that they did in principle favor the abolition of serfdom, but their agenda had much more to do with Russian national identity than it did with solving Russia's crushing social problems.

The idea and image of the *narod* helped the Slavophiles build their vision of Russia's superiority over Europe because peasant communalism did in fact exist and could be pointed to as a living repository of Russian social unity. Given that the concept "the Russian people" remained something of a cipher among the educated classes, appeal to the virtues of the *narod* was an effective device. "The people" remained a poorly understood abstraction, so it was malleable material for rendering into whatever form the outside observer chose to promote. To a degree the Slavophiles themselves recognized the social distance that made such repackaging possible. Kireevsky once confessed that both the Russian land and the character of its people were so enormous they could only be examined from a distance, a point especially significant in the context of ongoing empire-building. Still, the Slavophiles could portray the *narod* as the exemplar of that authentic Russianness they regularly affirmed as a representation of the nation as a whole. In its separation from *obshchestvo*, the *narod* had unwittingly preserved the uncorrupted values of the pristine past and could therefore be presented as the embodiment of those positive values that lay dormant in educated society. Ivan Aksakov called the Russian people "the keeper of our historical instinct, our religion, and of the whole element of our political organism."[28]

The centerpiece of Slavophile evidence for the innate Christian ethic of the *narod* was the village commune. The Slavophiles were the first to put forward the commune as an institution that held profound importance for all of Russia. They saw it as a demonstration of Russia's natural *sobornost'* and Christian self-sacrifice. It was also essential proof that Russia never really partook of Western individualism. The commune offered the object lesson that in Russia, as Kireevsky wrote, "private, personal character, the foundation of Western development, was as little known as democratic government, [and] landed property, the source of personal rights in the West, was here the property of society."[29] On the basis of communal land redistribution, as well as the fact that gentry lands had often been held on condition of service to the state, the Slavophiles argued that Russia had never fully accepted the notion of private property, one of the driving forces behind the damaging individualism of the West. In Russia, property was temporary and conditional, meted out on the basis of participation in society. As a result, Europe had succumbed to dishonesty and dissension in pursuit of personal gain while Russia perpetuated fairness, good will, mutual support, and social unity.

> The commune is an association of people who have renounced their personal egoism, their individuality, and express common accord: this is an act of love, a noble Christian act . . . Thus the commune is a moral choir and just as each individual voice in the chorus is not lost but only subordinated to the over-all harmony, and can be heard together with all the other voices—so too in the commune the individual is not lost but merely renounces his exclusivity in the name of general accord and finds himself on a higher and purer level, in mutual harmony with other individuals motivated by similar self-abnegation; just as every voice contributes to the vocal harmony, so in the spiritual harmony of the commune every personality makes itself heard, not in isolation but as part of the group—and thus you have the noble phenomenon of the harmonious coexistence of rational beings (consciousnesses): you have fellowship, the commune—the triumph of the human spirit.
>
> Konstantin Aksakov, quoted in Andrzej Walicki, *The Slavophile Controversy*

The Slavophiles regarded communal landholding as a central principle of Russian life, nearly comparable in importance to the Orthodox religion. Samarin saw the commune as "the foundation of all Russian history," while Khomiakov claimed that "upon its development can be developed the entire civil order."[30] Khomiakov once wrote that to the peasant "the commune supports his feeling of freedom, his awareness of his moral dignity and all the initiative upon which we expect his revival."[31] Konstantin Aksakov also stressed the ethical nature of the commune, calling it "the ideal of brotherly love, which forms the essence of Christianity."[32] Nor did the Slavophiles consider the commune merely a holdover from the communalism practiced in European history. Russia's communes and *arteli* were institutions that expressed the fundamental genius of the Russian people: "The people who understood the lofty meaning of the commune and took it as a principle were the Slavic people, primarily the Russian people who created the *mir* for themselves even before the coming of Christianity."[33] Konstantin Aksakov, again in stark contrast to Western individualism, conceived of the commune as a "moral choir." In the West and within *obshchestvo* individual autonomy produces a "useless egoism," whereas in communal unity "personality is not annihilated; it merely renounces its exclusivity in order to form a unanimous whole, in order to become the desirable creation of all. In the commune they sing not with separate voices, but like a choir."[34]

The Populist Slavophile: Konstantin Aksakov

As suggested by the statement above, Konstantin Aksakov was the most devoted admirer of the *narod* among the Slavophiles. So devoted was he to his vision of the Russian peasantry, and so innovative in his interpretation of the peasantry's significance in Russian history and society, that in spite of the multitude of differences between him and the later populists, one can make the argument that Aksakov represents Russia's first populist thinker. Thus, before we move on to explore the rise of Russian populism in its full-blown form, it is well worth examining Aksakov's early and original celebration of the *narod*.

Although other Slavophiles pointed to the importance of the peasantry and its communal economy from early on, both Kireevsky and Khomiakov wrote about the importance of the *narod* and the commune in rather vague and abstract terms. In their analysis, the peasantry and its commune are evocative of Russia's unique national character, but remain distant from contemporary educated society. It may seem strange that in trying to establish Russian nationality as *sui generis* Kireevsky and Khomiakov did not emphasize the importance of the *narod* and communalism in a more direct and explicit way. The lower classes comprised the vast majority of living Russians, and they could never be implicated in contact with the "corrupting" West. One suspects that their status in Russian society encouraged these senior Slavophiles (both more than a decade older than Aksakov) to resist delving deeper into the peasant question. Much of *obshchestvo* still considered the world of the *narod* alien, uncultivated, and in no way comparable to the European inheritance. Elitism was not a trait the Slavophiles greatly indulged in relative to their peers, but it ran rampant among those they were seeking to persuade. We must also keep in mind that Russian landowners, very much including the Slavophiles themselves, were actively involved in depriving the *narod* of its dignity as free individuals. Even though Kireevsky and Khomiakov affirmed that profoundly

Russian characteristics existed in embryonic form within the people, their own scruples as landowners, reluctant to upset the socioeconomic status quo, may have prevented them from advancing the social status of the peasantry. Using vague allusions to the authentic Russianness of the people enabled them to gloss over awkward questions about just how educated elites were to find a reflection of themselves in the impoverished, oppressed, and illiterate working classes.

Little of such equivocation can be found in Aksakov's writing. In his enthusiasm for the world of the *narod* and the lessons it had to teach the educated sector of society, any possible scruples slipped away. Aksakov dove straight in to the effort to demonstrate to the privileged classes the wonders of the Russian people, if only his peers would open their eyes and see. Although Aksakov was not the most eloquent of the Slavophiles, he was certainly the least restrained and most impassioned among them. On occasion, his arguments sound almost cartoonishly simplistic, but unlike his more philosophically minded cohort Aksakov had a concrete and activist turn of mind. More stridently than the others he rejected any Western influence in Russian life, often referring to the educated members of society as "clever Russian monkeys" for their propensity to ape European manners and embrace European ideas. He believed it was the job of educated Russians to free themselves insofar as possible from "the European yoke."[35] He considered the hybrid cosmopolitanism of his friend, the novelist Ivan Turgenev, an error and a sin, and he even sought to keep his houseguests from speaking French. Not surprisingly, the influence of German idealist philosophy is less evident in his writings than in the work of other Slavophiles. Aksakov's work instead emphasized the tangible, living manifestation of pre-Petrine Russia he found in the contemporary lives of the Russian people.

More than the other Slavophiles, who emphasized the contrast between Russia and Europe, Aksakov built his worldview on a contrast between *obshchestvo* and *narod*. As he wrote to Turgenev, "the old world has not disappeared. It is still powerfully in the grasp of the peasant."[36] In an open letter to the Tsar, he recommended himself as "one who loves the simple people, who is anxious at every opportunity to make their acquaintance not as a master or official but . . . as an intimate, a fellow believer, and a compatriot."[37] To add extra piquancy to the distinction between the social elite and the people, he referred to *obshchestvo* using the Russianized Latin term *publika* [public]. For Aksakov the superficial, well-fed public had all the material advantages, while the downtrodden, laboring *narod* was the storehouse of Russian grit and Christian morality. Aksakov's admiration for the people could at times resemble a religious faith. "How difficult it is for us," he wrote to Turgenev, "standing so far below the Russian peasant to [manage to] portray him."[38] The *narod* had so long lived in a pristine state, uncorrupted by the world outside their Orthodox sphere, that Aksakov boldly proclaimed, "the Russian people is not a people. It is humanity itself."[39] He similarly lauded the village commune in language that would hardly be surpassed by any of the commune's ecstatic populist admirers later in the century: "The commune is that highest principle which is not destined to find anything higher than itself, but which is destined only to flourish, purify, and elevate itself."[40] Aksakov's veneration of the peasant commune had nothing to do with its economic function. He regarded it, rather, as the prototype of an ideally integrated human community: "In communal union personality is not annihilated; only its exclusivity is renounced in order to create a unanimous whole, in order to become the welcome inter-connection of all." [41]

> The public subscribes to ideas and feelings from abroad, mazurkas and polkas; the *narod* draws its life from native sources. The public speaks French; the *narod* Russian. The public wears foreign clothing; the *narod* Russian. The public has Paris fashions. The *narod* has Russian dress. The public (at least the majority) eats meat; the *narod* must fast. The public sleeps; the *narod* long ago got up for work. The public disdains the *narod*; the *narod* forgives the public. The public is all of one hundred and fifty years old; the age of the *narod* cannot even be calculated. The public is ephemeral; the narod is eternal. In the public there is gold and filth, and in the *narod* there is gold and filth, but in the public the filth is in the gold; in the *narod* the gold is in the filth. The public has fashionable society (*monde*, balls, etc.); the *narod* has the village commune (peasant assemblies). The public and the *narod* have their epithets. The public's is "most honorable"; the *narod*'s is Orthodox.
>
> Konstantin Aksakov, *Izbrannye trudy* (303–4)

One way Aksakov sought to draw closer to the people involved dressing "in the Russian manner." Unfortunately, after an interval of one hundred and fifty years since the gentry had begun to dress in Western fashions, it was unclear what precisely a Russian landowner might don to make himself look traditionally Russian. Aksakov's answer, at least at times, was to adopt clothing that resembled a cross between a pre-Petrine landowner and a peasant in holiday attire. He was mocked for it, and it embarrassed some of his fellow Slavophiles. Chaadaev told the story that when peasants saw Aksakov pass by in his "traditional" dress they mistook him for a Persian. Nevertheless, he and other Slavophiles did exert an influence on gentry fashion. It was they who were most responsible for bringing the long beard into fashion among the gentry. At first, when Khomiakov grew out his beard, a high-ranking government official ordered him to shave it off. Aksakov's father bemoaned this temporary prohibition of gentry beards as "the end of the hope of turning toward the Russian orientation." [42] But during the second half of the nineteenth century long beards had came into fashion within *obshchestvo* as a whole. The Slavophiles took their beards seriously as a symbol of their solidarity with the true Russia of peasants, priests and the historical past, and they condemned the wearing of Western clothing as, in Aksakov's words, "the conductor of all Western raving, of all contagious sins, and of servility and liberalism." [43]

While Aksakov and the other Slavophiles had connections with the supporters of Official Nationality, they disagreed with them in many ways. Aksakov, for example, despised Gogol's obsequious "Selected Passages from Correspondence with Friends" for its rigid adherence to official doctrine. In turn, Aksakov's incessant insistence on the superiority of *narod* over *obshchestvo* never sat well with a government that took pride in

Figure 2.2 Yuri Samarin as an early Slavophile and later, once beards were accepted among the nobility © Both: Wikimedia Commons (public domain).

educated society's Westernized culture (as long as it remained unblinkingly loyal to the throne). Aksakov strenuously supported the free expression of public opinion, accusing the government of being oppressive when it rejected freedom of speech. He argued in his letter to Alexander II that freedom of speech could not possibly hurt the state since the Russian people, in conformance with Slavophile doctrine, wanted nothing to do with politics. There is a certain irony here since Aksakov's own insistence on correcting what he considered the autocracy's political missteps clearly revealed his interest in politics, and thereby exposed his own Westernization. In any event, as a result of his political views, the state treated Aksakov as a relatively subversive figure. They subjected his work to strict censorship, and they shut down his publications more than once.

In his ardent admiration of the peasantry, Aksakov unintentionally exposed some of the contradictions underlying the Slavophile position. For instance, he clearly suffered from that affliction common among privileged people when assessing unprivileged others whereby the "other" becomes a collective type rather than a set of distinct individuals. In his praise for Russian popular song, for instance, Aksakov rejected the possibility of regional diversity or individual creativity:

> Song belongs equally to all the people, therefore all the people sing popular song, everyone has an equal right to it, and therefore no composer's name is attached to any song ... A people remains a single undivided mass, engulfing individuality, and therefore unchanging and always true to itself ... Here there are no poets; here the poet is the people itself.[44]

As this passage suggests, a dark side lurks beneath Aksakov's exaltation of the *narod*. As one of Aksakov's biographers expressed it, "the muzhik was to be looked up to, not pitied, and in the process his plight was perhaps forgotten."[45] Aksakov's chief idea, that the peasants lived a life morally superior to that of educated society, ignored the everyday human difficulties the peasantry faced. In one notable passage, Aksakov marveled at the supposed blessings of peasant poverty and obscurity: "Located on the lowest rung of the material ladder, lacking any honors or external distinctions, the simple person still has the greatest of human blessings: brotherhood, an integrated life, and ... communalism in his everyday world." This interpretation of the peasant's situation enabled Aksakov to exclaim later in the same piece: "Oh what wealth this poverty!"[46] To see the *narod* in all its glory led to, or perhaps required, a degree of blindness. It is a blindness we will encounter later with respect to the populists.

Aksakov deserves credit as one of the originators of Russian populism. He was the first to insist that the *narod* played the lead role in defining Russian identity, and he was the first to insist that the peasants and their way of life would be the primary factor determining Russia's future identity. For Aksakov the peasants were a solid mass of essentially undifferentiated folk, unspoiled in a Rousseauian sense by the corruptions of worldly civilization and thus capable of remaining pious, hardworking, and genuinely living in concert with one another. This image of the Russian people as communally united and capable of raising mere individuality into mutually beneficial integration continued to beguile members of educated society for decades. It made a formidable contrast to the dual subservience of *obshchestvo*: subservience both to the imperial state and to the preeminence of Western civilization. As the notoriety of Chaadaev's letter had exposed, many Russians regretted that subservience and hoped to break free of its influence. The Slavophiles, and Aksakov in particular, pointed to one possible exit. Backward-looking gentry intellectuals who preached the wonders of those they owned, the Slavophiles probably never had much chance to garner any widespread appeal. Many would follow Aksakov in his conviction that the people held the key to the reintegration of all Russian society. Following the Slavophiles, the people had become the sphinx whose riddle had to be figured out before the traveler could move down the road.

As a solution to tangible problems in the real world, Slavophilism had little to offer. Its vision of Russian uniqueness and superiority served mainly to soothe the troubled souls of intellectuals who, as Chaadaev had, felt a kind of hopeless grief over Russia's status as an inferior outsider among European nations. Once the era of practical problem-solving arrived with Alexander II's promise to abolish serfdom, the national identity issues that concerned the Slavophiles had come to seem less relevant. Moreover, the Kireevskys, Khomiakov, and Konstantin Aksakov had all died before the emancipation, and while Samarin did make an important contribution to the emancipation settlement, he acted as a pragmatic government official with the landowners', rather than the peasants', interests uppermost in mind. Samarin and his Slavophile colleague Koshelev mainly regarded the commune as a vehicle for assuring that the peasants would keep up with their redemption payments to the state. But the Slavophiles had been the first to propose the peasantry and its communalism as the bearer of a future Russia, and they were also the first to argue that European society was bankrupt and would benefit by looking to Russia for direction. Reformulated by the populists according to their more secular and revolutionary aspirations, the original ideas of the Slavophiles would come to inform Russian thinking in unexpected ways that no Slavophile would have approved of. With their adulation of the *narod*, especially its communalism, they introduced the microbial form of a new thought that was later to grow, mutate, and eventually to pervade *obshchestvo*.

CHAPTER 3
FOUNDATIONS

The essence and the content of Russian history is the life of the people.

Afanasy Shchapov

Let us then, brothers, as one man, fling ourselves among the people.

Mikhail Bakunin

In 1847, fearing he would be sent into exile for a third time, the 35-year-old Alexander Herzen departed from Russia with his family for a long sojourn in Europe. As it turned out, he would never return home again. Herzen arrived in Europe on the eve of 1848, Europe's "Year of Revolution." Traveling through France and Italy, he was thrilled to find himself a living witness to revolutionary events and the birth of new republican governments. Not long thereafter, however, he wound up bitterly disappointed by the bloody French suppressions of the left and the general failure of democratic socialism throughout Europe. As Geoffrey Hosking has noted, "the West" for Russians in this era was less a set of real places with their own special problems than an ideal to be accepted or rejected, "an adventure playground of the imagination."[1] As a left-leaning Westernizer in Russia, Herzen imagined Europe to be a battleground between "bourgeois philistinism" on the one hand and socialist revolution on the other. Having experienced the revolutions of 1848, his deeper acquaintance with Europe shook his conviction that the West might somehow lead the way toward the eradication of social injustice and serve as Russia's guiding light. Soon Europe became the anti-revolutionary foil for Herzen, and his native land became the place where freedom for all would finally be realized.

Unable any longer to look to Europe for direction, Herzen needed some new promise on which to pin his hopes. Relying in part on the Slavophile admiration for the Russian peasants and their village commune, over the course of the next two years he developed a new theory. He began to argue that it was Russia rather than Europe that had the greatest innate potential to lead the way to socialism. He now recognized that Russia had been socialist all along, not of course in its political system, but rather in the overlooked world of the peasantry. Referring to collectivist aspects of the peasant commune, Herzen began to claim that, "what is only a hope for the West . . . is already an accomplished fact for us."[2] He had discovered what he would go on to call "Russian Socialism," and he would continue to spread its gospel for the rest of his influential life. Herzen's "Russian Socialism" was the first unambiguous expression of what was later called populism.

Herzen's "Russian Socialism," a term we must leave in quotation marks since it was far from the only Russian version of socialism, established the original set of assumptions and aspirations on which the populist movement was based. As we shall discover in this chapter, however, Herzen's ideas were by no means the sole origin of populist thought. All of the early steps toward populism rested on a common goal: the attempt to effect a rapprochement between *narod* and *obshchestvo*, to somehow unite the separate spheres of Russian society. The desire to unify society became increasingly acute when Alexander II took the throne in 1855 and soon announced the need to abolish serfdom. Whether it was a matter of the state finally tackling the logistical nightmare of emancipating the serfs and incorporating them into Russian society, of stories and novels that sympathetically explored the lives of the lower classes, or of the more radical forms of social integration espoused by the early populists, visions of a more united Russia came to pervade educated society in this epoch, today known as the era of the Great Reforms.

This chapter describes the contributions of several seminal originators of populist thought in this era. Each of them had a different view of how the desired unification might be achieved. Herzen's "Russian Socialism" designated the village commune as Russia's vehicle toward a socialist future. The firebrand revolutionary Mikhail Bakunin declared the peasantry a revolutionary force capable of bringing about a cataclysmic change. The historian Afanasy Shchapov discovered a socially integrated society in Russia's past and imagined it as the key to forging an egalitarian future. The wandering ethnographer Pavel Iakushkin attempted to erase the boundary between *narod* and *obshchestvo* in his own person, both by spending time among the peasants and by dressing and living in a way that erased the traces of his noble upbringing. The radical publicist Nikolai Chernyshevsky advocated for a socialist, egalitarian future in ways that inspired generations of revolutionaries. Each of these figures was joined by friends and supporters, and their ideas and activities came to color the age. The word "populist" [*narodnik*] would not come into use until the 1870s, but this cohort in the 1850s and 1860s set the tone for their populist followers in the 1870s and beyond.

The Ideological Foundation: Alexander Herzen and Russian Socialism

Alexander Herzen was a towering figure of the Russian intelligentsia. An occasional writer of fiction, he was better known for his journalistic polemics, while he also wrote scholarly studies on science and philosophy. He is best known for the journals he printed in London and intended for export back to Russia, journals that often espoused anti-autocratic and revolutionary views. In spite of the subversive nature of his writing, Herzen's journalism was widely read in Russia, even by government officials, and quite possibly the Tsar himself. As an intellectual, Herzen bridged the gap between the Romantic generation of the 1840s, with their agonized debates about Russia's place in world civilization, and the revolutionary materialists of the 1860s. In serving as a link between these generations he felt, perhaps more acutely than anyone else, the sting of their radical difference from one another. His theory of "Russian Socialism" provided an ideological foundation for the populist generation of the 1870s, and yet he staunchly resisted some of the obvious implications of the very doctrine he had created. Herzen contained multitudes. He never met his American contemporary Ralph Waldo Emerson, but no figure of the nineteenth century more perfectly embodied Emerson's epigram that "a foolish consistency is the hobgoblin of little minds." Aileen Kelly, writer of a recent, penetrating biography of Herzen, concludes that his most essential intellectual characteristic was an awareness of the contingency of history, even of the contingency of his own most cherished beliefs.

Around the time Herzen lost faith in Europe, he read a newly published study on agrarian Russia written by the German scholar Baron August von Haxthausen, a man he had met and admired before he left Russia. A deeply conservative member of the Saxon nobility, Haxthausen had spent six months traveling through Russia in 1843, seeking to understand the Russian agricultural system, with a particular interest in the peasant commune. Partly inspired by the Slavophiles, Haxthausen sang the praises of the commune as a bulwark against what he considered the pernicious influence of capitalism then sweeping across Europe. He argued that the commune had enabled Russia to retain the peaceful agricultural life of Europe's past that capitalism was rapidly destroying everywhere else. Haxthausen worried that Western Europe was succumbing to the evils of "proletarianism" and wage slavery, and he praised the Russian village commune as the institution which ensured the Russian peasants would continue to farm and live off the land. The commune would guarantee the survival of the very sort of traditional small farming of which Haxthausen heartily approved. Like the Slavophiles, Haxthausen admired the agricultural life as a moral realm in which salubrious, age-old traditions would be upheld. By protecting the peasantry against the incursion of destructive modern habits and ideas, the commune supported the intact family, a peaceful social order, and patriarchal values.

> At the present time in particular, the organization of the Russian commune is of immense political value for Russia. All the western European nations are suffering from an evil which threatens to destroy them and for which no cure has been found: pauperism and "proletarianism." Protected by its communal organization, Russia escapes this evil. Every Russian has a home and his share of the communal land. Should he personally relinquish his allotment or lose it in some way, his children still have the right as members of the commune to claim their own share. There is no *mob* in Russia, only a *people*. This will continue to be the case as long as new, unnational institutions do not create an unpropertied mob, which we hope is no longer to be feared.
>
> Baron August von Haxthausen, *Studies of the Russian Interior*,
> trans. Eleanore L.M. Schmidt

Directly influenced by discussions with Konstantin Aksakov, Haxthausen's understanding of the Russian peasantry shared distinct similarities with that of the Slavophiles. He romanticized the docility and overall satisfaction of the peasantry, even under serfdom, and he commended Russia for its national unity, a unity he believed originated in both the paternalistic bonds between landlords and serfs and the uniformity of peasant institutions across the land. Haxthausen even considered Russian landlords to be the main support for the commune rather than, as others held, one of the economic burdens the commune had been created in order to ease. He even made the claim that serfdom undergirded Russia's "healthy social organism," and insulated Russia from external influences so that Russia "has no reason to fear the revolutionary forces now threatening Europe."[3] It may seem astonishing that during his months-long journey through Russia, Haxthausen failed to discover the abuses of serfdom that Radishchev had found so appalling a half-century earlier, but it is well worth keeping in mind that Haxthausen's trip through the countryside had been organized with the help of government officials, and, not speaking Russian, he had to rely on officially appointed translators. This arrangement undoubtedly made it easier for Haxthausen to find in the Russian Empire what he hoped to find there. To his credit, however, Haxthausen's empirical study of peasant communalism went far further than the Slavophiles had gone to provide solid data and information about communal arrangements in the villages, and his scholarship would long serve as a bedrock for understanding rural Russia.

Haxthausen's book spread word of the wonders of the peasant commune much more effectively than Slavophile journals and commentaries had managed to do. It is notable that Haxthausen and the Slavophiles shared a common concern with the socialist left: a mutual hatred for capitalism. Agrarian conservatives wished to revive traditional social relations, where socialists hoped to usher in a more just and rational world. However distinct their ultimate goals, the proximate task of overthrowing the pervasive, and seemingly unstoppable, influence of capitalism was the first order of business for both parties. And although Haxthausen disclaimed the resemblance between traditionalism and socialism as superficial, he even suggested that Russia's peasant communalism had something in common with the Western socialist ideas of Saint-Simon, Fourier, and Owen. For these reasons Haxthausen was embraced by the far right and the far left, and only Russian liberals subjected his work to criticism. Haxthausen offered a good-news scenario that counteracted Chaadaevian despair and did so with the authority of a foreign expert in good graces with the Tsar. His book received praise from voices as disparate as those of Tsar Nicholas I and his self-appointed nemesis, Herzen.

Before emigrating from Russia, Herzen often displayed concern for the condition of the peasantry, but like Radishchev and the Decembrists he was less interested in Russian uniqueness than in basic human rights and social justice. Anticipating the "repentant noblemen" we will encounter among the later populists, Herzen understood serfdom as the great sin and shame of the nobility—something from which nobles had profited, yet for which they had incurred a huge debt to those they exploited. The problem was, as some of his diary entries from the early 1840s show, that he felt powerless to extricate himself from the socioeconomic logic of serf-owning in which Russian society was trapped. Instead, Herzen put his faith in the social and political progress of the West, believing that Europe's scientific and intellectual achievements would eventually point the way forward for Russia as well. Before departing Russia, Herzen had examined the peasant commune but dissented from the Slavophile idealization of it. Like other Westernizers at the time, he saw in peasant communalism a hidebound patriarchal obstacle to human freedom. Only later did his disillusionment with the European left, and his reading of Haxthausen, enable Herzen to consider the peasants and the village commune in a new light. If Herzen had earlier dismissed the Slavophiles as retrograde fantasists, his new appreciation for the commune helped him change his mind. Although he was far from agreeing with them in most ways, in his 1861 obituary of Konstantin Aksakov, Herzen acknowledged that "the turning point of Russian thought" was the Slavophile discovery of the commune.[4]

As early as 1843, even while still in the thick of his polemical disputes with the Slavophiles, Herzen had suggested in a diary passage that his opponents might have a point when it came to their praise for the commune. He particularly appreciated that redistribution of land enabled Russian peasants to retain their communal unity, enabling them to avoid individualized wage labor, which had been the scourge of many European peasants. At this point, however, he still considered the commune an accidental holdover brought about by Russian backwardness, not to mention an institution easily frustrated by the machinations of landowners and government officials. But by 1847 a seemingly Slavophile note crept into Herzen's thought when he contrasted the exclusionary and "sinister" character of European private property to the openness and inclusivity of Russia's peasant villages. It would not be long before these tentative notes of praise yielded to a full embrace of the commune and a celebration of Russian difference from Western Europe.

In the early 1850s, Herzen joined the Slavophiles in turning to Russian history for illumination. He concluded somewhat fancifully that the age-old existence of the commune had insulated the *narod* for centuries from all undesirable influences, all the way from Mongol invaders to modern-day rapacious landowners and self-serving state officials. He began to celebrate the commune as "deeply national" and "the vital principle of the Russian nation."[5] Yet at the same time and in stark contrast to the Slavophiles, Herzen began to argue that peasant communalism put the whole of Russian society in a position to build a homegrown and broadly national version of socialism. Despising Haxthausen's support for serfdom, Herzen nevertheless approvingly quoted his contention that, "each rural commune in Russia is a little republic, self-governing for its internal affairs, which knows neither personal property nor a proletariat; which long ago raised a feature of socialist utopias to the status of a *fait accompli*."[6] Were this transformation to a socialist system to be achieved, Russia would be in a position to establish its own communal government and then guide the rest of the world toward the promise of a socialist future.

To paraphrase Karl Marx, Herzen stood the Slavophiles on their heads in order to create his "Russian Socialism." Where the Slavophiles tended to place their faith in the communal character of the people, seeing the commune as a logical outgrowth of that character, Herzen saw the socioeconomic institution of the commune itself as the foundation. Once adopted, the practice of communalism went on to shape the character of the people. This reorientation enabled Herzen to eschew any spiritual interpretation of the commune and vest it instead with relevance for the secular world of progressive economics and politics. Herzen's understanding of the commune was secular, forward-looking, and practical, but for all that it was no less a fantasy projection than the commune the Slavophiles had imagined. In 1851 he wrote to the French historian Jules Michelet that "truth is always spoken among the *narod*. The life of the *narod* cannot be false."[7] Herzen held the commune responsible for creating the conditions that empowered this unshakable sincerity: "The Russian peasant knows no morality that does not arise instinctively and naturally from his communism; and this morality is deeply rooted in the character of the Russian people."[8] In passages like these Herzen's admiration for the peasantry rises to the level of ethnic nationalism, an emphasis that would continue to inform his populist views.

Contrary to the Slavophiles, Herzen envisioned the future of the peasantry as thoroughly reinvigorated by an admixture of European progressivism. Here we find the most essential difference between Herzen and the Slavophiles. Herzen had no interest in conforming to any long-standing inherited tradition. For him humanity's best days were not behind but ahead. Peasant communalism would serve as a foundation, but it would have to be transformed into something new, modern, up-to-date, capable of receiving into itself the most recent social and technological advancements. As he put it in his memoir *My Past and Thoughts*:

> Only the powerful thought of the West, stemming from its long history, is in a condition to be able to fructify the embryonic possibilities lying dormant in the patriarchal culture of the Slavs. The *artel'* and the village commune, the sharing out of profits and the redistribution of land, the village assembly and the unification of villages and townships, governed by themselves alone—all of those are the cornerstones upon which the temple of our future free and communal life will be erected. But all the same these cornerstones are nothing more than stones, and without Western thought our cathedral of the future will remain but a foundation.[9]

In the years following the development of "Russian Socialism," Herzen came to exert great influence on public opinion. His London journals, *The Pole Star* and *The Bell*, were smuggled into Russia by the thousands and gained a wide readership that enabled him to expound his views in a popular forum. He also had good timing in that his publications began to flood into Russia around the time when Alexander II (r. 1855–81) came to the throne and embarked on a series of reforms that would go on to vitalize the public sphere. Herzen's emphasis on the great potential of the *narod* voiced a message that *obshchestvo* was ready to hear at the time when serfdom was being abolished and Russia had somehow to reimagine itself as an integrated society. Considering that Herzen was asking small and isolated village communes in rural Russia, usually numbering not much more than a few hundred people, to form the basis of a transformed political system capable of coming to the rescue of capitalist Europe, his chutzpah is astonishing. Until his death in 1870, he would continue to propagate these ideas in his journals and other writings. As a result, more than anyone else, Herzen established the basis for a new populist ideology.

Herzen's Path to a Better Future

Herzen stoutly agitated for the overthrow of the autocracy and the march toward a democratic and socialist society, but with respect to revolution, he was more ambivalent. The Slavophiles had argued that the peasantry willingly lived apart from and in harmony with the state; Herzen conceived of the peasants as apart from and hostile to the state, and he sometimes pointed to the rebelliousness seething below the calm surface of village life. Yet he continued to express the hope that the renewal of Russia could take place without bloodshed. Prior to the abolition of serfdom he envisioned a peaceful social transformation, but when the emancipation settlement locked former serfs into a new kind of debt bondage, Herzen and his colleague Nikolai Ogarev called to reconvene the *Zemsky Sobor*, a Russian version of an assembly of the estates that had operated on occasion during the pre-Petrine era. They demanded the assembly proclaim that all the arable land should be handed over to the communes, the total eradication of social estates, and the popular election of all leaders. By such means, Herzen sought, as he put it in his customarily pithy style, "to unite the two Russias between whom Peter's razor has passed."[10] His desire for a transformation somewhere between bloody revolt and continued inertia anticipates a stubborn problem faced by generations of populists. *Obshchestvo* was too small in numbers to stage any sort of revolutionary transformation without outside help, but the *narod* was too geographically dispersed, as well as too ill-informed, to unite into any kind of revolutionary force. How were those who favored radical change to tap into the power of the masses, and convince them both of the need for change and of their own capacity to bring it about? And even if the *narod* chose to revolt, how could they ensure that a peasant revolt would push for anything resembling the aims of the intelligentsia?

Recognizing the divide that separated the urban from the rural, the educated elite minority from the laboring, impoverished majority, Herzen suggested other ways to bring the two separate Russias together. His rhetoric often collapsed the distinction between *obshchestvo* and *narod*, and he encouraged educated society not merely to admire and learn from the peasantry but to emulate it, even to merge with it. Ogarev first called for educated Russians, such as schoolteachers, to go into the village and work among the peasants, something he himself had attempted as early as the 1840s. In 1862, when the government had shut down Saint Petersburg University because of student demonstrations, Herzen appealed to the students to "go to the people," and use their educations not to become petty state officials but to serve as "warriors of the people." By 1864 Ogarev was suggesting that landowners should reimagine themselves as simple peasant farmers and "join the commune."[11]

We are not petty bourgeois—we are peasants.

We are poor in cities and rich in villages. All efforts to create in our midst an urban bourgeoisie in the Western sense have resulted in empty and absurd consequences. Our only genuine city-dwellers are government workers; the merchants are closer to the peasants than to them. The gentry are naturally much more rural than urban dwellers. Thus—the city for us is really just the government, while the village is all Russia, the people's Russia.

Our peculiarity, our originality is the village with its communal self-governance, with the peasants' meeting, with delegates, with the absence of personal land ownership, with the division of fields according to the number of households. Our rural commune has survived the era of difficult state growth in which communes generally perished and has remained whole in double chains, preserved under the blows of the owner's stick and the bureaucrat's theft.

Alexander Herzen, "Forward, Forward,"
trans. Kathleen Parthé, in *A Herzen Reader*

Such aspirations were not so far-fetched as they may sound when we consider that many Europeans were at that time bitterly condemning the evident defects of the newly industrialized Europe. "Russian Socialism" pitted two opposing forces: the debased, heartless, materialist, Western culture of the bourgeoisie against the liberated Russia of the near future. To Herzen the liberal Europe that arose from the French Revolution had grown stale and conservative in its middle-class insistence on the new rights and huge economic gains brought about by an unbridled capitalism. In Russia it was not the middle class that was holding society back but the state itself with its will to entrench and expand the Empire. In contrast to a capitalist Europe that benefited the stolid middle class, Russia's feudal-like, agrarian economy benefited only the autocracy, and no one but the government itself had any stake in maintaining the status quo. In Russia, in other words, there was nothing to lose in fighting for a better future. Therefore, according to Herzen's optimistic assessment, while Europe had grown overburdened by maintaining its commitment to the status quo, Russia was now beginning to step onto the world stage and, because of the essentially socialist character of its people, it was in a position to transform and revitalize the entire European world.

Since the peasants embodied the genuine Russian values that had been lost among the Westernized elites, Herzen concluded that not just the peasants but all Russians had a natural inclination to socialism: "Accustomed as we were to communes, land partitions, and workers' cooperatives, we saw in [socialism] an expression of sentiments that were closer to us than what we found in political doctrines."[12] Here Herzen makes a contrast that would become typical of Russian populism. He interprets socialism not only as antithetical to capitalism in economic terms, but he also contrasts it to liberal democracy in which power is wielded by elected representatives. He was not specific about how power would be held at a national level in a future socialist Russia, but he clearly implied that government would be carried out, insofar as possible, away from the center at a local level. In that respect, "Russian Socialism" was both anti-capitalist and anti-statist. It favored a new kind of national integration at the grassroots of society in direct and open contrast to the imperial ambitions of the autocratic state. Herzen was both a socialist and, in the broad sense of the word, a nationalist.

We can also compare "Russian Socialism" to the contemporaneous conception of socialism espoused by Marx and Engels. According to Marx and Engels, socialism would inevitably emerge from the increasing proletarianization that industrial capitalism produced. Herzen believed the rudimentary socialism preserved among the peasants of Russia already formed a popular basis on which an updated socialism could arise. The Marxian path to socialism relied on the expectation of radical transformation, while Herzen's path proposed the likelihood that communalism would expand from within and eventually take over. Marx dismissed Herzen as naive, and Herzen was unimpressed by Marxism. For these reasons Herzen's populism and Marxism are usually juxtaposed against one another, but certain interesting parallels between them are not always noticed. Herzen assumed that Russia was destined for socialism because the vast majority of Russians were equal in their shared poverty; Marx assumed a revolution would come about once a sufficient mass of proletarianized workers had become equal in their shared poverty. Both visions of the future provided comfort to those who found Russian and European economic inequality a continuing tragedy for which they desperately sought a remedy. If Marx treated industrialization and proletarianization as a demonstration of the unavoidability of communist revolution, Herzen treated the existence of peasant communalism as its own prophetic demonstration that socialism in Russia was rapidly advancing since the Russian people were "nearer to the new social system by their way of life than all the European peoples."[13]

Similarities aside, a crucial distinction between Herzen's and Marx's paths to socialism involved their points of origin. For Marx, socialism was to emerge and remain an international phenomenon because it would take shape as part of a global process. Herzen believed Russia itself would be the origination point, so that if European change were to come, it would have to pass through a period of Russian influence. Once awakened through intelligentsia intervention, the village would point the way toward an egalitarian future of democratic social justice. In this way, again, Herzen's socialism had an unmistakably nationalist flavor in its constant emphasis on Russia's destined future. As Anthony Smith has remarked, nationalists understand the nation "as a community of history and destiny, or better a community in which history requires and produces destiny—a particular national destiny."[14] Herzen held such nationalist views side by side with his cosmopolitan socialism. He likened Russians bestowing socialism on the rest of Europe to barbarians bringing Christianity to Rome. Both were destroying the reigning social system in order to usher in something better. Europeans, like Romans, were unable to move forward because they were tethered to a glorious past; Russians, like newly Christianized Goths, lacked such a past. Once the Russian people had liberated itself from autocratic domination, it would be "the freest people in Europe," entirely prepared to build a new and better society.

At times it seems as though something approximating the ideas Herzen espoused as "Russian Socialism" would have arisen with or without him. If Herzen had not come up with these populist ideas, one suspects someone else probably would have conceived some version of them. Russian populism was a comforting ideal that served many masters at once. It fed the desire for a positive sense of Russian identity, it gave assurance of the eventual rise of socialism in Russia, it provided a lever with which the autocracy could be removed and replaced, and it promised a path toward the end of the Empire and the national unification of a deeply divided society. Such a satisfying wish list, merged into a single theory, was clearly enticing to many minds, just as Marxism was enticing in its own context. Neither prophetic view of future socialism could be proven, but both profited from the fact they could not be disproven either. It is no wonder these two ideologies continued to appeal to future generations. In spite of the appeal of these ideas, it must not go unmentioned that Herzen had established a cruelly problematic set of principles for future followers. Under "Russian Socialism" all of the intelligentsia's hopes were held in trust to a particular image of the peasantry and to the faith that the *narod* would in future fulfill the revolutionary and communalist dreams the intelligentsia demanded of them. To put it simply, the potential realization of populist ideals relied almost exclusively on the conduct and choices of flesh-and-blood peasants with a necessarily different set of interests from those of the intelligentsia. Problems created by this incongruity would plague populism for generations.

The question of Herzen's direct influence on later forms of populism has raised much debate. Part of the problem is that Herzen's precise influence is hard to pin down. His writings received abundant attention in the 1850s and 1860s, the years when he was in the process of developing "Russian Socialism." But those years were fraught with other questions that demanded attention, among them the emancipation, the reforms, the student movement, and the uprising in Poland. As a commentator on everyday events, Herzen's message could grow diffuse. Yet his widely varied writings contain a great deal of material that directly anticipates the full-blown populism that would arise around the late 1860s. For example, like the later populists, Herzen promoted a socialist version of the "advantages of backwardness" argument. Chaadaev, in his "Apology," had argued that since Russia was a "blank page" it could adopt or reject the lessons of European history and thereby improve upon them. Herzen went further, contending that socialism in Europe was impossible because Europeans were fettered by what they had to lose. In his letter to Michelet, he proposed that Russians had a greater inclination for revolutionary change than Europeans did. "We are too oppressed, too unhappy to be satisfied with being only semi-free," he wrote, "Your scruples and your ulterior motives hold you back, but we have neither scruples nor ulterior motives ... We are independent because we don't own anything."[15] Herzen made the point in another way when he claimed that if Russia had been more closely connected to European history, Europe would have "sapped the life of the commune."[16] By the lucky chance of having retained its communalism, the *narod* was now prepared to leap beyond Europe into the socialist future where Europe dared not tread.

Herzen also anticipated later populists in his struggle with the problem of reconciling communal egalitarianism with personal freedom. In his own words: "How to develop the individuality of the peasant without losing the communal principle? Herein lies the whole tormenting dilemma of our era."[17] The challenge for Herzen was "to retain the Russian commune and give freedom to the individual."[18] Because of his deep concern for human freedom, some have labeled Herzen more a liberal than a socialist, a man who lacked the will to abandon the personal independence of the few for the greater good of the many. Herzen explicitly stated that, for all its good qualities, the commune could not in its present state serve as the basis for Russia's future because it lacked the Western insistence on human freedom. The problem is obvious enough: an institution developed to ensure social equality, and even political unanimity, is not very helpful when it comes to promoting freedom of thought. As Herzen might have said, Aksakov's communal choir sounds wonderful, but the world needs operas too, and what kind of opera can you have without the arias?

For Herzen, all the gains of European science, art, and philosophy, were the indispensable inheritance of Western civilization's humanism and concern for liberty. Such tremendous advantages could not be sacrificed in the march toward a socialist future. While Marx and his followers professed that history followed a predictable pattern toward a predictable end, Herzen and the later populists argued that history could move in any number of directions, or as Herzen put it "history ... knocks simultaneously at a thousand gates ... Who knows which may open?"[19] As a consequence, for Herzen and the populists, historical change was up to the individual. It required the voluntary, conscious collective action of thinking individuals in order to advance in the best possible direction. Herzen taught future populists that history had to be fought for by those who freely chose to guide it forward. It would not, as in the Hegelian or Marxian paradigms, largely take care of itself.

Through Herzen, the Slavophile admiration for peasant communalism was transformed into a plan for Russia's socialist future. "Russian Socialism" laid down most of the fundamental ideas upon which the "classical" socialist populism associated with the 1870s and 1880s would rest. Unlike Herzen, later populists engaged in rigorous study of the *narod*, developing new economic theories and new methods of political activism. They would be faced with the monumental task of trying to overcome many of the contradictions Herzen had the luxury to gloss over. But with respect to the mainstream of populist thought, Herzen's ideology mapped out most everything that would follow. From an ideological perspective, every subsequent populist position can be read as an interpretation of Herzen's "Russian Socialism." Herzen must be counted among the populists even though no one used that word during his lifetime.

Why Socialism?

Now that we have broached the question of Herzen's socialism, readers today might reasonably wonder why it was so common among the Russian intelligentsia to assume socialism was the obvious solution to the problems Russian society faced. In order to understand why socialism appealed to so many at that time it helps to consider our own presuppositions about the concept. Today, the idea of socialism resonates quite differently than it did in nineteenth-century Russia, especially given the fact that then it was a vision of the future but now has been experimented with in numerous different ways, times, and places. At least at the level of the nation state, we now use the world "socialism" primarily to describe one of two distinct political phenomena. On the one hand it can refer to a state that employs the partial redistribution of wealth under government auspices in a manner entirely compatible with capitalist markets and liberal democratic politics. On the other hand, it is associated with one-party states and centralized command economies, which seek to do away with capitalism and replace it with beneficial mechanisms of economic control and considerable redistribution of wealth.[20] Much of the developed world today looks at the former system as a legitimate form of government affiliated with the democratic left and the latter system as a form of social engineering doomed to failure as a result of overreaching the capacity of both government competence and human adaptability.

Europeans in the nineteenth century had very little experience with either of these forms of government, but at the same time most of them had tremendous faith, far more than we have today, in the potential of human ingenuity to solve the world's problems. It makes sense that they did. Beginning in the late eighteenth century, Europe had witnessed massive changes that seemed to promise inexorable human progress. In the realm of politics republican democracies were born and universal (male) suffrage promised to increase enfranchisement for all social classes. In the realm of industry, manufacture was providing a plethora of new goods and services, eventually bringing about higher standards of living. And in the realm of technology, new modes of transportation and communication were uniting the world as never before, while medical science had already begun to extend life expectancy. To be sure, conservative minds found many of these changes deeply troubling, and many so-called advances seemed in fact to make life worse for many people. Then as now, precisely what constitutes progress remains a matter of debate; however, in the nineteenth century the expectation that humanity had the ability to reshape the world for the better was near its apex. If European civilization had demonstrated its ability to bring about such rapid advancement in almost every area, then what was to prevent it from solving what many considered its most pressing problem of social inequality?

Revolutionary France had already sought to address the problem in the 1790s, and beginning in the early nineteenth century several European thinkers began to promote various proposals to address this inequality. Socialism, then, was born of a widespread optimism that human beings have the ability to solve their problems through the application of will and ingenuity. The problem was—and we continue to debate the relative merits of capitalism and socialism for this reason today—inequality looked like a bigger problem to some people than it did to others. Supporters of socialism have always either come from the working class or felt sympathetic with it. In Russia in particular, before the late nineteenth century the laboring part of the population had little access to these ideas, so it was the educated sympathizers from *obshchestvo* who pushed for a more egalitarian society by means of a revolutionary transformation. In Western Europe socialism had to compete with another model for bringing about greater equality by building up the middle class through the continued advancement of capitalism. Emerging out of a social system in which there had been very little of either capitalism or a middle class, this solution did not seem viable to most Russians. By contrast to the West, where it was possible for many to imagine a just democracy as a feature of an industrial capitalist society with the capacity to bring about greater equality by lifting the working class into the middle classes, Russia was so divided socially that it was difficult to imagine a just democracy in the absence of a social transformation that would lift the fortunes of the poor by redistribution rather than free markets and free elections. Either continued adherence to the autocratic state or tearing it down and establishing an egalitarian society in its place seemed to many to be the stark zero-sum choice Russia faced. For the majority among politically motivated Russians, between the emancipation in 1861 and the Revolution in 1917, the debate would not be that between capitalism and socialism; instead it would concern precisely what type of socialism was needed and how to bring it into being.

The Rebel: Mikhail Bakunin

If Herzen was the first populist theorist, Bakunin was the first populist revolutionary. Bakunin made a far less significant ideological contribution than Herzen did, but much of the enthusiasm for populist values existed at the level of emotion rather than ideology, and when it came to emotional appeal Bakunin's influence would prove enormous. In the early 1840s when Bakunin fell under the influence of left Hegelians in Berlin, he became an advocate for what may be summarized as the "creative destruction" wrought by revolutionary struggle. From that time on he devoted his energies to political activity on the far left. Participating in several revolutionary events of 1848 and 1849, he was arrested and managed to receive death sentences in both Germany and Austria. Eventually he was extradited to Russia where he spent seven years in Saint Petersburg prisons. His sentence was commuted to Siberian exile once Alexander II attained the throne, and after three years in Siberia he managed to escape across the Pacific, finally returning to Europe in 1862. From that point until his death in 1876, Bakunin continued to participate in revolutionary causes, always fighting for the emancipation of the lower classes.

More a figure of European radical politics than Russian, and most famous for his disputes with Marx, Bakunin did weigh in on Russian questions at many points. His views on his native country are what concern us here. While Herzen and Bakunin were close friends, they often disagreed with one another. If Herzen hoped for a relatively peaceful revolutionary transformation that would retain those blessings of the old regime he considered worth holding on to, Bakunin welcomed the kind of wholesale destruction of the old regime that might lead to the founding of an entirely new order. Herzen was well aware that revolutionary aspirations often went hand in hand with chaotic and damaging upheaval, but he rejected destruction for its own sake while Bakunin welcomed chaos and upheaval for its cleansing effect. Herzen considered Bakunin rash and immature. He once noted that in advocating for an armed uprising in Russia Bakunin "mistook the second month of pregnancy for the ninth."[21] For his part, Bakunin was frustrated with the plodding pace Herzen took to bringing about a change they both agreed was absolutely necessary. The biggest disagreement between the two of them, at least in the 1840s, involved the village commune. Bakunin condemned the commune for its patriarchal backwardness, its often inhumane ways of meting out justice, and its enforcement of social conformity. That the peasants still clung to their "naive monarchism"—the idea that the Tsar was the ultimate protector of the *narod*—Bakunin blamed on the benighted condition in which the peasantry lived. He also noted that unity within the commune weakened the revolutionary potential of the peasants by isolating them in small, walled-off units that prevented them from forging broader regional connections.

In spite of Bakunin's disdain for the commune, he still saw the peasantry as a political conduit toward radical social change in Russia. In 1845, in an open letter to a French newspaper, he noted that members of the young nobility in Russia "do everything possible to connect with the people," but that making the connection was extremely difficult since the two populations had long been "separated by an abyss." It is unclear which young nobles Bakunin had in mind as early as 1845. Likely this claim (made out of earshot from most Russians) was merely a rhetorical device to bolster his next point that radical change could arise from the other side of the abyss:

> For the Russian people, Sir, in spite of the terrible slavery that oppresses them, and in spite of the beatings that rain down on them from all sides, possess entirely democratic instincts and appearances . . . There is something in their half barbarity so grand and energetic, such an abundance of poetry, of passion and spirit, that knowing them it is impossible not to be convinced they already have a grand mission to fulfill in this world. The entire future of Russia resides within them, in this innumerable and imposing mass of people who speak the same language and who will be, soon I hope, animated by the same feelings and the same passions. For the Russian people advance, Sir, in spite of all the bad faith of the government. Those very serious periodic insurrections of the peasants against their lords, insurrections that are multiplying in a frightening way, prove it only too well. It may be that the moment is not far away when they merge together in a huge revolution.[22]

Bakunin here anticipates another essential component of Russian populism: that the peasantry was inherently rebellious and, under the right circumstances, perfectly capable of bringing about a revolution on their own. This fantasy was stitched together from a fabric of wishful thinking, but Bakunin would continue throughout his life to have faith in the rebellious spirit of the *narod*. Dreaming of the peasantry's revolutionary intentions was an intoxicant many populists over the years would find hard to refuse. Only two powers in Russia appeared capable of producing fundamental change—the Tsar and the *narod*. If the autocracy proved consistently disappointing, dreams of "people power" offered a tantalizing remedy to the state's inertia.

Aksakov had espoused the Christian brotherhood of the peasantry. Herzen had proclaimed the socialist communalism of the peasantry. Now Bakunin hailed the revolutionary will of the peasantry. All these populist ideals arose within the impassioned imaginations of outside observers. All three of them searched for that untapped potential lying dormant within the *narod* that could serve to fulfill their own goals and aspirations. All three of them were also outsiders who based their conclusions on what they supposed to be the uniformity of the peasants across time and place. Bakunin, for example, argued that all peasants in all parts of European Russia "share one common misfortune and therefore one common cause"[23] In his own way, in other words, he idealized the peasants every bit as much as an Aksakov or Herzen had. Also akin to the Slavophiles, Bakunin grounded his faith in peasant rebelliousness on a reading of Russian history. The crucial historical events, he believed, were the Cossack and serf rebellions of the seventeenth and eighteenth centuries, in particular those of Stenka Razin and Emelian Pugachev, which had been widespread and surprisingly successful in their day. Historians today would dispute that such rebellions were entirely based on peasant dissatisfaction with the nobility, but such dissatisfaction played a role in them, and Bakunin had little difficulty taking the part for the whole. In addition, as time wore on, Bakunin grew more willing to accept Herzen's view of the peasantry as innately socialist, and he came to believe over the years that the commune actually might serve as a proper basis for the postrevolutionary anarcho-socialist future he hoped would materialize.

Unlike Herzen, Bakunin had few pangs of concern that the peasantry might throw the baby of European civilization out with the bathwater of popular revolution. He believed that the revolution must come from among the people and that no measures could be taken to construct a new society until a revolution had first cleared the ground for it. In Bakunin's view the *narod* was already revolutionary because the people's anger burned beneath the injustice of its impoverished and servile position, because history had demonstrated they would join a revolt whenever a Razin or a Pugachev appeared on the scene, because they already despised the state in the form of those local officials who governed over them, and because they believed that the land belonged to them rather than the local landowner they felt they had the right to take full possession of it. For all these reasons, too, Bakunin tended toward the view that the peasants had more to teach the educated classes than the other way around.

> There is no village in Russia which is not deeply discontented with its condition, which does not hide, in the depth of its collective heart, the desire to seize all the land belonging to the landlords and then that of the richer peasants (*kulaks*), and the conviction that this is its indubitable right. There is no village which, with skill, cannot be induced to revolt. If the villages do not revolt more often, this is due to fear or to a realization of their weakness. This awareness comes from the disunity of peasant communes, from the lack of real solidarity among them. If each village knew that when it rises all others will rise, one could say for certain that there is no village in Russia which would not revolt.
>
> Bakunin, Letter to Nechaev, quoted in Michael Confino,
> *Daughter of a Revolutionary*

Bakunin reserved great scorn for those populists who hoped to nurture and educate the peasantry into revolutionary preparedness. He believed the role of radical outsiders was not to help the people become sufficiently enlightened to be able to sustain a successful revolution. It was, after all, not the intelligentsia's revolution but the people's. The revolutionary intelligentsia needed only to rouse the *narod* to recognition of their preexisting rebelliousness and to bring isolated peasant villages and townships into a united awareness of their mutual interests and combined power. The job of the educated outsider was to "create in our people a feeling and consciousness of real unity" and "to convince them that an invincible force lives [within them]."[24] Sometimes, unconvinced that educated elites were up to this task, Bakunin put his faith instead in the bandits and outlaws who had led earlier rebellions. Such outlaw revolutionaries could use their wider connections and supra-local perspective to unite isolated revolts into full-scale revolution. Herzen is correctly understood as the ideological founder of Russian populism, but Bakunin injected the movement with a headlong recklessness that strongly characterized its most radical phases, those periods which would in fact lend populism much of its later fame (as well as its infamy).

Populist History: Afanasy Shchapov

Another important contribution to the early formation of Russian populism was made by the figure who is rightly considered populism's first historian, Afanasy Shchapov. From today's point of view the word "historian" might be overly generous when applied to a writer who sought out and discovered in ancient documents evidence of the tendentious views he already wanted to promote. Shchapov's view of Russian history was highly speculative, and it arose less as a result of his historical research than his historical research arose from his populist convictions. His claims and rhetoric did, however, have an important influence on shaping populism as a whole, especially on how the intelligentsia came to understand the political aspirations of the *narod*. Whatever its accuracy, Shchapov's reading of Russian history is highly instructive as a window into the formation of a populist worldview.

Shchapov's social background was far closer to the people than that of most populists we will encounter here. He grew up in Siberia, the son of a church-sexton father and an indigenous Buryat mother. He seems to have developed his sympathy for the Russian peasant upon coming to European Russia for divinity school and then college, where he was forced to defend his status as a member of the lower classes. In his university years, his fellow students discovered they could tease Shchapov to the point of tears by criticizing the common people, for whom his collaborator and biographer, Aristov, claims Shchapov had "a romantic love."[25] A devoted student, Shchapov studied history at the University of Kazan, beginning to publish articles on ecclesiastical history in the mid-1850s. Already in his early works we find a naive, even fanatical, belief in the natural abilities of the peasantry. Even more than Aksakov or Herzen, Shchapov embraced the view that the peasantry was the only thing that really mattered in Russian life. Influenced in part by the Slavophiles, Shchapov's idolization of the *narod* was similarly based on his reverence for the village commune. The commune "proved" that the peasants lived in peace on the land, always willing to lend assistance to one another. Convinced of the innate goodness of the *narod*, Shchapov was one of the earliest populists to encourage educated Russians to humbly learn from, rather than to help or to teach, the peasants. He grew convinced that the political impassivity of the Russian intelligentsia rested on its inability to connect with the people: closer connection to the people would encourage educated elites to become more politically active because, like Bakunin, he believed the *narod* had a thinly veiled tendency toward rebellion. He discerned evidence for this tendency in the continued and widespread existence of those religious schismatics, the Old Believers and other sectarians, who had split from the Orthodox Church.

Although he would later play down the Slavophile influence on his reading of history in order to fit in with the progressive thinking of the late 1850s, following the Slavophiles Shchapov at first considered the state to be a protective bubble that enabled Russia's age-old communalism to have survived intact. He even described the commune as a form of *sobornost'*, and his florid yet highly abstract interpretation of Russian history resembles that of the Slavophiles and the German idealist thinkers who inspired them. Shchapov also lamented the loss of pre-Petrine Russian unity that he considered (again echoing the Slavophiles) to have defined Muscovite Russia. As with the Slavophiles, a strong strain of Russian exceptionalism pervades Shchapov's history writing. It is especially apparent in the emphasis he places on Russia's absolute difference from the modern West.

Yet in spite of the obvious Slavophile influence on his thought, Shchapov quite clearly parted ways with the Slavophiles, and went even further than Herzen and Ogarev in his utopian view that the educated classes should adapt the collectivism of the village commune to their own uses. In sharp contrast to the Slavophiles, he disdained the existence of the gentry in Russian society. The nobility was alien to the people, and aristocratic and popular principles could never be reconciled with one another. Shchapov was mainly interested in the political, rather than religious, significance of Russian Orthodoxy, so that in contrast to the Slavophiles he did not necessarily reject Western influences on the Russian peasant, as long as they had no deleterious effect. "It is necessary to introduce [among the peasantry] a European basis of thought," he wrote, "but neither can we forget the foundations of the people's everyday life because the life of the people isn't a *tabula rasa* but a force, creating history by its own inner laws."[26] As Aristov commented, the point was to introduce Enlightenment among the people while recreating Russian society based on the essential political structures of the village commune. Thus, although contemporaries sometimes considered him a Slavophile historian, Shchapov had much more in common with Herzen's interpretation of the *narod*. It is not surprising that Herzen heartily approved of Shchapov's work, finding in Shchapov a fresh and powerful new voice.

How did Shchapov manage to transform the analysis of historical documents into a platform for populist propaganda? One might say that he acted less as a historian than as a masterful user of Aesopian language, that technique Russian writers employed to get around censorship by telling their stories in veiled messages understood by their readers but not necessarily by government officials. He found he could write about one thing, history, while in fact intending to convey a separate message about Russia's national destiny and the role of the people within it. Like his contemporary, but rather more subdued fellow historian, Nikolai Kostomarov, Shchapov despised the state-centered historiography that went back to the eighteenth century, and he made every attempt to replace it with what he believed to be the untold story of the people's history. This task would prove Herculean. Since social history of any kind was in its infancy, and since the documentary evidence Shchapov had to rely on did not come from the *narod* itself, he was forced to depict the history of the *narod* using a very broad brush. This was a regrettable necessity, but it also made it easier to tell the story he wanted to tell. The Slavophiles had pioneered this interpretive technique in the service of portraying the *narod* as docile and Christian. Shchapov saw them as actively rebellious and focused his attention on popular rebellion and the struggle to maintain autonomy and popular democracy under the pressure of an expansionist Russian Empire.

In his effort to counteract the prevailing idea that the state was the axis and driving force of Russian history, Shchapov radically discounted any constructive role the state might have played, claiming that reading the original sources would convince anyone that "it was the peasants who were the builders of everything."[27] The novelty of Shchapov's populist approach to the history of Russia derived from his emphasis on regionalism. He believed that by concentrating their attention on the state, historians had inadvertently neglected the outlying areas (nearly all of the Empire's immense terrain); instead he framed those outlying areas as "the essential, productive element of our future civilization."[28] If the state had attempted, centripetally, to yoke the powers of the various peoples and regions to itself, Shchapov found that in such a sprawling imperial terrain the regions exerted an even more powerful centrifugal force working to remove the people from the state's influence. In essence, he posited, there was no single Russian land but simply many distinct regions, even if these regions had retained many similarities. Having established this basic approach to Russian history, he could then present the "losers" of Russian history—the formerly important cities of Kiev, Novgorod, Pskov, the *veche* [the old popular assembly], the peasants, the Old Believers [dissenters from Russian Orthodox leadership], and the commune—all as standing in opposition to the centralizing Muscovite state, not just as a vestige of history but as a living force for change. These popular, democratic elements of Russian history, which the state-centered historians considered the discarded detritus of autocratic consolidation, were for Shchapov continuing forces of destabilization in the contemporary world. They were the real Russia thinly veiled over by the flimsy veneer of state power. The implication was unmistakable: democratic Russia, still extant among the vast majority of the population living in the countryside, harbored the revolutionary power to bring about its own autonomy and in the end to render the autocratic state history's future "loser." To be sure, as history, Shchapov's ecstatic interpretation of the Russian past is one-sided and nearly impossible to defend. All the same, it served as an inspiration to those early populists seeking a path toward the reunification of Russian society.

Nothing is so needed for us now as precisely the spirit of communal unification, rapprochement, reconciliation, the spirit of communal assembly and consultation, the spirit of communal initiative and collective guarantee. It's time! It's time! Instead of empty conversation and journalistic exposition of our sympathy for the peasant, for the great peasant question, instead of the fruitless scholastic search for the grounds and abstract-theoretical judgments on various forms of association, we city dwellers must together search for methods of genuine living collective unification between ourselves, to learn from the village commune the practical social principles of communalism, to acquire, develop, strengthen, and perfect the spirit of peasant communal assembly and consultation in collective, amicable, communal initiatives ... The social principle of the commune is productive and full of life. To us, disconnected by the prejudice and hatred of the system of social estates, put at odds by abstract theories, fearing one another, suspecting duplicity and physically and morally emaciated, wasting away, in the closed-off circles of the military, the bureaucracy, estate castes, scholarly and literary, and so on ... we need the freshening, enlivening, calming spirit of the commune, the communal social life, communal socialism ... We need peasant communal tact, the spirit of the *artel'*, communal reasoning, and talent in the arrangement and undertakings of our associations.

Afanasy Shchapov, "The Village Commune" in *Sochineniia*

The one essential commonality that ran through the autonomous regions was communalism. Shchapov even found in the commune a sort of small-scale version of the hidden, but archetypal, characteristic of Russian history. As opposed to the Slavophiles, who conceived of the commune as existing in a mutually beneficial symbiotic relationship with the autocratic state, Shchapov linked the commune to those institutions in the Russian past that had been overthrown by Muscovite dominance. He considered the commune to be integrally related to the democratic assembly [*veche*] of Kiev and Novgorod, and thus inimical to autocratic power. He argued that although Kievan and Novgorodian democracy had been defeated long ago, in fact they continued to exist in miniature, yet virtually everywhere in Russia, in the world of the peasants, the Cossacks, and the Old Believers, and in any other elements that remained distinct from and alien to the state. If this alternative Russia was concealed from view by the dominant and grandiose Tsarist Empire, Shchapov believed it nevertheless remained active and full of potential. He went so far as to argue that modern Russia had the capacity to become unified on the basis of a merger between the existing commune and the political revival of Russia's ancient democratic traditions. Originally influenced by the Slavophile "discovery" of the commune's importance, Shchapov redefined the commune not as the guarantor of state power but as a stepping stone toward its final destruction. Shchapov played up the "otherness" of peasant religious practices and read that otherness as a form of rebellion. By highlighting what one scholar has called the "spectacular difference from the life of secular urban dwellers" among Russia's religious sectarians, Shchapov was able to suggest they were intentionally rejecting the Western ways that had been foisted upon Russia by the autocracy.[29]

The populist radicalism evident in Shchapov's historical writing was expressed in a sufficiently Aesopian language to evade censorship, and that is why the subversive nature of his views would come to the attention of the state in a different way. After a disastrous incident in 1861 in which a group of peasants demonstrated against the terms of emancipation and were violently suppressed, Shchapov gave a speech at a Kazan funeral service for the deceased peasants in which he denounced the government and, in essence, called for popular rebellion. Notwithstanding all his historical writing, Shchapov remains best known for this oration. It ended with a striking and as yet unheard of call for "a democratic constitution," by which Shchapov undoubtedly meant democracy linked to peasant communalism. Arrested and taken to Saint Petersburg for questioning, he was released within four months because the police could find no direct evidence of the content of his speech. Like Herzen, Shchapov was a populist *avant le nom* and prior to the formation of a larger movement. And yet he anticipated the disappointment felt by many later populists when the peasantry did not prove as revolutionary or as socialist as they assumed it was. Believing that the peasantry represented a higher form of Russian culture that had the capacity to point the way toward a better future, when such expectations went unmet Shchapov began to reject his populist views. During the last years of his life he turned away from the study of history toward an interest in the natural sciences.

Fashioning the Classless Identity: Pavel Iakushkin

As we have seen, one of the earliest attempts on the part of educated society to establish closer contact with the *narod* involved collections of folk songs. In the eighteenth century collecting had been a rather haphazard affair, often relying on songs and tales found among personal acquaintances or peasants who lived in the cities. Under the influence of both Slavophile nationalism and European ethnography, however, interest in folk materials eventually grew more systematic. A major figure in Russian collecting of folk materials was Ivan Kireevsky's brother Petr (Pyotr). Petr Kireevsky, as avid a Slavophile as his brother, wrote very little. Instead, hoping to shed light on "the formation of the national spirit," he devoted his life to gathering and cataloging as extensive a collection of folk materials as he could discover.[30] Classifying them both by type and by region, he collected songs, spirituals, legends, and tales mounting into the thousands, of which only a small fraction were ever published during his lifetime. Although Kireevsky sometimes went on his own to collect materials in rural Russia, he mainly drew on the services of friends and acquaintances, including some of the most renowned figures of the first half of the nineteenth century, such as Alexander Pushkin, Nikolai Gogol, the conservative historian, Mikhail Pogodin, and the linguist Vladimir Dal.

Ultimately, help from friends would not satisfy Kireevsky's desire to cover as much ground as possible, and he began to fund collecting trips to unexplored regions. The most important of his paid collectors was Pavel Iakushkin, who had been a student at Moscow University when they first met. Once Iakushkin abandoned his studies and went to work for Kireevsky in 1844, he devoted the next two decades of his troubled and fascinating life to collecting ethnographic materials. As one scholar wrote, Iakushkin made "going to the people" his profession.[31] During the summer months, he wandered, mostly on foot, through nine Russian provinces, collecting not only songs for weddings and dances, but also stories, legends, children's games, jokes, riddles, and sayings. Due to the usual peasant suspiciousness of outsiders, the practice of collecting those materials was no easy task, and Iakushkin had to develop an arsenal of techniques to gain him entrée among the locals.

On the advice of Kireevsky and Pogodin, Iakushkin adopted what must at first have felt like a disguise in order to ingratiate himself with the peasants he met. He began to wear clothing that clearly distinguished him from the gentry class into which he had been born, strategically dressing as, and playing the part of, a wandering peddler. In this guise, Iakushkin carried small goods he could trade for the recitation of a song. One wonders whether it helped him fit in that, while his father hailed from the nobility, his mother had been born a serf, a somewhat unusual situation that may have afforded him a rather multifaceted and nuanced view of social class. In the costume of a peddler he wore high boots, a long beard, and a rope around his waist, as he wandered through the villages trading wares for folk materials. He faced a serious problem, however, in that he had to wear spectacles in order to carry out his work, a thing most peasants had never witnessed on a member of their own social class. He made use of local taverns where he would soften the resistance of peasants with alcohol in order to coax the desired information out of them. Unfortunately, this technique was to have fateful consequences as it sustained Iakushkin's tendency to alcoholism, which would hasten his death at the age of fifty.

With his mixed parentage, in a certain sense Iakushkin biologically bridged the stark divisions of Russian society. Once he took on the guise of a wandering peddler, it was almost as if he attempted to reconcile that division within his life and person. His sphere of movement was neither rural nor urban, his dress was not really that of a peasant, nor certainly of a nobleman, and the lifestyle he adopted was divorced from both the world of agricultural labor and from the manners of fashionable society. Although he published his travel notes and wrote some short stories, he took no interest in "foreign" literature, dismissing and scorning anything he considered overly learned. On one occasion he was mistaken for a peasant by a member of the nobility with whom he shared a carriage. When, having realized his mistake, the nobleman begged his forgiveness, Iakushkin assured him he was "very glad" to have been perceived that way.[32] In essence Iakushkin created and staged a persona that refused the social segregation on which Russian society was built.

Iakushkin's dual (or blended) identity led to many misunderstandings and general awkwardness in a world so steeped in the norms of class difference. He himself admitted that the peasants looked at him as though he was a sort of actor. In such a stratified society, his attempt to erase the difference between one class and another only made him stand out everywhere. Yet in another way it afforded him a rather privileged position. Wandering year after year through the far reaches of the countryside, he developed a

Figure 3.1 Pavel Iakushkin © Out of copyright (public domain).

respect for the *narod* that, unlike that of his educated peers, was not based on the blind idealization of unfamiliarity. He may have been the first populist to appreciate the peasants without idealizing them. Unlike the peasant worship of his employer Kireevsky, who was searching for a spiritual truth in peasant folkways, or a Herzen, who placed his hopes in the "socialism" of the commune, Iakushkin portrays the peasants he meets on the road as ordinary human beings with plenty of faults, an often bleak disposition, and a healthy and well-earned mistrust of outsiders. Moreover, after so many years among the peasants, he was able to discern subtle local differences in a way that set him apart from other educated urbanites who could only think about "the" peasant and "the" village. Such an attitude resembles that found in Turgenev's *Notes of a Hunter* to a degree, but where Turgenev's narrators remain outside observers, Iakushkin took on the role of participant, in everything from selling wares to singing and drinking along with the peasants who were also the targets of his interest.

Unavoidably, but also rather deliberately, he brought the peasant side of himself back to the city whenever he returned. While Iakushkin's wanderings around the countryside left few notable traces on the peasantry, in the city he produced quite the reverse effect. He was remembered in Moscow and Saint Petersburg as a remarkable figure, both as an extreme eccentric and as an inspiration. He kept on his peddler's attire among his urban friends, moved from house to house to abide temporarily with those who agreed to take him in, and intentionally slept on the floor so as not to get spoiled by the "luxurious" life of his elite friends. He even claimed to own only one set of clothing at a time, wearing it until it wore down to rags, at which point he would buy a new outfit of the exact same type. It would not be fair or accurate to say that Iakushkin was bringing rural culture back to the city—especially since his drunkenness seems to have grown progressively worse over the years, and may account for much of his unusual behavior—but it does seem accurate to say that his persona and conduct served as a sort of one-man public demonstration of opposition to social difference.

Unfortunately, even though he struggled to erase that difference in himself, Iakushkin came across in both the country and the city more as an oddity than as a role model. He was once announced by a maid as "someone … at the door who is neither a barin [gentleman] nor a peasant."[33] On the other hand, Iakushkin inspired many young Russians in the 1850s and 1860s to look to the countryside in order to discover the heart and soul of Russian culture. V.P. Ostrogorskii remembered Iakushkin as "the first and only *narodnik* in the years of my youth, with deep respect for and faith in the spiritual strength of the masses, which he knew from personal experience [*ne iz knig*], and in which he clearly saw the dark ignorance and primitivity … He revealed Rus' to me in all its breadth and power, awakening a desire to know the treasures of popular life."[34]

The Paradoxical Populist: Nikolai Chernyshevsky

As Herzen's influence began to wane in the early 1860s, it was eclipsed on the left by that of the more radical Nikolai Chernyshevsky. Were we able to go back to the time when radical populism reached the height of its influence in the 1870s and ask one of the populist revolutionaries whether she had been more inspired by Herzen or Chernyshevsky, she would inform us in no uncertain terms that Chernyshevsky had been a far greater influence on her and the movement as a whole. This passionate devotion to Chernyshevsky is hard to reconcile with the fact that he rejected many of the populist articles of faith, including in particular the notion that the *narod* had some valuable lesson to impart to *obshchestvo*. In fact, it has been claimed that Chernyshevsky was really not a populist at all. One must keep in mind as we examine Chernyshevsky's contribution to the populist movement that Russian populism never espoused a particularly well defined set of principles. It lacked a manifesto, or to put it differently, it had too many manifestos. A variety of populist assertions—from Herzen's, Bakunin's, and Shchapov's to others we will encounter in the next chapter—were meant to be grasped with the intellect. But populism could also be assimilated at the level of emotion. It could mean merely sympathizing with and desiring to serve and elevate the suffering *narod*. Chernyshevsky, more than anyone else, endowed young radicals with the ardent and politically engaged commitment that came to characterize Russian revolutionary populism.

If Chernyshevsky was not a "classical" populist, his politics did at least arise from that outrage over Russian inequality that goes back to Radishchev, and he also shared with Herzen, Shchapov, and others the desire to bring socialism to Russia. But by contrast to most of the figures we have discussed, Chernyshevsky lacked the nationalistic commitment to proclaiming Russia's difference from Europe and special contribution to world history. Like Marx and Engels, he envisioned an international socialism of the future without any special emphasis on Russia's contribution. With respect to the *narod* itself, if we return to the distinction made in the previous chapter between those proto-populists, who defended the peasantry as ordinary human beings and those full-blown populists, who found something special in the peasantry, their culture, and their institutions, then Chernyshevsky was closer to the former. He openly disdained what he considered the conservative tendencies of the peasants, and he refused to idealize them as something to be believed in or worshiped. He merely fought for their economic and social rights as human beings worthy of dignity and equal opportunity.

Because of this difference, Chernyshevsky was able to hold certain views that would be antithetical to Herzen and other populists. Most notably, he did not particularly fear the advent of capitalism in Russia. For Herzen the growth of capitalism had the potential to undermine peasant socialism. As capitalism played an increasingly prominent role in Russia in the decades after the abolition of serfdom, other populists would take this threat even more seriously, as we will see. Chernyshevsky, on the other hand, had no difficulty envisioning a path to a socialist future that would lead through the rise of capitalism, and he did not fear the prospect of a Russian transition from an agricultural to an industrialized economy. Absolutely distinct from the Slavophiles, Chernyshevsky believed in the need to modernize peasant life rather than preserve the past. These views led some, like the Marxist Georgy Plekhanov, to claim Chernyshevsky had never been a populist at all. Some have even pointed to passages in which Chernyshevsky exposed the squalor and patriarchal backwardness of peasant life as evidence that he had outright contempt for the *narod*, wishing only to transform the peasants into something new, different, and better. In fact, Chernyshevsky refused to romanticize any class, ethnicity, or religion; he was more of a leveler, a supporter of absolute equality who rejected the idea that all people were not, at base, cut from the exact same cloth. He had a profound sense of the absurdity of any and all hierarchy. The inversion of social class that Herzen had adopted from Aksakov—*narod* above and *obshchestvo* below—an inversion that would become a characteristic feature of Russian populism, was not within Chernyshevsky's world view. The only thing Chernyshevsky idealized was the bright, modern, international socialist future of his imagination.

With the goal of attaining this future, as early as 1848 Chernyshevsky had supported Russia's need for a peasant-based revolution, and he accepted that certain features of the peasant commune could be helpful in realizing it. He did not conceive of the commune as the linchpin of his revolutionary interests, as it was for Herzen; rather, he regarded communalism as a primitive holdover from an earlier epoch in European history, but he called it a "sacred heritage" and welcomed the fact that in Russia it had lasted into the present. He understood the commune's coelacanth-like persistence into modern Russia to be a potential "advantage of backwardness" Russian socialists could make use of, referring to it as an "anti-toxin" against the debilitating side of capitalism and wage labor in rural Russia. Echoing Herzen's claim that Russia already had the socialist society Europe only hoped to achieve, Chernyshevsky remarked that: "the order of things for which the … West is now striving still exists in our country in the mighty national customs of our village life"[35] His novel *What Is To Be Done?* (1863) makes clear that he wished communal cooperatives to become the future of educated Russians as well. Both Chernyshevsky and his closest associate, Nikolai Dobrolyubov, saw the peasantry as more rebellious than docile, and at times they both appealed to educated elites to go out and work among the *narod*. Dobrolyubov, for instance, invited young Russians to "work among the people directly and immediately so as to call into being its fresh and redoubtable powers."[36] In these ways Chernyshevsky and Dobrolyubov clearly numbered among the populists.

Chernyshevsky's primary interest, however, was to be found not in the peasantry but in urban, educated Russia, and it was in this realm where he exerted his primary influence on the history of populism. He focused on encouraging young members of the educated elite to change society by remaking themselves. In this effort, Chernyshevsky, more than anyone else, set a new tone among the left-leaning and radical intelligentsia. He pointed the way toward a life of self-sacrifice and single-minded devotion to the cause that virtually all young Russian radicals found compelling. He even provided a sort of "how-to manual" in his novel and other writings by which young people could resist conventionality and fashion a counterculture of "New People." This counterculture would serve to demonstrate the benefits of such unconventional arrangements as open marriages, living communally, and working in cooperative *arteli*. By emulating the tone Chernyshevsky and Dobrolyubov set in their writings and public personae, and later by emulating the characters in *What Is To Be Done?*, they would struggle toward revolutionary change in the process of enacting the Chernyshevskian stance, embodying it in their speech, their dress, their attitudes toward others, and in their actions. All of these were marshaled to repudiate the old world of social hierarchy, elitism, and class advantage in order to replace them with full equality, rational decision-making, and political power in the hands of those who could use it to create the greatest good for the greatest number.

In practice, this politics of personal life could not bring down any preexisting political institutions, nor did it change the minds of liberals or conservatives, but Chernyshevsky's own life as a martyr to the cause—he was arrested in 1863, subjected to civil execution, and exiled to Siberia for the next two decades—and especially his novelistic instructions about "what should be done" proved empowering to generations of revolutionaries. In this respect, although somewhat removed from populism ideologically, Chernyshevsky can be considered the individual most responsible for the rise of populist activism. He helped light a burning desire within young radicals to sacrifice themselves for the good of the cause.

When populism emerged as the dominant ideology, it would be fueled by Chernyshevsky's exhortations and personal example. At the same time, both Chernyshevsky and Dobrolyubov were responsible for introducing a tenor of steely-eyed realism into the revolutionary movement, which remained central to the tone and posture of Russian radicalism for generations. As we shall see, populists of all varieties would struggle to find a position somewhere in between the willing idealization of the Herzens, Bakunins, and Shchapovs and the call for a sober assessment of unfortunate reality professed by Chernyshevsky, Dobrolyubov, and their followers. No one would find the conflict easy to negotiate.

A Populist Call to Arms: "To the Young Generation"

After the revolutionary year of 1848, in Russia there began a rigidly repressive seven-year period during the terminal segment of the reign of Nicholas I. But the Crimean War brought new drama, and Russia's loss in that war, coupled with Alexander II's ascension to the throne around the same time, galvanized both state and society into a vigorous and impassioned search for a new direction. The pivotal moment of this search was the February 1861 abolition of serfdom. From the state's viewpoint, emancipating the serfs constituted a bold declaration of a new path, and it was accompanied by a series of reforms calculated to introduce a calibrated measure of societal participation in public affairs. The period between the end of the Crimean War in 1855 and the 1861 emancipation witnessed the formation of a much more clearly defined and politically motivated left, center, and right wing of public opinion, each with its own journals in the newly open press. Of course emancipation had the most direct and extensive impact on the former serfs themselves, but it also had an explosive effect on *obshchestvo*. Under Nicholas I the Russian state was to be considered infallible, the social system sacrosanct. The abolition of serfdom constituted a tacit admission that the former regime had been wrong and its certainty in itself misplaced. If the serfdom that had been sanctioned by Official Nationality had been wrong, what else was wrong? What other aspects of the system needed to be questioned, or rejected?

For many on the left, even before emancipation, change emanating from the autocracy was proceeding far too slowly. If the state was willing to modernize Russia, it was only so as to advance the imperial project under autocratic rule. The autocracy considered counterproductive anything that might hinder that aim. Once the terms of emancipation were finalized, it became clear to the public that the peasants, while legally free, would remain in a state of long-term indebtedness, and their communes would lack the lands that had been settled upon the landowners. With less land than they had farmed under serfdom, and now legally responsible for paying off the government for the land they had received, their debt was onerous and not to be fully repaid for decades to come. The left saw the settlement as one that unfairly favored the gentry's loss of property (in land and in "souls"). Such "property" they considered immoral and illegal, not something that had any right to be reimbursed. Some of them saw the settlement as nothing less than a new form of serfdom. In reaction, beginning in 1861 a series of clandestine publications, typically referred to as "proclamations," were printed in secret and then disseminated among the public. Such proclamations openly stated opinions that would have been censored in the legal press. They made their appeals to various groups in the population and called for different kinds of progressive or revolutionary change.

The first of these publications, "To the Young Generation," hit the streets in the summer of 1861. Written by Nikolai Shelgunov and Mikhail Mikhailov, its contents reveal the degree to which by the early 1860s populist ideas had already become a fundamental feature of revolutionary politics. The document was no doubt inspired by Herzen's writings, and although Herzen disliked its strident tone he agreed to publish hundreds of copies in London, which were then smuggled into Russia and distributed all over Saint Petersburg. One likely reason Herzen disapproved of the document is that it also exhibits the influence of Bakunin and others in its acceptance of violent revolution. Mikhailov and Shelgunov were both associates of Chernyshevsky, so with all of these influences combined, "To the Young Generation" can be read as a reasonably faithful reflection of radical thinking in 1861. It blends appeals that would have been easily understood by Western liberals together with uniquely Russian demands that reveal its populist pedigree. As the title suggests, it was an appeal to Russian youth, particularly those in the universities; its mission was to inform them both how to foment revolution and what a postrevolutionary Russia ought to look like.

As mentioned earlier, the Russian words "populist" [*narodnik*] and "populism" [*narodnichestvo*] would not come into use until the 1870s, but "To the Young Generation" begins by referring to "the most educated, the most honest and the most capable" members of Russian society as the *Narodnaia Partia*. It would be possible to translate this term as "National Party," but the context makes clear that a better translation would be "Popular Party" or "Party of the People."[37] The proclamation refers to the educated young generation as "leaders of the people," asking them to speak to the *narod* face to face in an effort to prove to them the evils of the government and social system under which they are being exploited. It also, very much in anticipation of future populists, persuades young people to go forth and alert the *narod* to the cruel consequences the spread of capitalism could inflict. Shelgunov and Mikhailov trust that Russia can avoid the twin pitfalls of capitalism: proletarianization of the masses and political systems designed to keep power in the hands of the wealthy, but only because the *narod* is so inextricably committed to farming the land and living communally that Russian peasants cannot even imagine themselves living under different circumstances. Thus they declare it fundamentally necessary for the peasants to retain communal ownership of the land. They also assert that Europeans could not possibly understand this peculiarly Russian desire for communal land use. For these reasons they conclude that Russian landowners must prepare themselves to return to equal status with the peasants, themselves becoming ordinary members of the village commune.

Lifting a page from other populists, they take comfort in the supposed advantage of backwardness. "We are a belated people," reads the proclamation, "and that is our salvation." As Herzen had stated explicitly, apart from the commune the Russian people have no significant inherited traditions that would prevent them from leaping into a new socialist future. In consequence, Shelgunov and Mikhailov welcome violent revolution if it will wash away the injustice of the past: "We boldly march to meet the revolution; we even wish for it. We believe in its fresh forces; we believe we have been called to introduce a new principle, to say a new word, and not to repeat Europe's past." To this they add that they would not be afraid to slaughter "a hundred thousand landowners" if it would be necessary to fulfill their revolutionary mission. Some of that mission would familiarly involve the granting of individual political rights such as free speech, elected and limited government, the abolition of the estate system, equality of taxation, and the rule of law for all citizens. But the basis of the future government they envision would be the village commune itself. Not unlike Shchapov, they refer to the commune as "the fundamental unit," and declare that all those units collected together would add up, in some unspecified way, to the Russian political system as a whole.

Shelgunov and Mikhailov clearly note that starting from the foundation of the commune would mean an end to private property in land since Russia's land would automatically go over to village communities rather than individuals. Interestingly, however, the proclamation reserves the flexibility to stipulate that if communal property holding should prove unworkable in the future, Russian society would have the right to abandon it. Open-mindedness of this sort would be found less and less often as populism gained momentum in later years. "To the Young Generation" was only one of many proclamations that came out in 1861 and 1862. None of them was as obviously populist in tone and intent as this proclamation with its emphasis on the centrality of the peasant commune. At the same time, it is worth noting that none of the proclamations gained quite as much attention as this one, due both to the fact that it was the earliest, and because Mikhailov was discovered, arrested, and became the lead player in a well-publicized trial for having illegally written and distributed it.

In connection to this proclamation, it is worth noting that populist ideas also found expression among less radical groups. For example, the desire for social integration was clearly apparent in the views of the liberal history professor, P.V. Pavlov. Pavlov had begun the "Sunday School" movement, in which the members of educated society would volunteer to teach the urban working classes such subjects as reading, writing, and math on Sundays, the workers' only day of rest. The Sunday schools began in Kiev where Pavlov first taught history, and they quickly spread throughout urban Russia. Since the schools were entirely voluntary, lesson plans were not fixed, and it would hardly be a surprise to learn that some of the teachers used them to engage in political propaganda. In any event, according to state officials, some volunteer teachers at the Sunday schools began introducing political ideas into their lessons, and the schools were effectively shut down in 1862.

In March of that same year, which happened to mark the one-thousandth anniversary of Russia's founding, Pavlov gave a speech on the thousand-year sweep of Russian history in which he characterized nearly the entire period as oppressive and unchanging. In his peroration, however, Pavlov noted that the emancipation had been a great milestone of freedom, an epochal transformation. He advised the state that now that it had stepped out on the path toward freedom any attempt to regress would prove disastrous. Pavlov then stated that moving forward toward freedom meant only one thing: that the educated classes must reject their privileged position and blend their interests together with the interests of the lower classes. The single thing that can save Russia, Pavlov thundered, was the merger of these classes. In the final lines he proclaimed: "We stand on the edge of an abyss. We will fall straight into it if we do not immediately advance toward the only way to save ourselves: union with the people!!! If you have ears, then listen!"[38] Pavlov received a standing ovation in the lecture hall. The government considered the speech and its reception to have constituted an open political protest, and Pavlov soon found himself in exile. Dangerous as it was, the very fact that Pavlov risked giving the speech suggests how populist thinking by 1862 had made its way from the clandestine publications of radical propagandists into the public sphere of liberal society.

Observing the gathering storm of such proclamations and speeches, the autocracy moved quickly and effectively, at least for the present, to minimize open dissent. Not long after Pavlov's speech, the state cracked down on anything it considered subversive activity. Chernyshevsky, Shchapov, and Iakushkin were all imprisoned or sent into exile in the following years. When Russia put down a new Polish rebellion in 1863, it provoked a fresh wave of patriotic enthusiasm, and a similar wave followed the assassination attempt on the Tsar in 1866. All of this led for a time to the diminishment of revolutionary activity, the recrudescence of autocratic authority, and the subsidence of populist journalism. That subsidence was not to last. Populist ideals and activism burst into life again toward the end of the 1860s and began to exert a much broader and more dramatic influence on the ideas and events of coming generations. The next two chapters explore the theoretical views and political activism that characterized populism at the peak of its influence in the 1870s and 1880s.

CHAPTER 4
POPULISM IN THEORY

First and foremost we propose that the reconstruction of Russian society must be carried out not only with the *goal* of the people's welfare, not only *for* the people, but also *by means of* the people.

Petr Lavrov

The Scottish sociologist Donald Mackenzie Wallace lived for six years in the Russian Empire from the beginning of 1870 to the end of 1875. Traveling extensively through cities, towns, and villages, he attempted to gain a comprehensive understanding of Russia, which he would later report back to European readers in an extremely successful three-volume study, translated into several European languages. Before proceeding to the countryside, Wallace spent time in Moscow and Saint Petersburg where he "had often been informed by intelligent, educated Russians" about the importance of the village commune. "The rural Commune," they told him, "presented a practical solution of many difficult social problems with which the philosophers and statesmen of the West had long been vainly struggling." Wallace's Russian acquaintances argued that the West was rapidly approaching "political and social anarchy" as a result of expanding capitalism and the consequent proletarianization of the masses. England in particular was on the verge of losing its peasantry, they claimed, because "men who have long been exposed to the unwholesome influences of town life are physically and morally incapable of becoming agriculturalists." As a result of this corruption, England would soon be facing collapse while the Russian institution of the village commune, which had the capacity to "solve satisfactorily the most difficult social problems of the future," would save Russia from a similar fate.[1]

Wallace does not name his Russian interlocutors, but the conversations he describes convey how, by the early 1870s, populist ideas had grown common within educated society. He had good timing. At around the end of the 1860s Russian populism entered into its heyday. By the early 1870s populist ideals and values had come to dominate both the political and the cultural spheres. The radical socialist populism that had begun with Herzen and Bakunin now began to inspire the hopes of thousands of young people in *obshchestvo*, and the quest to reach and understand the *narod* flooded literature, art, and journalism. The present chapter examines the rise and development of radical populist socialism as a set of interconnected theories and debates about the nature of Russian society that shaped the socialist left and would ultimately exert a lasting impact on Russian society as a whole.

Populism Full-Blown

In the previous chapter we learned that several writers had, by the early 1860s, set down the fundamental concepts of Russian populism. These included the role of the peasant commune and *artel'* as a basis upon which to build socialism in Russia, the idea that the *narod* had the potential to become a revolutionary force, and the need for the intelligentsia to selflessly devote itself to the cause of revolutionary change. Such ideas had found full-throated support in the early 1860s, but they were partially subdued by the government crackdown that began in the spring of 1862 and persisted through most of the decade. One should keep in mind that even as populist ideas were taking root, social prejudice among the upper classes remained widespread. As Vasily Bervi-Flerovsky described the attitude, "in *obshchestvo* there reigned the crudest and most boundless contempt for the *narod*, as if to the lowest sort of human being, useful only for extracting his sweat and his strength."[2] All the same, populist idealization of the *narod* had a powerful resurgence in the late 1860s with the publication of three works that served to revitalize the movement. Bakunin, having spent more than a decade in prison and exile, published an essay in 1868 that appealed to young Russians to go to the countryside and help launch a peasant rebellion. In 1869 Bervi-Flerovsky published a long study decrying the widespread poverty of the Russian masses, and most influential of all, starting in 1868, Petr Lavrov published a series of letters (later collected in a book titled *Historical Letters*) that called upon Russians to serve the needs and better the lives of the peasant majority. Collected together, these texts inaugurated the "classical" period of Russian populism. They commenced the production of a new and more complete body of populist theory, and they helped instigate a new era of populist political activism (discussed in the next chapter).

As we have seen, Russian writers were often constrained by censorship to express themselves in subtle or coded language. Although contemporary readers understood their message well enough, for readers today it can be difficult to discern the intent behind some of their coded texts. Fortunately for our purposes, some of the populists of this era followed in Herzen's and Bakunin's footsteps, relocating abroad where they could express themselves freely. Sergei Kravchinsky was both an active terrorist and a prolific writer. Having assassinated the chief of Russia's political police in 1878, he left Russia and began to publish under the pseudonym Stepniak. One of the books he published in English, *The Russian Peasantry* (1888), summarizes in unambiguous terms what it was the populists hoped to achieve. In the book's conclusion, Kravchinsky lays out a nearly complete summary of the position that had become dominant among the left intelligentsia in the 1870s:

> Now if our people are so much accustomed to co-operation in general, and co-operate so frequently on a small scale, why should they be unable to co-operate on a larger one . . . why should they be unable to till the whole of their communal land with improved implements on the co-operative system, which would be immeasurably more profitable?

Why should not they in the natural course of their intellectual and economical growth pass from communal and local co-operation to general, national co-operation, gradually embracing all the branches of national industry, which is nothing but socialism? . . .

Or, to put it beyond theoretical controversy, supposing socialism is not entirely a dream, of all European nations the Russians, provided they become a free nation, have the best chance of realizing it. The future will decide as to how much the Russian nation is fitted for it . . .

A nation of laborers, she [Russia] is to bring to the brotherhood of nations something peculiarly her own, in the development of new forms of labour. If she cannot do this, if we are to suppose that the solution of the political crisis under which she is now struggling will come after the aspirations of labour shall have been stifled, and that Russia will have to plod on her painful way to social reorganization in the rear of Europe, she will be but a poor imitator, and a drag upon civilization for many generations to come . . .

We are not European enough to successfully imitate a progress based upon the fruition of individual interest.[3]

Having argued throughout *The Russian Peasantry* that no people in Europe is more suited to communal labor than the Russian people, Kravchinsky here concludes that a shift to socialism can be carried out more smoothly and easily in Russia than anywhere else in Europe. Elsewhere in Europe, as the final sentence of this passage implies, capitalism has already taken too firm a grip to allow a socialist economy to take hold. But Russia, with its commune-based agrarian economy, was not stymied in the same way. It could convert to socialism and then play its fateful role in world history by demonstrating the benefits of a socialist economy to the Western world. Here again Russia and the rest of the world will profit from the advantage of Russian backwardness. But Kravchinsky also voices some of the foremost populist anxieties in this statement. What if, as so many Europeans argue, socialism is not the future? Will Russia simply remain a backward country struggling to keep pace with the West? How can Russia ever keep up with the advanced West when the Russian people are not individualistic or competitive enough to survive in a capitalist world?

Petr Lavrov, another enforced exile, was compelled to live abroad after 1870. In 1873 he began to publish the journal *Forward!* [*Vpered!*] in which he could finally express his views about Russia openly and directly. He proclaimed as the goal of his journal the attempt to achieve "the predominance of the people" in Russia by means of "a popular uprising."[4] The introductory section of the journal, "Our Program," lays out Lavrov's vision of the populists' political aims. It announces that the hoped-for revolutionary uprising must come from among the rural people themselves. It was not to be a revolution carried out by the intelligentsia in the name of the people but a revolution that emerges from within the world of the Russian village. Lavrov also makes it clear that his journal will promote what he calls a social and economic, rather than a political, revolution. By this he meant that the goal of the revolution should not be to seize state power and set up an alternate government. Instead, the *narod* ought to take power at the local level through their communes, governing themselves and the land in communal fashion, if also drawing on the assistance and guidance of the intelligentsia. Educated society was tasked with the mission of helping to join together local, independent communes into a larger united government, while maintaining the grassroots autonomy of the local communes. Lavrov envisioned the future Russia as something like a vast anarchistic federation. His central aim was to subordinate all other classes to the interests and values of the peasantry while ensuring that communalism would prevail as the fundamental socioeconomic operating principle of that new federation.

The views of Kravchinsky and Lavrov were fairly representative of populist aspirations, but that is by no means to suggest their thinking was accepted and approved by all populists. As Andrzej Walicki has pointed out, "Populism was a broad current of thought differentiated within itself; it was a supra-individual ideological structure within which many positions were possible, sometimes complementary and sometimes symmetrically opposed to each other. It is clear, therefore, that it is hardly possible to find in an individual all the aspects and all the constitutive elements."[5] Because of its variegated and pluralistic nature, even at the peak of its influence populism took shape more as an endless, ongoing debate than as a coherent doctrine. It existed almost exclusively in the realm of the intelligentsia imagination, and that imagination was a hothouse in which ideas grew quickly into a tangle of overlapping and intertwining theories, plans, and practical goals. This chapter attempts to offer the reader a guide to the complicated aims, fraught debates, and troubling contradictions that characterized Russian populism at the height of its influence in the 1870s.

Few populist thinkers or organizations ever managed to escape from the woes of internal dissension. Underlying their debates was the frustrating predicament in which they found themselves. Inheriting the dilemma from Herzen, they demanded a revolutionary transformation of Russian society, and yet insisted that transformation must come from among the people. On trial in 1877 for agitation among the peasants, Ippolit Myshkin declaimed that "amidst all the differences of opinion on different questions, the adherents of social revolution come together on one thing: that the revolution can be accomplished in no way other than by the people itself."[6] What they could not control, and constantly fought over, was how to shape a revolutionary consciousness and elicit revolutionary activity from among the *narod*, a part of Russian society from which they were, of course, estranged. Both theorists and activists failed to find consensus on such basic questions as what kind of government and society should replace the autocracy, how to reach and organize the peasantry, and how to bring about a revolution.

Full-blown populism coalesced into such a complex and varied form that it became almost impossible to penetrate the tangled and knotted mass of overlapping and interweaving principles and ideas and tease out the individual strands of thought. One strand we have already referred to in the second chapter is Radishchev's approach to the people, the ambition to bring justice and equality to the lower classes by integrating them within the rest of society. All populists of any shade shared this aim, but the emphasis of later writers like Herzen, Shchapov, and Shelgunov had contributed another layer to the movement: the fundamental importance of communalism and the compelling idea that Russia possessed an innate socialist spirit that could be tapped into as the basis for a glorious socialist future. A powerful corollary to this cherished goal was the desperate insistence on preventing Russia from succumbing to the capitalism that had "overtaken" the West. If capitalism in Russia developed too quickly, the populists feared, it could destroy Russia's chance to leap past Europe into modern socialism. Educated Russians therefore had a duty to prevent the encroachment of this threat from abroad.

The Call to Serve

As noted earlier, the "Radishchevean" approach to the people—the fight to bring justice, welfare, and dignity into the lives of those who lacked them—cannot be thought of as synonymous with populism. What democratic movement, after all, does not share the same goal? The emphasis on social equality was especially evident among those populists who followed Chernyshevsky in resisting any idealization of the *narod*. Bervi-Flerovsky, for example, mostly portrayed the peasantry as downtrodden and miserable rather than cooperative and virtuous. He published hundreds of detailed, data-driven pages in an effort to prove "there wasn't a single country in which people were so poor, overworked, and unhappy as in Russia."[7] Like Radishchev, he regarded the peasants as nothing other than ordinary people unfairly treated; their impoverishment, hard labor, ill health, and many other problems sprang from the inequality built in to Russian society. Although relative to other populists Bervi-Flerovsky downplayed the importance of the commune, his work clearly supported the populist movement's calls for social change.

Lavrov went further and claimed that the solution to economic injustice and social inequality could be found within the peasantry itself. Following Herzen, Lavrov vested great hope in peasant communalism, arguing that the village commune required the intervention of the intelligentsia to steer it toward socialism at a national level. By wedding peasant communalism and intelligentsia support into a united effort to build Russian socialism, Lavrov injected new life into the disconnected populist views that had come before him. His *Historical Letters* was greeted by a new cohort of politically motivated youth in the early 1870s both as a moral exhortation to improve their world and as a plan of action for how to do so. The letters enjoyed immediate popularity and had an influence nearly comparable to that of Chernyshevsky's *What Is To Be Done? Historical Letters* did more than any other publication to establish populism not just as a way of thinking but as an active political movement. Understanding Lavrov's impact is indispensable for understanding the emergence and spread of populism during the 1870s.

Chernyshevsky had propagated a unique version of utilitarian ethics that would go on to inspire large numbers of Russian revolutionaries. The term he used to describe that ethics was "rational egoism." Rational egoism encapsulated Chernyshevsky's notion that right-thinking human beings always consider it in their interest, even in their self-interest (their egoism), to assist other people, and society at large, in order to improve the lot of humanity. Thus he interpreted any altruistic act as virtually the same as a self-interested act, at least in the behavior of a reasonable individual. Armed with this deliberately minimalist philosophy of human behavior, Chernyshevsky sought to convince the public that if they were among the rational and reasonable they would behave in such a way as to benefit their fellow human beings. On a different basis than Chernyshevsky, Lavrov proposed his own ethical philosophy intended to persuade readers to act for the greater good. Lavrov's philosophy rested less on an appeal to intellect than it did on tugging at his readers' emotions, in particular on their sense of guilt and responsibility. Like Chernyshevsky, Lavrov acknowledged self-interest as an essential human characteristic, but he also posited that, historically, once human societies had entered into complex social relationships, the sense of justice for all (which ultimately derived from a sense of our own need for self-protection) became the equal of self-interest in any moderately ethical and responsible individual. Possessing an internal demand for justice, human beings are, or at least ought to be, impelled to do what we can in order to ensure justice exists and continues to be enhanced and extended throughout the world in which we live.

In *Historical Letters* Lavrov contrasts this supposed innate sense of justice to the glaring social inequities in the modern world (especially in modern Russia). He then argues that civilization has only managed to make progress by dividing into a mass of physical laborers and a small, privileged group of educated people. Sadly this latter group has all too often accepted its privileges without accepting its concomitant responsibility to seek justice for the rest of humanity. As Lavrov expressed it in an oft-quoted sentence: "Civilization has paid dearly so that a few thinkers sitting in their studies could discuss its progress."[8] He asserts that such a state of affairs is nothing less than a moral outrage demanding immediate redress. For Lavrov, and this would separate his views from those of many other populists, the educated minority, as a result of their advantages, has a sacred duty to become the instrument to realize improvement in the lives of the many.

> Mankind has paid dearly so that a few thinkers sitting in their studies could discuss its progress. It has paid dearly for a few little colleges where it has trained its teachers—who to this day, however, have brought it little benefit. If one were to count the educated minority of our time and the number of people who have perished in the past in the struggle for its existence, and estimate the labor of the long line of generations who have toiled solely to sustain their lives and allow others to develop, and if one were to calculate how many human lives have been lost and what a wealth of labor has been spent for each individual now living a *somewhat* human life—if one were to do all this, no doubt some of our contemporaries would be horrified at the thought of the capital in blood and labor which has been lavished on their cultivation. What serves to soothe their sensitive consciences is that such a calculation is impossible.
>
> Petr Lavrov, *Historical Letters*, trans. James P. Scanlan

Not only has the educated minority been the group to benefit from the labor of the downtrodden working people, but they also happen to be the only group with the advantage of a conscious awareness of the obligation they owe. Lavrov argues that education has inculcated in many elites a keen awareness of the injustices that surround them because it has turned them into what he calls "critically thinking individuals." Such critically thinking individuals have the capacity to recognize the errors of their society, and they also possess the ability to actively band together in order to correct those errors: "Every civilized minority ... bears the responsibility for all the sufferings of its contemporaries and of posterity which it *could have* eliminated, had it not confined itself to the role of representative and custodian of civilization."[9] Ultimately, then, the goad Lavrov used to prod readers into action was guilt. Although they did not all have noble backgrounds, those who heeded the call of Lavrov's writings have been called "repentant noblemen." They responded to such conscience-needling passages as the following:

> He who feels or imagines that he has the strength has no moral right to waste it in a petty, private sphere of activity when there is any chance of broadening this sphere. The cultivated person, in proportion to the broadening of his own cultivation, must compensate mankind for the still greater sum which it has spent on that cultivation. Thus he is morally obliged to choose as broad a sphere of social activity as is open to him.[10]

Such urgent demands helped turn the relatively cowed and contemplative intelligentsia of the mid-1860s into a generation of political activists, and it had a particularly potent effect on its younger cohort.

When Lavrov wrote *Historical Letters* from within Russia he was constrained to express himself delicately, without mention of revolution, socialism, or anything potentially construed as political opposition. But even in this legally published text he somehow managed to assert that any educated individual with a modicum of self-respect ought to recognize the need to fight, even to die, in defense of "the dignity of others." To his Russian admirers Lavrov's revolutionary message was clear. *Historical Letters* managed to reorient the left away from the Chernyshevskian emphasis on self-improvement (a message fervently carried forward by the influential Dmitry Pisarev until his death in 1868) to a new emphasis on the call to serve the people. One of Lavrov's supporters described the impact of *Historical Letters* in the following way:

> At one time we were attracted to Pisarev, who spoke of the great use of natural science in the formation of "thinking realists" ... Suddenly this little book tells us that science is far from the only thing in the world; that dissecting frogs alone doesn't take you very far; that there are other important human questions: there's history, there's social progress, and finally there's the people, that starving, overworked people, those working people who take upon themselves the entire burden of civilization.[11]

Historical Letters generated among many readers a reverent enthusiasm. When published as a single volume, the book was said to be "kept under the pillow" of readers and "read until it was frayed and torn." A future member of the Land and Freedom Party called it "a book of life, a revolutionary gospel, a philosophy of revolution."[12]

Shortly after the publication of *Historical Letters* Lavrov went abroad and, like Herzen, lived out the remainder of his life in the West. Once he began publishing the political journal *Forward!* in Zurich (and later in London), he began to openly support the overthrow of the Romanov dynasty and its replacement by local socialist control originating within the *narod*. As a consequence of the freedom to state his positions plainly, the differences between Lavrov's views and those of other populists, particularly the coterie of radicals surrounding Bakunin, soon began to appear in high relief. Their differences were based primarily on the controversy over the intelligentsia's role in the coming revolution. Lavrov sought, a la Herzen, to find a beneficial synthesis between the communal principles of the Russian people and the blessings of European civilization the intelligentsia had received and could bring to them. Lavrov believed educated elites should improve themselves in order to be of use to the *narod*. According to Lavrov, no society could be called civilized in which the majority of citizens had not been "brought into the sphere of history," as full stakeholders, meaning they had their basic needs met and enjoyed fundamental human rights, like health, education, and freedom of speech and assembly. In Russia it was the duty of "critically thinking individuals" from *obshchestvo* to prepare the *narod* for the rights and responsibilities of full citizenship in the socialist future. As he put in in *Forward!*: "The role of the vanguard of our youth who desire the welfare of the people, consists first of all in drawing near to the people, secondly in preparing them to throw off the oppressive state order, to destroy the old restrictive social forms and to establish a new society according to *their* needs."[13] The only way to accomplish this involved "strict and diligent preparation" in order to "develop in oneself the possibility of useful activity among the people."[14]

Lavrov emphasized the fact that few among the *narod* were even literate, much less had the capacity to think critically or acquire a revolutionary consciousness. They were not yet in a position to help themselves. The task of integrating society would be very difficult, according to Lavrov, because of preexisting conditions in Russia in which "the division between the classes is not only distinguished by greater or lesser personal wealth but by all the details of everyday life."[15] Because of its subaltern status in the Russian Empire, the peasantry had retained outmoded and unattractive cultural practices as well as a kind of inertia that made change from within difficult. That meant the original impetus for change had to come from without, from educated and politically active individuals. In its present condition, Lavrov pointed out, it will be difficult for the *narod* even to believe what the members of *obshchestvo* have to tell them. Therefore great understanding of the people, thorough preparation in figuring out how to address their needs, coupled with an abundance of patience, would be required by the radical intelligentsia if it was to help the *narod* realize its revolutionary potential. As events would bear out, Lavrov's prediction that it would be difficult to open lines of communication between intelligentsia and *narod* was prescient.

But Lavrov's pragmatism and sober restraint worked against him among those revolutionaries who lacked his patience. The circle of revolutionaries surrounding and inspired by Bakunin looked upon that restraint as moral cowardice. Bakunin encouraged young Russians to go to the countryside and incite rebellion, claiming the people would respond warmly and swiftly to such a call. His followers felt little compunction about the supposed need to ready the people for the socialist future revolution. Given their multitudes and their ingrained traditions, any so-called preparation would be "lost like grains of sand in the steppe."[16] For Bakunin the revolution had to come first. After that things would sort themselves out. Bakunin mocked Lavrov for his unreconstructed sense of social superiority: "What are you going to teach the people? Is it not what you yourselves do not know and cannot know, and must first learn from the people?"[17] Lavrov retaliated that it was high time:

> to abandon the old view that a revolutionary idea created by a small group among the minority can be foisted on the *narod* … the civilized minority has the responsibility not to force its ideas on the *narod* …but to clarify for the *narod* its real needs, the best means of satisfying them, and the power to do so which lies within the *narod*."[18]

In point of fact, Lavrov and Bakunin were both revolutionaries and by this point both agreed that peasant communalism could serve as a solid potential basis for a more advanced form of socialism. Like Herzen's earlier argument with Bakunin, this debate was more emotional than rational. Bakunin saw Lavrov's patient gradualism as an anchor on the march of history, and his own enthusiasm for "revolution now" appealed to many others unprepared to postpone what they considered the inevitable conflagration.

The Coming Revolution

Bakunin's vision of a revolution "from below," a revolution made by the *narod* without outside assistance, would gain widespread appeal in the 1870s, but Lavrov's view that the intelligentsia had a significant role to play, both in fomenting radical change and in guiding the *narod* down the right path remained at least as common among the rank-and-file populists. Most of them believed they had a duty to help the *muzhik*, the younger brother, to build the new world they hoped to share together. One way or another, the new generation of populists aimed to revolutionize Russia, or even, as Lavrov declared in the very first sentence of *Forward!*, to revolutionize "the whole world." With such an ambitious goal in mind, they needed to formulate a theory for why the revolution must take place and how it would unfold.

In fact, the populists lived in a late-nineteenth-century Europe obsessed with explaining why and how historical change came about. At the beginning of the nineteenth century, Hegel had portrayed world history as the process of fulfilling a highly abstract, God-centered plan for human progress. Rethinking Hegel, Marx too saw history as a process with a known cause and a predictable outcome, but for him historical change emerged from the human struggle with material reality and class conflict. Auguste Comte's influential sociology also rested on an understanding of world history as the path of advancement through successive levels of development, from immaturity to maturity. Counter to these theories and from an entirely different point of view, Darwin's natural history explained biological evolution as adaptations to changes in the environment that operated outside of any particular plan. Social Darwinists like Herbert Spencer, however, drew on Darwin's explanation of biological change to create a theory of universal progress. Excluding Darwin, each of these thinkers explained not only how and why history progressed, but where it was going. With all these theories of what history is and where it must be going, it is no wonder Tolstoy devoted so much of *War and Peace* to the idea that history had no set purpose that could be grasped by humanity.

In this context, it is not so surprising that both Lavrov's *Historical Letters* and Nikolai Mikhailovsky's most famous work, *What Is Progress?* (1869), constituted extended musings on historical change. As opposed to Marx and other "historical determinists," populists like Herzen, Lavrov, and Mikhailovsky rejected the idea that history "had a libretto," or a knowable script. Instead they emphasized the power of individuals and motivated groups to consciously push history in the most sensible, just, and equitable direction. Where a Hegelian or a Marxist was armed with a reason why the world had to change, as well as a mechanism of change that lay beyond the power of individuals to influence, Russian populists believed they had the power to instigate the transformations they wished to bring about. This "voluntarism," the idea that society could change by force of will alone, went back to the Slavophiles and characterized almost all populist thought. It makes sense too that such a way of thinking was common in Russia but not Western Europe. The West could conceive of itself as a culmination of history, or at least as history's vanguard, and establish the "laws" that led to its position at the head of the line. Russia, both different from and less advanced than the West—in terms of wealth, technology, political freedom, sciences, and much else—had no such luxury. Their starting point had to be the freedom of action to produce change for the greater good. Even when Marxism, with its fixed trajectory of development, made inroads among the Russian intelligentsia, a strong strain of willful agitation characterized its most successful practitioners, the Bolsheviks.

Lavrov and other populists like Mikhailovsky devised a voluntarist approach to history and revolution they termed "subjectivism." The need for change in Russia and Europe was plain enough to them, and peasant communalism seemed to offer a special advantage for Russian progress, so they both argued that it became the job of the populist intelligentsia to consciously, or "subjectively" as right-thinking individuals, join the effort to fulfill the grand promise of peasant-centered socialist revolution. Their theories conceived of history not as a schema to be interpreted but as an alarm bell waking people up to their ethical obligations. The future course of history had to be guided by the intervention of the populist intelligentsia, the only segment of Russian society yet able to grasp the concept of "the good of all" and make the conscious choice to fight for it. History had laid that duty upon them. When a decisive revolutionary struggle finally arrived in 1917, Lenin, inspired in part by populist radicalism, would be thinking the same way.

Mikhailovsky, the most influential populist writing from within Russia in the late-imperial period, agreed with Lavrov that educated individuals had a duty toward the people. He argued that the historical determinism of Marxism was its greatest flaw because it substituted a prearranged expectation of how history would play out for something more important: the revolutionary's capacity to think and act at liberty, to react to circumstances as they presented themselves. With their high regard for free-handed activism the populists rejected anything that said you couldn't, given enough right-thinking allies, make the world what you wanted it to be. Marx and Engels regarded the populist trust in the power of the human will as naive and utopian. In "Our Differences," the first important Russian Marxist, Georgy Plekhanov (a former populist), labeled the populists unscientific and Romantic, afraid to face the raw facts of global historical development that Marx had understood. Interestingly, Marx himself was more receptive to the idea of a Russian shortcut to socialism through the peasant commune. One scholar has even gone so far as to say that Marx, with respect to Russian questions, should almost be classified a populist himself. But after Marx's death in 1882 Engels declared Russian populism a self-deceptive and useless idealization dependent on faith in the commune's magical potential to underwrite a socialist revolution.

Averse to the Marxist idea that revolution everywhere necessarily followed the same path through the rise of capitalism, the populists were naturally more receptive than Marxists were to earlier Western European socialists and anarchists like Saint-Simon, Fourier, and Proudhon, whom the Marxists had already rejected as retrograde utopians. Yet another model of ethical voluntarism the populists could pattern themselves on, even if they only followed it unconsciously, was Christianity. Christianity, of course, emphasized not revolution in this world but redemption in the hereafter yet, like populism, Christianity was premised on putting the last first, on fighting for the unfortunates of the world. Lavrov acknowledged in *Historical Letters* that the fight for a peasant-based revolution would be difficult, bitter, and slow. Those critically thinking individuals who would work for the people's betterment had to be prepared to engage in a kind of altruistic self-sacrifice akin to the martyrdom of the early Christian tradition. Some historians have placed great emphasis on the analogies between populism and early Christianity, and one finds many instances of the populists themselves making the connection. The populists did indeed look to the promise of the village commune in the hope of begetting what could be called a life free of sin and malice. Still, we must keep in mind that if Russian populism resembled Christianity it was only in its contours. It had a similar outward appearance, but at heart its adherents were mostly atheists who fought hard to extirpate the repugnant but deeply ingrained Orthodox world view they considered a harmful retardant among the *narod*.

Andrzej Walicki's study, *The Controversy over Capitalism*, defines populism as a movement that arose directly as a result of the populists' fear of Western capitalism invading the village. While we have treated populism here as a much broader phenomenon than Walicki does, he was certainly correct to emphasize the significance of its determined anti-capitalism. The populists saw themselves fighting a war on two fronts. They had to diminish the political power of the Tsarist autocracy while racing against time to prevent the further incursion of those capitalist productive forces that had already received a big boost from the abolition of serfdom and the labor market it provided. Larger and larger numbers of peasants were moving to the cities, both part-time and full-time, in order to supplement their incomes. While many of these workers retained the *artel'* system of communal labor, urbanization was changing their habits, and the old rural ways of life appeared to be under pressure among the very group of urbanized peasants with whom the populists had the most contact. Those who believed the commune could serve as the basis of future happiness dreaded that Western-style capitalism might be on the verge of destroying the commune by replacing it with individualized wage labor. As noted in the previous chapter, the fear of capitalism was shared by conservatives and socialists alike. Unlike the Slavophiles, the populists envisioned a modern future—non-Christian and non-patriarchal—founded on the basis of peasant communalism, but they also feared the advent of the sort of world that Marx and Engels had described in which a small minority of property-owning bourgeois were supported by multitudes of destitute wage-slaves.

While the Marxists saw the rise of capitalism as nothing more than submission to the laws of history, the populists believed the rise of capitalism would, as Lev Tikhomirov bluntly summarized in 1884, "lead to horror."[19] The threat of such socioeconomic conditions making headway in the village rumbles in the background of populist socialism, helping impart to populism much of its revolutionary urgency. As early as 1872, Mikhailovsky was arguing that people were acting naively optimistic when they claimed that industrialization and the proletarianization of the Russian peasantry could never happen in Russia. By contrast to the Marxists, the populists understood capitalist progress as a form of regression in the sense that it would impede the rapid shift they believed Russia could make toward modern socialism on the basis of peasant communalism and popular revolution. The populists were terrified of that very same relentlessness of capitalism the Marxists celebrated as the road to revolution. It was populism's collective nightmare that capitalism would roll in like a tsunami and destroy everything they held dear.

When the populists worried about the rise of a rural bourgeoisie, they thought less about European-style industrial magnates and more about wealthy peasants, those "fists" [*kulaki*] and "commune eaters" [*miroedy*] who had either separated from the commune or found the economic power to dominate it, and about former gentry landlords, who would enrich themselves by buying land and turning peasants into impoverished wage-laborers in their new "agribusinesses." These self-motivated, profiteering outsiders, in this disturbing scenario, would not only destroy collective landholding, but would, as one populist wrote, "exert the most destructive influence on the people's morality."[20] For these very reasons, Lenin in the 1890s referred to the populists as "economic romantics" and unwitting conservatives because they sought to "turn back the clock" and regain an ideal past that, according to him, had already vanished and could not be regained. Lenin's criticism was not unreasonable. Although populists never supported the continuation of the peasantry's patriarchal traditionalism, they certainly did idealize the culture and practices of the village commune as a stepping stone toward modern socialism, and overreliance on this uncertain ideal would return to demoralize them at a later date.

Most kept the faith that the peasant commune remained strong enough to serve as a rampart against the encroachment of capitalism. Some populists, most notably the economist Vasily Vorontsov, even argued that capitalism simply had no chance of gaining a foothold in Russia because Russian social, economic, and geographical characteristics could never be conducive to a system based on private property and wage labor. For Vorontsov, since capitalism could not ever gain a foothold in Russia, modernization would have no other way to occur but through the transition of peasant communalism into socialism on a broad scale. Vorontsov's major work, *The Fate of Capitalism in Russia* (1882), stole a page from Marxist determinism and vested the village commune with the weight of inevitability. The peasantry had no other choice but to strengthen their communal traditions. Such hopeful populists regarded the peasants, in their rootedness to the earth, their mutual obligations to one another, and their lack of crass materialism as the very antithesis of the European bourgeoisie. At the height of their enthusiasm, they even proposed that Russia, as a result of the communal principles of the people, already stood at a higher level than any society to be found in a Western Europe now degraded by the ravages of capitalism. Mikhailovsky approvingly quoted another populist who held that: "Commerce . . . still has not succeed in placing its fatal mark on our peasantry—in that is its great advantage . . . communal and *artel'* based customs are too deeply ingrained in our peasantry."[21]

Within this celebration of deeply rooted peasant communalism we again find the idea that Russia had benefited from the "advantage of backwardness." Vorontsov pointed out that the differences between Russia and the West were not founded on race or ethnicity. Instead they resulted from differing rates of development: "Our uniqueness comes from the fact that we started out on the path toward progress later than others," enabling Russia to retain "the spirit of the *artel'* and the commune . . . that other peoples long ago had already lost."[22] Mikhailovsky even used this backwardness argument to assert that Russians from the educated classes would themselves more easily be able to enter into peasant culture when the time came. Westernized as they were, even Russia's educated elite had not yet become corrupted by the extremes of capitalism, bourgeois modernity, and hyperindividualism that now existed in the West. Convinced of their capacity to defeat autocratic power and build a socialist society on the foundation of the village commune, while simultaneously terrified of a capitalist onslaught, the populists militated for revolution. The sooner the better.

The Dawn of a New World

Historians have sometimes inadvertently painted a confusing picture about populist attitudes toward the *narod*. Isaiah Berlin held that the populists "did not believe in the unique character or destiny of the people."[23] Richard Wortman, by contrast, found that "members of the intelligentsia of the 1870s ... envisioned the peasants as virtuous brethren in distress, whose life still preserved the elements of justice and humanity lacking in the urban educated milieu."[24] The degree to which the populists did or did not hold up the *narod* as an ideal to emulate has been an ongoing debate among historians. It has gone largely unresolved precisely because the same questions were already in dispute at the time. Populist sentiment consisted of an amalgam of idealization and disappointment with the peasantry; populists sang odes of praise to the peasants as well as laments bemoaning their inability to live up to their potential. The populist revolutionary Lev Tikhomirov wrote that "in neither moral strength, clarity of social self-consciousness, nor the resulting historical stability can we place a single one of our [educated] social strata on a level with the peasant and worker class."[25] Another radical populist, Iakov Stefanovich, wrote that when he went to the village he learned only that "the Russian *muzhik* is full of all kinds of prejudices. He believes in God and it is only to religion that he turns for an explanation of everything around him; he is ready to consider the tsar his benefactor and pin all hopes on him; finally, he is a despot in his family and beats his wife."[26]

It is at least safe to say that for a time, roughly between the late 1860s and the early 1880s, idealism predominated. The glorification of the peasantry was possible in part because populists inescapably saw the *narod* through the refracted light of their own social environment. Most populists were convinced in one way or another that their own culture was false and morally compromised. Praise for the peasant "other" often reflected dissatisfaction with *obshchestvo* and a wish for something better. The populist dream of merging together with the peasantry made it necessary to find among the *narod* those values—morality, endurance, social solidarity—they found lacking in themselves. Even today historians sometimes write about the populist "search for the peasant soul." Although phrases like this ring of mysticism, it is difficult to find another way to express what the intelligentsia was trying to locate among the people. Reverence for the life of the people offered many advantages. It assuaged guilt felt by those who didn't engage in manual labor, it gave hope for a solution to Russia's endemic poverty and inequality, and it offered a way to imagine the national character in a positive light. Confronted by contemporary Europe with the idea that capitalism was the only viable path to success, the peasantry seemed to embody an alternative way of organizing society that could pave a separate path forward. Since the idealization of the peasantry filled a need, it was easier to have faith in a bright Russian future. To borrow Wortman's term, the *narod* became a kind of "alter-ego" to the populists. In reality, the *narod* might not live up to the ideal the populists imposed on them, but at least they seemed to stand that much closer to the values the intelligentsia held dear. Within the peasantry, as one populist confidently averred, it was possible to envision "the foundation for the building of a future order, immeasurably higher than the existing one."[27]

The original apostle of the commune, Herzen, had died early in 1870, and by that time his public voice had grown much quieter than it had been a decade earlier. Nevertheless, his argument that peasant communalism represented exhibit A in the case for setting Russia on a path toward socialism persisted as the cherished hope of the new generation. Lavrov's *Forward!* praised the commune as "the single genuine element of political life existing in Russia."[28] On the surface the commune could appear chaotic, or it could seem a vehicle for one group of peasants to exploit another, but central to the populist faith was the idea that the seeds of a better life were to be found within it. Petr Chervinsky summed up the intelligentsia's Romantic fascination with the commune when he wrote that "the peasant's body, heart and soul are permeated with the sense of moral obligation to submit the 'egotistical I' to something larger and higher."[29] Bathed in such a hallowed light, it is no wonder the populists went to great lengths to preserve the village commune in its pristine form. Eventually they felt they themselves could somehow tap into that communal spirit and way of life. Communalism also seemed to demonstrate that peasants rejected the idea of private property, a rejection that prepared Russian society to accept and instinctively practice a modernized version of socialism. The commune could, in other words, mature into socialism, and that one advantage gave the Russian population as a whole a far easier path to a socialist future than was available for a Western Europe already corrupted by capitalism. Thus the commune, the psychology of communalism, and the sociability of the commune could not be sacrificed. It carried within itself the capacity to lead Russia, even perhaps all of Europe following in Russia's footsteps, toward the promised socialist future.

> The particular Russian goal to which every Russian hoping for the progress of his fatherland must contribute is to build up our commune, in the sense of communal working of the land and the communal use of its products, to transform the village assembly into the fundamental political element of Russian society, to absorb private property into communalism, to give the peasant the education and understanding of his social needs, without which he will never be able to take advantage of his legal rights, no matter how broad they may be, and without which he will never be able to extricate himself from exploitation by the minority.
>
> Petr Lavrov, "Our Program," in *Forward!*

The populists did of course understand that peasants themselves were human, and inevitably rife with mortal failings. But the same could not be said about the commune. Vorontsov went so far as to claim that the village commune,

> facilitates a sort of psychological education by means of its lofty and altruistic characteristics … it clears the psychological ground not for herd-like activity under the guidance of a leader, but for independent social creativity through the work of collective thinking, which absolutely ensures that the result of that activity will be practical, original and multisided, and therefore it offers the possibility in the future of developing into yet higher sociocultural forms.[30]

Mikhailovsky similarly saw the commune as a social space in which it would be possible not only to experience genuine social equality and solidarity but in which one could develop one's own inner potential.

As a result of this near worship of the village commune, one of the most characteristic and distinctive qualities of the populist movement was its very willingness to imagine Russia's future as one in which the culture of the elite would be diminished, or in some versions entirely erased, and immersed within the world and culture of the imagined peasant milieu. Populism was a movement of deep and sustained self-abnegation. Those who embraced the populist creed needed, to one degree or another, to reject their own cultural background and to acquire the knowledge necessary to support the national community of the future, a knowledge lodged exclusively within the *narod* itself. In effect, the populists were saying, "our culture has been poisoned by overwhelming alien influences, and we must embrace that part of society that yet remains untouched." Mikhailovsky, sounding not unlike Konstantin Aksakov, held that Russian elites would understand the peasantry only once they grasped that "ignorant and impoverished as they are, with respect to tranquility of conscience, they are higher than we."[31] In Mikhailovsky and others we find a Rousseauian strain of populism that rejected the benefits of the civilized world and readied itself for a more complete transformation in the image of the *narod*. Some even hoped, and literally trained (see Chapter 7), to become one with the people as agrarian laborers. Lavrov, Mikhailovsky, and others had substantial reservations about any complete loss of their Western cultural inheritance, but the group of populists who most fully accepted this "leveling" and merging into the peasantry were actually the first to refer to their worldview as populism [*narodnichestvo*].

The Romantic desire to blend with the people was not a matter of sheer mysticism. In a certain sense it actually rested on a foundation of political realism. The abolition of serfdom had been a declaration that the Tsarist empire, or at least the ethnically Russian part of it, must learn to conceive of itself as a national whole. As Shelgunov put it, "the union of the heights and depths, of intelligentsia with the people is not an empty dream. This union is an inevitable historical law. It is the path of our progress."[32] On one level, Shelgunov's point is undeniable. Two quite separate societies shared the same soil but not the same culture. If they hoped to form a single society they had to find the common ground on which to do so. Numerous governmental measures, involving law, governance, economic assistance, and social support in the village, would attempt to accomplish the desired unification in the wake of the 1861 emancipation. But the fact is that unification would never really come about—to the degree that it did—until the twentieth century under tragic circumstances. Even Lavrov, who continued to emphasize the importance in Russia of critically thinking individuals well read in European political thought, believed that other sectors of society, including state officials, the nobility, and the Church, were entirely unnecessary and would do best to disappear into the masses. These groups, he wrote, "have no place in the future structure of Russian society ... only by blending together with the Russian people, with the people of independent collectives and free unions, can the civilized person of the future morally exist."[33]

Many populists themselves sought the path toward unity by entirely shaking off their elitism, overcoming their educated, urbanized, and leisured ways, and fully immersing their own lives within the peasant milieu. Mikhailovsky, for example, believed it was necessary to "abjure every personal interest in the interest of the people," although he never wanted to leave behind his scientific and humanist education.[34] As the more radical populists, writing for the underground newspaper *Land and Freedom*, held, "We are convinced that the only cultural forms that have a historical future are those rooted in the minds and wishes of the popular mass."[35] Another underground paper called on Russians to "totally and absolutely merge with the popular masses in the process of gathering revolutionary strength."[36] The absolute rejection of "Western civilization" heard in these statements was premised on a kind of paradox: by abandoning their cultural inheritance the populists would be leaving behind the original ideas that had convinced them to reject that inheritance in the first place.

The irony was that highly individualistic thinkers, constantly at odds with other members of the intelligentsia who disagreed with them, somehow believed they would be able to adopt the spirit of communalism they admired and blend together with one another inside an alien culture of which they did not always approve. Therefore one must understand the drive to "abjure every personal interest" as an emotional response to the sociopolitical situation in which the populists found themselves. As Berdiaev has expressed it: the populist "was conscious of the fact that his position was not normal, not what it ought to be, and even sinful."[37] Mikhailovsky said as much, too. In his view, educated society lacked "the moral contribution from the people because the 'civilized' person truly finds himself in a false position with respect to the people."[38] Here was the reason for the remarkable, almost Christian, humility and self-sacrifice of the populist intelligentsia. A more liberal populist, Chervinsky, described this "urge to submit oneself to something broader" as a purely emotional response: "not intellectual like the ideological love for humanity with which it has much in common, but psychological, pervading body and soul."[39] Mikhailovsky was a complex figure, who harbored a great deal of ambiguity about this self-abnegation, but even he felt the deep psychological desire to immerse himself among the people. "Oh, if I could drown in that grey rough mass of people," he wrote in his diary, "dissolve irrevocably, preserving only that spark of truth and idealism which I succeeded in acquiring at the cost of that same people. Oh, if only all of you readers were to come to the same decision . . . what a great illumination there would be, and what a great historical occasion it would make! Unparalleled in history!"[40]

There is a strain of anti-intellectual sentiment here that Prince Petr Kropotkin made clear in his call to "close all universities, academies, and institutions of higher learning and to open instead trade schools."[41] Kropotkin held, as Martin Miller put it, that a genuinely revolutionary party would "orient itself exclusively to the *narod* rather than to the intelligentsia . . . The revolutionaries had to be prepared to live the daily life of the common man in order to spread propaganda and win sympathizers."[42] The figure who took this sentimental strain of populism furthest of all was the erstwhile terrorist, Iosif Kablits. Kablits believed the village commune represented a higher stage of human development than that attained in the most advanced Western society and considered the average peasant as morally superior to the average member of *obshchestvo*. The peasants were, in fact, more capable and intelligent than the intelligentsia. Therefore Kablits hoped to remove every trace of intelligentsia influence from populism and replace it with pure submission to the grassroots will of the people themselves. He and his followers were doing little more than pursuing the logic espoused by most populist thinkers all the way down the path it led. Where a Herzen or a Mikhailovsky managed to restrain themselves from a total glorification of peasant potential, Kablits argued that the peasants should work to recreate Russia in their own image. In his *Foundations of Populism* (1882) he argued that any intelligentsia influence over the people would do nothing but mar the popular effort to construct the future Russia: "It is necessary to recognize that populism's success would be larger than expected if we ceased to indulge the institutionalized egoism of the intelligentsia and its attempt to aggrandize itself at the expense of the popular masses."[43] Self-abnegation was a defining trait of the populist intelligentsia, but Kablits was not advocating listening more attentively and learning more fully from the *narod*. He encouraged the populists to flat-out erase the intelligentsia in themselves. The esteem granted for a time to Kablits's *reductio ad absurdum* of the populist position demonstrated that some were willing to forego any reasoned ideological position and instead raise their admiration for the *narod* to a form of pure unquestioned faith.

An Apolitical Movement

How did such a profound faith in the *muzhik*'s cultural inheritance gain traction? Mikhailovsky shared Lavrov's view that "civilization" had only been able to arise because of the "eternal suffering of the people." It was the wish to redeem that suffering in the future that lent Russian populism both its emotional weight and its call to arms. The longevity of this appeal can be explained by the self-catalyzing spiral it created. Those guilty before the *narod* wished to find in it that noble ideal lacking in their own social environment, and the more they represented the peasants in an idyllic light, the more agonizing the culpability at having shared in perpetuating their suffering. In this self-reinforcing process, it is easy to see how some populists could come to apotheosize the peasants for the martyr's cross they bore. Since virtually all populists were members of educated society, enjoying at least some degree of comfort and stability, they suffered from their own version of original sin.

The quasi-religious character of Russian populism had been noted early on by Turgenev in a letter he wrote to Herzen in 1862 taking Herzen to task for his blind worship of the peasantry. Turgenev pointed out that while Herzen posed as an enemy of mysticism, now he had begun "kneeling mystically before the sheepskin [peasant coat] . . . this unknown God." Turgenev also noted that this "God" gained its stature precisely because of its mystery: "Fortunately one does not know anything about it, and thus one can again pray, believe, and hope."[44] Much later, looking back on the 1870s, the populist Nikolai Morozov, said of the intelligentsia that since they were too weak to fight for their own freedom, "they turned the peasantry into a god."[45] James Billington no doubt exaggerated in his biography of Mikhailovsky when he dubbed Russian populism "a new Christianity," but the parallels to a religious faith are unmistakable.

At times the populist movement resembled a religious awakening or a crusade. Most of its adherents refused to see it as a political movement at all. Starting with Lavrov, they referred to their revolutionary socialism as "apolitical" in that they had no interest in taking over power at the top, as one would in a political revolution. Rather, they favored a transformation that came from below, a social, or better a socioeconomic, revolution. Today, in a world that understands politics as something that exists at the local, even the interpersonal, level, it would be an absurdity to disavow the political nature of a revolutionary movement attempting to remove power from the government and put it in the hands of the people. The populists, however, defined the term "political" exclusively as rule from above. Since they envisioned a social transformation that would begin among the *narod*, in which the *narod* continued to retain power communally in their local villages, they rejected the idea that such a transformation, as radical and absolute as it might be, could be understood as a form of political change. In Lavrov's own words: "For us the *political* question is subordinate to the social question, especially the economic question. States, *as they now exist*, are inimical to the workers' movement, and they must all conclusively disintegrate in order to make room for the new social order." He added somewhat incongruously that "only in the increase of autonomous small groups of communes and free alliances at the expense of centralized governments . . . consists the political progress of humanity."[46]

Raising up the banner of an apolitical transformation had a great deal to do with the populist fantasy that such a transformation would begin softly and unobtrusively among the people. Shelgunov, for example, imagined that the peasants on an estate would simply take over "their own" property (that which they farmed) and kindly inform the landlord it would be best for him to vacate the premises. It seemed so obvious to the populists where justice lay that they assumed both the peasants and property owners would eventually wake up to the problem of social inequality and clearly recognize the inevitability of popular control. This argument was based on the populists' theory of property. Ownership, they believed, had nothing to do with contracts or wealth. Rather they sided with what they understood as the peasant view of property—that ownership was created by labor. This view was indeed widely held among the peasantry. Mikhailovsky offered an example of it when he described how a peasant who had chopped down a tree in the forest nominally owned by somebody, found it impossible to consider such an act as theft because the tree had grown at God's will, and nothing that grew naturally could be owned by a person. However, if that same peasant had chopped the tree into logs and someone stole those logs from his yard, he would be outraged by the theft because his labor had transformed the wood into his personal property. The same theory applied to land farmed by the commune. The commune's arable land belonged to it while its members actively grew crops on it. From the populist point of view, once the peasantry's concept of ownership had been fully accepted, a political revolution would be rendered unnecessary. The shift toward widespread acceptance that land is not property would, in and of itself, entail a revolutionary transformation. Once this labor theory of property prevailed, the "revolution" already would have taken place.

> For a man who has tasted the fruit of the general-human tree of knowledge
> nothing is more attractive than political freedom, freedom of conscience, freedom
> of speech and freedom of the press, free exchange of ideas, free political meeting
> and so on. And, naturally, we want all this. But if the rights, which this freedom will
> give us, are to prolong for us the role of a coloured, fragrant flower—in such case
> we reject these rights and this freedom! Curse upon them, if they only increase our
> debt to the people, instead of enabling us to discharge it! ... By recognizing the top
> priority of the *social* reform we renounce the increasing of our rights and freedom,
> since we see these rights as instruments of the exploitation of the people and the
> multiplying of our sins.
>
> Nikolai Mikhailovsky, in *The Controversy over Capitalism*,
> trans. Andrzej Walicki

Yet another reason the populists denied their movement had anything to do with politics arose from their insistence that Russia was radically different from Western Europe. To Russians in the nineteenth century a political revolution meant, more than anything else, the French Revolution and those periodical Western European revolutions that followed it. Such events involved deposing a ruler or a government and replacing it with another form of government that continued to wield power from above. This type of revolution, as they had learned from European socialists, did nothing more than hand power to the middle class and the wealthy, who would continue to dominate over the working classes using the covering of electoral politics and political representation as a way to disguise their ongoing exploitation. This theory of political change rested on the populist conception of liberal democracy, for which the radical populists had great contempt. Lavrov, for instance, condemned representative government in capitalist societies as dismissive of the people: "in their eloquent debates about the subtleties of the constitutional system they always forgot about existing economic needs of the majority and remained opaque to them."[47] If in Europe liberals were merely powerful capitalists posing as democrats, then in Russia liberals were something even worse. As Bervi-Flerovsky put it, "The government ordered around [liberals] at will, subjecting them to the most humiliating insults, even if they only showed the slightest shade of independence."[48] He attributed this failing to the liberals' "absence of roots in the people."

In the positive sense of what they did hope to put into practice the populists embraced a vision of postrevolutionary Russia that was fairly close to a version of anarchism. Many populists believed that once the *narod* had seized control for themselves at the local level, the state would vanish, or at least diminish in size and importance, for lack of a purpose. It would become a vestige of the unhappy past. Although the term anarchism was less often used in Russia than in the West, two of its most prominent representatives in Europe, Bakunin and Kropotkin, were also Russian populists. Anarchism and populism both promote the idea that power should be placed in the hands of the people, and both hold that the people are most free when they govern themselves in small units. To return to the idea of populism as a form of faith, we should note that both anarchism and populism rested on a boundless belief in the good will, cooperative nature, and ultimate unity of humankind.

The Contradictions of Russian Populism

Any examination of populist views of the peasantry in the 1870s quickly reveals them to be frustratingly inconsistent and self-contradictory. Even the same individual will sometimes extol the wonders of the commune before going on to condemn those peasants who refused to live up to their image as communal, democratic proto-socialists. Now the *narod* is the vessel of social well-being the intelligentsia can only aspire to. Now it is retrograde, passive, undifferentiated, and in need of correction from outside. The devoted populist needed a high threshold for feelings of cognitive dissonance. The most obvious reason for all the incongruity was the false position in which the populist imagination had taken root. Like doting parents overly pleased with their children's accomplishments, populist intellectuals placed unfulfillable expectations on the peasantry, exaggerating their everyday survival strategies as a sign of future universal importance. In this way, the peasantry was set up to disappoint. On top of their overweening exaggeration of peasant potential, the populists struggled with the inheritance of two mutually incompatible intellectual traditions. The one, following Chernyshevsky and the "realists" of the early 1860s like Dmitry Pisarev, stressed the need for dispassionate understanding of the surrounding world based on a clear grasp of objective reality. The other, the idealization of peasant communalism as the kernel of Russia's destiny, had persisted through the 1860s and was revitalized in the early 1870s. Idealization of the *narod* sat awkwardly with demands for a coldly objective examination of the facts on the ground. These two inherited traditions of hard-headed "critical realism" and starry-eyed idealization were almost impossible to reconcile. Both had a profound influence on populism, and the contentious disputes of the populists arose in part from the difficulty of attempting to reconcile them.

Moreover, since the influence and staying power of Russian populism did not derive from precise doctrines as much as it did from emotional impulses like guilt, the desire to serve and sacrifice, and a wish for national redemption, it was all the more difficult to rally around any fixed principles in order to maintain a united front. For better or worse, the movement had no other choice but to live with its contradictions. The contradictions of classical populism can be broken into three groups. First, while the populist intelligentsia regarded peasant culture and everyday life as something to be admired and emulated, others treated the world of the Russian peasant as a culture of deeply ingrained and counterproductive habits and ways of thinking that could only be overcome with the help of outside assistance. Second, the populists prioritized the demand for revolutionary change, but they simultaneously insisted the coming revolution had to be carried out by the *narod* itself, in its own interest, even though the only group with any well-articulated interest in revolutionizing Russian society was the populists themselves. Third, as socialists, the populists strenuously rejected any hint that their motivations involved an element of nationalism, but the entire premise that the Russian *narod* exclusively possessed the necessary tools to create a socialist order made it difficult to ignore or disguise its underlying nativist agenda.

The Peasant Image

In the populist worldview, the basis on which the felicitous reconstruction of Russia would take place was the peasant commune. Such a reconstruction made sense, however, only to the extent that the commune actually embodied the beneficial characteristics of cooperation and self-sacrifice it was purported to possess. But the commune was simply the economic and political life of the village itself. As such it could not be separated from those other less-appealing aspects of peasant culture, including many characteristics the populists despised: its injustice toward women, its reverence for the tsar, and its parochial traditionalism. Since it was virtually impossible to extricate such traditions from the communalism that was bound together with them as part of a single culture, the populists found themselves hoping to forge a revolutionary new future on the basis of a relatively inflexible way of life. In this respect, Russia's vaunted advantage of backwardness posed a problem. The only way for Russia to move forward was for the peasant to remain backward. When one populist leader, Lev Tikhomirov, later abandoned his radical socialism and became a staunch supporter of autocracy, the Marxist Plekhanov claimed Tikhomirov's apostasy was "inevitable." To Plekhanov, anyone idealizing an outmoded institution like the commune would sooner or later end up reconciled with autocracy because traditional economic arrangements would never be supported by any society seeking genuine progress.[49] In other words, Plekhanov suggested, populist ideals could not rid themselves of the intrinsic element of conservatism lodged within them.

Among those who held fast to populist thinking, however, many attempted to address this very conundrum. As we have seen, Herzen himself was acutely aware of the problem and suggested, if in unfortunately vague terms, that the commune could never be the foundation of a new socialist society without first being revitalized by an injection of Western civilization. Chernyshevsky, in his defense of the commune, argued that history often moved forward by returning to some past principle, and hence peasant communalism would be able to form a new synthesis with modern socialism. Populists like Lavrov and Mikhailovsky, following Herzen, accepted that peasant culture and institutions must inevitably come under the influence of the gains made by the very Western civilization from which the peasantry stood apart. They both believed that one way or another the educated, urban elite would have to intervene in the village commune and direct it toward some improved version of itself.

But herein lay their dilemma, for in their idealization of peasant culture many populists viewed the peasantry's communalism as a social value and practice to which the intelligentsia should itself aspire. In overcoming this conundrum, the populists' voluntarism, or the idea that human beings have the capacity to direct history toward their own ends, offered a useful corrective. For instance, in his well-known essay *What Is*

Progress? Mikhailovsky found a way to refuse the contradiction all together. The essay is an extended polemic against Herbert Spencer's view that progress consists in the increasing differentiation and specialization, and hence increased capacities, of complex societies. Mikhailovsky argued the opposite, that modernity was eroding and degrading human integrity by creating so much diversity and specialization that individuals in advanced societies now functioned with increasingly limited knowledge of the world around them. Modernity was producing human beings who lived like tiny working parts of a vast machinery, leaving their integrity as individuals stunted and fractured. In opposition to Spencer, Mikhailovsky argued that genuine progress consisted in creating the least possible division of labor so that human beings could be holistically capable and knowledgeable throughout their intellectual and practical lives. Such individuals Mikhailovsky referred to as "integrated." The integrated person could be, like Mikhailovsky himself, the non-expert thinker—"layman" in his terms—whose ability to think broadly made him superior to the scientific specialist who only understood one narrow area well. Another exemplar of integration, although as Mikhailovsky made clear at a much lower level of development, was the Russian peasant, with his ability to master all the aspects of his environment in order to produce his own food, clothing, and shelter.

Mikhailovsky thus redefined progress as, in his words, "gradually drawing nearer to undivided wholeness."[50] In this way he managed to turn the tables on the whole question of how to reconcile backwardness with social advancement. As a quest for the "undivided wholeness" of the integrated individual, advancement meant something very different from specialization, social differentiation, and technical prowess. It could even mean a retreat from these aims into a simpler world, more integrated with nature and with other human beings. In this respect, the desirable wholeness of the integrated individual also had a social dimension. Since individuality is not born in a vacuum but created by relationships with other human beings, the unity and social solidarity of the commune and *artel'* also represented a higher stage of social progress. At least in theory, Mikhailovsky's reversal of normative notions of backwardness and progress minimizes the distance educated elites and communal laborers had to cover in order to merge with one another in a united society. Theory and practice, however, are two different matters, and under real conditions, for example when populists went to the countryside to live among the peasants, they found the social conservatism of rural Russia difficult to come to grips with.

The People's Revolution

The second intractable contradiction faced by the populists involved the problem of revolutionary change. Because no group other than the peasantry had the collective numbers and power to stand up to the government, the intelligentsia believed any revolutionary change necessarily had to come from below, from among the *narod*. As late as 1878, a populist underground newspaper was arguing that the coming of revolution was "as ineluctable and immovable as planetary motion through space" as a result of the inevitable backlash against the age-old and ongoing exploitation of the peasantry.[51] However, lacking any clear signal that the people were interested in rebellion, and aware

Figure 4.1 Two populist intellectuals: Petr Lavrov (left) and Nikolai Mikhailovsky (right). © Left: Wikimedia Commons (public domain). Right: Wikimedia Commons (public domain).

that the circumstances of Russia's social geography—with its small, isolated villages scattered across a vast expanse of terrain—would hinder a collective revolt, the populists grew increasingly aware of the difficulty they faced in attempting to foment revolution. Hopeful thoughts about peasant rebellions of the past tended to erode on contact with the people and the resulting awareness of their customary self-protective political quiescence. The populists were left in a self-contradictory, even absurd, position. How were they to step in from above and inspire a revolution from below?

This dilemma led to an odd inversion of the political spectrum. Those who had most faith in the capacity of the *narod* to effect change for itself, most notably the group of populists who published in the journal *The Week*, including Kablits, Chervinsky, and Vorontsov, discounted the need to agitate for revolutionary change. This attitude explains why Soviet historians labeled them "liberal populists." Those, like Mikhailovsky, who often disdained the peasants' level of cultural development, saw revolution as a needed corrective. For his part, Lavrov took the long view and accepted the necessity of patiently waiting for the peasants to gain a proper revolutionary consciousness once the intelligentsia had put in the painstaking work of living and laboring among them. As noted above, however, that position infuriated other populists who were both impatient for revolution and afraid that the imminent incursion of capitalism would destroy the communal values expected to sustain that revolution. Some less radical populists, like Tolstoy and Engelgardt (see Chapters 6 and 7), took a local approach to the question of change and began to work together with the peasants in the countryside in order to bring about a difference at a micro level that could perhaps serve as an example to others on a larger scale.

Petr Tkachev, in a view that was not widely accepted in his own time, advocated a method that would later be emulated by Lenin and the Bolsheviks. Despairing of the possibility of any peasant uprising as pure wishful thinking, he called on the populists to rise up and seize the state. Once they had control of the governmental apparatus, Tkachev believed, they would be able to implement their populist program. Without that control they would remain powerless to bring about a socialist future. In most ways Tkachev was not a populist at all, but his entire political philosophy may be said to have arisen out of his polemic against the populists. On the one hand, he did not merely lament the peasantry's lack of education but openly declared the purportedly glorious *narod* to be self-centered and psychologically immature. Tkachev's career as a revolutionary intellectual was founded on the desire to convince the populists of the error of their idealization and the consequent misdirection of their revolutionary struggle. On the other hand, Tkachev shared with the populists the fervent conviction that a revolution was necessary in order to repel the onrushing wave of Russian capitalism. Hence the desperate need to seize state power. There has been debate about the degree to which Tkachev inspired the revolutionary terrorism that is the subject of the next chapter, and even more discussion of the degree to which Tkachev should be seen as a key source behind the revolutionary tactics of Lenin and the Bolsheviks. During the 1870s, when Tkachev was debating Lavrov and his followers, others did begin to move in his direction once they had experienced the general unwillingness of the peasants to rebel. Although Tkachev was not their primary inspiration, those populists who turned to terrorism at the end of the 1870s did so in the vain hope that a strike at the top would somehow incite a peasant rebellion. All the while the peasants themselves remained impervious to the intelligentsia's revolutionary plans for them.

Covert Nationalism

There is no question that populism had its earliest origins in nationalism. Neither the overt nativism of the Slavophiles, nor the circumspect nationalism of Herzen attempted to conceal their aspirations for Russia's significance on the global stage. The socialist populists of the 1870s and after, however, uniformly rejected the notion that they stood for or supported any especially nationalistic aims. Socialism had evolved in opposition to nationalism as an internationalist movement, but the problem with the populists' claim to internationalism is inherent in the very ideas they espoused. Their entire vision of social progress relied on a specific form of communalism practiced by a specific population: the Russian peasantry. Still, Lavrov, Mikhailovsky, Bervi-Flerovsky, and others were at pains to minimize even the appearance of nationalist sentiment in Russian radical populism. Announcing his plans for a revolutionary struggle in Russia, Lavrov stated bluntly that "in our opinion, the *national* question must entirely disappear behind the important problem of the social struggle."[52] In a series of articles in 1876, Mikhailovsky strove to detach "the idea of the *narod*" from "the idea of nationality," and he regarded those who engaged in "a false idealization of the village" as patriotic epigones of the Slavophiles.[53] He minimized the outward appearance of a nationalist strain in Russian populism by portraying it as a matter of sheer coincidence:

> We see before us a valuable historical result: the predominance of the peasantry as a factor defining Russian life—a result upon which we can and must depend if we want to truly live and not just vegetate without faith, hope, and love. Given this, the epithet 'nationality' loses any sort of mystical and exclusive character and serves only as an expression of the, so to speak, historical foundation for a certain plan of action.[54]

It is not difficult to read between the lines of this statement how Mikhailovsky struggled to reject nationalism while at the same time taking pride in the homegrown blessing of the Russian peasantry. Even Chaadaev's lament that Russia lacked any achievements to stand up against Western civilization receives a response in Mikhailovsky's suggestion that merging with the peasant can point the way for the intelligentsia to regain "faith, hope, and love."

Similarly, the populist drive to stave off capitalism framed Russia's destiny not just as socialist but as anti-Western, as an antidote to Western errors. The most obvious thing the populists shared in common with the Slavophiles was disgust for modern Europe. We can also identify other links between the Slavophiles' and populists' admiration for Russia. Both Mikhailovsky and the Slavophile Khomiakov, for instance, pointed to the uniqueness of the Russian word *pravda*, which can mean either truth or justice, or even imply the unity of the two. Both of them took pride in the notion that such a concept was unthinkable in Western Europe. Mikhailovsky's promotion of the integrated person also echoes the Slavophile fear of the social disintegration they believed was taking place in modern European life. Further, Mikhailovsky, like all the Slavophiles, considered an organic connection to the past necessary for building toward a better future. Arguing against Marxist internationalism he complained that the Marxists "do not want to stand in any continuous relationship with the past and decisively cut themselves off from their heritage."[55] Plekhanov responded that populism was an idea founded on "the theory of Russian exceptionalism."[56] As a genuinely internationalist philosophy, Marxism could afford to place Russia on a continuum with other European states. Mikhailovsky's philosophy had no such luxury. It was beholden to the specific historical circumstances that brought the *narod* into being.

To be sure, populist socialism was far from xenophobic. It mostly welcomed connections to other working-class movements and other forms of socialism, and it easily envisioned a future of international cooperation. But Russian populists believed the attainment of such a socialism would most effectively be accomplished through the communalism already found in Russia. It seems fair to say that in most respects the populists engaged in an unconscious, "structural" nationalism, a nationalism built into the movement but not often emphasized or promoted. While they rarely spoke directly about the importance of nationality, they managed to bring in a nationalist perspective through the back door in their fascination with and idealization of the Russian, quite specifically Russian, *narod* and its mission to introduce socialism to the world by way of a Russian revolution. One can point to the dread expressed by Kravchinsky at the start of this chapter that if socialism would not take hold in Russia, then Russia "will have to plod on her painful way … in the rear of Europe." As Philip Pomper put it in his study of Lavrov, "like other members of the Russian intelligentsia, [Lavrov] struggled continually against a deep sense of national cultural inferiority, while simultaneously expressing great hopes for Russia's cultural future."[57]

In his *Condition of the Working Class in Russia* (1869) Bervi-Flerovsky made the point explicit: "The entire world would fix its attentive and curious gaze upon us if it saw that here the upper and lower strata of society all turned in the same direction to seek happiness along a single path … How great would be our strength if we joined together all parts of our society with such a powerful cement."[58] Bervi-Flerovsky felt the same anxiety as Kravchinsky that if Russia were unable to introduce socialism to the world, then the advantage of backwardness would be no advantage at all. It would only be backwardness, and "national pride" could not tolerate that:

> If we continue to go down the path which we have been on up until now, then we are inevitably bound always to remain at the tail-end of the civilized world; if I follow a person and go timidly step after step down the track he has left then I shall without any doubt always remain behind. The national pride of every Russian is bound to take offence at such a state of affairs, and it would be a different matter if there really were nothing more for us to do. But that is not so, is it? We see in modern civilization, at the head of which stand Europe and the United States, a fundamental defect, one of those defects which have dug the graves of civilizations and have made it inevitable that new leaders with fresh forces have come to take the place of the old ones.[59]

Bervi-Flerovsky reveals in clear terms here that, as removed as they were from the conservative nationalism of the Slavophiles, the populists were still motivated by national sentiment and national ambitions.

All of these abiding and intractable contradictions opened the populists to opposition, first from conservatives and liberals on the right and later from Marxists on the left. Many years of furious political debate would ensue. Somewhat less troubled in mind, on the other hand, were those populist political activists and agitators who had been inspired by the intellectuals. Since the populist faith rested mainly on an emotional foundation, revolutionary activists were less hindered by doubts that they might not have the proper philosophical principles on which to fight for change. The activists' main concern was to bring about popular revolution as quickly as possible by whatever means came to hand. In the struggle to find the proper method, they would go on to reshape radicalism for generations to come. Their story is the subject of the next chapter.

CHAPTER 5
POPULISM IN ACTION

The aim of all that reading and discussion was to solve the great question which rose before them. In what way could they be useful to the masses?

Petr Kropotkin

In 1876 Georgy Plekhanov, then a 21-year-old member of an underground populist organization, convinced a group of sympathizers to stage a pro-socialist political rally in the center of Saint Petersburg. Beginning in the summer of that year Saint Petersburg and Moscow had experienced an unprecedented storm of political demonstrations of a very different sort. The Russian public, in rallies and marches that sometimes mounted into the thousands, demonstrated its support for the liberation movements of Balkan Slavs seeking to throw off the control of the Ottoman Empire. Although the populist left had never managed to stage any comparably sized protests, Plekhanov argued that the time had come for public action. Many promised to participate, but most of them backed out. Nevertheless, Plekhanov succeeded in assembling a small group of a few hundred students and workers. Before a crowd in the portico of the Kazan Cathedral on Nevsky Prospect in the heart of the city a core group held aloft a red flag with the words "Land and Freedom" printed on it, while Plekhanov made a speech that lasted less than a minute. The demonstrators then began to march toward the palace, and a crowd of policemen and local shopkeepers descended on them, beat them, and hauled them away to prison. The demonstration and resulting melee had lasted only minutes, but some of those imprisoned wound up receiving long sentences in Siberian exile, the kind of sentence from which one was by no means certain to return. The autocracy had tolerated public demonstrations that promoted themselves as patriotic, but it regarded any demonstration by a left-wing organization as a serious crime and did everything in its power to prevent such events from taking place.

We begin this chapter with the story of this short and unsuccessful demonstration as a characteristic example of what populist political activists faced in attempting to get their message across. Their words were censored and could only be smuggled in from abroad or, at great peril, printed in local underground pamphlets and newspapers. The right of assembly for political purposes was also strictly forbidden. The history of Russian populist activism is the history of a movement convinced of the need for radical change yet in great danger whenever it attempted to give voice to its views. Constantly thwarted by the state, not to mention socially and geographically removed from the peasant masses, populist agitators had few effective ways to generate support in society. As we will see, radical activism went through stage after stage of new methods and new incarnations in the attempt to spread the word. Ultimately a group of populists landed on a method that did give them substantial publicity. It was virtually brand new: violence with the intention of generating attention for a political cause. They gave it a name which it still carries today: terrorism. This chapter will take us through the developmental stages of populist activism and attempt to explain why many of the populists eventually chose terrorism as their favored method for promoting revolutionary change.

The First Public Protests

Russia's first taste of modern political protest, the already-mentioned Decembrist Revolt (1825) took place not long after England's "Peterloo Massacre" protest (1819). Both occurred in the wake of the Napoleonic Wars, but the similarity ends there. It is instructive to contrast the two protests in order to understand the special differences faced by politically engaged Russians in the nineteenth century. The "Peterloo" protest arose in Manchester as part of the attempt to gain suffrage for members of the working class. It involved a mass rally of some fifty thousand workers and was violently shut down by a local cavalry unit at the expense of eighteen lives and hundreds of injuries. Dubbed Peterloo because it took place on Saint Peter's Field and recalled the recent battle of Waterloo, the mass gathering was part of an effort in the growing tradition of peaceful public protest built on the participation of politically active workers. The outrage generated by the massacre eventually led to the parliamentary reforms the protests had been calling for. Six years later the Decembrist Uprising took place in the Russian capital, Saint Petersburg. This revolt was the work of army officers not from the working class but almost exclusively from among the nobility. Given the autocratic political system, there was no tolerance for public protest, voicing complaints with, or asking for concessions from the government. In Russia the leaders of the Decembrist movement met in secret societies, and when Alexander I died, they marched at the head of three thousand soldiers onto the Senate Square in order to demand that a democratic constitution accompany the ascension to the throne of the next tsar. Like Peterloo, the Decembrist Revolt went down to defeat, but unlike Peterloo its aftermath was not democratic concessions. It resulted in the strengthening of autocracy under the next regime for the following three decades. The leaders of the revolt were either executed or exiled for life to Siberia.

If the long-term lesson of Peterloo had been that sacrifice can bring change, the long-term lesson of the Decembrist Revolt was that public protest brought destruction on its participants. No public protest would occur again in urban Russia until the 1860s under very different circumstances. Everyone who engaged in political protest throughout the history of Imperial Russia understood they ran a serious degree of risk. Dating back to the reign of Catherine II, windows of tolerance would open at times to allow a modicum of loyal opposition, or at least independent thought, but those windows were always subject to close at any moment. During the reign of Nicholas I, ushered in by the Decembrist Revolt, those windows stayed shut. That would change, however, early on in the reign of the next tsar, Alexander II, who recognized the need for a limited degree of open public expression [*glasnost'*] as a means to gauge the interests and concerns of the society over which he governed. From around 1856 forward, the legal press tested the limits of what it could say and still pass censorship, although no overt opposition to the government was legally allowed in print. Only foreign-based and underground publications, like Herzen's *Bell*, engaged in open protest. Because of the risks involved, it is not surprising that the earliest instances of political protest from within Russia arose among young people in the universities who had not yet developed the risk-aversion characteristic of more established members of society.

The limited tolerance of public opinion enabled by Alexander II's reforms was never intended to generate any genuine political protest, but by inviting society to participate, even in a limited way, in the post-emancipation rethinking and restructuring of Russian society, the Tsar inadvertently unleashed energies it would later prove difficult to rein in. Those who lived through the first years of Alexander's reign typically recalled the period in ebullient terms as a great awakening of Russian society in which the public finally began to take an active role in the formation of a new Russia. "Society strained its every power," recalled Nikolai Shelgunov, "in order to found for itself a new, independent position and shift the center of gravity of social initiative toward itself."[1] At first this participatory spirit was accompanied by warm acclamation for the Tsar and his initiatives. Even amid the impassioned political criticism regularly arriving with each copy of *The Bell*, Herzen took the time to lavish praise on Alexander and his accomplishment as the liberator of the serfs. It would not be long, however, before Alexander would learn that even limited freedom of expression leads to differences of opinion, fierce debate, open criticism, and finally outright attacks on the status quo. By the early 1860s the city of Saint Petersburg had turned into a hotbed of competing political views expressed not only quietly at home but in public venues like cafes, left-leaning bookstores, and even the public library. Public lectures grew more raucous and incendiary, and a space like the renowned Chess Club on Nevsky Prospect had become little more than a venue for open political debate.

As at many other times and places, institutions of higher education came to play a prominent role in the fervor of the times. Alexander lifted the restrictions on university enrollment that Nicholas had imposed, and enrollments nearly doubled in the first four years of his reign. The increase resulted in the admission of students from a more diverse array of social backgrounds than before. Combined with the tenor of the times, this enriched student body quickly established a new culture in universities and institutes across Russia. Many new students had only meager means to sustain them, so a variety of mutual aid associations sprang up in the universities in which students cooperatively helped each other acquire necessities like food and books. They even borrowed from the peasants the word *skhodka*, or communal assembly, and the student *skhodka*—a gathering of students to discuss some hot-button issue—quickly became a fixed feature of university life. An anonymous correspondent writing in to Herzen's *Bell* described the student *skhodka* as a training ground for student independence which instilled both responsibility and the potential for chaos within the universities since they took place entirely apart from the university administration. In point of fact these student assemblies did indeed provide an excellent platform for the generation of protest. The earliest protests involved unsurprising, intra-university issues, like whether students would be allowed to smoke on campus or wear beards with their student uniforms, but by the late 1850s student assemblies had become an almost constant feature of student life, and they began to focus more and more on current affairs and topics of national interest.

In the winter of 1861, almost simultaneously with the announcement of the emancipation edict, the University of Saint Petersburg threatened to prevent a lecture by the popular professor Nikolai Kostomarov for fear he had plans to discuss the emancipation. The students rallied and forced the administration to permit the lecture. Their success emboldened them shortly thereafter to use a funeral ceremony for the Ukrainian poet and artist, Taras Shevchenko, as an opportunity to express overtly political views. In the wake of yet another funeral demonstration in which students publicly decried the killing of Polish students by Russian troops, the government and the university administration wrote new rules to limit student engagement in the public sphere, including mandatory faculty supervision of every *skhodka*. When the university reopened in the fall, students immediately rejected the rules and met in their own independent assemblies to develop a response. At this point, the university closed the assembly halls to deprive the students of a meeting place. When the students broke in anyway, the government finally shut down the entire university. But the disturbances were not over. The next day around a thousand students met in front of the university and decided to march across the city to the home of G.I. Filipson, the administrator responsible for the closure. A long line of students, accompanied by bystander participants and a sizable police escort, marched through the city center. At Filipson's home, they demanded the new rules be abolished. The university refused, and after two more days of continual meetings in the university courtyard, the crowd of students was surrounded by Cossack troops and forced to submit. When the university was reopened two weeks later, further battles continued, and at that point state officials resolved to shut down the entire university. It did not reopen for the next eighteen months. Excluding the very different Decembrist Revolt, the students' assemblies and marches were Russia's first public political demonstrations. They ended in the arrests and expulsions of hundreds of students, but the students themselves were greeted by much of *obshchestvo* as heroic figures. Even the Tsar himself understood the situation not as a mere student protest but as "the first attempt of the revolutionary party to test its strength."[2]

The lesson the autocracy learned was that political discussion had to be kept in hand lest it break out into "revolutionary" public protest. The state's reaction in the early 1860s was a kind of microcosm of Alexander's entire reign. They shut down the possibility for public protest through arrest and intimidation, banned publications, arrested leaders like Chernyshevsky, and closed venues for interaction like the Chess Club. As a result, oppositional groups formed underground organizations that attempted to spread anti-autocratic and revolutionary views in clandestine ways. As one populist explained why radicals were going underground: "the reason is simple: if they do not allow the creation of open associations, then of course they will be created in secret."[3] At this early stage those underground movements would prove to be relatively small, disorganized, and ineffective, but in time their conspiratorial techniques would grow increasingly effective, and by the late 1870s they would begin to wreak havoc against the state. The exclusion of left-leaning speech and assembly in the public sphere, followed by the consolidation of political activity underground, constituted the pattern of political activism not only in the early 1860s, and not only during the reign of Alexander II. Until the Revolution of 1905, and then once again in its aftermath, the state limited public expression and assembly and curtailed nearly all protest on the left. The response was to engage in increasingly covert and increasingly violent attacks from below. This pattern persisted for decades and ensured that Russian populists would become pioneers in underground conspiratorial techniques.

Unsuccessful Conspiracies

Many years would elapse before the populists managed to form genuinely effective underground organizations, but that was not for lack of trying. Conspiratorial political organizations were far from new in the nineteenth century. They date back to the ancient world, and the populists could look to several modern models of political conspiracy that had appeared in the wake of the French Revolution. Even so, underground political activity was new under the circumstances of Imperial Russia. It was also dangerous because after the Decembrist Revolt Nicholas I had established an independent political police force which in theory reported straight to the tsar: the Third Section of His Majesty's Own Chancellery. The "Third Section," as it was known, had the advantage of decades before the 1860s to develop the techniques of spying and infiltration it was able to use effectively to combat sedition. In 1848 the Third Section had easily managed to infiltrate and disband a socialist organization that had been founded by Mikhail Petrashevsky. In response to Russian radical activism, especially the attempted assassination of Alexander II in 1866, it was strengthened with greater powers. If one understands effective underground organization as a weapon in the hands of an oppositional party, then the radical populists found themselves in a sort of "arms race" against the Third Section in which each side needed to bolster its operations and improve its techniques before the other learned how to counter. Through the 1860s and early 1870s the populists would find themselves the loser in this struggle, and since they would not develop effective conspiratorial methods until the latter half of the 1870s, they continued to pursue a variety of different paths toward the goal of the socialist revolution they hoped to bring about.

The first underground organization to gain notoriety received its name from Alexander Herzen. Representing what Herzen considered the two basic needs of the *narod* it was called "Land and Freedom," referring to arable land for farming and freedom from all forms of external control. Founded in the summer of 1861, it remains unclear precisely who the members of this mysterious organization were. The clandestine character of Land and Freedom rendered it unable to make any substantial progress toward their goal of overthrowing the state. It was hamstrung by its own conspiratorial methods, which kept its members in the dark even from one another out of an abundance of caution. Land and Freedom also confronted the problem that all populist organizations faced: its main goal was to push the rural *narod* on to the path of revolution, but it attempted to do so from the remote location of urban society, or in the case of Alexander Herzen and Nikolai Ogarev (who seem to have been at least peripherally involved) from abroad. The original, preliminary goal of Land and Freedom did not even involve the peasantry. They first needed to enlist a sufficient number of participants among educated urbanites in advance of making any headway in the countryside. In their small and shadowy state they managed to publish a few editions of an underground newspaper that proclaimed extensive revolutionary goals in dramatic language—"only the price of blood can purchase the rights of the people"—while in fact they were still just casting about for new members.[4] Indeed, some "members" were never really certain whether Land and Freedom existed. The first underground organization of the reform era does not seem to have lasted beyond the year 1863.

Around that same time another conspiratorial group was coming into being that had greater success and lasted longer. The Ishutin Circle benefited from the cover of already existing as a legitimate organization. Its name derived from its leader Nikolai Ishutin, and it began merely as an association of students at Moscow University who hailed from the provincial city of Penza. Inspired by Chernyshevsky, they soon turned toward radical politics, seeking in the usual populist manner to draw close to the *narod* in order to establish the commune as the dominant political and economic unit of rural life. Like Land and Freedom, however, the Ishutin Circle quickly recognized the limits on influencing, or even making contact with, the peasants. Instead they struck out in a dizzying array of new directions. Without any unified plan or steadiness of purpose, but with huge amounts of drive and ambition, they created a variety of leverage points from which they hoped to effect revolutionary change. They set up cooperative factories, organized student cooperatives, and even created a school for children into which they introduced progressive and anti-autocratic teaching. They hoped to establish revolutionary institutions in around Moscow and then to spread these projects out into the provinces, but as a small, covert organization they lacked both participants and financial resources.

In the end, like Land and Freedom, the Ishutin Circle provided an object lesson that revolutionary dreams and the practical capacity to fulfill them were not the same thing. It was a sign of things to come that once they began to recognize the limits of their broad social goals, they turned in a more conspiratorial direction, proposing to cut ties with family and friends, and even beginning to contemplate the use of violence. None of these plans got off the ground, however, because Ishutin's unstable cousin, Dmitry Karakozov, a peripheral member of the Circle, took it upon himself to travel to Saint Petersburg in an attempt to assassinate Alexander II. Although Karakozov was not acting on orders, his shot at the Tsar was also a harbinger of later developments. It seemed to him, as it would later seem to populists in the 1870s, that an event as dramatic as the assassination of the Tsar would send a wake-up call to the *narod*, alerting them that the government itself was the source of the poverty and inequality they suffered. Karakozov even left a letter in his pocket addressed to "my beloved simple Russian people."

Karakozov's shot unleashed a furious and powerful reaction from the government to the extent that the period after the assassination attempt in 1866 came to be called the epoch of "white terror." Arrests were made in the hundreds, and the government arrogated to itself the authority to close down any sort of public venue it deemed a threat. The only kind of revolutionary activism to make an impact in the next few years, perhaps the only kind that could have, was the duplicitous, ultra-extremist conspiracy led by Sergei Nechaev. Nechaev appeared on the scene in the late 1860s with a vision of the revolutionary activist as a desperado who rejects all creature comforts and human connections in order to coldly pursue the dream of total revolutionary destruction. Like Bakunin, and indeed in collaboration with Bakunin, he called for revolutionary destruction but without any well-developed corresponding vision of a postrevolutionary future. It cannot be denied that Nechaev's message appealed to a certain stratum of young radicals, drawn to its Romantic aura of outlaw abandon, but much of the attraction involved Nechaev's false claims that he was the representative of a powerful European organization. Without any time to gather steam, the whole Nechaev enterprise crumbled in a poorly executed murder of a core member of the group who had fallen out of Nechaev's favor. Nechaev escaped and remained abroad, managing to alienate most of the European socialists, while the trial of his collaborators unfurled in Moscow. He was finally extradited from Switzerland in 1872 and died in prison in Saint Petersburg a decade later.

Unfortunately, history has accorded a much larger place in the revolutionary movement to Nechaev than he really deserves. His "Catechism of a Revolutionary," possibly written with the help of Tkachev and Bakunin, makes fascinating reading for its radical absolutism, and the story of his rapid rise and fall is more dramatic than that of most revolutionaries, but in the history of populist activism he was more important as a counterexample. For as the story of Nechaev's organization was emerging in the public trial of Nechaev's co-conspirators in 1871 groups of young populist radicals came to see Nechaev's history as a cautionary tale. They began to set up their own organizations in deliberate contrast to the rampant destruction and conspiratorial methods he advocated. The best known and most important group to react against Nechaev arose in Saint Petersburg and eventually came to be called the Chaikovsky Circle. Where Nechaev had counseled secretiveness and isolation, the Chaikovsky Circle favored group cohesion and friendly interaction. Where Nechaev promoted violence, they turned first toward "self-education." Judging from numerous glowing memoirs, the Chaikovsky Circle had the brightest appeal of any populist revolutionary organization. It would leave a big stamp on radical populism as several of its members still at liberty would go on to participate in the notorious radical movements at the end of the 1870s. Although most of its members would be lost to arrest and exile, the framework of ideas the Chaikovsky Circle developed would serve as the basis on which those later organizations would evolve.

The Chaikovsky Circle had prominence and staying power that other revolutionary associations could not match mainly because they formed the kind of organization that people wanted to belong to and remain in. All group decisions were made on the basis of mutual consensus, and they eagerly agreed on the need for equality, gender diversity, personal morality, and lack of pretension. Any absence of ethical rigor, or ignoring these principles, was noted and mocked by other members as a means of maintaining group coherence; in fact the circle removed one of its earliest leaders for engaging in behavior others considered immoral. While enforcing such standards of personal conduct might sound like a recipe for a version of puritanical authoritarianism, by most accounts the members of the circle worked together happily and, although they engaged in vigorous political debate, managed to maintain a remarkable unity of purpose. In spite of its intentional blending of male and female participants, members recalled the circle as a "brotherhood." As one of them put it later, they operated on the basis of a "heartfelt simplicity of relationships that sometimes can be found in a good and friendly family circle."[5] To this sense of joyful unity they added a taste for Spartan living as a demonstration of their willingness to sacrifice, and of course as a mark of their solidarity with the impoverished *narod*. The name of the circle is itself revealing. Since they lacked any particular leading figure, they were named from the outside by non-participants only because Nikolai Chaikovsky happened to be well known as a gregarious recruiter. In opposition to the cloak-and-dagger schemes of Nechaev, the open, consensual, and self-sacrificing nature of the Chaikovsky Circle seems to have been attractive to a large number of populist radicals in the early 1870s, and they managed to establish several branch organizations across European Russia.

Impelled by the Chaikovsky Circle, the populist movement began its first period of sustained political activity. The evolution of the Chaikovsky Circle is instructive in this respect. Initially interested in self-education, they swiftly moved on to a project producing and distributing, at reduced rates, books on political subjects intended to educate and raise the political consciousness of workers and peasants, as well as to offer revolutionary political texts to educated readers. Soon this "book business" was not enough. By 1872 they had begun to hold meetings with factory workers to whom they gave basic lessons in literacy and arithmetic, while gradually adding political discussion into the mix. In some cases, they rented apartments, and had large numbers of workers coming to them for instruction. It was not particularly difficult for the Third Section, wary as it was of "worker/student" interaction, to discover these activities. At the end of 1873 the police arrested a number of radicals who had been meeting with workers, including several from the Chaikovsky Circle. These urban arrests helped set the stage for the next evolutionary leap of populist activism. It was to play out not in the city but in the countryside. They called it, quite simply, "Going to the People."

Bridging the Gap

"Going to the People" is rightly understood as one of the high watermarks of Russian populism. Never again would the populist impulse to merge with the peasants find such a pure form as it did during the summer of 1874 in the first and most buoyant wave of populists moving to the countryside to live among the *narod*. In a burst of unexpected enthusiasm, thousands flooded into the countryside in order to literally close the gap between the two isolated sectors of society. The first wave in that summer included between two and three thousand mostly young people, most of whom were unacquainted with one another. More than a decade earlier, Herzen had first admonished Russian students to "go to the people," and since the time of Iakushkin's travels in the village a handful of enterprising souls from the urban sphere had found a way to live among the peasants as teachers, farmers, medical personnel, ethnographers, or just summer wanderers. Precisely what changed that managed to provoke thousands from the populist intelligentsia to pour into the countryside all at once remains something of a mystery. The question becomes especially intriguing when we consider the difficulties they would face. It was well recognized that the peasantry was suspicious of outsiders, especially those outside of peasant society, and therefore anyone hoping to live among them had to, like Iakushkin, play the part of a local. Before going they had to find ways to dress, to speak, and to work among the people. Already by the winter of 1874, numerous populists were—rather arrogantly, it must be said—attempting to learn trades that would enable them to keep up with people who labored for a living, or offer them some useful service.

To understand why "going to the people" came together and was carried out with remarkable spontaneity, we can point to the writings of Bakunin and Lavrov, both of whom, in their different ways, had encouraged the members of educated society to go out and work among the people. Although they were quickly arrested, a group under the leadership of Alexander Dolgushin had set an example the previous summer by intentionally living and carrying out agitation in the countryside. Some have credited the movement to the influence of Chaikovsky Circle members who had gone to the village in the winter of 1873–4. When Kravchinsky, along with Dmitry Rogachev and Dmitry Klements returned they all proclaimed that living among the peasants presented little difficulty, and, even better, those they encountered in the village had been receptive to propaganda. Others have suggested the populists went to the countryside once they grew disillusioned with the limits of propaganda among the urban working class and now sought to acquaint themselves with the "real" *narod* in their authentic rural setting.

But none of these influences seems significant enough to have ignited a mass movement. The more plausible explanation already existed within the minds of those who chose to join the movement. As we have seen, fascination with that "other Russia" that existed side-by-side with, but separate from, the world of educated elites had been building for decades. The rural village had been vilified and oppressed of course, but more recently it had been idealized to a curiosity-provoking degree. The *narod* was said to contain the germ of revolutionary change, the makings of a socialist future, and the essence of authentic Russian identity. The fascination with the true Russia—the great majority of the population living separately and differently but not far away—was hard to resist. Considered from this perspective, "going to the people," collapsing the space between urban and rural Russia, was a movement waiting to happen. It took but a few small nudges to set it in motion.

As befits a movement involving thousands of participants, the populists went to the countryside not for any one or two reasons but for a number of interconnected reasons.

Perhaps the most prominent was curiosity: the quest to understand for themselves the *narod* they had learned to admire but mostly only read about. For many that admiration knew no bounds. As one of the participants recalled, the populists "loved the *narod* sincerely, open-heartedly, almost naively. To say anything unfavorable about the *narod* meant you'd earned an enemy for life. They idolized, bowed and prayed [to the *narod*] ... It was of course a dream and a 'soul-elevating scam,' but at that time it was inescapable."[6] Curiosity also prompted a desire to fully understand those mysterious "other" compatriots they intended to unite with as fellow citizens in the transformed Russia of the future. Who were they? On what basis was a merger possible?

Another driving factor was the desire to be of assistance, or as Lavrov had put it to "discharge the debt" they owed to the people. And yet to do so required serious and thoughtful preparation. Already living abroad, Lavrov was keenly aware of the difficulties they would face:

> It is not in theory only that the man of Russia's civilized class must prepare himself. He must prepare himself as well for life. He must use every effort in order, within him and around him, to smooth over those sharp differences the habits of life's circumstances placed between the social classes in Russia. He must be able to live with the *narod*, must accustom himself to speak with him, understand him, sympathize with him not only in general, but in specific lived questions.[7]

The solution was to present oneself, insofar as possible, as a member of the *narod*. More often than not that meant dressing in the clothes of a member of the working classes and learning some skill in manual labor. It could even involve changes in speech and mannerisms that seemed to the educated and urbanized populists to replicate country folk. But actually managing to pass for a local was, at a minimum, exceedingly rare.

Not unrelated to the desire to help and serve, many populists wanted to test themselves and discover their capacity for the hard physical labor they admired in the peasants. Their admiration for the peasants' long-suffering endurance under difficult conditions was matched by their desire to learn the culture and folk wisdom they believed lay hidden in the depths of rural society, and of course they hoped to imbibe the spirit of that communalism believed to characterize peasant culture. Many memoirs even recall a holiday-like atmosphere among the participants as they fanned out across the huge rural expanse of the Empire. They were, after all, literally engaging in a summer excursion to the country. Others were intrigued by arguments, like those of Shchapov, that sectarian religiosity acted as a covert form of rebellion among the *narod*, and they wanted to discover whether the exotic religious beliefs of a people so different from them could be activated in some form of secular rebellion. Relatedly, the reason official Russia adduced for populist treks to the countryside—that they had gone there with the aim of spreading propaganda to fan the flames of discontent—did in fact play a significant role as well. The opportunity to fulfill all of these goals via one apparently simple act of inhabiting rural Russia delighted those who participated; it rendered "going to the people," especially at the outset, the most joyous and optimistic phase in the entire populist movement. As one populist later described that initial moment: "We all had great faith in the future then . . . We felt in ourselves the presence of an unusual strength and the consciousness of this strength rested on our faith in the people."[8]

For some of the participants, this feeling of confidence and enthusiasm had a tendency to spill over into an almost religious ecstasy. They later recalled it as "the mad summer of 1874." One populist remembered the summer as "pure religious ecstasy, in which neither judgment nor sober thought had a place."[9] Kravchinsky refused to see "going to the people" as a political event and instead likened it to a crusade in which the restoration of the soul was as much a motivation as any external mission. One element of this quasi-religious feeling involved the desire on the part of some populists to abandon their former selves and adopt a new existence, even to gain a new personality, just as they had adopted new forms of dress and new modes of speech. One Jewish populist went so far as to convert to Orthodoxy. Some populists remembered getting carried away by the moment and losing the objectivity they prized in themselves as politically engaged intellectuals, but it was difficult for them to resist the multiple attractions of the adventure.

> A powerful cry arose from nowhere certain and spread through the land, beckoning all those with true compassion to the great deed of saving the motherland and humanity. And all those compassionate people responding to this cry, filled with sorrow and indignation for their prior life, abandoning their homes, their wealth, their honors, their families, gave themselves over to the movement with the sort of joyous enthusiasm and ardent faith that knew no bounds ... It would be hard to call this movement political. It was more like a crusade, with all the contagiousness and utter devotion of a religious movement. People strove not only toward distinct practical aims but also toward the satisfaction of a deep need for personal moral purification.
>
> From Stepniak-Kravchinsky, *Underground Russia* (1882)

Not only did they feel they were finding their way home again by returning to the "real" Russia of the *narod*, but they were also experiencing what many Europeans in the nineteenth century experienced when they vacationed in the countryside: the poetic and the picturesque side of rural life. Political mentors like Chernyshevsky had long since instilled in them strong objections to such frivolity, but not everyone is made of such stern stuff. One populist, having recalled "the picturesque banks of the Dnieper" and "the trills pouring forth from the nightingale," said "I soon forgot the bitter and unpleasant feelings I had prior to my departure."[10] On top of it all, many of them felt an empowering sense of actually making a difference in the new world they had entered: "Every minute we felt we were needed and not extraneous. Consciousness of one's usefulness was a magnetic force attracting our youth to the village; only there was it possible to have a clean soul and a peaceful conscience."[11]

For all the virtues of the village experience, in the long run many populists found life in the village difficult, even traumatic. Many of them wound up returning to the city under arrest. In fact, the most common story told about "going to the people" is that the populists went out with high hopes and had them dashed by the conservative recalcitrance of a peasantry which saw through them as educated urbanites no different than any landowner or government official. The real story was, of course, far more complicated than that. They found much to admire, from hard work to folk wisdom, and even a degree of receptivity to revolutionary views. Some of them managed to draw close to the peasants with whom they lived and worked. Nevertheless, few of them found life in the village to be what they had hoped for or expected. Part of the surprise involved sheer lack of knowledge. "Loving the *narod*," said Plekhanov, "I knew it very little, or better to say I entirely did not know it."[12] Even if there was a degree of success in attempting to draw close to the peasants and interest them in new ideas, the peasantry itself certainly could never have lived up to those high expectations that had been built up over many years in the urban world of the populist intelligentsia.

To begin with, that which the theorists revered as the very essence of the Russian village, the jewel in the crown of peasant life, the commune, makes only an occasional appearance in the memoirs of those who went to the people. If the young populists hoped to find the promised spirit of communalism in the village, there is very little evidence they did. As one of them put it, "the first thing I noticed among the peasantry was the lack of solidarity among them."[13] Nor did they discover a peasantry prepared to leap into rebellion at the slightest push. Some peasants were interested in political ideas; some reacted with suspicion and hostility. Others were simply indifferent, as Nikolai Morozov discovered when one of the peasants used his propaganda materials to roll cigarettes. What they found, for the most part, was hard-working, malnourished human beings suffering from a variety of ailments yet trying to scratch out a meager living. And they found them by the millions. One of them found himself too worn down by work to even engage in propaganda by the end of the day. After this he understood better how what he referred to as their "zoological" existence bred a tendency toward conservatism. Another common reaction was voiced by Vera Figner, who worked as a medical specialist. She found the peasants replete with chronic ailments and living under conditions that only exacerbated them. She was powerless to change those conditions and had very little to offer for a cure. Under the circumstances, she recognized just how difficult it would be to make any difference as one individual among such a mass of humanity. "I must confess," she wrote later, "I felt alone, weak and powerless in this peasant sea."[14]

Much the same feeling overtook those who sought to rouse the revolutionary sprit of the peasantry. One claimed that only one in a thousand peasants took an interest in his views. Another said that even the interested peasants listened to him the way they listened to the village priest, respectfully and with interest, and then went about their business just as they always had. For many it turned out to be more difficult than they had expected to embrace the grueling and monotonous life of peasant Russia. Even much later the populists admitted how difficult it had been to get along without their usual amenities. Far from the urban realm of exciting ideas or contentious debate, the village mainly turned out to be a place for long hours of hard work. Many populists wound up so worn down by the work that they returned to the city of their own accord. Another common reaction was simple loneliness. They felt disconnected from the urban environment in which they had formed bonds with like-minded others who had also wanted to experience life in the village. Unless they were traveling together, as some of them did, they had no one with whom to discuss their impressions and experiences. One populist was so desperate to speak "in his own language" to his peers that he questioned his sanity as he found himself talking to the stove in a peasant hut. Amid all of these difficulties, attempting to dress, speak, and work like the *narod* also led to feelings of hypocrisy. As Tikhomirov recalled: "We lied [to the peasants] at every step, and we lied in the name of truth."[15] Populists continued to venture out to the countryside throughout the rest of the 1870s and beyond. Many of them even remained there for years at a time. But the ultimate outcome of all the high hopes "going to the people" first inspired was a powerful sense of disillusionment. The movement did not lead to saving the *narod*, or to merging with them, or to raising their political consciousness. What it did lead to was a change in tactics. Now the populists moved back to the cities and began to rethink their approach to transforming Russia. In this respect, at least, "Going to the People" had made a difference.

Going Underground

The first sign of change arrived as a shift in tactics. A group inspired by Bakunin, who called themselves "Rebels," hit on a new method for rousing the peasantry to revolutionary action. The peasants harbored deeply ingrained distrust toward local landowners and rural officials yet still believed the tsar had their best interest at heart, a sentiment that has been termed "naive monarchism." To the peasants the tsar was, as one of them put it, "the friend of the simple folk and the enemy of the landowner."[16] Recognizing this conviction among most peasants, the Rebels decided to make cynical use of their simple faith in a beneficent tsar. Such a belief naturally instilled passivity and frustrated those who remained convinced that Bakunin had been right that the peasants were ripe for rebellion. The Rebels focused on the single Ukrainian district of Chigirin and convinced the peasantry there that the Tsar wanted them to revolt against local landowners and officials. To do so Iakov Stefanovich, one of their leaders, assumed a false identity as a peasant and brought the local peasantry a forged decree purportedly straight from the Tsar, a decree that commanded they band together in a secret organization in an effort to overthrow the local landlords. To the delight of the Rebels, their plan was remarkably successful. Hundreds of peasants joined the cause as a result of the deception. But before any rebellion could actually get underway, the local constabulary discovered the plot and put an end to it. The "Chigirin Affair," as it came to be called, differed from "Going to the People" in fundamental ways. Few of the Rebels even interacted with the peasants or spent much time in the village. When they did visit the village they were armed and prepared to join the revolt. Their weapons were a signal of the new direction then beginning to take shape in the cities.

By the middle of the 1870s, most populists had accepted the impossibility of fomenting revolution in the countryside. They refocused their attention on the urban sphere but remained as determined as ever to bring about a peasant-centered revolution. How that would be possible as yet remained unclear. When the urban public sphere came to life in 1876 with the protests in support of the Balkan Slavs, radical populists got involved as much as other parts of society. Some volunteered as soldiers and medical personnel, and these included prominent members of the Chaikovsky Circle, such as Klements and Kravchinsky. The demonstrations themselves appeared to the populists a hopeful sign that Russian society was awakening to its potential as a political force. Mikhailovsky cautiously greeted the pro-Slav demonstrations as a moment in which it was possible "to hear the sound of freedom."[17] In this atmosphere, even for many populists who were still convinced their work among the peasants would bear fruit, the cities began to exert a magnetic attraction.

Anyone familiar with [the revolutionary movement of the 1870s] says that Petersburg was its main hearth, the center of government and the focal point of all the country's intellectual forces. Year after year it was the place in which the oppositional elements accumulated. Precisely here were formed the most serious all-Russian revolutionary organizations ... the provinces were pulled into Petersburg and received their impetus from here ... All of the most important political trials, with their enormous agitational significance, took place here, and it was here that revolutionary uprisings found their greatest response. In Petersburg were concentrated the main literary strengths of Russia, along with those groups that sided most with revolutionary ideals. Revolutionary organs were published only in Petersburg and from here they were spread throughout Russia ... The population of workers in Petersburg ... was more prepared to grasp socialist and revolutionary ideas. Propaganda at the factories and workshops had been carried out longer here, more systematically and to a greater extent than in any other industrial center ... The students of Petersburg were more numerous than in any other city and more advanced than all other students in Russia: the student unrest in Petersburg universities gave the first signal to the movement and went in advance of it.

Vera Figner, from her memoirs

For the time being the creation of a more organized underground association seemed advisable. The Kazan Cathedral Demonstration described at the beginning of this chapter took place shortly after the Balkan Slav demonstrations. It unfurled a flag advertising a radical populist organization formed that same year and named after the earlier underground organization, Land and Freedom. Under the aegis of Land and Freedom the populists rerooted themselves in the city. Earlier that year, in March, they had transformed an ordinary funeral into a populist demonstration, and in June they carried out the spectacular prison break of Petr Kropotkin from a Saint Petersburg military hospital. Both events hoodwinked and humiliated official Russia and gave impetus to the new political strategy Land and Freedom now began calling "disorganization." This strategy was proposed as a way to introduce turmoil into government operations and expose the weaknesses of a state they sometimes referred to as "a colossus with feet of clay," meaning a power that could easily be toppled. By the fall of 1876 it seemed to many observers that a turning point in the populist movement had come. In spite of the fact that only work and propaganda among the peasantry upheld the doctrinal principles of populism, the success of "disorganization" in the capital cities became too hard to resist. The sense of enthusiasm for urban activism certainly helped inspire the Kazan Cathedral Demonstration, but when this demonstration ended in ignominy and arrests it was already clear that organized assemblies in the public sphere could not provide a road forward. Some other form of protest was called for at this point, but no one had a clear plan.

Many populists chose to return to organizing and agitating among urban workers. Organizational work included the earlier methods of teaching combined with gentle propaganda, but as the workers themselves grew more politically active, the populists helped them organize strikes, participate in carefully limited demonstrations, form labor associations, and even print a small newspaper. The state, of course, frowned on all such activity and attempted to shut it down as quickly and decisively as possible. Any hint of a strike, as Plekhanov recalled, brought forth Cossack guards and police at every street corner. In this same period, however, the state unintentionally obliged the urban populists by offering them an unexpected platform on which to air their views and convince urban society of the value of their cause. To adjudicate the cases of those hundreds of populists who had been arrested for going to the people in 1874, they organized two famous trials. The first, called "The Trial of the 50" for the number of defendants tried, was held in public so that members of society could witness for themselves the nefarious actions of the populists who had spread propaganda among the peasants. At this trial the defendants did not deny the charges but used the megaphone of the public trial to defend their actions as altruistic and self-sacrificing attempts to attain justice for the millions of Russians left behind in the miserable conditions of the peasant village. To the chagrin of the government, the populists came across as proud martyrs for a noble cause. The state reacted by removing the next trial, "The Trial of the 193," from the public eye. But because of its size and the fact that family members could attend, not to mention that the underground press had come into operation by this time, word of this trial circulated widely, and it grew to become an even greater sensation than the former trial. The populists at this trial were savvy enough to use it intentionally to orchestrate their message. In the trial's most famous speech, to the glee of his populist observers Ippolit Myshkin roundly denounced the senators presiding over the trial as something worse than prostitutes for doing the bidding of the corrupt and oppressive autocracy. These trials had such an effect that, as the historian and statesman Pavel Miliukov would later remark: "The political trials made the revolution popular."[18]

In its early stages Land and Freedom saw its main goal as support for those who went to the countryside to continue the work of propaganda among the *narod*. But as time went on and the lure of urban activism grew stronger, the populists recognized the need to increasingly refine their tightly organized and highly disciplined urban underground. The introduction of conspiratorial discipline was first undertaken by a former leader of the Chaikovsky Circle, Mark Natanson. While the Chaikovsky Circle had been relatively lax in its conspiratorial techniques, the intervening arrests and imprisonments had injected a new level of caution and secrecy into Land and Freedom. Vera Zasulich later recalled Kravchinsky saying that in terms of conspiratorial discipline Land and Freedom "exceeded the Chaikovsky like grownups to children."[19] When Natanson was yet again arrested in 1877, his organizational work was taken over primarily by Alexander Mikhailov, a figure who has not received full credit by historians for the seminal role he played in turning Land and Freedom (and its successor The People's Will) into a powerful and resilient underground organization. This was no small feat because these two organizations would go on to become the scourge of the autocracy, exert a profound effect on Russian history, gain international notoriety, and help bring into being terrorism as we know it today.

An unusual individual among the populists, Mikhailov was a born leader but without any taste for the spotlight. He worked tirelessly to bring about a revolution but did not seem particularly interested in populist ideology. At one point, in fact, Mikhailov openly rejected the notion that the radical populists needed to espouse a particular doctrine. Instead he sought out recognition and influence via demonstrations of power. For instance, he once remarked about the underground press he helped found and carefully guarded that "Whatever is written makes no difference. What matters is the mere existence of such a newspaper! The police search for it and cannot find it. That's what has an effect on the public."[20] Whatever his political views, Mikhailov's activity was almost entirely practical, and that was its stalwart advantage. He can be thought of as the embodiment of that populist voluntarism which dictated that revolution was not made by intangible historical processes but by flesh and blood actors in the everyday world. Vera Figner later said as much about the members of Land and Freedom: "By their strictness and loftiness they raised the individual beyond anything humdrum; a person felt more vividly that it was in him that the idea lived and must live."[21]

Mikhailov's genius lay in his ability to make use of state systems of control by turning them to the populists' advantage. Since all Russians were expected to carry a passport and register it with local officials, in nineteenth-century Russia the passport served as a crucial guarantee of legitimate identity. Many populists associated with Land and Freedom, however, hid their actual identities once the police were in pursuit of them. Under the circumstances they had to create high-quality passports of false or borrowed identities. As they liked to say, a high-quality forged passport could "wash you clean" by turning you into an ordinary upstanding citizen. At the same time, even among themselves they rarely used their own names but referred to each other by nicknames, and along with their new identities they changed their outward appearance. While it had been fashionable on the left since the early 1860s to "dress down," either in worker attire or bohemian-fashion like the so-called nihilists, the members of Land and Freedom chose to appear as ordinary "bourgeois," making them seem entirely

Figure 5.1 Alexander Mikhailov © Out of copyright (public domain).

harmless and apolitical. Their intentional ordinariness extended from their clothing to their domiciles. What they called the "conspiratorial apartment" was typically occupied by a fictitious husband and wife, made to look entirely ordinary and perfectly open to neighbors and building caretakers. They took great care to furnish these apartments with such features as china plates and portraits of the Tsar. The chain of conspiratorial apartments throughout Saint Petersburg, some in poor sections and some even along elegant Nevsky Prospect, functioned as living space, meeting rooms, and as workshops for such activities as printing newspapers and manufacturing dynamite.

Assisted by a large network of sympathizers and supporters, ranging from students to well-heeled liberals, and also benefiting from a remarkably effective mole whom Mikhailov had managed to place on the clerical staff of the Third Section, the members of Land and Freedom enjoyed a remarkable sense of impunity. Although Mikhailov frowned on it, in their ordinary dress they attended the theater, held parties at restaurants, and even visited each other's conspiratorial apartments. As their "disorganization" activities ramped up, increasing numbers of police spies were put on the payroll to hunt them down, but even in this case Mikhailov managed to find the solution. He taught all the members to know the city down to the smallest detail so that if they believed they were being followed they could use various courtyards, alleys, and back exits to elude the essential danger of revealing where they lived. Mikhailov not only gave instructions but even secretly tested members of the organization by following them the way a police spy would. Those who couldn't see well enough were furnished a pair of glasses. This elaborate network of concealment techniques made possible the next phase of populist political activism—the use of violent acts to send a political message, which they took to calling "terrorism."

Terrorism

The turn toward political violence did not take place all at once. To a degree it arose almost by chance, but it was also the result of multiple influences, far from the least of which was the continued determination of many populists to precipitate revolutionary change as soon as possible. We have already noted the attempt to fool the peasants of Chigirin into rebellion. A short while earlier the Kazan Cathedral Demonstration had revealed the hopelessness of public protest. In January of 1878 an event took place that combined the violent intentions of Chigirin with the aftermath of the demonstration that helped lift populist "disorganization" to a new level. Dismayed at the notorious prison flogging of the populist prisoner Arkhip Bogoliubov (an alias), a 28-year-old woman named Vera Zasulich decided to avenge his mistreatment. The flogging had been ordered in the summer of 1877 by Saint Petersburg's Governor General Fyodor Trepov for the trumped-up reason that Bogoliubov as a prisoner had refused to remove his hat in deference to Trepov as he passed through the prison on inspection. The real reason had been Trepov's indignation at those political prisoners, most of whom had been arrested for spreading propaganda, who had shown contempt for him during the inspection. To flog a member of educated society was nearly unheard of at this time. It provoked a prison riot, and Zasulich became the first to heed the loud calls for revenge against Trepov. On the morning of January 24, 1878, she walked into Trepov's receiving hours on a false pretext, pulled a revolver from beneath her shawl, and shot him in the abdomen at close range. Dropping the gun, she stood in silence awaiting her punishment.

The state decided to try Zasulich not as a political criminal in a closed court but as an ordinary criminal in a public jury trial. By the day of her trial on March 31, the Saint Petersburg public had developed a huge fascination with Zasulich and her deed. What was the reason this young woman had committed such a violent act and never sought to escape punishment? Since Zasulich had herself spent time as a political prisoner, her attorney masterfully portrayed her as the victim of a state that had abused her with its methods of cruel and arbitrary government. He managed to convince the jury that Zasulich was merely an honorable victim rightfully trying to avenge the innocent Bogoliubov for abuses she herself knew too well. Demonstrating that much of urban society had by now grown tired of arbitrary acts by the government, when the jury came back with a not-guilty verdict the hundreds of well-heeled spectators witnessing the trial broke out in an ovation of jubilant applause and tears of joy that lasted several minutes. When Zasulich was released, a cheering crowd of more than a thousand awaited her outside the courthouse. Although the government hurriedly tried to rearrest her, she was hidden away by supporters and soon escaped abroad. The Zasulich Affair, as it came to be called, sent a clear signal to the radical populists: violence against a state official had not only been tolerated but welcomed by Russian society. Violence, it seemed, was the answer.

Those who have attempted to account for the populist adoption of violent tactics have too often treated Zasulich and her trial as the exclusive cause. In fact, Zasulich's attempt to murder Trepov was already an act of political terror as much as revenge. Her attempt on Trepov was supposed to take place simultaneously with another murder of the chief prosecutor for the Trial of the 193. That attempt had failed, and her case could be treated as a simple act of vengeance when it was actually intended as a form of "propaganda by deed," a political spectacle meant to send a message to state and society. Zasulich assumed she would become a martyr to the cause rather than a model for a new method of political activism, but the populists greeted her act as the foundation for a new phase in the revolutionary struggle. Already in possession of a well-hidden underground "behind enemy lines" in the middle of the capital city, they would go to war with the state using the method of surreptitious attacks, and their war would serve to demonstrate the weakness and illegitimacy of the autocracy, thereby calling forth the anticipated revolution.

After Zasulich, Kravchinsky was one of the first to recognize the potential of political violence. Little more than three months after the trial, in early August of 1878, Kravchinsky accomplished his "homage" to Zasulich by killing the head of the Third Section in broad daylight in the center of Saint Petersburg. As much as this killing had been inspired by Zasulich, however, it was in fact something quite different than Zasulich's attempt. While Zasulich had awaited her punishment as a martyr to the cause, Kravchinsky was accompanied by two accomplices who helped him immediately escape into the heart of the city and back to safety in his underground stronghold. The plot had been assisted by Mikhailov and other members of Land and Freedom; it was an act of "propaganda by deed," in which Kravchinsky's safe escape was very much part of the point. Kravchinsky's intention to "remain an active soldier" became the standard model for Land and Freedom. Quite in contrast to Zasulich, if Kravchinsky and others could return again on another day to carry out another such attack it was a sign of their strength as an organization prepared to do battle against their enemy, the Tsarist autocracy. Kravchinsky felt so secure in his underground anonymity that he brazenly walked the streets without concern for capture to the point that another member of Land and Freedom had to explain to him that if he were to be caught "three fourths of the significance of your act is lost."[22] At this point, deliberate acts of violence for political purposes had become the new method of political struggle the populists would continue to practice for much of the next three years.

To capitalize on the murder, a week after the event Kravchinsky used the underground printing press to publish his anonymous pamphlet "A Death for a Death." The short essay justified the assassination and explained that many more such "executions" would follow if the state did not cease to support the wrong elements in society. This method of striking in a surprise attack and then explaining the attack through a communique—either Land and Freedom's underground newspaper or a specially printed proclamation—became standard practice for the radical populists. They bolstered the violent act itself by making specific demands and threats of further violence if their demands were not met. In the year 1878 alone there would occur four assassination attempts against government officials, three of them successful, and these were accompanied by other forms of "disorganization" that included assistance with worker strikes, successful jailbreaks, robbery of a treasury building, and the killing of a police informant. By this time the urban underground sensed its power as a force for destabilization, and it poured more and more of its limited resources into these kinds of activities.

Underground political violence had nothing to do with the original tenets of populism that, as we have seen, sought to promote local revolt from below among the peasants in the countryside, and this did not go unnoticed by those members of Land and Freedom who tried to maintain the original ideological purpose of "going to the people." They recognized that their initial plans were being derailed by, as one of them put it, the "fireworks" of urban attacks. At the same time, those fireworks were generating tremendous enthusiasm. The more the underground terrorists appeared to be the direct and merciless foes of the autocratic state, the more their supporters in *obshchestvo* celebrated them for their "heroic" and "daring" exploits. In turn this enthusiasm inspired the terrorists to believe they were generating the kind of societal fervor that could lead to revolution. But they were no longer talking about a socioeconomic and anarchistic takeover of the villages under the auspices of the commune. Now the revolution they began to dream of would come from an urban society that would put an end to the autocracy.

The growing taste for political violence and the financial demands it generated meant that resources for the original populism based on rural agitation and propaganda were drying up. More and more the members of Land and Freedom seemed to be split into two separate groups, the villagers, adhering to work among the peasants, and the urban terrorists, whose center of gravity was shifting decisively to the city. As a result the villagers, whom the urbanites sometimes mocked as "sleepy farmers," sensed their increasing marginalization within the movement. One of the populist "countryfolk" lamented: "things have gone so far that the active participants in one and the other place have completely ceased to understand and sympathize with each other."[23] It was not long before the tension came to a head and decisions about the future of Land and Freedom had to be made. In June of 1879 a meeting took place in the city of Voronezh at which the two sides debated the efficacy of terrorism and the ultimate purpose of Land and Freedom. In the end Plekhanov, the most important leader opposed to the terrorist struggle, walked out of the meeting. He and that segment of the populists still devoted to the original purpose of populism later regrouped as "Black Repartition," a name that referred to the communal redistribution of land, while Mikhailov and those urbanites who favored terrorist methods renamed their organization The People's Will. Land and Freedom was no more, and Plekhanov eventually went on to become "the father of Russia Marxism," but The People's Will was now in a position to carry out their plans unimpeded by competing interests.

One of the main factors contributing to the split had been an event that took place in April of 1879. Alexander Solovev, a populist disturbed by his powerlessness to improve the lot of the peasantry through work in the countryside, sought out the members of Land and Freedom and presented himself as someone with plans to assassinate the Tsar. The terrorists had to wonder: If the assassination of ordinary government officials had generated a fearful respect for them, then what might be the impact of the assassination of the Tsar, the very embodiment of the autocratic state? They lent Solovev no direct and open support but quietly offered their services in tracking the Tsar's movements and finding him a gun. Solovev eventually took several shots at the Tsar from close range on the Palace Square, but Alexander managed to evade every one of them. Refusing to confess who had helped him, Solovev was executed, but he had planted a seed in the minds of his abettors. Once Land and Freedom became The People's Will the remaining members decided to follow in Solovev's footsteps. In the fall of 1879 they declared a death sentence on Alexander II and began systematically to pursue his assassination, thinking it might finally precipitate the long-awaited revolution by unleashing mass unrest.

How did they convince themselves that assassination of the Tsar would lead to revolution in the Russian countryside when they were already well aware of the peasant distrust toward educated elites and parallel faith in the good wishes of the tsar? There is not a monocausal answer to that question. One simple, though insufficient, explanation is that they had exhausted all other options—from propagandizing among the workers, to living in the village and attempting to ignite revolution there, to the deception of Chigirin, to urban public protest. None of these had produced anything substantial beyond mass arrests of populist activists. Perhaps a spectacular act would finally shock the *narod* and/or *obshchestvo* out of its complacency. For lack of a better option, they thought it possible such an event would, as Nikolai Kibalchich hopefully expressed it, "give the signal to an uprising of millions of hungry peasants."[24] Many of the radicals were later to admit, however, that they never had great confidence in provoking revolution by way of political assassination. Some of them had even been aware that spectacular violence might incite an anti-Semitic pogrom, which in fact it did. Other motives inspired the "hunt for the Tsar" as well. One, as suggested by the title of Kravchinsky's "A Death for a Death" was revenge against a state that had persecuted the populists for pursuing their revolutionary goals. Another is reflected in the non-violent activities The People's Will was simultaneously engaged in. These involved outreach not to peasants but to the various sectors of urban society, including the liberal intelligentsia, the growing class of industrial workers, an members of the military. Many of the populists within The People's Will had concluded by the late 1870s that it might be possible to provoke revolution, not first among the peasantry, but within urban society. In this way, the signal sent by their terrorism was directed less toward the village and more toward the cities, and the sophisticated language of their underground newspapers and proclamations bears this out.

None of these motivations, however, yet fully explain the powerful magnetic tug toward acts of violence that became the central, overriding *raison d'être* for the existence of The People's Will. Violent acts of "propaganda by deed," together with their accompanying proclamations, had provoked a palpable degree of panic in both government officials and urban society at large. High-ranking officials believed the state was threatened with collapse and began to discuss the possible necessity of radical reform. In 1880 in the midst of a series of attempts on his life, Alexander II actually did disband the fifty-year-old Third Section and reorganized his government under Mikhail Loris-Melikov, who promised to establish a more humane form of governance. The members of The People's Will could see clearly that their terror campaign was exerting a powerful influence on the autocratic state, the only entity in Russia that enjoyed a significant degree of political power. By 1880 it had come to seem as though only two institutions had any significant power in Russia: the state and The People's Will.

Recognition of their newfound influence proved intoxicating to The People's Will. The weapon of an underground organization used to carry out violent attacks had given them a lever with which to shake the confidence of one of the most powerful governments in the world. Could it not also be a tool powerful enough to provoke a revolution? Some members of the organization, most explicitly Nikolai Morozov, were convinced they had found in underground terrorism not only a new but a less costly and difficult path to revolution. Even Lavrov, so instrumental in promoting peaceful propaganda among the people, eventually admitted that political conditions in Russia necessitated the use of an underground organization. The People's Will were probably more responsible than any other group for spreading the gospel of "propaganda by deed." One member of a later incarnation of The People's Will was still singing its praises in the 1880s: "[Ideas] will be incomparably more vital, vibrant, powerful and widespread," he insisted, "if they are proclaimed not by the mouths of separately verbalizing individuals but by the thunder of heroic facts, stunning the mind and fantasy with the brilliance of sacrifice, the brilliance of struggle, and the power of our faith in the justice of our cause."[25] Clandestine terrorism was lauded by adherents like Morozov for its supposed capacity to bring about change with a much lower body count than a violent uprising of the masses would have produced. The radical populists began to mistake themselves for a center of revolutionary change in Russian society as a result of the shock their underground terrorism managed to produce. The most convincing reason for the turn to terrorism and pursuit of the Tsar, then, was the mistaken perception that they had become a powerful revolutionary force.

When the supporters of freedom were few, they always closed themselves within a secret society. That secrecy lent them great strength. It gave a handful of bold people the possibility of struggling with millions of organized, overt enemies … But when to this secrecy is introduced political murder as a systematic method of struggle, such people become truly terrifying to their enemies. The enemies must at each moment tremble for their lives, not knowing when and from where revenge will find them. Political murder is the fulfillment of revolution in the present moment. Underground forces "unknown to anyone" call to judgment highly placed criminals, decree upon them a death sentence, and the powerful of the world feel the ground slip out from underneath them as, from the height of their powers, they fall into some dark and unknown abyss.

From Nikolai Morozov in *The Land and Freedom Leaflet* (1879)

From the fall of 1879 The People's Will pursued Alexander II, ruthlessly using every means they had at their disposal. As tsar, Alexander held in his hands not one but two of the most important political functions in Russia. He served as the autocratic executor of state policy, in which in principle his political will stood behind every decision and act the state made, and at the same time his person—including both his image, his personality, and his physical existence—embodied and represented Russia. To destroy such a target seemed to the members of The People's Will nearly tantamount to a revolution itself. Surely, if such a momentous event as an assassination of this august figure could take place, it would initiate a sea change in all of Russian society. Indulging in such heady expectations in the fall of 1879 they drew on two modern technologies in their initial assassination attempts: the railroad and dynamite. They chose three sites along the recently built rail line from the Crimea to Moscow as locations to destroy the Tsar's railway car with the use of huge amounts of the recently invented dynamite. The first site outside Odessa had to be abandoned when Alexander switched his travel plans for a different route. The second site near the city of Aleksandrovsk was prepared, but for unknown reasons the dynamite did not detonate. The third site, outside Moscow, had been painstakingly excavated for weeks. This time the bomb resoundingly exploded, derailing and overturning several imperial train cars, but it turned out they had attacked a supply train. The Tsar had passed by in a different train an hour earlier.

Three more attacks took place in the year 1880. Two of them failed, but one that had been prepared at the same time as the railroad bombings created massive casualties and shocked the world because it took place inside the walls of the palace itself. This attack was actually carried out by a disgruntled member of the working class who had enlisted the help of The People's Will. Stepan Khalturin, a carpenter, devised a plan to use his carpentry skills to get on the palace staff and then find a way to assassinate the Tsar. Once he gained access to the palace and became a live-in worker there, he first thought to murder the Tsar using an ax, but his friends among The People's Will convinced him it would be more effective to use their preferred method of dynamite. They developed a plan to place a bomb in the workers' quarters where Khalturin lived since his living quarters lay two floors directly beneath Alexander's dining hall, and the Tsar's dinner hours were well known. Every day Khalturin smuggled small amounts of dynamite into the palace and placed them under his pillow. This act became particularly perilous when his contact in The People's Will was arrested, and the police found a half-burned sketch of the palace dining room with a red cross marked on it. Khalturin, however, masterfully convinced palace guards and his fellow workers that he was a harmless peasant who understood little about city ways. He managed to continue to bring in small loads of dynamite each day. Ultimately, he smuggled in around a hundred pounds of dynamite. Although Khalturin himself argued for increasing the amount of dynamite, his contacts in The People's Will assured him it was enough. Having lit a slow fuse, Khalturin walked out onto the palace square. Just as he met his connection in The People's Will he turned around to see a huge explosion. The floor between the workers quarters and the Tsar's dining room had been occupied by military guards. The explosion killed twelve of them, wounded fifty-six others, and damaged the Tsar's dining room, but it turned out Alexander was late for dinner that evening. He had escaped again.

The palace bombing proved to be another failure, this one with tragic collateral damage, but the ability to place a huge bomb directly within the palace itself, less than three months after they had blown up the Tsar's train, fascinated the world. Even in the sanctuary of his well-guarded home, Alexander was not safe. The explosion at the Winter Palace earned The People's Will a degree of shocked notoriety both at home and abroad. It made them look, as Tikhomirov would later put it, all-powerful and ubiquitous. At this point, however sound or unsound their judgment in pursuing the assassination, the momentum of the assassination process had taken control, and they readied themselves for one final concerted attempt that would take place on March 31, 1881. As elaborate as their earlier schemes had been, The People's Will outdid themselves this time by uniting an arsenal of techniques, including new technologies, months of background research, simultaneous plots, and elaborate orchestration. After carrying out a time-motion study of the Tsar's activities, the plot began when two members posing as a married couple rented a storefront along one of Alexander's customary travel routes. They opened up a cheese shop, and from a side room they and their sundry nighttime visitors began to tunnel under the street. When neighbors grew suspicious because the owners seemed to know little about cheese, the police inspected the shop but, remarkably, managed to overlook the sealed barrels of earth scattered through the store.

The tunnel completed and the dynamite set, The People's Will remained aware that Alexander might or might not choose to pass the store and had therefore devised two backup plans. Plan B, almost as elaborate as the mine under the street, drew on the talents of The People's Will's resident scientist, Nikolai Kibalchich, to fashion a handheld bomb—a sort of early nitroglycerine-based hand grenade—that an individual could throw at a person or vehicle. Kibalchich produced four of them for use, and The People's Will stationed four bombers near the cheese shop. Plan C involved the physical stabbing and shooting of the Tsar by Andrei Zheliabov, who had taken over direction of The People's Will when in November of 1880 Mikhailov was finally captured. Three days

Figure 5.2 Journalist Representation of the Assassination of Alexander II © Ullstein Bild Dtl. / Getty Images.

prior to the planned attack, however, Zheliabov himself was captured. At this point only the underground mine or the handheld bombs were available. When on Sunday March 1, they discovered Alexander had chosen an alternate route that would not pass the cheese shop, the remaining leader of The People's Will, Sofia Perovskaia, understood which route the Tsar was likely to take and ordered her bombers to hurry with their unstable nitroglycerine hand grenades through the city to lie in wait along the Ekaterinsky Canal. When the Tsar's winter sleigh approached, she gave them the signal to advance. The first bomber hurled his weapon underneath the winter carriage. Several people were wounded in the resulting explosion, but the Tsar got out of the armored carriage unharmed to inspect the damage. At this point a second bomber approached and threw his bomb at close range at Alexander's feet. Both the assassin and his royal target would die within hours.

Some members of The People's Will retained the hope that when they assassinated Alexander II it would unleash a rebellion in the countryside. The assassination did lead to unrest, but that unrest manifested itself in the first major pogrom against Jews in the Russian Empire. Any hint of rebellion against the government, however, went unnoticed. Instead, public opinion turned decisively against the organization that had killed the Tsar. Perovskaia, Zheliabov, Kibalchich, and one of the bombers were executed, while the rest of The People's Will went deep into hiding, and carried on in desultory fashion (mostly abroad) until the middle of the 1880s, but the organization would never be resurrected in the same form again. In part as a result of the assassination, the next two reigns of Alexander II's son, Alexander III, and grandson, Nicholas II, would prove comparatively reactionary, and when genuine waves of revolution swept through Russia in the early twentieth century, the tactics, political goals, and world views of the participants would be markedly different from those of the populists in the 1870s. The legacy these populist activists left to the world was an inheritance most would rather leave behind. The People's Will, more than any other individual or organization, formulated the techniques, and spread the gospel, of underground terrorism. By embracing the name "terrorist" as an appropriate label for their activity, they popularized a new use of the word terrorism that remains close to the way it is typically used today. European anarchists seized hold of the new method, and one of them in Paris in 1894 took terrorism to the next level by deliberately throwing a bomb into a crowd of innocent civilians.

While The People's Will helped create terrorism as we know it, their adoption of terrorism also went a long way toward remaking them. The conviction that they had become a powerful force to be reckoned with in Russian society is obvious when one reads the pronouncements they made in their newspapers and proclamations. "Thanks to the battle with the state," one article gloated, "the party acquired the right of citizenship; the government keeps it alone in mind, considers it alone worthy of attention."[26] The People's Will had grown so fond of their newfound relevance in Russian society that it induced them to take yet another step away from the original tenets of populism. Over the course of constructing the urban underground and carrying out violent attacks, they began to think less and less about a revolution that would emerge among the *narod* and more and more about a revolution in urban society. They justified this shift by noting they would be able to use a political revolution and the creation of a government of elected representatives to gain sufficient power to then proceed to improve the welfare of the people. To further these revolutionary plans, they made connections with the various stakeholders in urban society—from industrial workers to the military to the liberal bourgeoisie—as a starting point in the move toward the removal of autocracy and the instatement of freedoms and rights around which all groups could rally, the very kind of "bourgeois" politics of elections and representation they had vilified only a few years earlier.

After the assassination, Tikhomirov, with the help of the populist theoretician Mikhailovsky, composed a letter to Tsar Alexander III. So significant did they consider this letter that a week after the assassination they printed and distributed thousands of copies, more than any proclamation or newspaper edition yet published. Alexander Mikhailov referred to it from his prison cell as the most perfect document The People's Will had created. The letter sympathized with the grief of the new Tsar, calling him "a citizen and an honest man," but it threatened to continue attacks if he did not accede to the populists' assertion that Russia could only be saved by "a voluntary rendering of the Supreme Power to the people."[27] But what, at this point, did the populists mean by rendering to the people? No mention is made of the peasantry, communalism, or social revolution. Instead the letter called for amnesty for all political prisoners, the convocation of a general assembly chosen through a national election, and freedoms of speech, press, and assembly. In the weeks and months that followed the publication of this letter, The People's Will would disintegrate, but in a sense the populists' revolutionary ideology had already burned to ashes amid the flames of terrorism. And yet it was too deeply ingrained to go away. Populism had reached a crisis point, but it would live on in the realms of art and ideas, and it would gain new life as a political movement in the early twentieth century.

CHAPTER 6
POPULIST ART

The peasant is the hero of our time.

Mikhail Saltykov-Shchedrin

What almost every imaginative writer of the age had in common was the desire to discover the people of Russia, including themselves, and present them as they were. For they did not know who they were.

Edward Crankshaw

The great poet of the Russian peasantry, Nikolai Nekrasov, died late in the year 1877. His funeral in January 1878 was recalled as an event of such civic magnitude that it almost amounted to a political demonstration. It began at nine in the morning and did not disperse until dusk. "Petersburg," as a witness recalled, "had never seen anything like it." Attendees included the student youth of Saint Petersburg, much of the literary world, and even members of Land and Freedom, then just about to embark on the spree of political violence that would culminate in the assassination of the Tsar. Also in attendance was the 24-year-old Vladimir Korolenko, by now a convinced populist radical. Korolenko managed to shimmy along the top of a stone wall to a place near the edge of the grave. The conservative writer Fyodor Dostoevsky had been asked to speak, and Korolenko recalled his oration as quiet but passionate, in a voice that sounded "moved and prophetic." Dostoevsky praised Nekrasov as "the last great gentleman-poet," and vowed that "the time would come, and it was already near, when a new poet, equal to Pushkin, Lermontov, and Nekrasov, would appear from the people itself." Korolenko got so excited that he almost fell off the wall. He later wrote, "I was to remember Dostoevsky's words for a long time thereafter as a foretelling of the imminence of a fundamental social revolution, as a sort of prophecy about the people's entry into the arena of history."[1] That Dostoevsky, a reactionary nationalist, managed to so inspire a radical socialist in the shared space of their ardent populism suggests the main theme of this chapter: Russian populism spread far beyond the revolutionary variety described in the last two chapters.

Were we to limit our examination of populism to nothing more than a peculiarly Russian socialist movement we could tell a simpler story and rest satisfied with a relatively clear and comprehensible understanding of the subject. But the rise of socialist populism was in fact part of a larger and more complicated story, a story that explains why Russia's two greatest novelists (Dostoevsky and Tolstoy), the most prominent school of nineteenth-century painters (The Wanderers), and one of Russia's greatest composers (Mussorgsky) were neither socialists nor revolutionaries but sufficiently close to populism that they have all been referred to as "populist" artists. Nor was it just that these artists were "under the influence" of populist thought. Russian artists of this era did not take up their chosen themes in imitation of the views and values espoused by well-read publicists and critics like Herzen or Chernyshevsky. They acted on their own accord, inspired by many of the same issues that inspired socialist revolutionary populists. Political radicals and artists all emerged from Russia's small urban intelligentsia, sometimes knew one another personally, and certainly knew of and commented on each other's activities. They were all engaged in a similar conversation about the future of Russia and the nature of the Russian people. Journalistic polemics, revolutionary acts, works of political philosophy, and works of art all emerged from the same public discourse.

In fact influence could, and often did, flow not from politics to art but from art to politics. As one instance, Vladimir Bonch-Bruevich recalled the impact of realist painting on revolutionaries in the late nineteenth century:

> It is still poorly known what powerful experiences the revolutionaries had, the oaths we swore there in the Tretiakov Gallery looking at such paintings as "Ivan the Terrible and His Son Ivan" or at "Princess Tarakanova," or at that painting in which a proud member of The People's Will, full of conviction, on the scaffold refuses the blessing of the priest. We also contemplated "Unequal Marriage," considering it an expression of the age-old oppression of women, dwelled in detail on "Bank Crash" and "March of the Cross," and for hours we studied the martial, cruel, and horrifying epics of Vereshchagin; we endlessly gazed upon our own political fate in "At the Halting Place," and closely understood "Boat Haulers on the Volga" and thousands of other paintings and drawings from the lives of the workers, the peasants, the soldiers, the bourgeoisie, and the priests.[2]

Alongside the revolutionary populism we have discussed thus far, other less aggressive expressions of populist views continued to exert their influence on Russian society. One might say that side by side with revolutionary populism there arose several other "populisms" in this period. As much as the politically inclined revolutionary populists, Russian writers and artists also followed down trails first blazed by Radishchev, Chaadaev, the Slavophiles, and Herzen. They made it their business to find meaning among the *narod*, seeking to heal their divided society. In art, as in revolutionary politics, there arose an intense desire to understand where Russia was going, and perhaps to nudge it in the right direction. Artists found ways to represent, make sense of and re-envision the world of the *narod* in writing, music, paint, and other media.

Russian Art in the Nineteenth Century

Percy Bysshe Shelley famously claimed that "poets are the unacknowledged legislators of the world." In Western Europe this statement seemed provocative and outlandish. In nineteenth-century Russia, without legislators but with a tradition of politically engaged writers and artists, it comes a bit closer to describing the position of the artist in society. The arts in Russia had a much more open and intimate relationship with the realm of politics than they had in Western Europe. That is not to say that all art does not have its underlying ideology, what Frederic Jameson called its "political unconscious."[3] Nor does this relationship imply that Russian artists necessarily expressed themselves in an especially tendentious manner. In a world in which the expression of overt political views risked not only censorship but jail and exile, political discussion tended to take place obliquely in the realm of literature and literary criticism. Many of the most influential figures of the mid-nineteenth-century intelligentsia acted either full- or part-time as critics. These included the original Russian exemplar of politically engaged criticism, Vissarion Belinsky, followed by the previously mentioned Chernyshevsky, Dobrolyubov, Pisarev, and Mikhailovsky. To them we must add the most important critic in music and visual arts of the populist era, Vladimir Stasov. Such prominent and politically engaged critics held the feet of writers and other artists to the fire, urging that their work expose corruption and promote change for the better. Artists themselves, not surprisingly, often spurned and repudiated their critics, but in many ways they rose to the general challenge laid down and created art that responded in some fashion or another to the burning issues of the day.

The powerful voice of both artists and critics in Russia had everything to do with the absence in Russia of a civil society engaged in public affairs. Lacking freedoms of speech and press, and without any mechanism for involvement in national politics, the Russian public found itself at the mercy of the autocracy and the extensive bureaucracy that ran it. For the most part, Russian critics, journalists, and writers of fiction had to express themselves "in disguise," in what has been likened to the language of Aesop's Fables—a sort of parable form that was evocative rather than direct, saying one thing but implying another. In journalism such limitations had the effect of muting the voices of those writing for the tolerated press, although at times the guessing game played between journalists and their audiences had the effect of exaggerating the implications of their suggestions and hints. In fiction, novelists and short-story writers were often empowered by these same limitations, which forced them to imply what might otherwise have been stated directly. Paradoxically, perhaps, the limitations created by censorship could sometimes arouse impressive flights of artistic and imaginative power. In visual arts and music, a similar suggestive creativity held sway. The absence of direct participation in politics or public affairs meant that the civil society which took shape in Russia during the latter half of the nineteenth century operated first and foremost around the fulcrum of art and art criticism. Despite the obstacles placed upon it by the autocracy, *obshchestvo* began in these years to build a public sphere that would eventually have the muscle to assert itself in the Revolution of 1905. The tradition of an active and politically engaged art world played an important role in building up this muscle.

The power of criticism and the limits placed on expression were not the only influences that determined the nature of artistic output during the second half of the nineteenth century, for Russian artists were also beset by the very same set of problems radical populists were confronting. The autocracy had long relied on Russia's social divisions for its economic sustenance and the maintenance of political control. How to conceive of and bring about a united national community under these circumstances plagued all of *obshchestvo*, including those "unacknowledged legislators" in literature and art. The words *narod* (as applied exclusively to the laboring classes) and *intelligentsiia* both came into being in the middle of the nineteenth century as recognition of Russia's unsustainable social fragmentation grew. The abolition of serfdom implied a challenge to rethink and recreate Russian society, not as a docile collection of dutiful subjects to the Crown but as a unified community of citizens with a duty to the collective whole. To accomplish such a change required a radical reconsideration of the relationship between *narod* and *obshchestvo*. That reconsideration was the task the intelligentsia set for itself. Nathaniel Knight has characterized this situation in vivid terms and shown how it led to the emergence of populist art:

> The intelligentsia could realize its highest mission as the consciousness of the nation only by alienating itself [in cosmopolitan thought and culture], albeit temporarily, from the source of national uniqueness and returning to look with new eyes on the national essence embodied in the *narod*. The intense creation of national culture in the period following the emancipation can be seen, in effect, as the unfolding of this process. From the "mighty handful" in music and the "wanderers" in art to the flowering of the Russian novel, intellectuals were channeling the skills and techniques of European civilization toward the particularity of the Russian national tradition, producing works that have since achieved iconic status as the ultimate expression of Russian cultural achievement.[4]

Many artists in this era did convey—often far more eloquently and movingly than the revolutionaries—an expression of what can only be called populism: they identified in the lower classes the key to solving Russia's problems. But Russian artists were far less committed to fixed principles than those who wrote about socioeconomic and political questions, so populism in the arts was more impressionistic, more ambiguous, and less devoted to any one truth. It had an exploratory rather than dogmatic character. From early in the reign of Alexander II (r. 1855–81), populist ideas entered into and transformed the major branches of Russian art. The difficulties of reimagining and reuniting a post-emancipation Russia helped lend Russian literature and art its famous agonized introspection. Populist artists were not only seeking to understand the *narod* and its place in Russia's future; they simultaneously sought to understand their own role in that future.

As contributors to the populist epoch, artists confronted the same contradictions that bedeviled radical populists: at one and the same time they had to adhere to the critical realism advocated by extremists like Dobrolyubov and Pisarev and also somehow find room for celebration of the *narod*. The former objective emphasized a dispassionate and thoroughly empirical approach to the arts. Both Chernyshevsky and Pisarev rejected aesthetics as a pointless aspect of art, believing art and literature useful only insofar as they exposed social problems or functioned to improve society. Their approach to art was unabashedly didactic, and it was extremely attractive to a certain type of thinker who, by mastering its reductive emphasis on observable facts alone, gained an authoritative tone and a ready world view. It was also in many ways an imperative under the special historical circumstances of Imperial Russia. In a world where freedom of expression was extremely limited, readers cherished any unvarnished representation of the world they lived in. The viewpoint of critics like Chernyshevsky exerted a powerful influence on many writers and artists throughout the reform era. It managed to delegitimize the importance of any art that lacked social content. This austere version of realism was part of a larger vogue for realism throughout Europe in the mid-nineteenth century, but Russia took it in a unique direction, strongly emphasizing political engagement and denunciation of the status quo.

At the same time, the influence of populism suggested the need for a positive program able to show the way forward. Neither hard-headed realism nor devoted altruism and idealism could be abandoned; instead they had somehow to be combined. The distinctive style in Russian literature, which Geoffrey Hosking describes as "realist, identifying with the *narod*, informed by deeply held social and political convictions, and haunted by the question 'What is Russia?'" characterized the world-famous literature that came out of this period.[5] Most Russian writers and artists one way or another had to navigate the perilous waters between critical realism and populist ideals. As we will see, much of the tension found in Russian art in this period resulted from the effort to successfully carry out this difficult negotiation. Finding a way to combine the two contradictory demands helped create works of art that remain powerfully resonant to the present day.

Literature and the People

In his career as a literary critic during the first half of the nineteenth century, Vissarion Belinsky did more than anyone else to ensure that socially conscious work would dominate the Russian arts. He established the role of critic as arbiter of the moral and political values behind the literary production of his day, and he did as much as anyone to raise the status of Russian literature as the chief expression of the national consciousness. Belinsky respected writing for its aesthetic value, but had higher praise for its social and political content. The ability of a work of art to expose prejudices, undermine tired conventions, and express the national character constituted its most important function. The concept of a work of literature (or art in general) as socially valuable would anchor itself deeply in the thinking of the intelligentsia where for a time it became nearly a reflexive understanding of the purpose of art. One literary historian has described Belinsky's "immense influence" in the following way: "Russian writers and critics tended to follow him in believing in a literature totally committed to social, political or religious ideas yet true to the autonomy and authenticity of the creative imagination."[6] Although he would later be criticized for his destructive influence on the artistic freedom to create beauty for its own sake, Belinsky had a palpable and virtually inescapable impact on the literature of the populist period, even though he died before it had really begun.

One friend and admirer of Belinsky, Ivan Turgenev, focused extensive and direct attention on the Russian peasantry. Oddly enough, however, Turgenev cannot easily be ranked among populist writers. The stories collected in his famed *Notes of a Hunter* (1852) are presented as unassuming vignettes taken from the observations of a gentry hunter who stumbles across various incidents in rural life as he walks about in search of game. In the context of Russia in the late 1840s and early 1850s, which would turn out to be the eve of emancipation, Turgenev's stories exerted a powerful effect on the reading public. Progressive Westerners took them as an exposure of the damage and absurdity of serfdom, while Slavophiles appreciated that the peasants came across as ordinary, even sometimes impressive, human beings. When the stories in *Notes of a Hunter* are collected together they clearly advance an argument against serfdom by giving the impression that the variety of experience and depth of humanity in the peasant milieu was at least as multifaceted as that among the educated elite. Because Turgenev's characters do not come across as wooden or idealized, these stories can be thought of as an artistically powerful update on the very same theme as that found in Radishchev's *Journey*. They affirm the fundamental humanity of those living under serfdom. Not quite as effectively, but in a similar fashion, the roughly contemporaneous fiction of Vladimir Dal, Dmitry Grigorovich, and Aleksei Pisemsky sought to achieve a similar goal. The first appearance of these works in the 1840s, especially *Notes of Hunter*, helped to disgrace those who still treated the common people with scorn.

But we must be careful to distinguish Turgenev from those writers and artists more directly associated with populism. To expose to the public the inhumanity of Russia's own "peculiar institution" was not yet to take the next step essential to a populist world view: to locate within the *narod* some feature capable of redeeming and reconstructing the whole of Russian society. The Slavophiles discovered that feature in the native *sobornost'* of the commune; Herzen found it in the commune's innate socialism; Lavrov thought the peasantry held the keys to a revolutionary transformation. Others too discovered in the bosom of rural culture a way to capture and improve the Russian national character. As for Turgenev, while his stories contain certain admirable peasant types, like the mystical Kasyan, fine-tuned to the natural world, or the heroic woodsman trying to save the forest from depredation, never do his peasants seem to embody any kind of higher principle applicable to the whole of society. His peasant characters, like Turgenev's educated readers, are merely people with the potential for serious errors and feats of moral strength. Turgenev was a liberal who spent much of his time in Western Europe. He had even been nicknamed "American" for his admiration for liberal democracy. It is no wonder that Slavophile attempts to draw him into their admiration for the *narod* as true and uncorrupted Russians had little success.

When Turgenev describes the character Khor as an admirable individual, it has nothing to do with the peasantry as a whole: "Khor had attained a highly ironic view of life. He'd seen a lot, knew a lot, and I learned a lot from him."[7] Turgenev maintains this general tone throughout the stories. The peasants are distinct individuals; only rarely do they come across as a "type," and never as a collective unit. Turgenev's great service was to show that peasants behave and react in ways that are entirely predictable according to character and circumstance. Their motivations, whether noble, despicable, or comically absurd, are as recognizable and comprehensible as those among the educated classes. We find in Turgenev virtually no sense that there is something useful to be learned or gained from the peasantry as a social class. Nevertheless, *Notes of a Hunter* does intersect with populist concerns at several points. It movingly demonstrates the injustices of the serf system, especially regarding the arbitrary power vested in the hands of the gentry, and it intrigues the reader by acting as a portal into the hidden fascination and mystery lurking beneath the surface of rural life.

Most of Turgenev's later work explored the gentry and the intelligentsia rather than the peasantry. By contrast, the aforementioned Nekrasov, a contemporary of Turgenev's who also had an illustrious literary career, devoted the bulk of his work to an exploration and defense of the *narod*. Nekrasov suffered from a more profound sense of social guilt than Turgenev did, and his work is suffused with a feeling of civic duty to awaken *obshchestvo* to the hardship, obscurity, and limited options of peasant life. At the same time, unlike in Turgenev's stories, Nekrasov's poetry calls forth an image of the Russian peasantry as a unified culture that can be studied, sympathized with, and admired. In this way Nekrasov stood much closer than Turgenev to a populist worldview. The peasants in Nekrasov's poems appear not so much as a social class; they seem to comprise the nation itself, a nation that has long suffered at the hands of a small group of miscreants—from landowners and state officials to any member of the educated elite unsympathetic to the plight of the people.

Nekrasov's poetry was loved and admired by many of his contemporaries, but his detractors criticized him for its overt didacticism, arguing that Nekrasov placed denunciation and exposure of injustice above the aesthetic quality of his verse. In the context of his time, the criticism made sense since Nekrasov quite consciously prioritized the need to inform educated society of the injustice he saw in his native land. Eventually, however, his particular blend of denunciation, poetic description, and empathy for the people would be fully accepted in the canon of Russian literature. In addition to exposing inequality and hardship, his poems evoked the people's admirable perseverance, capacity for improvement, sense of humor, and occasional joys. In Nekrasov's work, the *narod* is on display as an embodiment of the national character. Thus even as Nekrasov developed a poetry of social themes and brute reality, his best poems are not only didactic but poignant, multidimensional, and often aesthetically pleasing, works of art. In fact, he claimed not to be writing for the intelligentsia at all but rather for the Russian peasants who would read him in the future once they had acquired literacy.

Like all other populist writers, Nekrasov had to find a way to negotiate between the demand for unvarnished realism and the attempt to portray the *narod* in a nobler, more optimistic light. To this end, he developed several techniques. One of them, found in his best poems, was a constant shuffling between voices, perspectives, and styles of writing, so that no single voice or view predominates. We might find, stuffed side by side into a few verses, a lyrical landscape, a lament about unceasing hardship, a folk song in rural dialect, the musings of the intelligentsia narrator, and a sudden moment of levity. This approach gives even some of his short poems a kind of epic, if somewhat dizzying, quality; it also enabled him to avoid the purely condemnatory realism of some of his peers while sidestepping the accusation that the brighter passages constituted unrealistic idealization. Nekrasov's poetic voice shuttles back and forth between sentient intelligentsia observer and omniscient narrator, and he uses that alternation both to carry his educated readers into the world of the peasantry and to portray that world as if from within.

Nekrasov was closely associated with radical populists like Chernyshevsky and Dobrolyubov. He sympathized with many of their views and hired them at *The Contemporary*, the journal he edited. It is not surprising that his poems sound many of the same themes voiced by his younger, more politically engaged, peers. "Railroad" (1864), for example, anticipates Lavrov's theme that *obshchestvo* owed a great debt to the *narod*. In this poem, a child riding on the railway between Saint Petersburg and Moscow asks his father who built the railroad. When the father answers that the project executor, Count Kleinmikhel, built it, the narrator is prompted to explain in lurid detail that it was the brutal suffering and death of thousands of workers that built the railroad. Enjoying their ride on the train thanks to the sacrifice of those railroad workers who have received no credit, the narrator suggests to the boy he should be thankful to the peasantry rather than Kleinmikhel: "bless the work of the *narod*, and learn to respect the peasant."[8] Nekrasov's radicalism shined through elsewhere as well. Even though it was difficult for any Russian writer to get dissenting views past the censorship, Nekrasov's poetry often drips with hatred for the ruling classes, and some poems like "Song for Eremushka" (1859) contain subtle but unmistakable appeals to revolution. In person, as in the following speech he gave in 1875, he could be much more blunt:

> Yes, our history is written in blood! Yes, it is no surprise that we are so timid and cowed! Yes, we need a generation of heroes [*bogatyri*] like the nihilists [radicals], so we can tear out this miserable fear from the heart of the people! So that we can set on its feet our village, our brotherly commune, our new liberties! Well, and yes, I see them, these needed heroes, I feel their presence![9]

One of Nekrasov's greatest poems, "Red-Nosed Frost" (1863) provides an excellent example of how he was able to convey the virtues of the *narod* without seeming to glorify them. He places the main character Darya in a brutally difficult situation. At the sudden death of her husband, with two small children to feed and keep warm, she must venture into the forest to chop firewood even though the cold is overpowering. Given the plight of immediate need, overwhelming grief, and the prospect of a miserable future, her tears that "drop without ceasing" do not seem lachrymose. Her death in the forest as the cold deepens and she falls into a reverie, enables Nekrasov—through her family recollections, the poet's narrative observations, folk songs, and folk imagery like that of Grandfather Frost—to produce a panoramic evocation of peasant life that is both admiring and hopeful. Darya herself is a deeply tragic heroine because of her great potential and her huge capacity to suffer. She represents peasant women as beautiful, noble, strong—the type who can capture a runaway horse or calmly walk into a cottage on fire. Yet in spite of her prototypical heroism, a pall hangs over the entire poem: this is the tragedy not of a notable figure but of a person who will die in voicelessness and obscurity. The reader recognizes that for every Darya whose story is told, millions of similar stories go unheard.

Nekrasov's most ambitious poem, usually translated as "Who Can Be Happy in Russia?," which he worked on for many years, mimicked a common populist theme found in Bervi-Flerovsky's *The Condition of the Working Class in Russia* and Fyodor Reshetnikov's *Where Is Better?* As a sort of travelogue, it moves from place to place in search of some release from seemingly universal bitterness. Seven peasants meet and travel around Russia (with the aid of a magic tablecloth that offers them food and drink) to answer the question "Who lives happily and freely?" in their native land. On this platform Nekrasov builds a sort of epic novel in verse that mingles the comic with the tragic. Not only does Nekrasov place the peasants at the center of the action, but the poem comes close to treating Russia as a country made up of the *narod* alone, without any significant role for the urban elite. In this poem, the peasants ask their own vexed question about the fate of Russia, a form of inquiry typically reserved for the intelligentsia alone. The peasants, in other words, take charge of the narrative, and each of them is treated as a distinct individual, not lumped together as a unit in the manner of the Slavophiles or Herzen. At times they behave nobly and heroically; at other times they are hedonistic and self-centered. In this respect "Who Can Be Happy in Russia?" attempts to accomplish something no other writer had yet attempted: it was a fictionalized portrayal of what purported to be the popular point of view.

In the end the seven peasants do find an individual happy and free enough that they call off their search. Interestingly, unlike the rest of the characters, he is not himself of peasant origin. Grisha Dobrosklonov, the son of a priest, is probably meant to remind readers of Nekrasov's by then long-deceased colleague at *The Contemporary*, Nikolai Dobrolyubov. Dobrosklonov fulfills their search for happiness and freedom because he is ambitious to fight through the difficulties of the present in order to bring about a better Russian future. In other words, and Nekrasov's readers no doubt understood the implication, the only path toward happiness in Russia would be that of revolutionary struggle. That Dobrosklonov is not himself a peasant but from a middling social class may be an appeal for intelligentsia activism, and it also might have been a way for Nekrasov to suggest that in a future Russia the idea of separate social estates will have been forgotten.

Nekrasov irritated the old guard in his nonconformist and politicized use of verse, but among the left-leaning populists he became a hero. Before he died he received a letter from a group of students that read:

> We shall mourn for you, our beloved one, dear singer of the people's woe and suffering; we shall mourn for one who kindled in us a powerful love for the people … We shall not forget your name, and we shall hand it down to the … people so that they may also know him whose many good seeds have fallen on the soil of the people's aspirations.[10]

Nekrasov managed to strike a balance between celebrating the *narod* and denouncing the dismal conditions in which so many of them lived. In the aforementioned funeral oration, Fyodor Dostoevsky summed up both sides of the balance: "He saw in them more than just the image of creatures humiliated by slavery, a bestial image; through the strength of his love he was able, almost unconsciously, to comprehend the beauty of the People, their power, their intellect, their suffering humility, and even to have some faith in their future mission."[11]

The soul aches, despair grows.
Narod! Narod! I was not granted the heroism
To serve you, poor citizen that I am,
But a burning and holy impatience
For your fate I've carried unto old age!
I love you and sing your suffering,
But where is the hero to carry you from darkness
Into the light?

Nikolai Nekrasov, "Despondency" (1874)

Apart from Nekrasov, much of the immediately post-emancipation literature represented the dark side of popular life. Populist writers like Nikolai Uspensky, Fyodor Reshetnikov, Vasily Sleptsov, and Nikolai Pomyalovsky published numerous works of fiction intended not only to expose and denounce the hardship in the lives of the people, but even to demonstrate the cruelty and degradation that, they suggested, had come to characterize the culture of the lower classes in general. How could it be that detractors of the common people are still counted among the populists? The answer involves the intellectual ferment of the times. As Alexander's reforms brought diminished censorship and an upwelling of debate surrounding the abolition of serfdom, influential critics like Chernyshevsky and Dobrolyubov supported literary depictions of the *narod* that refused to shy away from the miserable state to which they believed it had fallen. A portrait of the people that drew attention to their degraded condition would demonstrate the necessity for radical change to bring about its improvement. The ills of Russian conditions under which the *narod* suffered had to be diagnosed before they could be cured.

Exaggerating considerably, Chernyshevsky argued with acerbic sarcasm that those gentry writers, like Turgenev, who had written about peasants "idealized peasant life, portrayed for us such noble, exalted, virtuous, patient, and energetic beings, that we could not but be touched by the description."[12] In his praise for young non-noble writers like Nikolai Uspensky, whose stories did little more than appall readers with their evocation of the frightful condition of the popular masses, Chernyshevsky was able to demonstrate his support for a politically engaged realism. The early voice of sympathy for the peasants was replaced by a picture of the peasantry as drunken, ignorant, and self-serving, all those qualities the populist intelligentsia despised and hoped to eradicate.

As diametrically opposed as the stories of Turgenev and Uspensky were, both portrayals of the peasants can be understood as populist at least in the sense that both found their justification in the improvement of the lot of the people. Not only Chernyshevsky but even his avowed opponent Dostoevsky found Uspensky's work an expression of "loving the people . . . just as they are."[13]

Fyodor Dostoevsky

No less than Nekrasov, and indeed no less than the socialist revolutionary populists, Fyodor Dostoevsky held up an idealized image of the *narod* as Russia's destiny and salvation. For a number of reasons, however, Dostoevsky is generally considered to be separate from and antagonistic toward the populists. Most importantly, his understanding of the *narod* and its place in Russia's future was in fact quite distinct from the radical populist conception of the people's significance. Dostoevsky's world view can be thought of as a highly original blend of Slavophilism, imperialist, messianic nationalism, and populism in which a unification between *narod* and *obshchestvo* would bring about a Christian moral transformation of Russia that would eventually lead the Russian nation to a position of world-historical prominence. Dostoevsky's brand of Orthodox nationalism had little to do with the socioeconomic concerns of the populist left, and yet Dostoevsky shared with them the idea that the *narod* carried within itself the makings of a revolutionary transformation that would enable Russia to point the way forward to a Europe that had lost its way as a result of capitalist modernity.

Those who have read only Dostoevsky's prominent novels might well find it surprising that he is included among the populists at all. In his most famous works—*Crime and Punishment, The Idiot, The Devils*, and *The Brothers Karamazov*—Dostoevsky demonstrates a fascination for abnormal psychology, angst-ridden philosophical problems, interpersonal relationships, spiritual redemption, urban squalor and scandal, and the errors of the Russian intelligentsia and Western rationalism, but we find few hints that Dostoevsky, like his character Shatov in *The Devils*, found the role of the *narod* in Russia's future a central and overriding concern. As Linda Ivanits has shown, however, everywhere in the philosophical subtext of these novels one senses the lurking presence of the people. Like God or some overriding principle Dostoevsky's *narod* is at once everywhere and nowhere.[14] Fortunately, we do have more direct access to Dostoevsky's populist outlook in his nonfiction where the question of the *narod* plays a leading role. Dostoevsky makes an excellent case in point about what we lose if we define populism too narrowly. To remove him (and others like him) from the equation because he wasn't socialist or revolutionary would undermine our ability to grasp the broad set of interlocking values that enabled populism to take hold so widely among educated Russians. The risk of overstuffing the concept of Russian populism with too many conflicting perspectives is thus outweighed by the reward of being able to see populism in its proper light as a healthy profusion of interconnected, and widely divergent, views.

Like other populist thinkers and artists, Dostoevsky had to find a way to navigate the narrow straits between celebrating the people and portraying them in the cold light of reality. His method typically involved a narrative trajectory that began in abject degradation and led in one fashion or another to redemption. Not only characters from the intelligentsia, but many of the peasants he writes about followed a path from suffering to salvation. He raised this essential theme of Christianity to a national trait by portraying Russians as uniquely capable of both pure debauchery and absolute deliverance. Dostoevsky himself experienced such a cycle in his early years as a writer. For participation in a clandestine circle of socialists, he was condemned to death by Nicholas I and put in front of a firing squad, only to be reprieved at the last minute. Sent instead to hard labor at a prison camp in the Siberian city of Omsk, he spent nearly a decade in Siberia. He later wrote about his prison experiences in a fictionalized account called *Notes from the House of the Dead* (1862). This novel would seem to describe his actual experiences in prison, but it was published several years after his release, and it is impossible to learn from it precisely how the prison experience affected him. It can be said with certainty, however, that his time in Siberia marked a turning point in Dostoevsky's life. When he returned to European Russia in 1859 he had undergone a personal and ideological transformation.

Among Dostoevsky's novels, *Notes from the House of the Dead* spends more time than others describing the lower classes in the form of the narrator's fellow inmates. It also seems to reveal much of the new thinking about Russia and religion Dostoevsky acquired while in Siberia. In prison he did in fact experience something few populists ever did: unbroken daily contact with the masses. Not surprisingly, given that he was imprisoned among hardened criminals, much of that experience was miserable, but with time and reflection Dostoevsky took away from the experience more of a love than a loathing for the people. The novel's protagonist learns that there is an unbridgeable chasm between the classes: "the estrangement happens without any malice ... He's not one of us, that's all."[15] But in Dostoevsky's fiction no statement can ever be taken at face value, and the very tone of the narration hints at a unity between gentry narrator and the lower-class prisoners. *Notes from the House of the Dead* is peppered with third person plural statements such as "Everyone of us felt ..." and "We all now understood that ..." Reflecting the novel's constant tension between social unity and mutual incomprehension, the narrator states that the gap between the classes "can be *fully* noticed only when the *nobleman* ... is really in fact deprived of his former rights and turned into a simple man," a comment that leaves the reader to wonder whether the narrator has in some sense lost his noble status and detachment.[16]

Dostoevsky would develop the conviction that he had come to understand and appreciate the *narod* through long contact with them. What he found among them was an external tendency toward brutality and debauchery that masked an inner, hidden Christian morality. That morality consisted of a deep thirst for justice, a tolerance for human error, a great capacity for suffering, and a sympathy for the suffering of others, all Christ-like qualities he typically finds absent among the educated classes. Evil is often evident on the surface of life in prison, but the presence of God lurks deep within the prisoner. Here for the first time Dostoevsky expresses a populist theme he would return to more than once later on: "There is not much our wise men can teach the people. I will even say positively—on the contrary, they themselves ought to learn from them."[17] Although the *narod* had many useful tools to gain from *obshchestvo*, in the final analysis the most fundamental life lessons were those *obshchestvo* would need to learn from the *narod*.

In the early 1860s, Dostoevsky, along with his brother Mikhail, published two journals. Together with the writers Apollon Grigoriev and Nikolai Strakhov, the Dostoevskys carved out a philosophical position intended to lie between those of the Slavophiles and Westernizers. They called themselves *pochvenniki* [men of the soil], suggesting that where Slavophilism was stuck in the mud of Russia and Westernism had its head in the clouds of European thinking, like a tree they would be rooted in the soil but grow toward the sky. The soil was a metaphor for native culture, particularly that of the *narod*, with which these writers hoped to reconnect. They believed the educated class needed to find its roots within the people. They argued that the divided nature of Russian society had to come to an end but that it had been a necessary temporary division which had enabled *obshchestvo* to acquire self-awareness. In no way advocates for socialism or revolution, the *pochvenniki* did recognize the village commune's importance in the ethical, Slavophile sense as a reflection of peasant brotherhood and mutual aid. In order to unite the divided halves of Russian society, Dostoevsky not only called for the abolition of social estates but argued that all Russians could find a common purpose in Orthodoxy and certain collective "national characteristics" like a capacity for suffering and a thirst for broad experience. In the opening announcement of his journal *Time*, Dostoevsky claimed for the *pochvenniki* that "unification whatever it may cost, regardless of the sacrifice, and the sooner the better—this is our foremost idea."[18]

The unification of *obshchestvo* and *narod* would remain a lifelong obsession of Dostoevsky's. In his *Diary of a Writer*, a mouthpiece for his personal views published periodically during the final decade of his life, he suggested that not only among the intelligentsia but also among the people the emancipation had unleashed a clamor for change: "the same seething ferment is going on in the depths where [the peasant] lives as it is higher up."[19] Unlike the view held by the radical populists, however, Dostoevsky argued that ferment did not hail revolutionary change. It mainly signaled the rise of a new, energized, more self-confident, and more globally powerful Russia. Admonishing the intelligentsia he wrote:

> To become Russian means to stop despising our *narod*. And as soon as the Europeans see that we have begun to respect our people and our nationality, then they will immediately begin to respect us ... And in fact we ourselves will then understand that much of what we despised in our people is not darkness but precisely light, not stupidity but precisely wit, and once we have understood this we will indubitably utter in Europe such a word as has never been heard there before.[20]

This message was echoed in Dostoevsky's famous "Pushkin Speech" at the 1880 Moscow celebration of a monument to Alexander Pushkin. In this speech, which was greeted with wild applause, Dostoevsky rather implausibly suggested that the national spirit of a unified Russia had already been propounded in the poetry of Alexander Pushkin. Pushkin becomes the torchbearer for Russian national identity through his supposed capacity to articulate the voices of both the eternally Slavic *narod* and the Westernized *obshchestvo*. "Had Pushkin not existed," Dostoevsky proclaimed, "it might well be that our faith in our Russian individuality, our new conscious hope in the strength of our People, and with it our faith in our future independent mission in the family of European peoples, would not have been formulated with such unshakeable force."[21] This was a remarkable statement about Pushkin. Some years earlier the critic Pisarev had written the precise opposite, claiming that no Russian writer was as good as Pushkin at inspiring in readers "limitless indifference to the people's suffering."[22] Dostoevsky managed to convince his audience not only that Pushkin's work bridged the divided sectors of Russian society, but that in doing so he demonstrated that Russia, and only Russia, would be in a position to point the way forward to the Western world, showing them how to unite in peaceful, brotherly affection. The argument rested on the notion that Pushkin, like other educated Russians, had been broadened by a dual inheritance that included both the Russian experience and a passionate devotion to the cultures of the West. Pushkin had integrated into his world view a great breadth of social and cultural influences in a way that Europeans could not because they were prevented by the overriding influence of their own well-developed national perspective. It is not difficult to hear the populist echoes in Dostoevsky's unique take on the advantages of backwardness. This variant of the populist message suggests that within all Russians lies a spirit of global unity so potent it contains the capacity to reshape the world. The Pushkin Speech was the latest version, almost the apotheosis, of the advantages of backwardness idea.

> The question of the People and our view of them, our present understanding of them, is our most important question, a question on which our whole future rests; one might even say it is the most practical question of the moment. "Who is better, we or the People? Are the People to follow us, or are we to follow them?" This is what everyone is saying now, everyone who has even the tiniest thought in his head and some concern in his heart for the common cause. And so I reply frankly: it is we who ought to bow down before the People and wait for everything from them, both ideas and the form of those ideas; we must bow down before the People's truth and acknowledge it as truth, even in the terrible event that it comes from the Lives of the Saints. To put it briefly, we must bow down like prodigal children who have been away from home for two hundred years but who, however, have returned still Russians ... But, on the other hand, we should bow down only on one condition and that is a sine qua non: the People must accept much of what we bring with us.
>
> Fyodor Dostoevsky, *Diary of a Writer*, trans. Kenneth Lantz

Dostoevsky's faith in what might be called a revolutionary transformation in the moral sphere ultimately rested on his own special idealization of the Russian people. Even though at times he acknowledged that "the people are still a theory for all of us and still stand before us as a riddle," he believed in their hidden inner character, the Christ-like message they were preparing for the world, in the way that the radical populists believed in their communalism.[23] In both cases, despite all signs to the contrary, the *narod* would triumph over its own shortcomings and restore Russia and the world with their hidden reserves. Dostoevsky had faith that the *narod* had never lost those Christian characteristics and convictions that had dried up elsewhere. The almost motherly kindness he detected in the gruff peasants, in spite of their failings, was even apparent in his fellow Siberian prisoners. When describing the peasantry he lauded their "frankness, honor, sincerity … purity, meekness, breadth of outlook, and lack of malice." He held these characteristics aloft as the key to Russia's future in spite of the fact that he also saw in them what he called "depravity" and "abominations."[24] The moderate liberal Konstantin Kavelin would later object to the Pushkin Speech that "one can hardly ascribe moral virtues to an entire people," but it was precisely this untapped collective virtue Dostoevsky trusted would soon come to Russia's rescue (and to the rescue of the world).[25]

Dostoevsky did not so much argue that specific individuals were Christ-like or devout; rather the people as a whole had suffered to such an extent that they had become what he liked to call a "God-bearing" people, reflecting his view of Christianity as a process of suffering and redemption. As a collective whole the *narod* was "incomparably purer in heart than our upper levels of society."[26] Dostoevsky's fevered prose managed to get across a feeling of urgency reminiscent of that demonstrated by the radical populists in their urge to foment immediate revolutionary change. The intelligentsia, he argues in his *Diary*, is "worse in almost all respects" than the *narod* and it thus lacks any basis on which to solve Russia's social and ethical problems.[27] The character Shatov in *The Devils*, whose views bear a striking resemblance to those propounded by Dostoevsky, proclaims: "The purpose of the whole evolution of a nation, in every people and at every period of its existence, is solely the pursuit of God, their God, their very own God, and faith in Him as in the only true one. God is the synthetic personality of the whole people taken from its beginning to its end."[28] Shatov's ultimate source of meaning is not scripture, the Church, or even God. It is "the whole people," a point he is grudgingly forced by the character Stavrogin to admit. In pursuit of this dream, Shatov finds a solution that would be remarkably similar to one chosen by radical populists a few years later. The intelligentsia must go out and work among the people in order to forge the social bond that is missing. In his own conservative way, Dostoevsky seems to have recommended "going to the people."

To be sure, some of Dostoevsky's views differed radically from those of the populist left. In particular, he showed great admiration for the gains of Empire as a symbol of Russian nationality. He often displayed what Olga Maiorova has called "that peculiar blend of national sentiment and imperial pride—so typical of Russia in the nineteenth century."[29] Moreover, in his adamant Orthodoxy, his admiration for the meekness and self-sacrifice of the *narod*, his sense that modernity was leading to a disintegration and mechanical secularization of society, Dostoevsky was close to the Slavophiles, and at times acknowledged the similarity. But just as populism had strands of Slavophilism in its genetic code, Dostoevsky's thinking was imbued with values that connected him to the populists. Like some of the revolutionaries, he preached to educated Russians the need to "bow down" to the people and to await their "new word." Like others he struggled with the question of whether the intelligentsia should lead the people or follow them. Like Lavrov he wrote that the intelligentsia has a debt to the people who have served them so long. Like all populists he bemoaned the growing materialism of the *narod* as a corrupting influence and attacked the European bourgeoisie for facilitating the proletarianization of the masses. Not surprisingly, then, as the radical populist idealization of the *narod* grew in the 1870s, even in spite of his religious conservatism and vehement nationalism, Dostoevsky had something of a rapprochement with the left. Nevertheless, unlike Herzen, Lavrov, or Mikhailovsky, he never found a way to accept any revolutionary solution. Such solutions always demanded social equality, an aspiration Dostoevsky regarded as inimical to human freedom. He romanticized the spiritual wealth of the people, but instead of stressing the need for meekness and redemption he focused on the impact he believed the Christ-like *narod* would have on the secular world.

Leo Tolstoy

Embarking on a brief description of Leo Tolstoy's contribution to Russian populism may be the ideal place to recall the point that no writer or artist who espoused populist views was necessarily restricted to those views alone. Least of all Tolstoy, whose multiplicity of talents and interests seems almost without end. But for Tolstoy the Russian people, in particular the peasants, served as an essential touchstone. Contemplation of what he saw as the people's outlook on life led him to a religious awakening and a lifelong struggle to live in accordance with a strict set of ethical and spiritual principles. Quite dissimilar in their political views, Tolstoy and Dostoevsky joined with each other, and with other populists, in the belief that the *narod* possessed qualities that could positively transform Russia and bring valuable lessons to the rest of the world. Neither the revolutionary socialism of the radicals, nor the nationalism of Dostoevsky held any interest for Tolstoy. Rather, he came to advocate for the personal adoption of the Christian values he found in the gospels, which he thought were reflected more in the Christianity of the people than in the teachings of Russian Orthodoxy. He believed these popular Christian values could finally lead individuals toward a genuine Christian ethic and a true understanding of their place in the world. So devoted to the peasantry was Tolstoy that even Mikhailovsky criticized him for his excessive deference to the virtues of the people. Yet although Tolstoy's writing and activities (especially after his turn to Christianity) consistently gave a prominent place to the *narod*, the great author and religious seeker was such a protean figure that critics and biographers don't always prioritize the populist orientation of his life and work.

Unlike Dostoevsky, who acquired his populist outlook gradually in adulthood under the pressure of circumstances, Tolstoy professed a Rousseauian world view from early on that fueled his admiration for the peasantry. The feeling that civilization had a corrupting effect, that one must strive toward the kind of humble truths that are innately understood at all levels of society, was never far from Tolstoy. He had a lifelong talent for getting along easily with people of all social classes and a lifelong interest in the lower classes. His Rousseauian perspective may have been an innate part of his nature, but it was also a matter of steeping himself in Rousseau's thought from an early age. At some point in his teenage years he even wore a pendant around his neck with a picture of Rousseau inside. The Rousseauian principle that civilization endangered individual morality, and that enlightenment consisted in finding a path to natural simplicity, resounds throughout Tolstoy's fiction and spiritual nonfiction. In the Russian context it naturally led him to valorize the peasantry. In the words of Isaiah Berlin, "Rousseau must have strengthened, if he did not actually originate, [Tolstoy's] growing tendency to idealise the soil and its cultivators—the simple peasant, who for Tolstoy is a repository of almost as rich a stock of 'natural' virtues as Rousseau's noble savage."[30] Following Rousseau, over the course of his life Tolstoy came to see educated society as corrupt, and unsophisticated working people as honest and righteous.

Tolstoy's eventual repudiation of the social milieu in which he was raised required decades to materialize and was never absolute. As we learn in his *Confession*, he attempted for years to reconcile himself to educated society, taking a sort of guilty pride in his glory as, in Turgenev's phrase "the great writer of the Russian land." But keen awareness of the "false honor" of his situation would be compounded by a succession of experiences that indicated to him the bankruptcy of the civilized world. In a famous example, he described witnessing an execution in France and recognizing that "no theory of the reasonableness of our present progress could justify this deed."[31] Over time, Tolstoy lost the sense that progress and modernity could bring benefits to society. He lumped together both technological and institutional forms of modern life under the derogatory label of "liberalism," a term he used to suggest that lazy embrace of unearned privilege among the elite which only served as a veil to conceal the unabated suffering of the vast majority. A "liberal" to Tolstoy was anyone who complacently or unthinkingly emulated European social and political norms.

Teaching peasants became a sort of second vocation for Tolstoy after his primary career as a writer. In the late 1850s, he opened his first school for peasant children on his estate, and began to take trips abroad to study educational methods in Europe. The underlying idea that informed all of his teaching was typically populist: the *narod* does not need to be lectured to, nor even given a curriculum. Tolstoy believed the people, in their millions, would be creating the world of the future according to their own ideas, so he tried to keep any possible elite prejudice out of his instruction. The slogan hanging on the wall of the school read "Do What You Want." Relying on Rousseau's novel/educational treatise, *Emile*, Tolstoy attempted to educate the local peasants in an entirely non-compulsory way. The title of one of his pedagogical essays suggests the nature of this approach: "Who Ought to Teach Whom How to Write: We Our Peasant Children, or Our Peasant Children Us?" Already in the early 1860s Tolstoy had anticipated one of the central questions the radical populists would be asking in the 1870s. At times he seems to have taken his teaching more seriously than his writing. He called his experience teaching peasant children "my church in which I sought and found salvation from all anxieties, doubts and temptations," and he went on to write popular instructional supplements for other teachers.[32]

Tolstoy's celebrated emulation of peasant dress may be attributed in part to the fact that he appreciated physical labor and came to feel more and more that human beings were born to exercise their bodies in the manual labor the gentry and the urbanized elite had largely abandoned. Later in life he would refer to agriculture work as "the only basis for an honorable and reasonable life."[33] Tolstoy regularly participated in manual labor on his estate, and the homespun clothing of the peasantry enabled him to do so in a way that urban fashions did not. Even at his home in Moscow he would at times disguise himself as a manual laborer and go out to chop wood with workers along the Moscow River. After his religious conversion he would dress as a pilgrim, attempting to pass as a peasant when circumstances allowed. Later in life he could sometimes take his new identity to extremes. As time went on Count Tolstoy's wife began to complain about his increasing disinterest in washing and the consequent smell.

Not only in his life but in his writing Tolstoy sought ways to identify with the *narod*. It is customary to consider this identification something that did not take place until after his awakening. Tolstoy described it that way himself. But his tendency to find a truth and goodness in the peasantry as opposed to the duplicity and self-deception of educated society was already long present in his novels and stories. A good example would be his early story "Three Deaths" (1859), in which the dignified death of a cart driver is contrasted to the misguided and pathetic death of a noblewoman. Tolstoy's novels also gesture toward the personal transformation he would later experience in the form of a deep wisdom he ascribes to certain peasant characters. The most indelible of these is Platon Karataev in *War and Peace* (1869). Tolstoy describes Karataev as a blend of traditionally masculine and feminine characteristics. He is kind, observant, skillful, sage, ethical, resilient, self-confident, and at peace with the world. Outwardly a grizzled soldier, inside Karataev is compassionate and empathetic, able to recognize and soothe the suffering of the central character, the nobleman Pierre Bezukhov. Karataev only appears in a few brief chapters, but Bezukhov holds on to his memory as a kind of idealization "of all that was Russian." What makes him an embodiment of Russianness is the possession of a kind of wisdom that has been trained out of the elite: "The chief peculiarity of his speech was its spontaneity and shrewdness. It was obvious that he never considered what he said or was going to say, and this lent an especial and irresistible persuasiveness to the quick, true modulations of his voice."[34]

Tolstoy's portrayal of Karataev also anticipates Mikhailovsky's theory of the integrated individual: "He knew how to do everything, not particularly well but not badly either. He could bake, cook, sew, carpenter and cobble boots."[35] When *War and Peace* was written in the 1860s the left criticized Tolstoy for idealizing the peasantry in the manner of a gentry apologist, but for Tolstoy the character of Karataev was less an apology than an ideal to which he himself aspired. In "Three Deaths," the final death was that of a tree which died, as Tolstoy put it "quietly, honestly and beautifully" in the unconscious "recognition" that death was part of life. Tolstoy portrays the death of Karataev in a similarly "honest" way, as the sort of dignified and resigned death he would later aspire to: "His life, as he looked at it, held no meaning as a separate entity. It had meaning only as part of a whole of which he was at all times conscious."[36] To characterize Karataev's death in such terms sounds as though Tolstoy wanted to stress the futility of Karataev's existence, but in the context of the novel, which fits in well with other passages in Tolstoy's oeuvre, Karataev's lack of personal concern for his own demise reveals an Edenic state of mind, a perception of the world that has not yet lost its innocence.

Tolstoy's search for meaning in a finite life once again led him to the *narod* in *Anna Karenina* (1877), the writing of which coincided with the personal crisis he describes in his *Confession* (1882). In the middle section of the novel, written in the wake of the "Going to the People" movement, Tolstoy describes how the character Levin—in many ways a self-portrait—joined in to work at mowing rye with his own peasants. The extended description is memorable both for the difficulty Levin has in approximating the skill of the peasant farmers and the joy he experiences working with them as a team. Tolstoy offers the reader a brief glimpse of an undivided Russia, but he also makes sure the reader remains aware the glimpse is not reality. Levin returns to his estate at the end of the day: unlike the peasants he can choose whether or not to work. To drive the point home, in a later section of the novel Levin grows so enamored with the lives of the peasants that he resolves to discard his old life and take up a new one with the peasantry, marrying a peasant woman and residing in a peasant hut. Filled with the glory of this new resolution, Levin stays awake all night in a field entirely convinced he will now enjoy a life that is "simpler and better." Walking home, however, he encounters the young noblewoman who is to become his wife and immediately abandons his plans. The disdain with which Tolstoy conveys Levin's light-minded resolve keeps the novel on a footing of disinterested realism, and yet Levin's wavering does not discount the narrator's point that he was in fact "distinctly conscious of the simplicity, purity and rightness of that life."[37]

The "rightness of that life" would soon reappear in the novel, and with more fateful consequences in Tolstoy's own life. In the final section of *Anna Karenina*, Levin is reaching the peak of an existential crisis that has been building throughout the novel. He learns about a peasant who "lives for the soul and remembers God." This simple expression strikes him as carrying the very meaning of existence for which he has long been searching. In a moment akin to Rousseau's own famous philosophical awakening, Levin sits down under a tree and contemplates this revelation. He realizes he has learned from the description of this peasant that "I know the meaning of my life is to live for God, for the soul . . . And such is the meaning of all existence."[38] The Levin of this final chapter bears a strong resemblance to Leo Tolstoy in his *Confession*. In this brief memoir, in some ways a fictionalized distillation of a spiritual dilemma he had been experiencing throughout his adult life, Tolstoy confessed to an existential crisis in which he, like Levin, had to hide lethal objects from himself in order to resist suicidal temptation. Although *Confession* plays somewhat creatively with the facts of Tolstoy's life and thought, it offers a reasonable picture of his spiritual struggles in this period. Searching for a solution to his crisis in the realms of science and philosophy, he remained dissatisfied, but when he began to explore the lives of "the believers among the poor, simple, unlettered folk: pilgrims, monks, sectarians and peasants" he believed he had discovered a "real faith" in contrast to the irrational faith of Christians from "our circle":[39]

> Thanks either to the strange physical affection I have for the real laboring people, which compelled me to understand them and to see that they are not so stupid as we suppose, or thanks to the sincerity of my conviction that I could know nothing beyond the fact that the best I could do was to hang myself, at any rate I instinctively felt that if I wished to live and understand the meaning of life I must seek this meaning not among those who have lost it and wish to kill themselves, but among those milliards [billions] of the past and present who make life and who support the burden of their own lives and of ours also ... Rational knowledge, presented by the learned and wise, denies the meaning of life, but the enormous masses of men, the whole of mankind, receive that meaning in irrational knowledge. And that irrational knowledge is faith.[40]

Ultimately, Tolstoy arrived at the conclusion that educated elites have been living meaningless lives, and he began the attempt to take up a simple Christian life modeled after that which he found among the *narod*.

The *Confession* was written in 1879 and published in 1882, and over the years Tolstoy would reconcile himself to a degree with his former life, but the transformation he experienced was lasting and profound. At this point, living and dressing peasant-fashion became habitual. His new appearance, in tandem with the temporary abandonment of fiction writing for the publication of nonfiction tracts on spirituality and social problems, established his image throughout the world as an ascetic visionary. Berdiaev referred to the post-conversion Tolstoy as a religious *narodnik*. In the same moment of converting to devout Christianity he also converted to a life of simplicity through which, in his own person, he would attempt to reconcile the divided nature of Russian society. Where Dostoevsky had drawn on the *narod* for a confirmation of his political views, Tolstoy founded a new belief system and a new way of living. From the early 1880s, almost all questions that interested him involved a personal and collective ethic, and how to take action based on that ethic. Tolstoy had become a populist in the sense that, like Dostoevsky, he declared there was no people in the world as devout as the Russian people. Yet he was no nationalist. The religious and ethical ideals he preached applied freely to people of all nationalities. Indeed, "Tolstoyan" communities, of which there were more than a dozen in Russia, began to spread throughout the world in places as far flung as Chile and South Africa. Tolstoy's philosophy even had influence beyond the West through his impact on Mahatma Gandhi.

Tolstoy's recreation of himself would have multiple effects. Although he later returned to it, at first he abandoned the writing of fiction as a frivolous pursuit. He found he was unable to accept Russian Orthodoxy, for all the "mythology" that had grown up around it and instead, Luther-like, struck out on his own reading of the Gospel in order to discover a Christian approach to life that made sense on his own terms. For proclaiming an anti-Orthodox Christianity and denouncing Church abuses, eventually the Church censured him in a way that was tantamount to an excommunication. During Tolstoy's lifetime his religious writings were in many ways more influential than his famous novels, and a movement developed around him that involved both a religious and a social rethinking of the modern world. Based mainly on his own interpretation of the Sermon on the Mount, Tolstoy's religious views involved personal asceticism and an emphasis on love and service. He greeted with ambivalence the Tolstoyan movement that arose around his teaching, inviting readers of his work to discover their own personal path to Christianity as he had. On the other hand, he was gratified in his wide-ranging influence, and he seems to have been sufficiently content in the role of preacher, sometimes even prophet. His followers, led by Viktor Chertkov, did what they could to establish an organized movement based on his ideas, and a smattering of Tolstoyan communities still exist today.

> And I began to draw near to the believers among the poor, simple, unlettered folk: pilgrims, monks, sectarians, and peasants ... And I began to look well into the life and faith of these people, and the more I considered it the more I became convinced that they have a real faith, which is a necessity to them and alone gives their life a meaning and makes it possible for them to live. In contrast to what I had seen in our circle—where life without faith is possible, and where hardly one in a thousand acknowledges himself to be a believer—among them there is hardly one unbeliever in a thousand. In contrast with what I had seen in our circle, where the whole of life is passed in idleness, amusement, and dissatisfaction, I saw that the whole of life of these people was passed in heavy labour, and that they were content with life.
>
> Leo Tolstoy, *A Confession*, trans. Aylmer Maude

Tolstoy's position as both religious teacher and global celebrity, coupled with his high social status, gained him a kind of impunity to punishment unusual in Russia that enabled him to express radical political views without undergoing the usual prison or exile, although much of his more controversial work did not pass censorship. After his religious awakening, Tolstoy's populism emerged as an odd blend between social conservatism and radical politics that is sometimes referred to as Christian anarchism. On the one hand, he wrote morality tales, like the play *The Power of Darkness* (1887) that brutally conveys a warning about the wages of sin. On the other hand, like the radical socialist populists, he railed against capitalist exploitation and industrialization and argued that no one could more effectively point the way out of the evils of capitalism than the Russian people. Toward the end of his life, he attempted to avert plans under Prime Minister Stolypin to curtail the village commune. Although he opposed all forms of political violence, as early as 1865 while in the midst of writing *War and Peace* he had concluded that "the Russian Revolution ... will not be against the tsar and the despotism, but against landed property."[41] At the end of *Anna Karenina*, Levin famously refused to accept his brother's vulgar populist stance that "the people" support Russia's war effort. Later in life he advocated eradicating the money economy and private land ownership and replacing them with local self-governance and communal farming, an anarchist version of socialism not unlike that of the populists. He also became both a vegetarian and a thoroughgoing pacifist, proposing that all national governments disband their armies. He even called for a passive revolution in which peasants would simply "cease to obey any kind of force-using government and refuse to participate in it."[42] Tolstoy's vision for society was in many ways as radical as that of any populist revolutionary. He supported an almost complete return to the soil in which all people, including the intelligentsia, would engage in agriculture and live in Christian harmony.

The Visual Arts

Relative to literature, during the first half of the nineteenth century the Russian visual arts remained fairly conventional. Once the ferment surrounding emancipation got underway, however, artists began to experiment with new themes from contemporary life in a newly realistic manner. The crucial turning point took place in 1863 when a group of artists resigned under protest from the Imperial Academy of Arts and set up a painter's *artel'*, inspired by Chernyshevsky's workers cooperative in *What Is To Be Done?* Under the formidable influence of the painter Ivan Kramskoi and the critic Vladimir Stasov, these artists sought to depict scenes from Russian life, concentrating in particular on images that critiqued the social ills and injustices they saw around them. The *artel'* did not last, but in 1870 Kramskoi and a separate group of painters established the Society of Traveling Exhibitions, from which they gained the name "The Travelers," which is usually translated into English as "The Wanderers." They created their association as a method for displaying their art in cities around the country, and they were remarkably successful, eventually becoming an influence on the Russian art world that rivaled the Academy of the Arts itself.

In the emancipation years, realist painting tended to turn a critical eye on Russian society in the same way as the literature of that period did. Painters used their canvases to expose poverty, death, hard labor, drunkenness, and the mistreatment of women and peasants. Vasily Perov, for example, painted somber images condemning the provincial Church as well as Nekrasov-like depictions of peasant hardship. Some realist paintings were more explicitly political, like Valery Yakobi's "Prisoner's Stop," which portrays a long convoy of prisoners being escorted to Siberia under armed guard. One of them, a political prisoner being carted on a wagon, has died. An officer looks at him impassively, while another prisoner has crept under the cart to steal a ring from the deceased's fingers. Encouraged by left-wing critics to use their art to expose Russia's failings, the work of these painters tends to be dark in hue, uncomfortable to look at, and didactic in intent. It is not surprising that painters eventually rejected the critics' injunction to pass judgment on the world around them. In extricating themselves from this appointed role, they received a boost from the rising tide of populist enthusiasm contemporaneous with the establishment of the Traveling Exhibitions. Admiration for the *narod* and interest in Russian national identity gave them an excuse to create positive representations of the peasants, country life, the urban lower classes, influential public figures, current affairs, and episodes from Russian history. Many of their paintings generated a great deal of interest and discussion in the press, and some of them even became classics of Russian art. Kramskoi, who painted many portraits of peasants, considered the *narod* as an artistic subject to be, as he put it, "a tremendous wellspring."[43]

As the realist painters' denunciatory impulse began to subside, their work grew more colorful and lively, and as their imagery progressed from didactic to relatively ambiguous it also became more intriguing to consider. The peasant portraits created by the Wanderers do not seem to resolve the peasants into a mass or a subset of "types"; they animate them as distinct human beings. Their emphasis on individual character may have resulted in part from the fact that the painters themselves often hailed from less exalted social backgrounds. Vasily Maksimov, born into a peasant family, left the Academy early in disgust over the intelligentsia idealization of the *narod*, an idealization he referred to as "pretty words about 'the people' made over a glass of beer."[44] Later, as a member of the Wanderers, he did his best to provide an accurate representation of peasant life in his paintings, neither a socially critical evocation of rural squalor nor an idyllic picture of harmony and virtue. Another reason for the empathetic yet seemingly unmediated expression of peasant character involves technique. The Wanderers' finished works were typically completed in urban studios, but they often rested on sketches made *in situ* in the Russian countryside. Both studies and the finished studio works differed substantially from French and British depictions of the working poor during the same era. European painters often emphasized the dignity of labor within a rural landscape, while portraits by Perov, Kramskoi, Maksimov, and Repin seat the subject close at hand and provide little to no background; they look the peasant subject square in the face. In this way, peasant portraits were produced in the same manner as portraits of the famous and wealthy. Such paintings stressed personality and psychology, seeming to peer into the eyes of their subjects in the attempt to determine who they were. Russian realist peasant portraiture treated the little man, the *muzhik*, as a psychologically complex, three-dimensional human being.

Interestingly, the portraits these artists created, as much as they set out to portray human character, often received widely varied interpretations from contemporary critics and later art historians. Is Perov's *Fomushka—the Owl* (Figure 6.1a) a portrait of gravitas and purpose or does it portray an embittered, defensive, and worn-down elderly man? What of Kramskoi's *Portrait of an Old Peasant*? (Figure 6.1b). On the one hand, he could be ready to use the stick in his hand for no good. On the other hand, he looks downward in contemplative fashion, not entirely unlike Kramskoi's *Christ in the Wilderness*, painted during the same year. Other peasant portraits were less ambiguous, either by leading the viewer to an obvious conclusion through the painting's title, as in Repin's *Peasant with an Evil Eye*, or by evoking certain qualities like otherness or warm sympathy, as with Kramskoi's smiling *Mina Moiseev* (see Figure 1.1, in the opening chapter). But the majority of these portraits leave it up to the viewer to decide what to think about the

Figure 6.1 Peasant portraits: Vasily Perov, *Fomushka—the Owl*, 1868 (left) and Ivan Kramskoi, *Portrait of an Old Peasant*, 1872 (right) © Left: Wikimedia Commons (public domain). Right: Out of copyright (public domain).

subject. And that uncertainty invites the viewer in for a closer look, welcoming the members of *obshchestvo* to recognize their shared humanity with the newly freed peasantry. Placing them against a stark background on the wall of one of their well-attended and widely discussed exhibits, often on the very same walls that held portraits of great cultural figures, these images elevated the status of the rural people they portrayed to a level of civic importance. It implied that the peasants constituted essential contributors to the national character. The paintings ask the viewer to pose an essential question: not "who are they?" so much as "who are we?"

Although such portraits reflect a fascination with the lower classes, they do not involve any of the typical populist idealization of them. They do not set up the peasant as the key to understanding Russia's future. Some even better known canvases did, however, suggest a fully populist orientation and contributed to populism as a whole. What is arguably the single best known Russian painting of the nineteenth century was admired from its first appearance for dignifying the *narod* and locating within the people fresh strength. Ilya Repin's *Boat Haulers on the Volga* (1873; Figure 6.2) managed to unite into a single image a condemnation of popular travail and an appeal for a better future. Yet it was presented with sufficient ambiguity to please a variety of different viewers. First created on a summer journey to the banks of the Volga River (during which Repin got to know his subjects personally), *Boat Haulers* depicts a then common form of labor in which workers on the banks of a river are harnessed to a ship and physically pull it upstream as a team. Boat haulers had long fascinated the intelligentsia as a species of human oxen, a forceful reminder of the dehumanization of the working class, and it was already a popular subject in literature. Nekrasov wrote a poem about boat haulers, Reshetnikov had used them as a symbol of popular degradation, and Chernyshevsky's revolutionary hero Rakhmetov had demonstrated his unity with the people by serving as a boat hauler. Some populist activists, like Nikolai Rogachev, went out among the boat haulers to spread propaganda.

Repin's painting gratified a conservative like Dostoevsky for its lack of tendentiousness and warm depiction of the individual boat-haulers, and it appealed just as much to the far more liberal Stasov, who found in it a recognition of popular suffering and future potential. Many competing interpretations of the painting have been proposed, but Dostoevsky and Stasov together captured the two sides of its appeal. Although interpretations of the painting's "intention" have varied considerably, it seems quite clear that Repin meant at least to draw viewers closer to the world of the laboring classes, a world from which he himself had come. In 1872, as the painting was being completed, Repin wrote to Mussorgsky that "the peasant is the judge now, and we must reproduce his interests."[45] By contrast to other well-known contemporary depictions of manual labor, like Courbet's *Stone Breakers* or Millet's *Gleaners*, in Repin's painting the point of view is intentionally low. The viewer is almost looking up at the boat haulers. This vantage point enables us to witness the strain in their legs and also to contemplate the varied expressions on their faces. Each one is unique, as in the aforementioned peasant portraits: some clearly admirable, others shirking or exhausted. Most of the team seems almost to blend together with the natural environment, an environment they literally carry on their dirty skin and clothing. With its subjects in harness like beasts of burden and either long-suffering or entirely worn down, the painting certainly plays on the convention of boat hauling as a symbol of the people's dehumanization. It would be difficult to find an image more resonant of hard physical labor. Yet the way the boat haulers are portrayed as a group of distinctive, though somehow familiar, personalities—one of them even gazing straight at the viewer/painter with a challenging glare—imparts great warmth to the painting. Both *Stone Breakers* and *Gleaners* obscure the faces of the workers they portray, so that one would say the viewer of those paintings is invited to observe not individuals so much as labor itself. The viewer of *Boat Haulers* looks at laboring people and finds a great deal of humanity in each of them.

Obviously the grueling work in the hot sun, along with the paucity of recompense that is indicated by their ragged clothing, conveys a clear rebuke of Russian conditions. But notes of genuine optimism are woven into the painting. The bright sunshine imparts a kind of hopefulness to the scene, and some of the boat haulers wear sympathetic expressions. Most importantly, the boy at the center of the painting looks fresh, stands up straighter and taller, has not yet had time to acquire the same smudged and sunburnt appearance as the rest of them. He gazes far off into the distance, as if envisioning a better future, and while one might think he is adjusting the strap across his shoulder, it would be just as easy to imagine him, in a bold or even rebellious gesture, throwing the harness from his body in order to seize his liberty and regain his dignity. Repin has found many ways to make this figure the focal point of his painting. He stands in the center of the

Figure 6.2 Ilya Repin, *Boat Haulers on the Volga*, 1873 © Wikimedia Commons (public domain).

group, close to the viewer, lit by the sun, and painted in colors that sharply contrast to the dark boat haulers. Among them all, only he wears a cross around his neck. More in line with the palate of the sky or the bright ship they pull, he seems to represent not oppression and degradation but something of that hope for the future the populist intelligentsia had vested in the people. Repin adds one more almost hidden sign of optimism in the steam ship far behind the hauled sailing vessel. In spite of its connection to capitalism and industrial technology, the steamship, which was already by this time the predominant mode of travel along the river, seems to suggest that one day soon the future will eradicate the need for the suffering and dehumanization represented by the boat haulers. More than just its initial impression of humans in harness, the wealth of contrasts and the food for thought Repin's painting offers help explain why it became an iconic image of the populist era.

Another remarkable painting from this period was Vasily Surikov's *Boyarina Morozova* [The Noblewoman Morozova] (1887; Figure 6.3). Although Surikov did not necessarily intend any overt political message in his image, like the historian Shchapov he found in pre-Petrine history a way to imagine the Russian people before they had split into two distinct social worlds. In this painting a woman of noble birth during the outbreak of Russia's religious schism sides with the Old Believer religious dissenters refusing to accept the dictates of the Orthodox Church. The dissenters included members of all social classes, and in the populist age they were commonly identified with the laboring poor and those unwilling to accept the status quo. The Boyarina, in other words, is still at this time "of the people" in a way that a member of the nobility could no longer claim to be in the nineteenth century. We see her carted through the streets on the way to confinement in a nunnery, followed not long after by imprisonment and death. The crowd surrounding her includes supporters and detractors from all sides.

Apart from Morozova, who stares up at the holy icon on the side of a church, the central figure in the painting is a holy fool (or "fool for Christ") who looks up at her in

Figure 6.3 Vasily Surikov, *Boyarina Morozova*, 1887 © Wikimedia Commons (public domain).

the same manner that she looks at the icon. Mirror-like, both form the Old Believer two-fingered sign of the cross. As in so many of these busy, operatic paintings created by the Russian realists, this one includes a large cast of characters meant to evoke the motley and mixed crowd of medieval Moscow. The bond between Morozova and the holy fool—both are in chains (his of repentance and hers of criminal martyrdom)—suggests the social unity that has been lost in modern Russia, and it also suggests something that many populists since Shchapov found appealing: the idea that Old Believer communities might play a useful role in reconnecting Russia. Their religious views per se were not necessarily of interest to the populists, but their rejection of expected norms was admired as proto-revolutionary. The "disgrace" of Morozova and the Old Believers in the face of authority appeared here as a mark of her heroic character, just as the exiled and executed radical populists appeared heroic to many Russians. Although Surikov's personal political views were moderate to conservative, and some critics greeted the painting as reactionary, its potential connection to populist radicalism was not lost on the revolutionary populist Vera Figner, who admired it as a depiction of someone fighting to the death for a cause she believes in.

Relative to other contemporary movements in the visual arts, the Wanderers tended toward the view that the purpose of art was to serve society. They set a mission for themselves, at a time when even photography (much less more advanced visual media), was still in its infancy, to create a visual representation of the whole of contemporary Russia. During the 1870s and 1880s, depictions of the *narod* remained a dominant theme, and those portrayals continued to vary from critical exposure of the hardship in which Russia's working classes found themselves to more hopeful expressions of the people's cultural attractiveness, endurance, and potential for the future. A painting like Grigory Miasoedov's *Busy Season (The Mowers)* (1887) idealizes agricultural labor in its portrayal of peasants reaping a bountiful harvest among the wildflowers and butterflies of their grainfields. The mowers seem less "hard at work" and more "at one with nature." Konstantin Savitsky's *Meeting the Icon* (1878), in which a group of peasants comes to revere an icon being carried through the countryside, evokes peasant piety while also hinting at the social distance of church leaders from the people. Repin's *Religious Procession in Kursk* (1883), offers a monumental panorama of provincial life in the form of an enormous parade of marchers carrying religious objects through the countryside. It conjures up a baneful display of religious faith marred by secular reality. Even as all social classes march together in their Orthodox faith, their radically different social status, and the overt police violence used to maintain it, seem to be more on parade than anything connected to Orthodox spirituality. As different as they are, in all of these paintings the *narod* is presented to the viewers of *obshchestvo* as an enigma, a blend of promise for the future and the deep scars of the still unsettled past.

The Mighty Handful and Modest Mussorgsky

Like the Russian visual arts, Russian classical music took longer to develop originality than literature had. Once it did, however, it produced work that would eventually acquire worldwide renown. The shift toward a national school and national themes in Russian music occurred in a rather conscious and deliberate way. Under the tutelage of the powerful critic Stasov, who spent a life time pushing for a realist-national turn in both art and music, a group of five composers formed around Mili Balakirev. Stasov dubbed them the "Mighty Handful." The other four were César Cui, Alexander Borodin, Nikolai Rimsky-Korsakov, and Modest Mussorgsky. They understood themselves as composers in the classical tradition, but they willingly abandoned many conventions of classical music in the West in the hope of creating a new national style of music based on Russian folk melodies, national themes, and at times a realist, rather than romantic, presentation of their work. Some of their melodies they discovered on summer trips to the countryside—their own version of "going to the people." For themes they often turned to folk tales and history. Rimsky-Korsakov drew on historical themes and several Russian folk tales for the sources of his operas, while Borodin chose the history of Kievan *Rus'* and Mussorgsky focused on pre-Petrine Russia.

Among the five, the composer who has been most closely associated with populism was Mussorgsky. From an ancient noble family, Mussorgsky chose a traditional career path through the military, but at the same time he developed remarkable talent as a concert pianist. Balakirev became his mentor in the late 1850s and taught him about musical structure, at which point he resigned his commission from the army and devoted himself full-time to music. Without an income and because of financial difficulties that grew acute when his family had property removed from them in the emancipation settlement, Mussorgsky lost his former privileged position and had to find work as a low-ranking civil servant. Balakirev was not classically trained, and he intentionally protected the Mighty Handful composers from too much musical theory, believing it would hinder their unique Russian voices. Stasov encouraged Mussorgsky to think of art as something that served a social purpose, although Mussorgsky always remained interested in purely formal questions as well. In the early 1860s Mussorgsky first visited Moscow and began to develop a fascination for Russian history. Moscow's pre-Petrine architecture gave him the sense that he had come into contact with "the real" Russia, a world entirely unlike that of the Europe-inspired architecture of Saint Petersburg. Like Surikov, Mussorgsky found in the pre-Petrine past a time when the Russian people was more intact as a single whole. While Soviet scholars connected Mussorgsky to radical populism, recent scholarship has refuted the notion that he held any radical views. Mussorgsky's fascination with the Russian people fits more comfortably with conservative strains of populism. In his work the *narod* does not come across as ideal, and certainly not communal, but especially in his operas the popular masses play a central role. In both *Boris Godunov* (1873) and *Khovanshchina* the key to an understanding of Russia can be found less in the main characters and more in the people as a whole; in both operas the fate of the country is the fate of the whole people.

Music, an art steeped in emotion, lends itself easily to sentimental and romantic themes, and while Mussorgsky's work is broadly classed as part of the European romantic tradition, like populist writers and visual artists he was interested in using his compositions to convey complex ideas in a realist fashion. His realism ranged from the attempt to approximate in music the rhythms of human speech to operatic themes that drew on historical events and represented them in a seemingly raw and unpolished manner. His realist style was also bound up with the attempt to resist imitation of conventional European models and instead create an entirely native musical art. A relatively early work, the familiar *Night on Bald Mountain*, Mussorgsky considered successful because it had avoided "German influence" and was, in his words, "grown on our native fields and nurtured on Russian bread."[46]

Subsequently, his opera *Boris Godunov* would blend an attempt to evoke in music the mood and speech of ordinary people together with a critical appraisal of a traumatic episode in Russian history. In this opera, Mussorgsky's masterpiece, he sought to create a libretto and score that would offer a serious and honest representation of history, making use of native voices and native melodies as his building blocks. It was an interpretation of history that drew on the latest populist historiography, in particular the work of Nikolai Kostomarov, whom Mussorgsky knew personally and read avidly. Kostomarov was a populist historian somewhat in the vein of Shchapov, though a much more distinguished scholar. He believed the motive force and final inheritor of Russian history was not the autocratic state but the people itself. It was this understanding of Russian history that Mussorgsky strove to render in music and adapt for the stage in *Boris Godunov*.

Like his populist peers in literature, Mussorgsky sought to reimagine artistic beauty as something that did not whisk you away from the world so much as plunge you into it. As one scholar writes, Mussorgsky wanted to create a music capable of incorporating "the cries of beggars, orphans, young children, holy fools, shrewish wives cursing their drunken husbands, impoverished peasants."[47] This approach enabled him to put the people on center stage while still treating them with the critical eye demanded by realist critics like Stasov. In the introduction to the libretto, Mussorgsky wrote that he considered the *narod* to be "a great individual, inspired by a single idea."[48] The depiction of the people as "an individual" is a key to the entire opera, for "the people" is a central character, arguably the main character of the opera in spite of its eponymous tsar. A traditional chorus, like the chorus in a Greek play, comments on the main action, which is carried out by the tragic hero. In *Boris Godunov* the chorus declines this role and speaks for itself. "Musorgskii's masses," as W. Bruce Lincoln describes, "bowed down to authority, rose up against it, prayed before it, and cursed it."[49] The chorus that represents the Muscovite crowd is dynamic, in constant motion and sometimes speaking or gesturing in contradiction to the main characters. It also helps advance the dramatic action. Mussorgsky made the role of the *narod* explicit in a letter to his friend Repin: "It is the people I want to depict; sleeping or waking, eating and drinking, I have them constantly in my mind's eye—again and again they rise before me, in all their reality, huge, unvarnished, with no tinsel trappings! How rich a treasure awaits a composer in the speech of the people."[50] In *Boris Godunov* the chorus/people are oppressed and capable of violence and cruelty. It is an elemental force, potentially powerful, but pitiless and without direction, a mob-like rudderlessness that comes fully into view at the end of the opera when they sing the praises of the false pretender seeking the throne.

Only a holy fool in the crowd, and of course the members of the audience, understand that the crowd's support for the pretender heralds the beginning of a terrible decade in Russian history known as the Time of Troubles. Mussorgsky used the story of Boris Godunov to create one of the great populist works of art, and yet the people are portrayed as a rabble, ready to do violence to a disgraced nobleman, as easily swayed to engage in rebellion as to fight for the Polish pretender who appears with a Jesuit retinue. If the people are portrayed in such an amoral and incoherent way, how can the opera be considered a populist celebration of the *narod*? While the first critics, with their fastidious musical standards, savaged *Boris Godunov*, the public treated its composer to several standing ovations. It is difficult to know precisely what the audience admired, but today we can see clearly that Mussorgsky did not really write a tragedy about the character of Boris Godunov, who dies before the final scene in the play. It seems rather that the fate of Russia is the tragic meaning of the drama. Boris has led the *narod* astray, and now they must continue a long period of suffering, which is conveyed in the holy fool's song that concludes the opera:

> Pour out, bitter tears! Weep, Orthodox soul!
> The enemy approaches and darkness falls.
> The darkest of impenetrable darknesses.
> Rus' alas, alas!
> Weep, weep, you hungry Russian people.[51]

In this way *Boris Godunov* reflects the populist epoch from which it emerged, an age when the ruler had ceased to be the central character because the people as a whole had taken his place. Beyond that, as Stasov put it, Mussorgsky captured "the innumerable nuances of the people's spirit, of their mood, intelligence and stupidity, strength and weakness, tragic quality and humor."[52]

Mussorgsky's own life would end tragically a few years after the triumph of his opera, due to poverty and alcoholism. He attempted to write another historical opera, *Khovanshchina*, which remained unfinished at his death. Similar to *Boris Godunov* this opera did not idealize the *narod*, but it did put them—the Moscow crowd, rebellious musketeers, and Old Believers—at the center of the action. *Khovanshchina* emphasized mystical and religious themes and seems to treat any form of rebellion as a doomed affair. It portrays endurance and suffering but offers no escape from the negative forces of modernization coming from Europe and Peter the Great. At the end of the opera the Old Believers, as happened historically in some cases, immolate themselves rather than subject themselves to the coming era. One contemporary critic wrote that *Khovanshchina* captured, "the very essence of the Russian people, its forces, its sense of the starkness of life, the inevitability of suffering, its Asiatic fatalism."[53] But what Mussorgsky intended to communicate remains unclear. More than anything it seems a paean to fatalism and hopelessness. Yet it still retains his earlier Kostomarovian fascination with the importance of the people in shaping Russian history. The anguish over Russia's inability to find its proper path that Mussorgsky seems to express in *Khovanshchina* has been one reason some have found it difficult to identify Mussorgsky with Russian populism. One study locates Mussorgsky "far from . . . [a] populist and progressive materialist," because he "did not glorify the Russian people," but then quickly turns around and refers to the populist nature of his work.[54] It is an understandable confusion that derives from the overly narrow use of the term "populism." If we include among the populists only those who were politically radical and subordinated rational analysis to simple glorification, it would be impossible to understand the ideological breadth, the fertile contradictions, and the ferocity of debate that characterized the populist age.

Repin and Tolstoy did not meet until the 1880s after Tolstoy's religious turn. Tolstoy in this period now proclaimed his reverence for the simple life of the peasantry, sometimes in his asceticism even envying them their manual labor, their meager fare, and the Spartan existence of their lives. Although Repin had great respect for his friend and visited him often, he disavowed what he saw as Tolstoy's hypocritical admiration for the peasants, an admiration that celebrated their hard and tedious lives as an object of emulation. For Repin, born among the peasantry, what poor working people needed was help and education, not to be admired for some elusive inner quality. He captured in paint Tolstoy's reverence, portraying him barefoot in peasant dress and at work behind the plow (Figure 6.4). Repin's desire for justice for the poor, by contrast to Tolstoy's Christian glorification of poverty underlines Tolstoy's populism and marks Repin as a liberal modernizer. By the late 1880s, Repin's view would be ascendant and populism in crisis.

So much more could be (and has been) written about the art and literature of the populist age. This chapter has examined only a minuscule sampling of the lives, ideas, and work of some of the best known and most talented artists of the period. Scores of

Figure 6.4 Ilya Repin, *Tolstoy at the Plow*, 1887 © Wikimedia Commons (public domain).

other writers and artists merit further exploration. In fact, the following chapter will shine a light on some more of them. It does so, however, not to understand their work or admire their creations but to show how their creativity reflected the agony of the populists as they began to recognize the limitations of the high hopes they had placed upon the *narod*.

CHAPTER 7
REGRETS AND REVISIONS

All of us who love the People look at them as if at a theory and, it seems, not one of us loves them as they really are but only as each of us imagines them to be. And even if the Russian people eventually were to turn out to be not as we imagined them, then we all, despite our love for them, would likely renounce them at once with no regrets.

Fyodor Dostoevsky

In the year 1876, Fyodor Dostoevsky wrote the above skeptical thought in his *Diary of a Writer*. Couched as this statement was, inside of Dostoevsky's call to educated society to "bow down" before the people, it seems to have been more an ironic jab at those who didn't share his convictions than a confession that his own faith in the *narod* may have been misguided. As it turned out, however, the statement would prove an insightful prediction of things to come. The *narod* did in fact come to disappoint many populists. As we have seen throughout the foregoing chapters, populism contained a number of fallacies and contradictions. Somewhere in the early 1880s, these flaws began to catch up and overwhelm those who had placed in the peasantry their highest hopes for Russia's future, for the improvement of society, and for a better understanding of themselves. Many began to resign themselves to consternation and regret. The 1880s became a period of retrenchment in which formerly enthusiastic populists began to rethink the conviction that drawing on the hidden resources of the *narod* would transform Russia for the better.

In retrospect it seems the turning point was March 1, 1881, the day The People's Will finally managed to assassinate Alexander II. Up to that point populism had transferred its focus from treks to the countryside to anti-governmental terrorism, believing it had found a recipe that would produce revolutionary change. Dostoevsky died a month before the assassination, but his final entry in *Diary of a Writer* for January of 1881 spread a hopeful message about the intelligentsia uniting with the *narod* and enlightening all of Russia. After it was clear the assassination had produced little effect on either *narod* or *obshchestvo*, it seemed to send a clear message that something was wrong. Whether the problem lay in their methods or their foundational principles remained to be decided. Most of the radical populists' eggs had gone into the basket of disorganization and terrorism, yet once they had succeeded in destroying Russia's most prominent target nothing resulted but the ascension of a new tsar. Alexander III's reign, born of violence just as Nicholas I's had been, adopted a similarly reactionary and intractable stance.

Worse still for the populists, under Alexander III and Nicholas II the progress of capitalism in Russia accelerated in the city and the countryside, and it became clearer and clearer to many that the commune did not provide a bulwark against the evils of self-interest and social fragmentation. It offered little defense against the temptation to better one's own or one's family's economic position in the situation of a market economy. Finally, on an emotional level the closer the populists drew to the *narod* the further removed these human beings seemed to be from the ideal of the populist imagination. This slow-rolling discovery caused great distress to those who, in the 1860s and 1870s, accepted on faith that the peasant village held the key to a better future. So jarring and widespread was the disillusionment that it has been the central theme of two books on the populist movement. Richard Wortman's title for one of these books, *The Crisis of Russian Populism*, would serve perfectly well as a title for the present chapter, which will focus entirely on that crisis and its effects. Cathy Frierson's *Peasant Icons* uses the evolving image of the peasant to document a similar breakdown. Perhaps inevitably, the intensity of populist enthusiasm led to an equal and opposite disenchantment.

The Populist Dilemma

As early as the rough awakening that attended "Going to the People" in the summer of 1874, doubts had begun to set in. Throughout the foregoing chapters, we have confronted many of the conflicted positions in which the populists found themselves, but these were always smoothed over in some fashion—either by accepting the ongoing debate, by shifting tactics, or by patiently accepting that the future would eventually resolve the problem. One way to resolve the doubts, of course, would be to get more and better information, and an urgency to learn more about the *narod* lay at the heart of the work of many writers and scholars in the 1870s and 1880s. Statisticians, ethnographers, reporters, and writers of fiction went to the countryside and brought back voluminous accounts of peasant society across various parts of the Empire. As it turned out, the gathering of information had the opposite effect from dispelling doubt. The more direct research there was, the more it tended to undermine populist ideals. Like those who had "gone to the people" before them, when intelligentsia observers went to the countryside they began to discover disquieting facts. The presumptive communal peasant happily practicing a version of socialism in the countryside, if there ever had been such a creature, seemed to be rapidly evolving into something else under the post-emancipation influence of freedom in a money economy. The commune seemed to exist more to line the pockets of the wealthier peasants than to share the burden of economic hardship throughout the community. Self-interest, illness, drunkenness, and squalor seemed more to characterize peasant life than did the idyll of collective farm labor the populist intelligentsia had portrayed to itself. When the revolutionary solution of striking violently at the government proved ineffective, populist faith in the *narod* began rapidly to give out. By the 1880s, disappointment, lack of direction, and fear for the future had replaced the earlier optimism.

At the same time as the intelligentsia was raising up the people as its idol, emancipation had in fact enabled peasants to make more choices about their role in the world. Taxes, redemption payments, and the often iron-fisted control of peasant elders certainly constrained the peasant's options, but peasants did have an increasing range of choices, including for some migrating to the cities full- or part-time. Some, the so-called *kulaki*, were enriching themselves; poorer peasants were hiring themselves out as paid labor. As a result, the cooperative nature of the village commune—to the extent that it had ever existed—was no longer a hallmark of peasant life. The populist intelligentsia searching for redemption in the "peasant other" found instead groups of distinct individuals with greater autonomy in thought, moral standards, living circumstances, and personality than they had expected. The commune had been supported by the state itself in the emancipation settlement primarily as a way to ensure the regular inflow of capital, and it continued to help village households survive under straitened circumstances, but it looked less and less like the ethical community of cooperation and mutual assistance that would underpin a socialist future. The populists were looking to the *narod* to show the way forward just at the time when the peasants were trying to take advantage of their limited freedom to improve their lives. The irony is palpable. Populists hoped to retard the economic growth and dynamism of those they wished to rescue from economic immiseration.

The reason populism reached a crisis almost at the very moment of its full flowering has everything to do with the wishful thinking that had always driven the populist faith in the peasantry. Whether the intelligentsia hoped to find communalism or deep-seated morality, rebelliousness or Orthodox spirituality, all of these hopes were projected on to the *narod* from the outside, and that projection was not in the interest of the *narod* so much as it was in the interest of the intelligentsia. As a result, the hopes of the populists tended to rise and fall according to a repeated pattern of great enthusiasm followed by bitter disappointment. Recalling Russian society in the 1870s, the writer Vladimir Korolenko noted how quickly and completely populist ideas took hold of the public: "everyone, without distinction of viewpoint, recognized that in those peasant masses there was ripening, or perhaps had already ripened, some Word that would resolve all doubts." It seemed to him that all of Russian society looked to the *narod* for "some kind of formula for a new life." Looking back he could see that such a hope was naive, but he justified it as a kind of necessity: "this naivety was shared by the least romantic representatives of Russian educated society at that time ... It offered our generation what the previous generation of thinking realists had lacked: it brought faith not in mere formulas and abstractions. It gave our aspirations a kind of wide, vital foundation."[1]

From the time of the Emancipation the idea of the *narod* loomed very large in the mind of Russian society as a whole. The people lay on our horizon like a cloud into which men peered, trying to discern or guess the shapes swarming within it. In so doing, different men saw different things, but they all peered anxiously, with great interest, and they all invoked popular wisdom. Without dealing with the Slavophiles, in whose system the people played such an important part, one might mention that even Katkov and the conservatives pointed to the "wisdom of the people": in their view the people consciously upheld the foundations of the existing order. For Dostoevsky the people was *bogonosets* (God-bearer) ... The very fact of peasant origin conferred a sort of patent on the possession of true popular wisdom.

Vladimir Korolenko, *The History of My Contemporary*,
trans. Neil Parsons

But remembering the 1870s from decades later, Korolenko recognized the illusion for what it was. Given the flimsy basis of factual evidence on which populist aspirations rested, that the platform of self-delusion would finally give way cannot be surprising. Nevertheless, it was a rude awakening to recognize the painful and depressing collapse of one's cherished hopes. It compelled the populists to rethink their own position in the world, the meaning and goals of their own lives, and the actions they would take in the future. The populist movement had brought disparate people together around a common purpose. Its undoing would push them in a variety of different directions. Despite its seeming self-assurance, the populist movement had been assailed by doubts all along. Lavrov had predicted in the first issue of *Forward!* that there was too much distance between the two parts of society for "going to the people" to have an immediate effect. Looking back thirty years later, he argued that the populists had been suffering from a "pathological disorder." Excessive optimism, he argued, led first to the naive assumption that work in the village would prove a turning point, and once that did not materialize it led to "sinking spirits and hopelessness."[2]

This is the pathos that characterized the populist movement. An enterprising and idealistic generation set out to unite their divided society and help those who were disenfranchised and excluded from opportunity, but those who fought the hardest were the first to run up against the very wall of social separation they were struggling to overcome. As much as the populists wished to connect with the peasantry, few if any of them were ever to shed their outsider status. The inability to do so had long been predicted. In 1862, for example, Turgenev's character Bazarov, noted throughout *Fathers and Sons* as an educated man with the ability to converse freely with the local peasantry, turns out in their eyes to seem more like a "village idiot." As late as the year 1908, Alexander Blok would continue to feel befuddled by the perpetual distance between the *narod* and the intelligentsia:

Between the two camps—the people and the intelligentsia—there is a line at which they can meet and agree ... But how tenuous the line is today between the secretly hostile camps! How strange and rare are the meetings! How disparate the "tribes, tongues, conditions" that come together here! Workmen, sectarians, tramps, peasants meet with writers and public figures, officials and revolutionaries. But the line is tenuous. As before, the two camps do not see and do not want to know each other; as before, most of the people and most of the intelligentsia tend to regard all who desire peace and accord as traitors and defectors.[3]

Blok was right that the struggle to end the divided character of Russian society had made little headway almost a half-century after the emancipation.

The Engelgardt Experiment

The most widely read and discussed investigations of the peasantry were found in the popular scholarly journals of the day, mostly so-called "thick journals," which discussed contemporary issues at length. Of the numerous articles written on the subject, arguably the most beloved and eagerly anticipated, were the yearly "Letters from the Countryside" written by one Alexander Engelgardt, former rector of the Saint Petersburg Agricultural Institute. Like so many others at the time, Engelgardt had a passionate interest in the *narod*. He wanted both to understand them and to help them emerge from serfdom in a better condition. But he had never intended to be in a position where he could directly interact with the rural population. That would change as a result of his arrest in 1870. As rector of the Agricultural Institute he had been responsible for overseeing a series of student discussions that met each Saturday. Rumors reached the Third Section that these meetings had begun to take on a political character, and police reports about them led to Engelgardt's arrest in December of that year. The government sentenced him to internal exile, barring him for life from living in Saint Petersburg, and he chose to return to his family estate, Batishchevo, outside Smolensk. In this way Engelgardt "went to the people" under force of circumstance. There he would remain for the following two decades. Mikhail Saltykov-Shchedrin, editor of the day's most popular thick journal *Notes of the Fatherland*, requested Engelgardt to write about his experiences in the country amid the local peasantry. Engelgardt complied, and saw his first letter published in May of 1872.

In the early 1860s Engelgardt had written about his admiration for the village commune as a genuinely cooperative institution. He even made an appeal to young urbanites to go to the countryside to offer their services and to profit from living a simple country life. Now more mature and an accomplished scientist, he set out in a seemingly nonpartisan way to understand country life, agriculture, and the world of the Russian peasant. Engelgardt's letters consist mainly of commentary on everyday life in the countryside, weaving his own experience as a gentry farmer together with that of the local community. The letters are written in a plain literary style, emphasizing simple reportage to a curious urban audience. Like other writers in the populist era, Engelgardt had to meet the twin demands for unadorned realism and portrayal of the *narod* in a positive light. He accomplished the balancing act by blending a tone reminiscent of a field biologist describing an ecosystem—that is refusing to intrude his own judgment on what he observed—together with the repeated theme that he was studying and learning from the remarkable know-how of the peasantry, a know-how hard won in the daily struggle to manage a grueling life devoted to subsistence agriculture. That Engelgardt's letters gained so much attention is itself intriguing. It is hard to imagine that descriptions of everyday life on a farm, without much in the way of storytelling, plot, or character, would become fascinating at other times and places. Part of the appeal involved the author's trustworthiness as a guide to country life, but even more importantly the letters appeared at the right place and time. On the heels of the emancipation, urban Russia was hungry for information on the changes and developments of a poorly understood rural world that accounted for more than four-fifths of the Empire's population.

That urban audience had long been receiving plentiful amounts of conflicting information about the *narod*. Depending on the source, the people could be ethically advanced or rabidly debauched, rebellious or passive, mutually cooperative or self-interested. Engelgardt, a dispassionate stranger to country life, might be just the inquisitive, rural Cicerone to resolve these disputes. Over the course of fifteen years of letters, his depiction of the peasants is notable mainly for its detail and complexity rather than any sort of tendentiousness. In the fourth letter, published in 1874, Engelgardt states outright: "I do not want to idealize the *muzhik*," and contemporary readers probably came away from the letters with a sense that he met his goal.[4] Engelgardt combines great admiration for the peasantry with a feeling of foreboding that their way of life is quickly vanishing. When read together as a single text, the letters contain a great deal of self-contradictory argumentation, but considering that they appeared annually over many years, some of that contradiction can be attributed to Engelgardt's ongoing reassessment based on continued experience, not to mention those actual changes in rural society taking place across the years. Moreover, while readers hoped for an account of "the" peasantry, Engelgardt was in fact reporting on nothing more than one specific community of individuals in one small corner of an enormous country. One hears much in these letters about how Engelgardt learns from the local peasants at least as much as he teaches them. He claims all his German texts on agronomy are worthless compared to what the local peasants know about farming. For this reason, he adopts peasant farming methods, abandons "German" clothes for a sheepskin coat, and attempts to eat meals that resemble the local peasant diet. The peasantry's knowledge of how to get along in the northern countryside has accumulated over centuries, and Engelgardt enjoys demonstrating the absurdity of attempting to fit urban ways into a rural context. At the same time, he brings the reader into an intimate understanding of the hardship of peasant life, in which subsistence living means alternation between meager fare and starvation. He shows the reader how it takes great ingenuity on the part of the peasants merely to survive.

Although Engelgardt's portrait of peasant life is multi-faceted, if anything it must have disappointed the hopes of his readers. The commune does little to redistribute wealth, and it has a tendency to favor the strong. Strictly patriarchal, even despotic, households thrive while the weak are subject to further deprivation, and the peasants he describes are deep down as self-interested as their educated, urban counterparts. Each head of household would gladly become a wealthy *kulak* if he could, and any sort of ethically-based mutual aid would seem from these letters to be a myth invented elsewhere. Engelgardt emphasizes the male muzhik's "natural" tendency toward cooperation, but he claims that the women are the village exponents of selfish individualism, the small-time capitalists of the Russian countryside. On top of this, drink gets the better of many peasants, as it does for a time of Engelgardt himself.

On the other hand, Engelgardt manages to find examples of communalism that function extremely well for economic purposes. Of course, the crucial question many of Engelgardt's readers wanted an answer to involved the peasantry's reliance on communal mutual aid. Not until the seventh letter from 1879 do we get a sense that he values the commune, but the communal functions he describes are not that of any village commune, redistributing land. He studies an *artel'* of diggers organized economically to carry out local projects. In the *artel'* "there is no drunkenness, no noise, no fighting, no stealing, no swindling," and the work is done efficiently and to a high standard. But the reason Engelgardt gives for the existence of such *arteli* has nothing to do with an "innate spirit of cooperation." The *artel'* exists, and its members behave well, for purely economic reasons: they get well paid for half the year. The ultimate message of this key letter, written at a time when populist terrorism was in full swing in the cities, was that communalism offered the only viable method for agriculture to advance in Russia, even if in the decade after emancipation the peasantry had turned toward greater individualism and as a result lost its ability to function in the communal way it needed to.

Thus Engelgardt's letters did not provide his countrymen with a remedy for the contradictions of the post-emancipation countryside, and the populists were no closer to knowing what was to be done. Engelgardt himself had wanted to find a solution to the alienation from society and general misery and poverty of the peasants, but he discovered no path forward in the peasants themselves. Russian conservatives still argued that farming in Russia would not be possible without a system like serfdom that disciplined the peasants to concentrated labor, and Engelgardt sought to disprove them by becoming a farmer himself to show that farming could be carried out profitably. Both a scientist and a writer, Engelgardt was a man of great talent, charisma and drive. His relentless pursuit of a remedy for what ailed the countryside provided a fascinating experiment because of his tenacity in pursuing a solution by whatever means available. He believed his example would help the local community prosper. If so it could become a model for the rest of Russia, demonstrating how farming could be carried out successfully by anyone undertaking it in the correct manner.

When he returned to his estate in the winter of 1871, Engelgardt found the local region depressed and the farms dilapidated. The peasants did not seem to be adjusting to their new economic circumstances brought about by the emancipation a decade earlier, so Engelgardt used his academic training in agriculture, combined with what he learned about farming from the peasants, to create a model farm, growing flax and instituting an elaborate new method of crop rotation. The experiment turned out to be a profitable success in its first year, and it produced the desired catalytic effect when some local peasants began to imitate Engelgardt's methods. When, however, he reported on his techniques and the fact that he paid local peasants to do the work, he was accused by the populist intelligentsia of being a country capitalist and destroying the cherished commune by turning communal farmers into hired laborers. By this point, Engelgardt was convinced that emancipation had brought out the self-interested individual in the peasant farmer, and considered the commune no longer an institution of genuine mutual aid and cooperation. On the other hand, Engelgardt did not want to abandon the communal principle in farming since he saw it as the only realistic way for Russian agriculture to flourish. In short, according to Engelgardt, the peasants needed to farm communally but no longer recognized that need, so he sought out an alternative. He reasoned that if he could demonstrate the power of collective farming, just as he had demonstrated the benefit of improved techniques, he would show the peasants the best way forward. But the only possible way to do this would be to find people convinced that communal farming was superior. He had nowhere else to turn but to the urban intelligentsia itself. He advertised for people willing to transform themselves from city-dwellers into farmers, and remarkably he found them. He located his new recruits among those who had either gone to the people in earlier years or who had regretted missing out on the adventure and saw working with Engelgardt as a safe opportunity for their own rural experience.

Engelgardt opened a training center to create what he called "educated peasants," young people from the universities who would live on his estate and learn to work and live as peasants. They would not "go to the people" so much as become the people. Or rather, they would become a new sort of people that had not existed before, a superior type which combined the strength, endurance, and agricultural acumen of the peasants with the cosmopolitan knowledge and specialized skills of people with a university education. They would be *"peasant mechanics, peasant engineers, peasant architects."* They would "live with [the peasants] with one life and one thought."[5] This meant that Engelgardt's training consisted both in learning all the small details of farming—such as how to milk a cow, plow a field, or know when to plant and harvest—and how to live roughly, get by on simple fare, and work long days. His trainees had to eat the same foods as the peasants, work for little pay, and forgo all luxuries. The training was supposed to last for two summers. It is a remarkable sign of the times that even given these stipulations Engelgardt managed to attract a large number of young people prepared to take on the challenge. One of them recalled thinking: "Here is real life, a difficult life perhaps, but in it there is such freshness, such a powerful tranquility that it was worth trying and finally, on the spot, deciding your relationship to the peasant."[6]

I recognize only one science in farming for educated people who want to settle on the land—learn to work, work as the muzhiks do, yes, even in the muzhik's skin. I say to the person who wants to learn how to farm, "become a worker, work, plough, mow, thresh, work like a muzhik, live a bit with the workers, be in their skin" . . . I value an educated person who wants to be a farmer only to the extent that he is a muzhik. I am convinced that more than anything else we need educated muzhiks, villages of educated people, that our future depends on this. If only 1,000 young people of the educated class who had received an education, every year, instead of becoming bureaucrats, become muzhiks, settled on the land, we would soon see results that would amaze the world.

Alexander Engelgardt, *Letters from the Country*, trans. Cathy A. Frierson

Most of Engelgardt's recruits left quickly, unable to tolerate the new life, but seventy-nine remained to move on to the next step of forming a commune. As it turned out, the peasants and the populists did not get along with one another. The peasants scorned the city-dwellers as "skinny legs" and saw them as a threat to their livelihood, while the educated outsiders found their own company more interesting than the company of the peasants. Engelgardt accepted the cultural dissonance as inevitable, and when it came time to set up the first commune, he established his new "educated peasants" in a commune of their own. The first such commune had excellent success in bringing in a crop, but the majority of its members had not received Engelgardt's full agricultural immersive training, and after a series of interpersonal disputes they failed to last out the year. The next commune was formed exclusively from Engelgardt's students. He urged its members that in order to work and live together amicably they must take on an entirely humble and self-effacing attitude. According to reports, this approach was successful until the leader of the group died and once again the experiment fell apart. At this failure, Engelgardt concluded that communal arrangements could work only under his supervision. He drew up strict rules for the next commune that all members had to work, eat, and live collectively, and he bought land near his estate so that he could maintain a watch on its operation. Nevertheless, this commune suffered from internal strife brought on precisely by Engelgardt's rule that all work had to be shared equally. Within a few years this final experiment too had failed.

Engelgardt had financed and supported these projects, but all of them foundered on the interpersonal difficulties brought on by attempting to work and live in common. The series of attempts lasted nearly a decade, but the upshot seemed to reveal that communalism itself was the problem. Engelgardt reconciled himself to the notion that cooperation and mutual aid were not in the nature of either the intelligentsia or the peasantry, and he transferred his faith in the *narod* to the lesser conviction that while the peasants were self-interested they had still maintained their fellow feeling of sympathy for unfortunates. His grandiose scheme to reinvent the peasantry in the form of educated farmers had done little more than demonstrate that populist admiration for peasant communalism had been misplaced. Engelgardt returned to chemistry, while some of his former students comforted themselves with religion and entered Tolstoyan colonies.

Uspensky and Zlatovratsky

The two writers of fiction most closely associated with the radical populists of this period were Gleb Uspensky and Nikolai Zlatovratsky. Both published in popular journals and had a wide following in their day. Their stories and novels appeared in the 1870s and 1880s, at the height of the populist movement, and both during this period were almost exclusively interested in the changing identity and ultimate significance of the rural *narod*. Although their outlooks were quite different, their mission to understand the peasantry was virtually the same, and the two of them often seemed to be in dialogue with one another. They both sought to understand who the "real" peasants were and to convey that understanding to their audience of urban readers. That audience was demanding. It preferred unembellished and objective reporting over any type of idealization, and yet it desperately desired to find in these communiques on rural life something to cherish and respect in the *narod* they had learned to celebrate as their admirable counterparts. Uspensky and Zlatovratsky took separate paths to fulfilling these demands, but because they took up the same questions, we will discuss them here as two examples of the same phenomenon.

It is often noted that as writers of *belles lettres* neither Uspensky nor Zlatovratsky had great success. Nor did they want to. As a well-known scientist, Engelgardt could duly report his observations on the peasants he interacted with, but how were Uspensky and Zlatovratsky to be trusted not to be "telling stories"? For this reason, they needed to differentiate themselves from the established pantheon of Russian writers. To excite the reader with bold ideas, beautiful descriptions, or philosophical observations would have detracted from their purpose and aroused accusations of literary foppishness. Their fiction was much closer to straight reporting that included unassuming personal commentary on what they directly observed in the village environment. The bland style and narrowness of interest that has excluded them to a degree from the canon of Russian classics did not diminish the interest of their own generation. Vera Figner, reflecting the view from the left, called Uspensky "the best loved author of her generation" while Fyodor Dan referred to Zlatovratsky as a classical populist.[7] If Zlatovratsky was the optimistic idealist, always on the lookout for the praiseworthy sides of peasant life, Uspensky more easily gave way to despair and had to dig deeper and deeper to discover any positive message in the rapidly modernizing countryside. Even though Zlatovratsky was often accused of putting the peasant on a pedestal, he too exposed the dark side of peasant life, subjecting the evolving peasantry to "merciless analysis" with the intention, as he put it, "to reveal their depressing ulcers in order to cure them more quickly and truly."[8] Uspensky began his career writing in the expository form of hyperrealism favored by his cousin Nikolai Uspensky in the 1860s, but as time went on he became more of a theorist than a reporter.

Both Zlatovratsky and Uspensky went through a phase of absolute commitment to populist principles. Zlatovratsky's populism was more homegrown. Rejecting what he considered the miseries of urban life, he returned to his native Vladimir Province and spent time with local peasants, who confirmed the admiration for them he claimed to have had as a child. Uspensky had been writing—often about the degradation of the urban lower classes—since the early 1860s, but on an extended trip to Europe in the 1870s he went through the not unusual Russian experience of disillusionment with European society. At the same time he grew acquainted with a number of convinced populists abroad, including Lavrov, and they helped instill in him a new respect for the rural *narod*. When he returned to Russia, Uspensky took up residence in the countryside in the hope of finding the calm and comfort he had not found in Saint Petersburg or Western Europe. Zlatovratsky's and Uspensky's personalities, too, reflect different sides of the populist mentality. Zlatovratsky had a tendency to reject all that could be construed as elite or pretentious. He fancied himself personally close to the peasants, and liked to speak in a folksy idiom and repeat popular aphorisms. When he received criticism for excessive idealization, he defended himself by saying that he understood the peasantry better than other people. Uspensky resembled one of Dostoevsky's tormented characters; he was overcome with guilt and longed for some great act of suffering that would enable him to atone for it. For a time he nurtured the populist faith in a peasantry that had the capacity to save *obshchestvo* from its own mistakes, but not long after he moved to the countryside he recognized that his thinking about the peasants had been fanciful and wrong. Like Engelgardt and Zlatovratsky, he too hoped to use his diagnosis of peasant conditions and mentalities as the road to a remedy, but he struggled mightily to find the redeeming side of peasant life.

The chief difference between the two authors' understanding of the peasantry arose from the same sticking point Engelgardt had wrestled with—the village commune. Uspensky's experience in Samara Province was not dissimilar from Engelgardt's. He found that the peasant commune was not a social "space" of mutual succor and support for all. It was an institution easily exploited by the powerful for their own economic gain. He frankly disavowed any ethical component of communalism as well. In his words, "The first thing one notices from observing the contemporary rural order is the almost complete absence of moral bonds among members of the village commune."[9] Uspensky claims, ironically, that it is only as a result of their emancipation from serfdom, when they had been united by their common debt and mutual opposition to the landlord, that they lost their former moral unity. If there ever had been that vaunted mutual harmony the populists believed in, Uspensky laments in 1878 that there is nothing left of it now, and as a result the wealth has gone into the hands of a few locals, impoverishing the majority in the process.

Sharply contrasting with Uspensky, Zlatovratsky clearly discerned the persistence of communalism in the countryside. One must keep in mind something the populists themselves often forgot: the peasantry was not monolithic. Zlatovratsky focused on the lives of a peasant community in Vladimir over three hundred miles away from Uspensky's first base of operations in Samara. And both of them were far from Engelgardt's region near Smolensk. For this reason, when Uspensky claimed to be describing "the contemporary rural order" in his examination of peasants outside Samara, he was engaging in considerable exaggeration. Rural society varied from place to place, even village to village. That variation could possibly account for the fact that Zlatovratsky developed a very different interpretation of peasant communalism than that of Uspensky. For Zlatovratsky the commune was fundamentally capable of adapting to all kinds of new circumstances because he understood it less as a socioeconomic institution and more as a spirit of collectivity deeply rooted in peasant attitudes. As we read in his novella *Peasant Jurors*, for example, the principle of justice among the *narod* was not ingrained in any sort of institution, like it was in the justice system of urban and official Russia. It was ingrained in the popular consciousness. The rest of the world could and would change, but that popular spirit would remain a constant. To be sure, Zlatovratsky stresses that the commune is under threat. The essential narrative behind most of his stories and novels involves morally upright, traditional peasants besieged by an alien modernity and doing their best to stave off the attack. Factions and individualism take hold of village life and as a result the sense of mutual responsibility decreases. The peasants seem to be succumbing to the enticements of a money economy in Zlatovratsky's stories too. But where Uspensky found communalism moribund, Zlatovratsky managed to keep the faith.

> That kind of peasant always gives me an odd impression. The type is already dying out, like the heavy, awkward, contemplative kangaroo of the Australian forest, perishing in the struggle for existence with the agile, slippery predators of the newest forms. He's already a rarity in the villages near the city, although in the hinterlands he is still met with entirely in his original state. The more you get to know him, the tenderer the feelings you have for him, but at the same time in your soul lurks an irritating melancholy. Does the strict law of the struggle for existence really rule over humanity all powerfully? Can't a person try to take a stand against this horrifying, anti-humanitarian phenomenon?
>
> Nikolai Zlatovratsky, *Izbrannye proizvedeniia*

As for Engelgardt, so for Zlatovratsky and Uspensky the great threat was the *kulak*, the peasant capitalist, exponent of self-interest and destroyer of communal values. The new struggle all three of them found to be taking over rural life was that between the poor and benighted peasant with no tools to defend himself, and the *kulak* with the will, the power, and the wealth to build up his own mini-empire at the expense of everyone else. As moneylender, landlord, and self-serving individualist, the *kulak* played all the roles of the rapacious capitalists in the city, and he did so right there in the midst of the Russian village. The main concern that terrified the populists was increasing wealth discrepancy in the village. Such differentiation threatened the commune and loomed like a harbinger of rural capitalism, the top two perceived dangers to populist ideals. The figure of the *kulak* was more vilified than understood. As the most enterprising of peasants, the *kulak* was often regarded by other peasants both as an exploiter and as a pillar of the community, and even Engelgardt showed grudging respect for such figures. Most populists, however, demonized the *kulak* as a *miroed* [commune eater], the person and the principle that needed to be defeated in village life. To understand the populists' desperate fear of the *kulak* we might return to the anxiety Kravchinsky had expressed in an earlier chapter that if peasant communalism in Russia was undermined, then Russia would never be able to play its destined role on the world stage, and Russia would remain "but a poor imitator, and a drag upon civilization for many generations to come."[10]

Despairing of communalism yet unprepared to give up on the *narod*, Uspensky began to cast about for an alternate set of traits to admire. Moving to an even more remote location, deep in what Russians call "the bear's nook" (in English something like "the middle of nowhere"), he lived near and got to know a peasant profoundly devoted to farming. Finding this devotion to agriculture, as well as a concomitant lack of interest in other human beings, somewhat incomprehensible, Uspensky studied him intently and one day had a revelation. An artist he had known in Europe seemingly with little reason had grown irate about a small scratch on the Venus de Milo, a reaction that surprised Uspensky in a similar way to the obsessed farmer. Thinking back to the artist's reaction, Uspensky analogized that the peasants felt about agriculture in the same way this artist felt about great art. It was not just their source of livelihood but their source of meaning and value in the world. Like an artist passionate about his craft, the peasant was ardently devoted to the craft of farming. Thus Uspensky concluded that communalism had never really been the key to an understanding of the peasantry. What motivated the rural *narod* was that force he would use as the title of his next novel, *The Power of the Earth*. The peasants lived in union with the land, and their own fates were tied to the fate of the land. For a time Uspensky saw this deep attachment as an Edenic solution to life's problems in its unconscious simplicity. If a peasant farmer was able to feed himself and his family he could be perfectly content, lacking other sources of anxiety. It was an individualistic rather than a communal worldview, but it seemed to Uspensky worthy of respect, especially because it immunized the peasants from all other concerns. The *narod* was blessed by its total devotion to farming. It prevented them from having to eat from the tree of knowledge, the fruit of which, by contrast, *obshchestvo* had already had its fill.

And the secret is truly enormous and, I think, lies in the fact that the great majority of the mass of the Russian people will be patient and powerful in misfortune; they will be spiritually young, both courageously strong and childishly meek—in a word, the people who on their shoulders carry everyone and everything, the people whom we love, to whom we go for the healing of spiritual torments, will preserve their powerful and mild type, so long as the power of the earth rules over them, so long as at the very core of their existence lies the impossibility of disobeying her commands, so long as those commands rule over their mind and conscience, so long as they fill all their existence.

Gleb Uspensky from *The Power of the Earth*,
trans. Cathy Frierson (in *Peasant Icons*)

Attachment to the land was certainly a new ideal, but it lacked two features that made the idea of communalism so appealing. First, it did little to further the revolutionary socialist hopes of the populist intelligentsia, and second it had no power to prevent the malevolent incursion of modernity into peasant life. The novel *The Power of the Earth* takes up this latter concern in its description of a peasant hopelessly debauched because he is powerless to resist the temptations of money and alcohol that arrive in the countryside with the coming of the railroad. The very "power of the earth" had rendered the peasantry easy to exploit. This novel, Uspensky's best known, offers little hope for either the betterment of the peasant or the future of Russia. In the end, Uspensky gave up on the idea that the *narod* could point the way forward for the rest of Russian society. His

171

last stories focus not on the power of the earth but on the power of capital and the rise of a money-based economy.

Written at roughly the same time as *The Power of the Earth*, Zlatovratsky's novel *The Foundations* was intended to provide a different solution to the coming of the *kulak* and the weakening of the commune. By "the foundations" Zlatovratsky meant those presumed ancient, traditional values the *narod* lived by. They included piety, kindness to one another, homespun sagacity, and devotion to communal unity. This was a populist version of simple "heartland values," those principles preserved over time by rural isolation, which the city-dweller had long since abandoned. If these values stressed mutual aid and communal cooperation, they also meant a commitment to truth and fairness as well as the capacity for endurance and self-sacrifice. *Peasant Jurors* treats the *narod* as having an entirely different mentality from that of *obshchestvo*. It is a morally superior mentality because the peasants judge questions based on internal convictions rather than external, rationalist standards. They are good judges, and yet they are incapable of functioning in the city courts because their judgment functions on a different basis, alien to formal legality. Uncontaminated by Western thought, they serve as the moral guarantors of the authentic Russia that still exists within them, and thereby remains an accessible, if threatened, part of Russian culture. The drama that propels most of Zlatovratsky's work emerges from the tension between an encroaching and destabilizing urban modernity and the noble struggle by the uncorrupted peasants to retain "the foundations." The character of Petr, aptly named given the historic role of Peter the Great (Petr I) as Russia's first Westernizer, abandons "the foundations" and finds himself led astray in the big city of Moscow. He eventually returns to the village to find new meaning within the old ways. As much as Zlatovratsky sought to convince himself and his readers that "the foundations" were unshakable, the general impression of the novel is that these old ways were caught up in a fight they might well lose. Even in Zlatovratsky's benevolent reading, when the modern world was not rushing in through the front door of the peasant hut, it was creeping down the chimney.

It cannot be said that the work of Uspensky, Zlatovratsky, or Engelgardt was the sole cause of populist disillusionment, but collectively their work offered a powerful reflection of the growing sense of despair that populism's optimistic hopes for Russia's future may have been illusory. Accustomed to great confidence in the *narod*, the reading public was left confused by the new tone, like that of Zlatovratsky, which mixed optimism with discouragement and anxiety. One critic condemned these texts for exuding "a pronounced uncertainty, lack of definition, at times a pathological duality of views, a disjointedness between the various scenes, a vagueness or even a poverty of evidence and argumentation despite all the signs of great conviction." This reviewer also noted the "flagrant contradictions of ideas on significant problems: on what is meant by countryside, the rural commune, the intelligentsia's attitude toward the people, etc."[11] Fyodor Dan, a Marxist who opposed populism as an ideology, regarded Uspensky as a sort of stealth Marxist as early as 1876 who "mercilessly unmasked the power of money, the triumph of the 'kulak' ... and the progressive dissolution and degeneration of the commune."[12]

Uspensky would never have accepted such a characterization of his work in 1876, but by the middle of the 1880s he was becoming a defender of Marx. By this point he had come to focus the bulk of his attention on former peasants who were now wage laborers, trapped in a cycle of poverty and moving from place to place, cut off from the old consolations of the village, without any hope for improvement or stability. In despair, Uspensky spent the final years of his life in and out of mental asylums, struggling with depression and a tenuous grasp on reality. The cumulative effect of these writings was to strike down the original conviction that the peasantry was "naturally" socialist. Many rebuked Uspensky for ceasing to fight for the cause. Zlatovratsky continued to insist on the inner consistency of peasant communalism, but he could offer no proof of its existence. In his later years, he began writing on other topics.

Worse yet, the principal anxiety conjured up by these writers—that the communal spirit was under siege—was largely confirmed by scholarship and statistical research on that fate of the commune in various regions of Russia. Ongoing studies getting fully underway in the late 1870s cast doubt on the continuing strength of communalism. Many of those who helped collect the data were veterans of "Going to the People," and they hoped to enlist the information they gathered in service to the *narod*. Esther Kingston-Mann has fittingly described their research as "activist social science."[13] Like the difference between the despair of Uspensky and the confidence of Zlatovratsky, these studies too differed in their assessments of the prospects for the village commune. Also like the populist writers, these researchers were steeped in the emphasis on empiricism that was paradoxically such a hallmark of the populist age, and yet they too struggled to find within the raw data some confirmation of the continued relevance of peasant communalism. They developed cautious methodologies to ensure they gained the most accurate information possible, and, as a side effect of their efforts much of their work exposed the corruption of local landowners and officials. Conservatives vilified them as dangerous nihilists, shutting down their operations, and even burning some of their data. The research did show the peasantry's continued reliance on the village commune, but it also indicated that capitalist labor practices had made deep inroads into the countryside.

The most impressive of these studies was V.I. Orlov's exhaustive, multivolume, data-driven *Types of Peasant Landholding in Moscow Province*. Orlov's work demonstrated that communalism in villages near the city had been declining for precisely the same reasons Engelgardt and others had proposed: the rise of the *kulak*, the hiring of wage labor, and the unwillingness of commune members to cooperate for their mutual interest. Orlov's conclusions had been based on thousands of detailed interviews with local peasants, commune elders, regional landowners, and many others. Although he had wanted to prove that the peasants remained firmly attached to their communes, distressingly his examination disclosed that, at least in the Moscow region, communalism was giving way to capitalism, precisely the development the populists were working to forestall. Two followers of Marx in the populist camp, the economists Nikolai Rusanov and Nikolai Danielson, used Orlov's data to show that capitalism was rapidly penetrating the village. As a result, although the commune still existed it seemed to have lost its original purpose and was churning out a group of landless wage laborers, Russia's rural "proletariat." All of this depressing news would be amply driven home by the great famine that gripped the countryside in 1891 and 1892. That famine would once again bring urbanites out into the village, this time in the process of relief efforts, and they were able to see for themselves the miserable state into which the peasantry had fallen. In a blow to Russian populism, visitors to the village could also see clearly that the commune had done little, if anything, to relieve the peasantry of its economic plight. Far from nurtured by cooperation and mutual assistance, "the foundations" did not even seem to offer any psychological comfort. The *narod* would not be coming to anyone's rescue. It needed rescuing itself.

New Directions

If there was no precise turning point that marked the onset of populist disillusionment, it is at least clear that the apex of populist enthusiasm had been passed by some point in the early 1880s. For all populists the 1880s was a time for rethinking and regrouping. As we have seen, once Land and Freedom had split the newly formed People's Will Party each shifted its tactics and rethought its original aims. By the time of the assassination, members of The People's Will were agitating for elections and representative democracy rather than expecting an apolitical, decentered revolution to break out in the countryside among the *narod*. Then, when the assassination itself led to a reassertion of autocratic power under Alexander III, not to mention the decimation of the remaining organization, it once again opened the door to a fresh rethinking of populist tactics and aims. With most of the remaining leadership of The People's Will in self-imposed exile abroad, the one weapon the party still possessed was the reputation its members had earned as bold combatants in the struggle against autocracy. This reputation was their greatest asset in keeping up recruitment. Thousands of recruits continued to join one or another subsection or offshoot of The People's Will. But these groups possessed little of the organizational discipline that had distinguished the original People's Will, and they were consequently arrested in the thousands during the 1880s.

In the south, organizations affiliated with The People's Will continued to practice disorganization and terror, while in the north the most important of these new recruits were students in Saint Petersburg, including "The Union of Youth of the People's Will" led by Petr Iakubovich. This young man openly sought to shift the direction of the party away from its earlier focus on the urban public and back toward forging closer connections with the masses. The plan would be to carry out acts of terror in the factories and villages in order to impress and unite with working people. To a degree Iakubovich sought a return to the program of Land and Freedom, although he and his followers intended to retain the tactic of terrorism pioneered by The People's Will.

Iakubovich's leadership was only strengthened by the fact that the ranking member of The People's Will in Saint Petersburg, Sergei Degaev, had been discovered reporting his activities to the police and exposing members of the organization to arrest. The Executive Committee in emigration, headed by Lev Tikhomirov and Mariia Oshanina, directed Degaev to arrange the murder of the man to whom he had been reporting: the chief of the political police, Grigory Sudeikin. With the help of two associates, Degaev carried out the murder in December of 1883. In return for committing the assassination Degaev's life was spared, but now his former populist cohort despised him, and he emigrated to the United States. The Degaev Affair helped spread disillusionment among those affiliated with The People's Will, and after a wave of arrests in 1884 the party lost all sense of direction and purpose. A former member said in 1884 that The People's Will no longer had any clear orientation and had become little more than a mere tradition.[14]

Despite the party's loss of focus, one more episode connected to The People's Will took place in 1887. The event is widely known and remembered because of its link to the first leader of Soviet Russia, Vladimir Lenin. Lenin's older brother, Alexander Ulyanov, was a student at Saint Petersburg University where he got involved in politics, eventually joining a group that called itself "The Terrorist Fraction of the People's Will." Just as the earlier terrorist movement had its roots in government intolerance for public protest, this terrorist organization had been formed in the wake of public protests put down by the police. Ulyanov and others had organized protests in 1886 only for some participants to face arrest and exile as punishment for their participation. Prevented from demonstrating, yet again they turned to terrorism as what they believed to be their only remaining option. In 1887, only six years after the assassination of Alexander II, this group hatched a plot on the life of Alexander III. Drawing on the method that had been used in assassinating Alexander II, Ulyanov, a gifted student in the natural sciences, devised handheld bombs for three would-be terrorists to hurl at the tsar when he was en route to a planned visit at St. Isaac's Cathedral. The plot was discovered at the last minute, and Ulyanov was arrested and executed two months later. The then seventeen-year-old Vladimir Ulyanov (Lenin) admired his brother and was impressed by his revolutionary zeal, but it remains unclear to what extent the assassination attempt, or his brother's execution, had an impact on his own development as a revolutionary. There is no doubt, however, that Lenin learned from, and in some ways learned to emulate, the original People's Will that had inspired his brother's assassination attempt.

One notable figure who emerged from the shakeup of Land and Freedom was Georgy Plekhanov. Plekhanov had turned against Land and Freedom's adoption of terrorism in 1879, arguing that those who waged a battle to overthrow the state were giving up their original purpose of agitation among the *narod*. Plekhanov formed a new organization, Black Repartition, which renewed emphasis on the communal redistribution of land. Having intended to go back to work in the countryside, the members of Black Repartition were quickly discovered by the police, and the majority of them were arrested. Plekhanov had gone abroad by this point, and like others wanted by the police in Russia he would remain there for decades to come. Living in Geneva, over the course of less than two years, Plekhanov entirely shed the populist philosophy of which he so recently had been an eager defender and became the first Russian to fully adopt a Marxist worldview. Thus he became, as he would be known in Soviet Russia, "the father of Russian Marxism."

In principle, Russian populism and Marxism are extremely incompatible philosophies. Marx was hostile to the peasantry as a retrograde and petty bourgeois class while the populists saw the peasantry as the road to the socialist future. Marx argued that a revolution would necessarily take place as a result of the expansion of capitalism while the populists hoped for nothing so much as to forestall the advance of capitalism. Marx favored the creation of a revolutionary state while many populists favored the destruction of the state, typically to be replaced by a federation of independent communes. It is true that Marx had been widely read and admired by Russian populists, but they either misunderstood his work or cherry-picked it for arguments friendly to their own thinking. While still in Russia, Plekhanov had been one of those populists who drew on Marx's views to bolster his own arguments, but he remained thoroughly populist in orientation. He had been particularly close to the urban working class, and noted that they were more responsive to agitation than the rural peasants had been, but given their relatively minuscule numbers he had seen the urban workers merely as supporters of a struggle that could only unfold as an agrarian revolution. Different from most members of Land and Freedom, who fought for the revolution without needing any firm theoretical foundation, Plekhanov had always been a revolutionary intellectual with a profound desire to root his activism in a solid ground of rational principle. In Geneva, removed from political activism, he redoubled his study of the economic and sociological theories behind revolutionary socialism.

Intending to bolster his faith in the foundations of populism, instead Plekhanov found himself embracing the views of Marx and Engels. By 1882 he had begun actively to promote the need for the expansion of capitalism as the road to the Russian Revolution he had long fought for. Plekhanov was drawn to Marxism for a variety of reasons. First, he was losing faith in populism. Like that of many others by the 1880s, his confidence in the revolutionary and socialist nature of the village commune had begun to falter. Second, in contrast to the loose, self-contradictory, and shifting views of the populists, so contingent on the mood and actions of the peasants themselves, he discovered in Marxism a set of theories which suggested that rational processes, applicable everywhere, drove history forward toward an eventual socialist revolution. He also read Engels's powerful 1875 critique of Russian populism in which Marx's collaborator scoffed at the idea that the Russian peasantry had any revolutionary potential. Engels was already in 1875 claiming that peasant communalism was on the way out, an argument which, in the interim, had come to look increasingly likely.

In supporting a fully Marxist view, however, Plekhanov faced towering difficulties convincing the Russian left. Marxist ideology insisted that only the progress of capitalism could lead to a genuine revolutionary society and only the industrial proletariat was an authentic revolutionary class. That meant that in a society still mostly rural and an economy still mostly agrarian, Plekhanov had to welcome the rapid advancement of the precise bourgeois capitalism his associates so deeply despised. Many of them had been jailed, exiled, and had died in the effort to repel it. Under Russian circumstances, Marxism was saddled with the inescapable irony that socialist supporters of the working classes were compelled to usher in a liberal democratic revolution in the name of the capitalist bourgeoisie. Any Russian Marxist also needed to abandon, at least to a degree, the populist "will to power," that voluntaristic idea that conscious choices made by individuals and groups governed the direction of historical change. A proper Marxist had to accept that individuals and organizations had only limited power to budge the great socioeconomic forces that determined the direction of history. Plekhanov managed to make the titanic shift from populism to Marxism in part because he came to believe the rise of capitalism in Russia was inevitable. Given that inevitability—which turned out to be an accurate prediction—he designated the role of the Marxist intellectual in Russia as a supporter and enlightener of the expanding proletariat. Plekhanov and other Russian Marxists were to work on behalf of industrial labor, helping workers attain the political consciousness they would need in order to overthrow the liberal capitalism that would initially bring about a Russian bourgeois revolution. By the end of 1883, with a small coterie of like-minded associates, he had formed in Switzerland the first Marxist political association in Russian history, calling it "The Emancipation of Labor Group."

It had been astonishing to the populists to discover Plekhanov, one of their former leaders, adopting a view that upheld the necessity of capitalist development, but news of the transformation experienced by another populist leader, Lev Tikhomirov, came as a body blow. In the early 1880s Tikhomirov had been both the leader of The People's Will after the assassination and the foremost defender of radical populism against Plekhanov's turn to Marxism, but in 1888 this major figure in The People's Will announced himself an anti-revolutionary and Russian Orthodox supporter of the throne. Together Plekhanov and Tikhomirov had been editors of Land and Freedom's underground newspaper. After their respective political conversions, Plekhanov still supported an eventual revolution, but Tikhomirov rejected every aspect of his former convictions. He justified his new world view in a pamphlet called *Why I Ceased to Be a Revolutionary*.[15] The autocracy was delighted to have a convert and, against the objections of many conservatives who could not countenance Tikhomirov going unpunished, he received a full pardon from Alexander III. Attacked daily in the leftist press, considered by his former populist associates to have gone insane, and probably fearing for his life, Tikhomirov returned to Russia in 1889 and began to work as a right-wing journalist and editor for a Moscow newspaper.

What could have been the reason for such a complete break with his former views? Many have sought to answer this question, but the answer remains elusive. His fellow revolutionary, Nikolai Morozov, on learning of Tikhomirov's apostasy, claimed he had always had royalist tendencies, but this makes little sense. Some have painted Tikhomirov as a sort of agnostic political animal only interested in having the power to sway others, a power he did in fact possess both in The People's Will and later as an ideologist for monarchism. While it is true that he was capable of chameleon-like change even during his time as a radical, the shift he made as a leader of The People's Will from peasant-focused populist socialist to terrorist in favor of a representative democracy had been carried out in cooperation with most others in The People's Will. Certainly part of his political conversion involved that shaken confidence in the correctness of populist views experienced by so many in the 1880s. In his memoirs, Tikhomirov noted his discouragement that by 1882 "we revolutionaries … were completely destroyed."[16] Having gone abroad in that same year, Tikhomirov found the nationalist elements of his populist love of Russia coming to life. His love for country, combined with a sense that "the revolution" had failed, were exacerbated by deep debt and a need to provide for his family, especially after his son grew ill from spinal meningitis and needed long-term care. Turning to religious faith for support, he began to consider his former faith in revolution to have been devotion to a false idol. He grew convinced that "our ideals, liberal, radical and socialist, are the most enormous madness, a terrible lie, and furthermore a stupid lie."[17] We can hear in this statement the voice of a person incapable of existing in the absence of some definite faith, not unlike his position as a convinced revolutionary terrorist. Tikhomirov went from helping to kill the tsar to spending the rest of his life supporting Tsarism. When he died in 1923, however, Bolshevik socialists were in control of the former Tsarist Empire.

It may well be that Tikhomirov's dramatic repudiation of his former views was based on a psychological need for a political faith that would offer him a sound set of principles. But there was also a philosophical aspect to his transformation. The Jacobin language of Tikhomirov's pronouncements as late as 1883 gave way to a conservative analysis of society that led him to conceive—or at least enabled him to justify—an entirely different world view. As a revolutionary he had originally believed that change could come about through force of will and a correct analysis of the alteration society needed to undergo, but now he came to believe that change could only take place gradually as a result of building on what came before. Petitioning the Tsar for amnesty he wrote:

> I understood that the development of people, as of everything living, takes place only organically, on the basis on which they had been historically formulated and nurtured and that a healthy development can only be peaceful and national. I understood the falsity of ideas which destroy society by fostering ideas of limitless freedom and rights of the individual . . . I came to an understanding of the power and the honour of our historical traditions which reconciled spiritual freedom with an unquestioned central authority, raised above all personal ambitions.[18]

It is an argument similar to the one Edmund Burke propounded against the French Revolution. Unlike Burke, however, who could consent to an American model of revolution while rejecting the French model, Tikhomirov's extremism reemerges here as a mirror image of his original absolute rejection of authority. Now it was tsarist authority that had to remain absolutely unquestioned. Plekhanov found an alternative to populism within which he could compromise with both liberals and radicals. In a certain sense, Tikhomirov remained a radical, this time fighting for the other side. Plekhanov made a similar point when he used Tikhomirov's apostasy to demonstrate, with a degree of exaggeration, that deep down Russian populists were nothing other than Russian nativists and exceptionalists and as such already not far from Tikhomirov's pro-autocracy position.

Legal Populism

Once they recognized the flaws in their original thinking, Plekhanov and Tikhomirov gave up on the populist ideals they had earlier promoted with such ferocity. A more common response in the 1880s was to note the underlying problems of the original populist position and try to rectify them in order to salvage the movement. The most notable exponents of this effort came to be called "legal populists," a label which suggested that rather than overthrow and replace the political system in a burst of revolution, they would instead work within the system in order to gradually improve the lot of the peasantry while continuing to promote the benefits of communalism. This moderate stance made it possible for legal populists to publish their views in the press, which gave them considerably greater attention. Soviet historians, following Lenin, referred to the legal populists with disdain as "liberals" in socialist disguise. As a result of the battles that arose in this era between Marxists and populists, the legal populists have latterly been maligned as naive counterrevolutionaries who did not understand that the autocratic system could not be reformed from within. Under the circumstances, however, legal populism constituted a perfectly reasonable response to the loss of confidence in peasant communalism and rebelliousness and a good-faith effort to maintain populist ideals. While the views of the legal populists did not lack their own flaws, they appealed to many among the intelligentsia. They also helped to keep populist embers smoldering during this time of disillusionment and regret.

The movers and shakers of legal populism were not radical agitators but economists, scholars, and writers publishing their work in thick journals. Rusanov and Danielson, mentioned above, had argued from a largely Marxist point of view that the penetration of capitalism into the countryside was changing the nature of rural life and threatening the commune. Vasily Vorontsov, briefly discussed in Chapter 4, spearheaded legal populist thinking in his 1882 study *The Fate of Capitalism in Russia* by refuting this argument. The chief contention in his treatise was that, even if it appeared capitalism was making inroads into Russian life, under current conditions Russia still did not stand a chance of becoming a capitalist country. Vorontsov's reasons included the fact that Russia lacked sufficient external markets for manufactured goods since markets abroad had already been cornered in the Western scramble for empire. In other words, Russia had already been crowded out of lucrative markets abroad, and thus could not generate a pattern of sustained industrial or large-scale agricultural production. On the domestic side, Vorontsov contended, agrarian Russia was too poor to stimulate a thriving market based on manufacture and trade; it lacked transportation networks across its vast territory of dispersed communities, and it could never compete with the technological progress that had already cranked into overdrive in the West. All of this might sound like a lament for the sorry state of the Russian economy, but instead the conclusion Vorontsov and his followers drew produced a collective sigh of relief. That Russian capitalism had no chance of large-scale survival meant that Russian traditions, and especially the village commune, would continue to thrive and eventually settle in as the main basis for the socioeconomic system. Vorontsov even argued that the direction of Russia's economy should gain impetus not from economists like himself but from "the people's collective thought."[19] Elsewhere he held, similar to Kablits, that the most important task of the intelligentsia was its own self-destruction. Vorontsov's claims amounted to a fresh spin on the old notion of the advantages of backwardness.

Unfortunately, Vorontsov's thinking ran counter to the historical processes actually unfolding in the countryside at the time his study appeared. As so many were coming to recognize, the rural economy based on property ownership and wage labor was enriching some in trade, manufacture, and farming, while it was turning others into disposable labor. The state in fact actively encouraged these innovations as part of its economic policy. Beginning in the late 1880s, Russia pursued loans from abroad and instituted policies to stimulate the growth of capitalism. Lenin, by the 1890s an increasingly central figure among Russian Marxists, attacked the legal populists in his sarcastically titled article about "The Friends of the People." He referred to them as "petty-bourgeois opportunists" whose ideas were doing nothing so much as furthering the spread of capitalism into the countryside. There was truth to Lenin's attack. Wortman has rightly described *The Fate of Capitalism* as "a triumph of abstract theory over the mass of factual material flooding the Petersburg intellectual world."[20] Vorontsov and those who agreed with him saw what they wished to see rather than what was actually taking place. In defense against the weaknesses in their position, the legal populists portrayed the commune as an endlessly flexible institution. It could be used to spread advanced technology far and wide, it could facilitate large group projects like building roads or draining swamps, and of course it would make the eventual transition to national and international socialism far less troublesome.

In fact, the legal populists hoped to convince the state to use its wealth and political power to strengthen the commune. They suggested the state should intervene to lessen the tax burden, promote the spread of agricultural technology, and eventually help to build a socialist economy. This position seems absurd given not only the reactionary conservatism of the autocracy under Alexander III and Nicholas II but also their strenuous promotion of capitalism. But the legal populists pinned their hopes on state intervention for simple and obvious reasons: in spite of their faith in the great future of the peasantry, they did not trust that the *narod* was capable of solving its own problems at the present time. Nor could they side with the liberals, who favored capitalist development. As a result, they lacked any natural constituency of support in society and turned to state intervention as their last and only resort. Opponents of autocracy, both liberal and radical, noted that since the state also saw the commune as being in its interest, Vorontsov and other legal populists were effectively in cahoots with the government in trying to promote communalism without also promoting revolution.

This dilemma would vanish, however, during the revolutionary years of 1905 and 1906 when Nicholas granted the October Manifesto that enabled the creation of an elected assembly and empowered the Russian people to vote and run for election. In these years the legal populists formed the People's Socialist Party in order to work within the system toward the achievement of socialism. When they ran for election in 1906 they managed to garner a mere sixteen delegates out of 478, although they did exert some influence on the 107 independent peasant deputies who called themselves "Laborites" [*Trudoviki*]. In the West, they might have held the entirely ordinary status of liberal socialists with a natural constituency of left-leaning, law-and-order moderate progressives. In Russia they found themselves outnumbered by the revolutionary parties who had their natural constituencies in peasants and workers looking to better their lives through radical change. The People's Socialist Party tended to side with the views of the neo-populist Socialist Revolutionaries (the subject of Chapter 8), but they disagreed with their radical methods of terror against the government and returning all the land to the peasantry without compensation to property owners. At the same time they could not fit in with the liberals who rejected their long-range socialist goals. In the end their liberal brand of socialist populism made sense only to a thin sliver of the intelligentsia.

Legal populism exposed a serious flaw in the populist world view: as much as they wanted it to, Russian backwardness was not turning out to offer any advantages. The legal populists even came to recognize that economic lack of development enabled those other countries that had earlier embarked on industrialization to take advantage of Russia, whether by expanding production and distribution to Russian markets for their own profit or, as in the Russo–Japanese War, using industrial superiority to defeat Russia militarily. By the early twentieth century Vorontsov himself had come to favor the expansion of the industrial sector. In 1882 Vorontsov had come out as a staunch defender of small-scale, communal farming and rejoiced in his claim that capitalism would prove to be stillborn in Russia. As time passed, however, history proved him wrong. By the early twentieth century, he had given up support for small-scale farming and accepted the need for massive expansion in both agriculture and industry.

Legal populism proposed that populists need not fight for revolution but could and should work within existing institutions. The populist role should be to support the people peacefully through practical tasks that would help alleviate the peasantry's difficult post-emancipation economic condition. Fortunately there was a structure in place that made such efforts possible. In the 1860s, as part of the Great Reforms, the state had established an elective body known as the *zemstvo*, with the purpose of enabling the provincial population of all social classes to contribute to the welfare of the village. The *zemstvo* was a sort of rural civic center that would help manage local affairs and improve local conditions. It provided the best venue in which to carry out the new gradualist approach to supporting the peasantry which an associate of the legal populists, Iakov Abramov, famously promoted as "small deeds." The theory of small deeds rested on the conviction that sweeping revolutionary transformation not only had failed to gain power or offer any help to the peasantry, but as a result of terrorism had made the autocracy far more reactionary and punitive. After Abramov, this push for gradual improvement was also called "Abramovism," which in Russian is *Abramov-shchina*, a suffix that does not have the neutral connotation of "ism," but suggests a somewhat scandalous affair. In today's English it would not be as obviously negative as "Abramovgate," but it was certainly more a negative than a neutral term. The generally negative reaction this term implied can be attributed to the epoch in which it was made. As suggested by the unrest at the beginning and end of the reign of Alexander II, not to mention the coming mass revolutions in 1905 and 1917, it was still an era of revolutionary aspirations. Small deeds was a good-faith effort to provide aid to the rural *narod*, but in this period any turn away from radical change was liable to be greeted with contempt from the left as a form of socialist backsliding or even as collaboration with a corrupt regime.

Today repudiation of Abramovism seems rather unrealistic and unfair. The small deeds philosophy offered a needed corrective to the over-idealization of the peasantry, a means of getting to know the *narod* from personal experience in a less revolutionary form of "Going to the People," and it provided a genuine opportunity to help out in a limited and local, but practical, way. Any deed carried out through the *zemstvo* was, unfortunately, almost guaranteed to be small, since Alexander III had in 1882 expanded the power in the *zemstvo* of local gentry officers, who tended toward conservatism, at the expense of what came to be called the "third element," referring to those educated professionals from the cities who came to the countryside to offer their services. Such services came in many forms. Vorontsov, for example, typical of the legal populists, supported the necessity of education among the *narod*, of removing the impediment of the illiteracy that did more than anything else to remove them from public affairs. Large numbers of teachers came to work in the villages in the late nineteenth century, doing much to change village culture. Other third element services included medical treatment, the gathering of statistical information, building projects, veterinary medicine, even banking and insurance. It was a matter of taking reasonable, pragmatic, humanitarian steps in the right direction. As Abramov put it, "from these small deeds comes together the life of millions."[21] Heroism did not have to mean putting your life on the line in a revolutionary act; instead it could mean putting in long, grueling hours without the expectation of any immediate reward. It should be kept in mind, however, that in one way Abramovism marked a step away from populism in that it served the people but did not necessarily find any hidden importance within them for the future of Russia, and in this way it seemed to radical populist critics little more than a form of liberal charity. Revolutionary populists saw such Abramovism as a populism manqué, emphasizing pure obligation without any complementary expectation of the redemptive future that obligation would reward.

Disappointed Dreams

One reflection of the populist intelligentsia's shift in thinking from widespread enthusiasm in the 1870s to general disappointment in the 1880s and 1890s can be found in realist paintings by the Wanderers. Contrast, for example, the hopeful and sympathetic portrayal of the peasants we find in Repin's *Boat Haulers* with Sergei Korovin's 1893 *At the Commune* (Figure 7.1). The latter painting conveys the dark and divided side of the village commune. It could be an illustration of one of Uspensky's stories. The white-bearded *kulak* in the foreground laughs as a poor peasant pleads with him, tears of grief in his eyes, for something we can see he desperately needs but will never receive. The crowd around him seems, for the most part, as unmoved by his desperation as the wealthy peasant himself. It is an image of pure dissension and cruelty. The commune here, as in Uspensky's work, does not function as a form of proto-socialist unity; it functions as a mechanism in which the power of wealth ruins lives. Sergei Ivanov's 1889 *On the Road. Death of a Migrant* (Figure 7.2) tells an even grimmer story. An impoverished

Figure 7.1 Sergei Korovin, *At the Commune*, 1893 © Wikimedia Commons (public domain).

Figure 7.2 Sergei Ivanov, *On the Road. Death of a Migrant*, 1889 © Wikimedia Commons (public domain).

family, clearly in search of a better situation somewhere else has stopped by the side of a road seemingly far from human society. They have a cart but lack a horse. Their meager belongings are strewn about the road, and the father, wearing homemade bark sandals, lies dead with his face covered. The mother lies face downward, prostrate with grief, and a child sits up, staring at her dead father in mute incomprehension. Every detail of the painting conveys a painfully raw hopelessness. If the expression on the face of the peasant in *At the Commune* might evoke sympathy, this image evokes little more than despair.

These realist paintings are akin to much of the writing about the peasantry in the late nineteenth century. As in Uspensky's often grim portrayal of the world of the Russian peasant, they offer the viewer little reason for hope. On the other hand, like Zlatovratsky, who finally gave up on describing peasant life and turned toward writing about the intelligentsia and his own past, many painters in the 1880s and 1890s abandoned the expository realism that had dominated the 1860s and 1870s and turned to other themes. In the new paintings, artists still mostly favored the realist verisimilitude typical of the Wanderers in the attempt to capture the "soul" of Russian life, but they no longer looked as often to the *narod* as the source of that soul. Now Russian identity was to be found in history, religious themes, native landscapes, or in representations of everyday life within *obshchestvo*. Some painters went further afield and created images that strayed far from realism, as in the romantic fairy-tale paintings of Viktor Vasnetsov, the mystical spiritualism of Mikhail Nesterov, or the reconstructions of medieval Moscow portrayed in the work of Apollinary Vasnetsov and Andrei Riabushkin.

The "crisis" in Russian populism was brought on in large measure by a series of gradually accruing discoveries. The village commune did not, it turned out, offer an easy path to a socialist future; the peasantry was not after all a tinder keg of rebelliousness; and peasant culture was not in reality the preserve of long-suffering virtue. These were painful realizations because the populist intelligentsia had all along been searching for a reflection of its better self in the *narod*. Populism was, as Wortman put it, "an integral and essential part of the personality of those espousing it."[22] Petr Chervinsky admitted this freely in his description of what he hoped to gain from closer acquaintance with the peasants: "A great feeling lies here in embryonic form—the urge to submit one's egoistic self to something broader and more elevated to which man has moral obligations and on occasion may wish to sacrifice his individuality."[23] As Dostoevsky had suggested in his *Diary of a Writer*, for the populist intelligentsia, "love of the people was but an outlet for personal sorrow about [themselves]."[24] While the chief image of the populist has come down to us as a radical socialist, Anna Geifman has made an interesting observation about the degree to which this personal search for a native identity pervaded populism, noting that Jewish radicals sometimes held their distance from the populists because of populism's suspicious odor of "the traditional Russian ethos with its undertones of pogroms, reaction, obscurantism and Slav chauvinism."[25] In many cases this characterization would be inaccurate, but it does suggest an important and often overlooked aspect of the populist movement. The search for a native identity in the populist age was only partly about finding a path to a more just and socially inclusive Russian future. It also rested on a deeply personal set of beliefs—a "value system"—and like a religious crisis of faith the process of questioning and then abandoning one's beliefs felt for many like a disorienting loss of identity. The lapsed populist, like the lapsed believer, was left without a sense of meaning and purpose, almost in need of a new personality.

Returning to the first half of the nineteenth century, we can see that this psychological dimension had long underwritten the intelligentsia's sense of purpose. Chaadaev had given pure expression to what has been called Russia's "unhappy national consciousness," a feeling not only of dissatisfaction with the country but of a mismatch between nation and self, exclusion from one's own culture, and often a desire to rethink or recreate the national community.[26] Given the state's unflagging emphasis on furthering its imperial aims more than bolstering Russian national unity, it is unsurprising that those, like the populists who were more interested in Russian ethnicity and nationality, would find it difficult to overcome this sense of dissatisfaction. An unhappy national consciousness fosters the need for some compensatory antidote. In Russia that antidote was first supplied by the Slavophile reimagination of Russia as morally superior to the West. In turn, when he formulated the notion of "Russian socialism," Herzen had done so with an eye to leading Europe forward. Populist ideals had always contained a large dose of psychological self-medication for the unhappy consciousness of the intelligentsia. Although the populists of the 1870s, at least those on the left, refrained from open assertions of nationalism, we have seen how they too were concerned with Russia's importance vis-à-vis Western Europe. To have to give up on the idea of the *narod* as Russia's saving grace constituted a loss of self-worth, both personal and national.

Once that loss had fully registered, treatment of the peasantry in literature could be savage, far worse even than what we find in Uspensky's embittered portrayal. Perhaps the best expression of an anti-populist literature is Anton Chekhov's *The Peasants* (1897). In this extended short story, or novella, Chekhov adopts the dispassionate stance of a detached observer in conveying the lives of a peasant family and village that begins in abject misery and only gets worse. The story offers the reader virtually nothing redeeming about the titular peasants. It is not much of an exaggeration to say the inhabitants of the village, Zhukovo, come across as subhuman. So befuddled are they by poverty, illness, drink, labor, and ill-treatment from the authorities that they lack any sympathetic qualities. They can only be pitied for their misery since Chekhov offers the reader nothing to respect in them. The elders look back on serfdom as the best time in their lives, one daughter throws the family's night soil just outside the door of their hut and then unconcernedly trudges through it, while another daughter rejoices when her children die. All of them blame their troubles on the local *zemstvo*, the only local institution with the mission of improving their lives. Olga, an outsider from Moscow who comes to live with them as a daughter-in-law but leaves after her husband dies, ends the story with these parting thoughts:

Over the course of summer and winter there were hours and days in which it seemed that these people live worse than cattle, to live with them was horrible; they were crude, dishonest, dirty, drunk, and constantly fighting with one another since they disrespected, feared and were suspicious of each another. Who has a tavern and makes the *narod* drunk? The peasant. Who wastes and spends on vodka the money of the commune, the school and the church? The peasant. Who steals from his neighbor, burns down his house and gives false testimony in court just for a bottle of vodka? The peasant. At the zemstvo and other meetings who speaks out against the peasant? The peasant. Yes, to live with them was horrible, but all the same they are people, they suffer and cry like people, and they always had an excuse for everything. Hard work that makes the body ache all over at night, cruel winters, meager harvests, close quarters, and no hope of help from anyone.[27]

So bleak is Chekhov's story that it comes across as a sort of counter-exaggeration in opposition to the long-standing tendency to idealize the peasantry. Nor was it merely a matter of isolated personal expression. *The Peasants* was Chekhov's greatest success outside the theater and caused a sensation when it was first published. Chekhov received praise for his unflinching honesty, and reignited a vogue for frank and painful descriptions of life among the *narod*. Chekhov's younger contemporaries, Maxim Gorky and Ivan Bunin, often showed a similar contempt for the peasantry. One scholar wrote that Gorky regarded the peasants as "weak, cowardly, lazy, greedy, submissive, intolerant, irrational and violent."[28] Part of this literary disdain for the rural poor was in keeping with the strictures of critical realism. Chekhov's story can be justified either as an honest look at the peasant world in all its unvarnished reality or as a critical call for renewed attention directed toward the impoverished Russian people. The famine in the early 1890s had, after all, exposed the dire straits into which so many peasants had fallen after the emancipation. But for some among the intelligentsia it would seem that disappointment in the peasantry had led not just to renouncing the *narod*, as Dostoevsky predicted would happen, but to laying some of the blame for Russia's troubles on their "bad habits." Not everyone held this view. Tolstoy, to his death a believer in the innate worth of the common man, wrote that Chekhov did not know the *narod* and called his story "a sin against the people." But in spite of increasing scorn for the world of the peasant in the 1880s and 1890s, both "small deeds" and radical acts in the name of the *narod* continued to simmer at a low level. Around the turn of the twentieth century a novel form of populism, often referred to as "neo-populism," arose to play a central role in revolutionary Russia.

CHAPTER 8
NEO-POPULISM

Marx is our great common teacher in the realm of economics, but we do not feel constrained to make him an idol.

Viktor Chernov

In the year 1897, Chekhov was hard at work writing *The Peasants* on his estate of Melikhovo. That same year, the 24-year-old Viktor Chernov, who had been exiled from Moscow for radical activism, lived some three hundred miles to the south in Tambov Province, where he was working to organize the local peasantry into a revolutionary force. He began by distributing books, having discovered that some of the workers and peasants in the local region were, far from the brutes Chekhov had described, literate and eager for information. He visited a group of rural protestant sectarians, known as *Molokane* [Milk Drinkers], in an attempt to turn their religious dissent in a political direction. Working among the people, he learned how to avoid intelligentsia jargon and speak about socialism and revolution as a form of justice and right, in moral terms local people understood and appreciated. Together with an intelligentsia associate and a small group of peasants he organized a revolutionary association they called a "Brotherhood for the Defense of the People's Right," and they hoped to establish a web of such brotherhoods on a national level. Unlike populists of an earlier generation whose inspiration had been drawn from an external idealization of the *narod*, and who had gone to the people without knowing much about them, Chernov's political activity came into its own within the countryside, among the people who lived there.

He soon went abroad in pursuit of funding, and there among a cohort of populist exiles his optimism and erudition as a revolutionary theorist enabled him to help revive the fortunes of a moribund populism and rechannel it into the revolutionary force it would become in the early twentieth century. The sometimes blinkered idealization of the *narod* that accompanied earlier populist thinking, and did in many ways merit criticism, went into remission during the final two decades of the nineteenth century, but that did not mean the peasant question lost importance for educated society. The famine of 1891 and 1892 in rural Russia provoked another sort of movement to the people, this time as a matter of hunger relief, and the "small deeds" approach to building better conditions in the countryside, mostly through the *zemstvo*, continued unabated. The *narod* remained important for the intelligentsia both as Russia's struggling majority population, in need of their help and as a potential force of revolutionary power if only their resentments could be harnessed to a larger cause.

In the meanwhile, a new approach to revolution was gaining credence among the intelligentsia. Plekhanov's shift to Marxism in the early 1880s at first left him whistling into the wind of general indifference, mainly because Marx's analysis of history did not conform to Russian circumstances. But over the final decades of the nineteenth century Russian industrialization began to undergo a period of rapid development. As a result, former peasants were streaming into cities and factory settlements by the millions and, facing low wages and miserable conditions, were often becoming politically active as a new Russian proletariat. Some of them began to resemble the politically conscious working class upon which Marx and Engels had rested their expectations for revolutionary change. A Russian bourgeoisie of a sort was also taking shape. As a result of this turn, an increasing willingness arose among politically engaged intellectuals to adopt Marxism as Russia's path toward overthrowing the autocracy and establishing a socialist state. By the early twentieth century, Plekhanov had been joined by many thousands of allies (and Marxist competitors) drawing on Marxism as their source of revolutionary inspiration.

Still, as much as the advent of industrialization and Marxist ideology transformed the political landscape, it did not change the fact that Russia remained a predominantly agricultural country, whose majority population remained the peasantry. The Marxist view that a rising bourgeoisie would lead, in Russia as it had elsewhere, to a liberal democratic revolution, eventually to be followed, it was hoped, by a communist revolution of the proletarian masses, looked increasingly possible. But what role would be played by Russia's peasant majority? There was no significant place in Marxist thinking for the great majority of the Russian population. Marx and Engels considered the peasantry an archaic social class, a "petty bourgeoisie," destined over the course of history either to rise into the bourgeoisie or to get swept into the proletariat as wage laborers. The intelligentsia had either to reject the applicability of Marxist theory to Russia, to accept Marx and ignore this incongruity as a passing phase, or to somehow redirect Marxist theory so that it could apply to Russian circumstances. It fell to the inheritors of the populist tradition, the neo-populists such as Chernov, to follow the final course and rethink how revolutionary Marxism might more successfully correspond to Russian conditions. Populism survived the onset of Marxism, but it did so, as M.C. Howard has noted, "only by transforming its stand in ways which made major concessions to the Marxian critics."[1] Indeed, one of the best ways to think about neo-populism is to consider it populism under the influence of, and in direct competition with, Marxism.

The "New" in Neo-Populism

Chernov had gotten his start in radical circles working with the long-standing socialist leader Mark Natanson, a founder of both the Chaikovsky Circle and the second Land and Freedom. In 1894 Natanson organized the People's Rights Party, which advocated public, rather than underground, protest as a method of agitation. Not surprisingly, given the state's usual aversion to public protest, such open demonstration only led to the party's rapid eradication. Both Natanson and Chernov were arrested and sent into exile. In Tambov Province, between 1895 and 1899, Chernov cut his teeth as a revolutionary in collaboration with local peasant activists. The idea behind the peasant brotherhoods—

whose activities were mainly peaceful forms of protest like rural labor strikes and boycotts—was to create an entity that had not existed in the 1870s: a political organization that originated with and was carried out largely by the peasants themselves. It is doubtful that such organizations would have emerged in the absence of outside intervention, but they were willingly joined by politically active peasants who demonstrated in some local skirmishes that they had the capacity to effect positive changes in their material well-being. To some extent, then, the revitalization of the populist movement in this period was not just attributable to revived intelligentsia enthusiasm but to changing facts on the ground in the countryside.

Due to a wave of arrests that imprisoned dozens of his colleagues, Chernov decided to go abroad and seek help from the populist emigration in the attempt to set the peasant brotherhoods on a more national footing. To expand the reach of his local organization, Chernov published the constitution he had written for the first peasant brotherhood. Among the populist exile community this publication generated some enthusiasm and raised Chernov's stature. Not long after Chernov's arrival in Western Europe, the grandfather of that community, Petr Lavrov, died in Paris in 1900. His funeral inadvertently set the stage for a gathering of veteran populists from various parts of Europe. This event gave them an opportunity to reunite and reinvigorate the movement, and it led to the formation of the Agrarian Socialist League, primarily a publishing venture intended to generate propaganda materials for populist activists back home in Russia. It also launched the journal, *Revolutionary Russia*, edited by Chernov, in which they debated and worked out the new theories and tactics that became the heart of neo-populist thought.

On the pages of *Revolutionary Russia* Chernov would become the chief theorist of neo-populism and a towering figure within the soon-to-be-founded Socialist Revolutionary Party. His primary contribution involved combining and rethinking populism and Marxism. Important as his contributions were, Chernov was by no means the sole originator of neo-populism. A renewed populist movement based primarily on agitation among the urban working class had been gathering momentum in several Russian regions during the late 1890s. In 1896 Andrei Argunov founded the Union of Socialist Revolutionaries while another group took the name Party of the Socialist Revolutionaries. By 1901 these organizations would merge into a single Socialist Revolutionary Party (PSR, commonly known as the SRs), which soon joined forces with the Agrarian Socialist League to comprise a united front of SRs that would become synonymous with neo-populism. The original merger was concluded in an agreement made by two populist leaders still in Russia, Grigory Gershuni and Evno Azef, who together would go on to lead the revitalized terrorist wing of neo-populism. Chernov, as theorist in exile, played for the Socialist Revolutionary Party a role comparable to Lenin's intellectual role in the Bolshevik Party, but where Lenin assumed all leadership capacities Chernov was supported by the organizational, recruitment, and tactical talents of Gershuni, Azef, and Abram Gots. Since the new populism was largely the brainchild of Chernov, we must begin with an examination of his theoretical renovation of populism.

Chernov's contribution to neo-populism has been portrayed alternately as a continuation of classical populism and as a reworked form of Marxism, but there is little

Figure 8.1 Viktor Chernov © Out of copyright (public domain).

reason to emphasize one side over the other. In many ways Chernov's views did resemble those of the earlier populists. He had worked with Natanson and Mikhailovsky, he was deeply influenced by the poetry of Nekrasov, and he had great respect for the "heroic" terrorist underground of The People's Will. But as we saw in the last chapter, much had changed in the 1880s and 1890s. The central assumption of the original radical populists, that communalism made the *narod* receptive to modern socialism, had been discredited over and over again, and that other cornerstone of the populist faith, the peasantry's supposedly dormant rebelliousness, had begun to erode as early as the summer of 1874. Moreover, as Marxism grew more and more familiar to the Russian intelligentsia the theory and thought of Marx and Engels became impossible to ignore. Chernov understood the intellectual task before him as a matter of uniting the best parts of populism with the best parts of Marxism, while jettisoning any intellectual errors or contradictions. This task required adapting the large and growing body of Western European revolutionary socialist literature to conditions on the ground in Russia. It was a monumental undertaking, it was never completed to anyone's full satisfaction, including to Chernov's, but the work he did eventually led to the first Congress of Socialist Revolutionaries formally ratifying a party program, a summation of the neo-populist creed and statement of its aims and intentions.

As a first step, Chernov discarded the utopian vagaries about the promise of the commune and peasant-centered revolution that had bedeviled populism in its heyday. He put in their place an honest recognition of the rise of capitalism in Russia, the revolutionary importance of the urban proletariat, and a more fully worked out set of guidelines for how to foment revolution throughout Russian society. The immediate aim was to overthrow the autocracy and introduce full democracy, while the ultimate aim would be to bring economic equality to the whole of the working class, proletarian and peasant alike. Chernov did not entirely abandon the notion that peasant communalism could play a role in achieving these aims, but he rejected the "mystical halo" it had worn in an earlier phase.[2] Faith in communalism had made populism appear foolish and turned it into an easy mark for the growing number of Marxist opponents. In general one no longer finds in neo-populism any expression of a hidden inner spirit or a special destiny in the Russian peasant, nor does one find any disdain for the urban worker as a degraded example of the exalted rural prototype. Chernov, like his Marxist rivals, was a Westernizer. He considered the Russian peasants to be a part of the European population, if a part that had long suffered as the upper class's beast of burden, rather than the nationally unique stepping stone toward a socialist future the original populists considered them. He also abandoned the older generation's desperate resistance to capitalism and industrialization, accepting them as an inevitable part of economic growth and needed modernization. He even accepted the inevitability of capitalism's encroachment on life in the countryside, having seen with his own eyes just how common wage labor and the rent and purchase of land had become in rural Russia. But to accept these developments he had to commit the "heresy" of a fundamental rethinking of Marx. For Chernov and the SRs the peasantry was not a social archaism as it had been for Marx. At least under Russian conditions the peasantry could be considered an exploited class with reason to rebel. It did not stand in contrast to the urban proletariat. It was part of the proletariat, if a less politically conscious form. Chernov rethought Marx to develop the view that "proletarian" peasants might also be radicalized by capitalism, so warding off capitalism was no longer a life or death necessity as it had been to the earlier populists.

Chernov's realism with respect to historical changes taking place in Russia marked a sharp difference between neo-populism and the urgent idealist insistence on preventing change that had defined the previous generation. It is, then, a reasonable question to ask: How, lacking those earlier ideals of classical populism, could Chernov and the SRs retain the confidence to fight for revolution? Part of the answer is that the neo-populist's conditional acceptance of Marxism convinced them that a powerful new force of revolutionary dynamism had arisen in the form of a growing urban proletariat. Recognizing the tactical strength of the industrial working class, the neo-populists stood them at the center of their revolutionary plans. Unlike the Marxists, who separated the proletariat from the peasantry, and focused their attention almost exclusively on the urban working class, the SRs envisioned both classes together engaged in a single struggle to overthrow the autocracy and establish a more egalitarian society. In fact, they believed a revolution would not even be possible without the help of both sectors, even though they placed the workers in the forefront as the vanguard of the revolutionary forces and saw the peasantry as the proletariat's large reserve army. Michael Melancon in particular in recent years has driven home the point that while the SRs are known for their peasant focus and their emphasis on the usefulness of terrorism, the primary focus of their agitational activity was the factory and the industrial workforce, a point that had gotten lost in the attempt to establish clean lines between the Marxist Social Democrats (SDs) as the party of the working class and the SRs as the party of the peasantry. Orthodox Marxists did look down on Chernov's revolutionary plans as a misunderstanding and bastardization of Marx's view of history, but Chernov retorted that he was reading Marx differently, following his thinking down the road it would have taken Marx himself had he lived longer. He also rejected the need for an orthodox understanding of Marxism, making the statement in this chapter's epigraph that "Marx is our great common teacher in the realm of economics, but we do not feel constrained to make him an idol."[3] That restraint notwithstanding, a great deal of Chernov's thinking, even the language he used, was indebted to Marxism, as when he wrote about the peasantry as a class whose labor was "still not alienated from the means of production" and therefore "approximating the proletariat."[4]

The open-ended and flexible nature of neo-populism was both its great strength and a fundamental weakness. It facilitated quick shifts in tactics, but it also left neo-populism open to a great deal of internal dissension and also somewhat rudderless in the absence of a firm guiding plan. In creating the SR party program, Chernov sought to address the lack of guiding principles, and while the party did grow more organized, it still suffered from a huge amount of inner conflict. It is true that Russian Marxism also split into two separate and competing parties, Bolsheviks and Mensheviks, but both of these were more clearly defined according to specific, spelled-out principles and dogmas, and both were firmly convinced about the accuracy of their understanding of historical destiny and political strategy. The neo-populists, by contrast, sought to keep a single party united by offering disparate elements each their own sphere of influence. That approach rendered the SR Party something of a patchwork organization, stitched together loosely, and the internal divisions would continue to plague them, just as the formal split of the two Social Democratic parties sapped them of a collective potential they may have had had they managed to remain unified.

Because of their big-tent approach, the SRs could boast of being a large and popular party, larger than either the Bolsheviks or the Mensheviks, and nearly as large as both combined. At the same time they had to struggle to define themselves and try to live with the internal feuding and the multiple cleavages that defined them. They had somehow to fuse together within one party an agitational campaign to rouse the masses to revolution and an underground organization engaged in political violence against state officials. They had to grapple with how much agitational effort to devote to urban workers and how much to the peasantry. They fought over whether to move decisively toward a socialist revolution in the name of the people or whether to join with the liberals in accepting an initial phase of "bourgeois" revolution. These and many other issues had to be dealt with during the revolutionary period of the early twentieth century that witnessed a constantly shifting political landscape.

Neo-Populists, Workers, and Peasants

A large source of the tension among the SRs sprang from a problem any revolutionary party would like to have: they found themselves in a society growing much more politically active than it ever had been in the past. In the nineteenth century virtually the only politically active Russians came from among the intelligentsia. Those few peasants and workers who did join the revolutionary forces were often labeled "former" workers or peasants because their political consciousness seemed to place them among the intelligentsia. But by the early twentieth century it was increasingly possible to retain one's original social status while holding newfound political convictions, to be considered, for example a "peasant revolutionary," or a "Marxist worker." Under the new circumstances, the SRs had to decide where their constituency lay, among the peasants or the workers. On the up side, they could and did pursue connections and influence among both groups because as a result of their general adaptability, unlike the SDs—who were hamstrung by a less flexible set of assumptions about how revolutions come about—the SRs had the freedom, even the moral compulsion, to fight for a change in any way they deemed effective. On the down side, it was more difficult for them to retain a clear identity as a political party, their efforts were spread thin across a larger group of supporters, and they had a tendency to shift from one primary goal to another.

For this reason historians have found it difficult to agree on the central objectives of the SRs. As noted above, there has been a long-standing tendency to define them against the SDs, the party of the industrial worker, as the party of the peasantry, whose main aims and activities were focused on agitation in the countryside. But this distinction does not hold up to scrutiny. Within Russia, Chernov's positive experiences with the peasant brotherhoods had been an anomaly. Most neo-populists continued to believe the peasantry lacked revolutionary potential, and they focused their agitational efforts on the urban working class. They certainly considered the peasantry worthy of consideration as a huge part of the working class, and in that way they made a valid contrast to the SDs, but it was widely accepted in all socialist parties that only the proletariat possessed the potential to ignite a revolution. "Our Tasks," an early statement made prior to the unification of the SR Party, was unequivocal in its position that "a conscious *mass revolutionary* movement of the peasantry is at present impossible."[5] The SR focus on the working class is one good reason to regard them as neo-populist rather than simply retain the old word *narodnik* [populist]. In the SR party program put forward in 1906, one finds limited mention of any difference between peasants and workers. Instead, the document emphasizes conflict on a broader scale, that between exploiters and exploited. It even proclaims as a central objective "to make all layers of the toiling and exploited people awake that they are one working class."[6] In setting out their specific goals the program prioritizes as its first item SR policy toward industrial workers, although the second item, their policy toward the peasantry receives equal attention.

In Russia most workers hailed from the peasantry and were still connected to their rural roots. Marx's rather absolute distinction between peasant and worker thus seemed somewhat artificial in the Russian context. The focus on factory labor was not only perfectly natural but also extremely useful for the SR Party. The majority of their supporters were found among the urban working classes, and their ability to declare themselves representatives of all working and exploited people in Russia gave them an advantage over the SDs. For many Russian workers, with roots in the country and the city, the SRs were speaking to both sides of their personal interest. In fact, the great success of the SRs in attracting workers infuriated Lenin, who felt they were malevolently stripping away supporters who should have "naturally" gravitated toward Marxism. Gershuni claimed Lenin feared the SRs more than he did the autocracy. Partly to counter SR influence, the 1903 Bolshevik Party program included a whole section aimed at ameliorating the condition of the peasantry where the Menshevik program, in proper Marxist fashion, ignored the peasantry almost entirely. As such a Bolshevik countermeasure suggests, the SRs and SDs, enemies as they were, helped to shape the other's policies and agenda.

It is possible that the SR's original focus on the urban worker may have grown even more central over time had not the peasantry itself begun to demonstrate a more rebellious character in the year 1902. We need not reiterate that, contrary to populist habits of thought, there was no such thing as "the" peasantry, since peasant society varied socially and culturally across the enormity of the Russian Empire. Any attempt to understand the *narod* in its entirety grew even more complicated after 1861 when the emancipation and reforms created a new dynamism in the village, rendering the rural population a rapidly moving target. Russia as a whole in this period was undergoing seismic change, mostly as a result of trying to keep up with a rapidly modernizing world. Industrialization, the increasingly sophisticated tools of capitalism, the effects of technological advancement, and demands for greater participation in public affairs all worked to reshape Russian society in the early twentieth century. Far from immune to these changes, in some ways the countryside was affected even more than any other sector. As a result of its relative isolation, it had the furthest to go. Some changes in peasant life during this period resulted from direct and intentional efforts by the state. Establishment of the *zemstvo* helped expand education and increase literacy among the peasantry, and that literacy, accompanied by a rapidly expanding press, in turn afforded rural people greater access to information and ideas that hitherto circulated almost exclusively in the cities and among the well-educated. Even more significantly, the industrialization that had gotten underway at midcentury with the building of railroads was bolstered by the state through new economic policies beginning in the late 1880s, and more and more peasants began to migrate temporarily or permanently into the cities as workers where they inevitably began to gain a larger and more complex conception of the world. The large worker strikes that took place in the middle of the 1890s even helped contribute to an expanded understanding of political rights and demands. In short, the *narod* to whom the populists flocked but found unreceptive in the 1870s was no longer the same *narod* at the turn of the century.

While literacy and a growing connection to the rest of society were positive gains for the peasants, persistent and growing economic troubles affected them as much or more. Not only was the peasantry the sector of society responsible for the large majority of the tax burden, even as they continued to make redemption payments, but a population explosion in the countryside in the post-emancipation period meant less land per capita and consequent loss of income. On top of this, an increasing social differentiation led to grinding poverty for those who were left behind. One thing was clear throughout rural

Russia in the post-emancipation years: the peasants wanted and needed more land. They had long complained that the landowners had received an unfairly large proportion of the land in the emancipation settlement. After a poor harvest in 1901 and under threat of another famine in the spring of 1902, revolts broke out near Kharkov and Poltava, which subsequently spread to the Volga and Urals regions. Although the revolts were carried out and justified in different ways depending on the region, they functioned according to a broadly similar pattern that would reemerge in 1905 and 1917. The peasants, often justifying their actions based on rumors (or perhaps self-protective protestations) that the Tsar had commanded them, took over lands owned by local gentry in the name of the village commune. Most of these actions were peaceful, although gentry estates were often burned to the ground as a signal that the landowner should not return. Seizing land in the name of the commune and then redistributing it through communal structures shows that peasant communalism remained alive at least as a tool with which to confront opponents outside the village. To take the land in the name of the commune was a good way to minimize personal responsibility, and it is clear that the peasants were shedding some of their former docility. In some parts of the countryside there was growing awareness of the fact that the peasantry was bearing much of the labor and poverty burden for the rest of Russia. Maureen Perrie has described this attitude, however rare in 1902, as a recognition of the demand for social justice: "why should they starve, when the *pomeshchik*'s [landowner's] barns were full of grain and hay which they, the peasants, had labored to produce; and why should the gentry claim land, when they did not work it with their own hands?"[7]

The SRs responded with enthusiasm to the unexpected revolts. They revitalized the old hope that that the peasantry might constitute a revolutionary force, although this recognition of the peasantry did not entail the SRs abandoning the urban working class in order to become a peasant party as some have suggested. Even after 1905 the populists would still consider industrial workers to be the leading edge of the coming revolution. In order to connect with and encourage the peasantry the party instituted the SR-Peasant Union, which expanded their base of support. Some party members went physically again to work in the villages and to help radicalize the people they found there, who included the "village intelligentsia" of educated peasants and the "third element" of *zemstvo* workers, many of whom chose to join the Socialist Revolutionary Party. Under these circumstances it seems less surprising that the neo-populists had greater success than previous generations making inroads into peasant communities and finding a mutual language in which to discuss political and economic concerns.

As we begin to publish *Krest'ianskoe Delo* we ought to tell you who we are and what we want. First of all—we are town dwellers and know village life only from the sidelines. And yet we have taken it upon ourselves to discuss peasant needs and peasant affairs. Whether we are capable of this task, our village readers will decide for themselves. We ourselves see the matter like this: perhaps we shall make mistakes in little things, in details; perhaps we shall not express ourselves the way the peasants are used to talking; perhaps as a result of this the peasants will fail to understand some of the things in our newspaper, or will not understand them in the way we intended. But we are convinced that we have a more correct understanding of the causes of peasant poverty than have the peasants themselves, and that we know better than they do how they can escape from their unhappy position. And this being so, it would be a sin for us to keep silent.

> First issue of *The Peasant Cause* (1901), trans. Maureen Perrie,
> in *The Agrarian Policy of the Russian Socialist-Revolutionary Party*

Socialist Revolutionary Ideology

The SRs did not like to put limits on themselves. Emphasizing the need to work among both peasants and urban workers, combining elements of Marxism with earlier populism, still relying on terrorist attacks to destabilize the government, and hoping to unite all of these separate elements into a single common cause, neo-populism employed multiple separate strategies which never really came together as a unified plan of action. Radkey noted long ago that "chaos might be termed the normal state of affairs within the SR organization."[8] This quip exaggerates their disorganization to a degree because they all did share the unifying purpose of curtailing autocratic absolutism. That basic aim seems to have been enough to see the party through to 1917. In the meanwhile, they had little choice but to coexist as a tangle of sometimes overlapping, sometimes competing, views under the broad umbrella of ending the old regime and ushering in, sooner or later, a socialist future.

Chernov's party program joined the demand for all the rights and freedoms of elected government together with laws to improve conditions for factory labor (on the path toward full socialism). With respect to the peasantry the SR program was unique and centered on Chernov's original concept of the "socialization" of the Russian land. Oddly enough, to the untrained eye a comparison between the SD and SR party programs would appear nearly identical. The differences appear to consist more in tone and subtle distinctions than in clearly articulated differences. In truth, such subtleties masked huge underlying differences that, the parties believed, determined whether or not their revolutionary efforts had a chance of success. There was, however, good reason for the apparent similarity. All revolutionary parties were hoping to appeal to the Russian masses and thus to offer each sector of society what it desired. As for the SRs, to build an acceptable party ideology they had to perform a balancing act. They had to show themselves capable of competing with the attractions of the orthodox Marxist path to socialism while also remaining true to what was left of their populist conception of the peasantry. To compete with the Marxists, the populists needed to attract the support of both workers and peasants and to provide a plausible road map to the revolution that would find a place for all the Russian "toilers." Because they were in competition with the SDs, it behooves us to begin with a comparison between what the SD and SR parties had to offer.

Many of the classical populists had read at least some of Marx. They did not necessarily dispute his diagnosis of Western European conditions, even to the point of accepting that a proletarian revolution was imminent in the West, but that analysis left Russia out of the loop as a kind of latecomer to socialism, a revolutionary afterthought. As the equation changed with the advent of Russian industrialization, it became increasingly difficult to deny that Russia now possessed a small but not insignificant bourgeoisie and proletariat. According to Marx, the struggle between these two classes would lead to a proletarian revolution. This fact alone offered only a thin and distant hope that Russia might, one day, follow in Europe's footsteps. It was bland fare compared to the wildly optimistic promise classical populism had held out to its adherents that they would act as the vanguard of socialism and lead the rest of Europe into the socialist future. But the appeal of Marxism did not rest only on the need to adjust to changing conditions. In a series of studies Plekhanov, like Marx himself a brilliant writer, was able to contrast populism's faith in a false idealization of the *narod* with the compelling argument that Marx's understanding of the course of history had developed not out of hopes and dreams but on the basis of the latest and most up-to-date social science. Plekhanov held that Marx had established a new science of historical development, that his views, although understood variously, were supported by the large majority of European socialists in the late nineteenth century, and that they applied not only to one country, or only to Europe, but to all of human history. Moreover, from a socialist perspective Marxism furnished the satisfyingly optimistic claim that a revolution of the working class was historically inevitable. Marx's authority was difficult to refute. By contrast, the populists had lost confidence in the communal and revolutionary spirit of the *narod* and lacked any theory of history to stand up against Marxism.

On the other hand, Marxism still faced some major difficulties when applied to Russia. For Marx, history moved in stages determined by social classes and socially organized forms of production. The revolution that put the middle class (bourgeoisie) into power had to precede the revolution that put the working class (proletariat) in power. But even after the emancipation in most ways the Russian Empire still somewhat resembled a feudal system, with a landed gentry, an autocratic ruler, and a mass of subsistence farmers supporting them. Russia's future had to proceed through a liberal revolution to put the industrial middle class in power before the working class could become sophisticated enough to develop the "class consciousness" and revolutionary vigor it would need to overthrow the bourgeoisie, a so-called "inevitability" that nonetheless had not yet occurred in a single European country. Russian Marxists found themselves in the awkward position of supporting the working class and a radically transformed future while still advocating for a revolution to empower middle-class liberals. Partly as a result of these problems, just as they were gaining strength in the early twentieth century the SDs fell into passionate conflict with one another and in 1903 split into two separate parties of Mensheviks and Bolsheviks. The Mensheviks tended to favor working with liberals to bring about a bourgeois revolution, even while supporting and nurturing the revolutionary spirit of the working class. The Bolsheviks under Lenin saw Russian circumstances as unique and stole a page from the populist underground, favoring close party unity, conspiratorial techniques, and enlisting the support of the peasantry. The Bolsheviks also expressed ambivalence about revolutionary stages and welcomed the early advent of a workers' revolution.

Meanwhile the SRs continued to press a number of advantages they enjoyed. Unlike the SDs, especially the more conservative Mensheviks, they had no compunction about working toward an immediate popular revolution, nor did they feel compelled to limit their activism to a single social class. The populists could stand up for all the working poor. The proper Marxist approach to the countryside was to assume the rapid advance of capitalism and do nothing to hinder its advent—even at the expense of increasing impoverishment among the peasant have-nots—for the expansion of capitalism would all the sooner lead to revolution. This position could not have endeared them to those peasants, who wished to take over gentry-held private lands as their own. The neo-populists, on the other hand, supported the continuation of communal relations. They could accuse the Marxists of betraying the *narod* in their support for the rising "bourgeoisie" of *kulaki* and gentry landowners, and it was indeed difficult for the uninitiated peasant or worker to understand why a revolution should benefit the wealthy. Chernov absolutely opposed the Marxist idea that the peasantry was a force of reaction as a small-time bourgeoisie. He refused to see independent farming as "owning the means of production." For Chernov the peasantry was just another variant of exploited labor, only in their case they were exploited by taxes, high rents, low wages, and redemption payments. He held that the peasantry had an enormous revolutionary role to play. Since they paid the majority of the taxes and supplied the majority of the army's soldiers, removing those advantages from the autocracy would weaken it more than anything the still comparatively diminutive proletariat could accomplish. Unfortunately, most peasants did not yet recognize the power they held, but that did not mean they never would.

One other advantage neo-populism enjoyed involved populism's traditional voluntarism. While it was certainly an attraction of Marxism that it seemed to foretell an ineluctable socialist revolution, the neo-populists brandished the contrasting, but no less attractive, argument that human beings had the capacity to shape history. In place of a teleological march of history, the populists held up a bold call to action, rejecting the idea that history has a foreordained path and claiming for themselves the role of, especially by contrast to the passive Marxists siding with liberals, courageous revolutionary fighters. From a Marxist viewpoint, events mainly beyond our control led history forward, but for the populists it was comforting to know that individual will and action still mattered. This proposition had great appeal among revolutionary activists, not the types to twiddle their thumbs and let history take its course. Even Marx himself would show impatience with the quietist element of his philosophy of history: "the philosophers have only interpreted the world in various ways; the point, however, is to *change* it." Another Marxist, Lenin, would take revolutionary matters into his own hands to such an extent that his views can be regarded as a voluntaristic repudiation of Orthodox Marxism.

For the neo-populists socialism was not, as Herzen and others had argued, an especially national character trait. It was simply a more advanced stage of human development that, at best, Russia might more easily adapt to because of the relatively recent arrival of capitalism and the ingrained habit of communal practices. Marx himself had written a letter to Vera Zasulich in 1881, near the end of his life, in which he claimed to be convinced that the commune "is the mainspring of Russia's social regeneration" even though "deleterious influences . . . assail it from every quarter," so the neo-populists had no theoretical reason to deny it might be helpful.[9] One could say that neo-populist thinking about peasant communalism borrowed from both Uspensky's pessimism and Zlatovratsky's optimism. Like Uspensky, the neo-populists accepted that the commune was not a form of socialism, not necessarily beneficial to the majority of the peasants, and easily corrupted. Like Zlatovratsky, they found in communalism a mentality that would ultimately make socialization of the land easier. When challenged about the efficacy of their program in 1908, the Central Committee actually fell back on something close to Zlatovratsky's defense of communalism not as a concrete practice but as a set of internalized values: "Our expectations and hopes, our program rest not upon the fact of communal land ownership . . . itself, but rather on the complex of ideas, feelings, and customs, on that collective psychology bred into the peasantry by the whole previous history."[10]

In keeping with populist tradition, the SRs continued to ponder the optimal means of rousing revolutionary and socialist passions in the countryside. In this regard, Chernov's most innovative idea was the concept of "socialization," the jewel in the crown of neo-populist plans for the peasantry. From a modern Western vantage point socialization is an undoubtedly foreign concept. To explain it we can begin by contrasting it to three related but separate and distinct ideas: communalism, nationalization, and socialism. Communalism, of course, was the form of social organization by which a peasant village parceled out its land according to need. It was local and limited, while socialization was to be carried out on a national level. Nationalization, a more familiar idea whereby the state takes over ownership of some formerly private property in order to benefit society, was also distinct from socialization because socialization did not come from above at the state's behest. Finally, socialization was only a stepping stone toward full socialism, which would comprise a society and economy based on cooperation and equality, rather than economic competition.

Socialization was Chernov's plan for taking a widely held view among the peasants—that land should not be regarded as personal property but rather as a resource that every human being had the right to access—and turning it into a vehicle for the transformation to a socialist society. As one peasant representative put it at a meeting of the All-Russian Peasant Union in 1905 "The people see the land as the gift of God, like air and water. Those who need it should receive it."[11] As a policy, socialization meant first to eradicate the validity of property in land. The land would belong to no one, not even to the state; it would be the property of the whole society. In Chernov's words, "we shall make it no one's and precisely as no one's does it become the belonging of all."[12] As a result of the new legal standing of the land, regional authorities like townships and villages would begin to farm the privately owned lands they understood to be rightfully theirs because they were making that land productive. Such local entities would parcel out land according to need, in an egalitarian fashion and always with the view in mind that agricultural usage determined possession but not legal ownership.

The idea that socialization could take place from below was just the sort of thing the Marxist parties scoffed at in the SRs as utopian socialism. For the Marxists, sweeping change like this could not take place without putting the state in the hands of the working class. The Mensheviks as a rule wanted to expand the social power of the property-holding bourgeoisie so as eventually to expand the proletariat and usher in a revolution in the name of the workers. The Bolsheviks sought to nationalize the land as part of a forced-march revolution in the name of the working classes. The policy of socialization reveals one aspect of the distinct character of the SR Party. They continued to hold the faith that the *narod* had the capacity to work things out for themselves at the level of the village. They were, as Chernov put it, "great friends of decentralization."[13] The neo-populists no longer, as their predecessors had, trusted the peasants to make a quick transition to socialist cooperation on the basis of the commune, but their method of arriving at a socialist future was strongly democratic in that they believed the *narod* could and should conclude in their own minds what that future use of the land would look like. They realized a centralized state would be necessary but wanted to limit it and create a socialist future that would be federative, with as much local control as possible.

As much as the neo-populists may deserve credit for their democratic instincts, it cannot go unnoticed that the realization of a policy like socialization lay somewhere between the realms of the impossible and the disastrous. Keeping their policies vague, they never faced up to the real problems that would surely have followed any attempt to put socialization into practice. The first obvious problem is the division of the land. How would it be possible to parcel out land in equal shares when land itself is not equal? Rich, fertile soil predominates in certain areas, and in other areas the soil is unproductive or overused. Second, as Engelgardt so often emphasized, the quality of the farmers themselves varies a great deal, and some would quickly get wealthier than others. Third, population density was much thicker in some areas than in others. While socialization would certainly mean the peasants would acquire a great deal of extra land on the aggregate, it proposed no mechanism by which to ensure that likely struggles over access to the best lands would not occur. Not only could the inability to ensure equality lead to violence and renewed exploitation, but it would be the duty of the governing authority to intervene, thereby setting up the state the SRs hoped to lead as the necessary guarantor of law and order, or as a body that functioned to control the people.

Socialization was one platform of the SR Party program that was adopted at their first party congress in Imatra, Finland at the beginning of 1906. That program, although continuously in dispute, managed to last unchanged all the way to October of 1917. By 1906 Chernov, the program's primary author, had been working out the details for several years. In 1902 he had introduced the concept of a minimum and a maximum program, which he might just as well have called the short-term and long-term goals of the party. The minimum goal included socialization of the land along with democratic rights and major improvements for industrial workers (an eight-hour workday, a high minimum wage, and unionization), while the maximum goal called for a fully socialist economy in both manufacturing and agriculture. The two-tiered process aimed to ensure that the SRs in power would not overstep the limits of the possible and thereby conjure up disaster. The 1906 party program draws a great deal of its language and thinking from Marx. It speaks of the socialist struggle as "international in nature" and it claims as its primary goal "the intellectual, political, and economic emancipation of the working class."[14] Although the SRs, under the influence of Marx, assumed an immediate post-revolutionary world would be dominated by the liberal middle class, they refused to accept any form of constitutional monarchy, and they even added a proviso that in case of need they would resort to a temporary revolutionary dictatorship as a means of moving toward the maximum program.

Closing ranks around a specific program, however, had the practical effect of generating factionalism with respect to the more contentious issues the program raised. Party unity had been at its peak in the years leading up to the congress, but after the congress the fissures grew increasingly apparent. Chernov's very language of a minimum and maximum program provided an excuse for a splinter group on the far left of the party to break away as "maximalists," i.e., those who favored immediate adoption of the maximum program and refused to sit through the "bourgeois" phase of the minimum program. The maximalists favored relying on a small band of professional revolutionary terrorists and reproached the party's Central Committee for placing too much faith in an indeterminate popular uprising. They also objected to the hierarchical structure of the party. After further contention over the role of the party's terrorist wing, in 1909 the right wing of the party began to voice strong objections to the use of terror as an illusory projection of strength, and they tried to turn the party exclusively toward work at a grassroots level among the peasants and workers, noting that the *narod* was everywhere growing more politicized. As S.N. Sletov put it: "Today is needed the organizer of the future victory, who is able to organize on the basis of local interests."[15] In this way the SRs were continuing to grapple with those same questions that had first been raised in the 1870s and 1880s. Should we return to working among the people in order to bring about a revolution based on mass participation, or should we continue to fight for political power through the use of violent attacks against government officials? The Central Committee had depended on a combination of the two, but in 1908 the use of clandestine terror would blow up in their faces as a catastrophic mistake.

The Combat Organization

In spite of the various innovations of neo-populism, the SRs held true to the old idea that terrorism was a useful weapon in the revolutionary arsenal. Today the use of violence for political purposes (outside of a military context) is usually condemned as illegitimate even in a revolutionary context. Even the Bolsheviks who, once in power, relied on massive use of violence typically showed disdain for terrorism as a form of political struggle. The SRs, on the other hand, had inherited from the populism of the 1870s and 1880s the conviction that terrorism could serve to promote their cause. One reason they put their trust in it had to do with the particular form of terrorism they engaged in. Their political violence targeted not civilians but active government officials easily portrayed as enemy combatants, although "collateral damage" to innocent bystanders did sometimes occur. The neo-populists who engaged in terror set themselves up as heroic warriors in the fight to bring down a corrupt and oppressive autocracy on behalf of a society in desperate need of a democratic government. Even to relatively moderate public opinion this characterization often seemed reasonable. In a detailed analysis of the SR terrorist Maria Spiridonova, Sally Boniece notes that the use of "heroic" terror by the members of The People's Will had produced what she calls a "behavioral text" that neo-populists could and did latch onto in order to justify their own violent acts in the service of revolution.[16] As early as 1901 the SRs began to plan terrorist attacks, and they claimed their first major victim, Minister of the Interior Dmitry Sipyagin, in April 1902.

The reason terrorist methods would prove a thorn in the side for the SR Party had a great deal to do with the secretive manner in which they chose to carry them out. Two decades earlier The People's Will had conducted their terrorist battle against the autocracy by going entirely underground. As we have seen, all members of The People's Will lived disguised and concealed lives in order to operate from their underground base. The SRs, however, sought to be perceived as a mass party attractive to a large part of the public. Going entirely underground was not an option. Like Herzen and Lavrov, Chernov and the other SR leaders operated mostly from abroad, relying on rank and file organizers inside the Empire who did not risk excessive punishment for agitation and propaganda. Those engaged in terrorism, on the other hand, required absolute secrecy. In order to keep both functions in operation the SRs established the Combat Organization, responsible for political violence, with Gershuni at the helm. They offered this underground party all the funding and resources they needed, tacitly allowing them to conduct their affairs in nearly complete independence from the party. This structure seemed at first to provide a workable solution to the problem of underground terror carried out by a mass political party.

From its earliest origins the SR Party had differences of opinion about the use of terrorist methods. When the original two parties united in 1901 to form the first SR Party, one understood itself more as a successor to The People's Will, expecting to use terrorism as its primary weapon while the other envisioned itself more as a party engaged in agitation among the masses. Once the Combat Organization was already in full swing, and drawing a great deal of notoriety to the SRs, another faction sought to emulate it through the use of "agrarian terror," or violence directed toward people and property in the countryside, but the Central Committee squashed this idea as counterproductive to peasant interests. In 1906 the Maximalists pushed for the expansion of terrorism as part of their attempt to radicalize the party. But they had to split from the party in order to put their plans into action and soon wound up decimated by arrests. The party leadership long held to the middle path that afforded the Combat Organization a free hand to act as it saw fit. Even though the party's own dictates said the Central Committee would have full control over all decisions, in practice the party leadership ceded control to the underground and never managed to get it back. The SR Party was well funded, in part because they received generous help from abroad, and much of that funding went straight into the coffers of the Combat Organization. That wealth and autonomy did in fact boost the effectiveness of the terrorist apparatus, although not always in ways which the Central Committee approved. The Combat Organization engaged in its own intricate plots and, living in isolation from the rest of the party, carried out its terrorist program almost entirely without consultation with party leaders. While the party hoped to explain to the press its rationale for violent attacks in terms that would do them credit with at least some of the public, the Combat Organization usually made decisions based on their own special concerns. They chose targets of convenience, for example, whose killing could not be easily justified, and they sought to grab headlines by killing influential officials the leadership had never singled out as politically viable victims.

One wonders why the Central Committee, which controlled funding, did not keep the Combat Organization on a shorter leash. There is no single answer to this question, but it is worth noting that Chernov himself was a strong advocate of terrorist activity. In his 1902 article "The Terrorist Element in Our Program" he justified political violence on the grounds that it used attacks on state officials to redress the violent actions they had perpetrated in the first place. He made many of the same arguments earlier advanced by The People's Will that terror can "disorganize" state power and force officials to think twice before they committed their own acts of violence. He also claimed terrorist acts had a powerful propaganda effect, rallying the masses to the revolutionary cause. It must have helped that the Combat Organization had spectacular success early on in killing several high-ranking and thoroughly despised government officials. What effect terrorist assassinations of government officials actually had in fanning the flames of revolutionary sentiment is debatable, but political violence certainly played a role in making the SR Party seem powerful and deadly serious. It helped them generate a great deal of attention in their competition with the SDs. Finally, it was evident that intellectuals like Chernov still cherished the image of terrorist fighters as dynamic, heroic martyrs, sacrificing themselves for the greater good. The Combat Organization was playing a role the party leaders could not play, yet no party member could escape the moral burden of the violence the party supported. To be a terrorist party, wrote Chernov, was to remember that you were a party actively committed to violence "every day, hourly, as a *memento mori* standing before every member."[17]

The autonomy and underground isolation of the Combat Organization, along with the celebration of its members as freedom fighters, influenced its methods and its self-conception. As the isolated "warriors" risking their lives for the greater good, they had a tendency to look down on the "mere civilians" in the rest of the party. The Combat Organization became a kind of cult unto itself, regarding its own activities as exclusively important and the rest of the party as hangers-on to their celebrated deeds. The terrorist Ivan Kaliaev, who murdered Grand Duke Sergei Aleksandrovich, once said that "A Socialist-Revolutionist without a bomb is no longer a Socialist-Revolutionist."[18] Remarkably, the leaders of the Combat Organization showed little concern for ideology. Boris Savinkov, one of the main leaders of the terrorists, later wrote a memoir and two novels about his activities. All three of them reveal an almost total lack of interest in the political reasons for committing acts of violence. Instead, the terrorists he describes seem to act mainly out of a mercenary thirst for action. Like soldiers in battle, their only motivation in these texts seems to be comradery and self-sacrifice. Savinkov was never noted for any ideological commitments, and similarly the head of the entire Combat Organization, Evno Azef, was referred to as "the liberal with the bomb" because he openly showed disdain for the socialism that was the *raison d'être* of the SR Party. The Combat Organization, one might say, elevated the means above the ends. As despicable as their clandestine killing may appear in hindsight, in the context of a Russia in the midst of revolutionary upheaval, they generated not only admiration but imitation. They helped to inspire literally thousands of acts of terror, carried out mostly in the provinces by local terrorists hoping to share in the heroism and martyrdom of the revolution. But as Anna Geifman has shown, the exaltation of revolutionary political violence had a tendency to spin off into realms of pure criminality and sadism.[19]

The cost of the party's unbending support for the Combat Organization was finally paid in full when it was discovered in 1908, to the shock and chagrin of SR Party leaders, that Evno Azef had all along been in the service of the police as a double agent. He had assisted in organizing the killing of Interior Minister Von Plehve, who was his own higher up, but he had also done great damage to the party by exposing leaders like Gershuni to the police. Azef had long been accused of treachery, but the Central Committee resolutely defended him against these accusations until they learned of irrefutable proof that he was on the police payroll. When they were fully convinced and reported Azef's status to the rest of the party, the revelation proved a disaster. In spite of efforts to revive it, the Combat Organization ceased to have any meaningful existence, and even the party's continued existence was called into question. While the Central Committee managed to hold the party together, Azef's betrayal led to further factionalization. As it had with The People's Will, terrorism brought great notoriety to the Socialist Revolutionaries, but relying on it probably caused more trouble than it had ever been worth.

The SRs in a Time of Revolution

The Revolution of 1905 arose gradually and took few by surprise when it came to its culmination in October of that year, but the increasing fervor and the participation of nearly every sector of society were unprecedented in Russia. Amidst rising unrest, in part as a result of Russia's humiliating defeat in the Russo–Japanese War, an otherwise peaceful march of Saint Petersburg workers was fired on by government troops, killing around 150 and wounding hundreds more. This "Bloody Sunday" massacre signaled the start of months of protest that led to a massive general strike in October and finally forced Tsar Nicholas II to proclaim the October Manifesto. The manifesto granted civil liberties and elections to a democratic assembly. These concessions appeared to have transformed Russia into a constitutional monarchy. Nevertheless, Nicholas and his ministers continued to understand Russia as an autocratic state. Russia's political parties had to adjust their philosophies and tactics to fit the rapidly evolving series of events and the increasing politicization of the populace. By 1905, four broad revolutionary groups had come into being. Just as the spread of Marxism had been a logical response to Russian industrialization, the growth of capitalism had also brought into being a confident liberal party. Russian liberals had the support of the more conservative Mensheviks who were now, according to a strict reading of Marxism, welcoming a liberal democratic revolt. The Bolsheviks were characterized by their more strident support for the working class as well as their enmity toward the bourgeoisie and support of the peasants. In all these respects they were closer to the SRs than were the Mensheviks. All these parties and most of the population could agree on the immediate need for civil liberties, universal manhood suffrage, and a graduated income tax, although the radicals looked down on electoral politics as incapable of bringing economic justice to the working classes.

In the countryside the revolution was in many ways more far-reaching than it was at the national level of electoral politics. Across a much larger expanse of territory than in 1902, peasants took the revolutionary unrest emanating from the cities as a signal to commandeer landowners' property. Events in rural Russia during the Revolution of 1905 suggested once again to the SRs that the peasantry might constitute a revolutionary force. Emboldened by witnessing the revolutionary potential of their two main constituencies, the workers who had gone on strike and out into the streets, and the peasants who had seized property, the SR Party regarded 1905 as the beginning of the social revolution they hoped would take place. Between early 1905 and 1907 party membership expanded from around 3,000 to almost 60,000.

The SRs continued to boast of strong representation in urban factories, but they also used upheaval in the countryside to make deeper inroads among the peasantry. Peasant uprisings had broken out in virtually every corner of European Russia and beyond, and even though these were local and disjointed revolts, over the course of 1905–6 nearly 3,000 gentry manor houses were burned down. Members of the SR Party helped encourage various forms of peasant revolt, from the seizure of land to rural labor strikes and refusal to pay taxes and redemption payments. The All-Russian Peasant Union was formed in 1905 in an attempt to organize peasants into united regional groups and forge a national organization of peasants. Within a matter of months the Union had over 200,000 members and 359 separate village organizations. Some of these were closely connected to the SRs, who attended their meetings in an attempt to influence them. The overlap between the SR party program and peasant wishes was clearly evident in a statement made by one of the peasant delegates echoing Chernov's socialization: "Land is the mother of us all. It is not the product of human hands, but of the Holy Spirit. Therefore, it must not be bought and sold."[20] One of the peasant unions, in Sumy near Kharkov, managed in essence to take over local government for a time. In a tacit admission that rural Russia might not be as docile as they had hoped, in 1907 the state cancelled redemption payments outright.

In spite of the Peasant Union and the evolution of the peasantry toward a more conscious defense of their rights and demands, it was never going to be easy to mobilize the peasantry as a united revolutionary force. Peasant interests involved local questions, they tended to act spontaneously rather than in accordance with any outside plans, and they were spread out across such a vast extent that any meaningful unity of purpose remained virtually unattainable. The neo-populists had not outlived the problem that faced their populist predecessors: the peasantry was by far the largest population in Russia and therefore the most likely wellspring of revolutionary force, but how would it be possible to turn the dispersed peasants into a united body, acting for the benefit of Russia as a whole? The SRs pinned their hopes on the abolition of private property in land, and they continued to imagine "the" peasantry as a monolithic culture that would automatically act in concert with one another if they were properly motivated from outside.

Russia's prime minister from 1906, Petr Stolypin, took roughly the opposite approach from socialization in his famous "wager on the strong." Betting that the communal peasants deep down hoped to become smallholders of their own private farms, he instituted a land reform to encourage them to break away from the commune, becoming independent farmers. As such, he believed they would emerge as the foundation of a large Russian middle class. The plan offered loans and other incentives for easing the burdens associated with owning property, and it had some success. Between its implementation in 1906 through to 1917 it helped create a large number of privately owned peasant farmsteads independent of the village commune. It attracted some 2.5 million peasants before 1917. Although the majority of the peasantry did not opt for this approach, Stolypin's reforms lowered the proportion of communal peasants by about 10 percent. Stolypin's relative success disheartened many SRs. It was yet another sign that peasants could be lured away from the revolutionary and socialist impulses they hoped to find or instill in them.

In 1906 and 1907 two *Duma*s [parliaments] were convened which, in spite of the weighted electoral laws, attracted liberal and socialist majorities, and both parties sought first and foremost to address the issue of peasant land hunger. The autocracy used its authority to shut down the first and second left-leaning *Duma*s, so that neither lasted longer than three months of what was supposed to have been a four-year term. The autocracy then used the "failure" of the *Duma*s as an excuse to further restrict popular representation. That effort finally won them the sort of conservative *Duma* that would not conflict with the autocracy's aims. The victory of the Tsar and his ministers in the wake of 1905, Stolypin's land reform, splits from the party toward the left and the right, and then in 1908 the revelation that the leader of the Combat Organization was in the employ of the police, combined to form a dark period in the history of the SR Party. Some predicted the party would not last. At the grassroots level inside Russia, however, party organizers managed to continue their work, while Chernov and the Central Committee steered a middle course between defections of the more radical and more conservative wings. At the start of the First World War in 1914 a wave of arrests decimated party activity within Russia, and reactions to the war served to further divide party membership into those who supported Russian war efforts and those who considered Russian involvement yet another reason to overthrow the autocracy. As Russian war efforts foundered, however, party activism revived. By late 1916, activism was thriving in all revolutionary parties, and a spirit of working in concert prevailed across all the socialist parties. Bolsheviks, Mensheviks, and SRs worked together to organize strikers, marches, demonstrations, and planning meetings. The tipping point arrived in late February of 1917 when a march in Petrograd (Saint Petersburg) on International Women's Day shifted into a series of non-stop marches and rallies that escalated over the next several days until the entire city was in the hands of the revolutionaries. On March 1 Nicholas II abdicated the throne, and this time the Tsarist autocracy was gone for good.

It is not possible here to enter into the vast complexities of the Russian Revolution, constantly shifting over the next several months, and eventually witnessing the Bolshevik Party acquire power in October. But from the SR perspective it must be mentioned that an outcome of this kind was far from inevitable in February 1917. The most popular party in Russia in February, October, and beyond was the Socialist Revolutionary Party. While in late February the SRs and other socialist parties kept a low profile for fear of arrest, by early March they had come out into the light as some of the new leaders of Russian society. In May Chernov accepted a position in the Provisional Government as Minister of Agriculture, and in July the right-leaning SR Alexander Kerensky took the office of Prime Minister. In elections to the Constituent Assembly in October the SR Party gained more votes than any other, and Chernov was elected Chairman of the Assembly. Historians of the neo-populists have often noted how the Bolshevik victory consigned the SR Party to near oblivion by privileging the role of Lenin and the Bolsheviks as the inheritors of the Revolution. For our purposes the question we must pose is why the Socialist Revolutionaries failed to capitalize on their widespread popularity and wound up, as Trotsky famously put it, "in the ash heap of history."

The question is complex and remains controversial to the present day. Two essential views, not necessarily incompatible but entirely distinct in their level of sympathy for the SRs, form the poles between which historians have approached the SR collapse amid the Bolshevik assumption of power. On the one hand, the SRs have received recognition as a party that believed socialism and democracy had to go hand in hand. As a result of their trust in democratic principles and belief that the people as a collective whole should determine the direction and pace of the revolution they were defeated by a Bolshevik Party willing to take control in the name of "the dictatorship of the proletariat" and to govern without consideration for any opinion outside their own party line. This view emphasizes the humanitarian and democratic side of the Socialist Revolutionaries by contrast to the tyrannical rule of the Bolsheviks. The other side accepts the revolutionary *realpolitik* of Bolshevik tactics, suggesting that by contrast to the Bolsheviks the SRs were hapless players of revolutionary politics. In the words of Oliver Radkey, the SRs were inferior to the Bolsheviks "in point of unity and cohesion, discipline and organization, in leadership and in fighting spirit, in everything except mere numbers."[21] Both of these arguments hold weight and even complement one another. The reasons for the Socialist Revolutionary embrace of democratic politics and their inability to stand up to the Bolsheviks were not just of the moment. They had deep roots in their ideology, their sense of purpose as a party, and the special conditions in which the Russian Revolution took place.

To begin with, one needs to understand the source of SR popularity, which involved continued support from urban workers and the intelligentsia, but rested mainly on their identity as the party of the peasants, by far the largest voting bloc in the country. SR agitation in the countryside had dwindled between 1906 and 1917, so that by February 1917 the SRs had a more solid base among workers and soldiers than among the peasants. That pattern would quickly change, however, under the circumstances of 1917 when the neo-populists' original focus on the peasants, and lack of disdain for them as a class relative to both SD parties, made them an ideal match for the huge population of rural Russia which was all of a sudden in need of political leadership. During 1917 the SRs became "the muzhiks' party."[22] If the village commune had been undermined to a degree by the combination of capitalist practices and Stolypin's reforms, in 1917 its importance as a mechanism for the seizure of land came roaring back. This time landowners could no longer turn to the government for help, and throughout most of the countryside the peasantry confiscated gentry land in the name of their communes. In effect, they carried out an independent form of socialization before any law abolishing landed property could be enacted. The commune, it turned out, had remained a sufficiently important institution that it became a vehicle by which the peasants voted for political parties, *en masse* through a decision made by the entire communal assembly. Some of the land seizure was carried out violently, but much of it was peaceful, as members of the former gentry had no ability to defend themselves. A small percentage of local landlords actually remained in the countryside as small farmers with landholdings equivalent to those of the local peasants, even becoming members of the village commune. The former Stolypin landholders were often reincorporated into the communes in the same way. As this grassroots "socialization" and recommunalization of the villages unfolded, it became clearer to both the SR Party and the peasantry that they shared a common cause, and elections showed that the peasants identified with the SRs more than they did with any other political party. In this way in 1917 the peasantry became the mainspring of SR political strength, even as urban workers shifted toward the Bolsheviks.

But gaining greater electoral support than any other party in the country did not ensure the SRs greater political power under the special circumstances of the revolution. Once Nicholas had abdicated, two distinct centers of power arose to take the place of the autocracy. On the one hand, a Provisional Government was established by the *Duma*. It was a government that had appointed itself and did not yet enjoy the sanction of full and free elections. On the other hand, there immediately arose the councils (Soviets) of workers, peasants, and soldiers to look after the affairs of the lower classes. When united into national elective bodies, these Soviets stood as an alternate center of power. Most assumed this situation, known as "dual power," would be resolved by the election of a legitimate government later in the year, but in the meantime a dawning awareness of class interest and the spread of new ideologies as a result of genuine political freedoms was rapidly ushering in a process of polarization by social class and political opinion. Those relatively conservative revolutionaries—who supported the Provisional Government, the middle classes, and continued conduct of the war effort—grew more entrenched in their position while the more radical revolutionaries increasingly supported the demands of workers for economic improvement, including control of factories, the demands of the peasants for gentry land, and the demands of the soldiers to end the war. This polarization notoriously fed into the hands of the Bolsheviks. It also split apart the SR Party.

As we have seen, the SRs had been a contentious party from the beginning of their formation. Different SR newspapers had been published to propagate the views of each separate faction even before the war broke out. The First World War helped crystallize these differences by further splitting the party into defenders and detractors of the war. Once the revolution took place, the right SRs sided with the liberal Constitutional Democrat (Kadet) Party, while the left SRs tended to agree with the Bolsheviks and finally joined forces with them in November of 1917. Party leaders, among them Chernov, hewed to the center, which won them the contempt of both sides. Chernov and the old party leadership chose to maintain the illusion of unity but were paralyzed by the reality of the schism between the two radically different world views that had arisen among them. Hence they found it extremely difficult to act decisively as a revolutionary party ought to during a revolution. The attempt to maintain SR unity may well have been Chernov's biggest mistake since it was already quite clear by the middle of 1917 that the left and the right had little but mutual enmity in common.

Leading up to the Revolution, the SRs had been a big-tent party, able to accommodate a wide variety of views in their united struggle against autocracy. Once the autocracy was gone, those disparate views were left in naked face-to-face confrontation. The war had encouraged the party's right wing to openly express that covert nationalism which had always been an aspect of populism. Some right SRs argued that revolutionary Russia should retain sovereignty over breakaway parts of the Russian Empire, even over formerly autonomous countries like Poland. In a statement that could have been made by a conservative like Dostoevsky, the right SR V.V. Rudnev concluded that "The Great Russian Revolution has a great world task to perform, a transcending mission for all of humanity, in the name of which it has the right of revolutionary dictatorship—the right to violate the guarantees of peoples—and not only of those peoples associated by fate with Russia, but also of those elsewhere throughout the world."[23] The right SRs also played a role in sabotaging Chernov's attempt, after he became the Minister of Agriculture in the Provisional Government, to put his plan for socialization into place.

As for the left SRs, as early as April some of them had come to align themselves with the Bolsheviks and other left-leaning parties in their opposition to the war and in the need for a more dramatic and immediate shift toward socialist policies in both the city and the country. They grew disillusioned by what they saw as the SR party leadership's vacillation, and considered the right SRs, as Maria Spiridonova put it, to lack "any elements in common with socialism."[24] Their biggest objection was the centrist SRs' support for the war, which they considered an unnecessary and unconscionable sacrifice of the lives of soldiers. Over time they came to side with the Bolshevik conviction that all power should be placed in the hands of the Soviets and stripped away from the Provisional Government. At the center of the SRs, Chernov favored pursuing the war now that it had become a defense of the revolution rather than of the autocracy. He attempted to use his government role to introduce socialization, but when the attempt was thwarted the left SRs felt betrayed. When they finally allied with the Bolsheviks, it gave the Bolshevik government a useful cloak of legitimacy as if it were something more than just a one-party government. Chernov dreamed of establishing a mostly socialist government after elections to the Constituent Assembly had taken place, but the left SRs considered the right's acceptance of the war effort and continued capitalism to be a rejection of socialist principles.

> Russian democracy is now the mainstay of the international socialist movement, its main fortress and bastion ... If the revolution were to be routed, that would be an irreparable calamity for the whole International. If the Russian revolution were to fall now under the blows of German militarism, that would not only be the end of our freedom, but a death sentence on those internationalist currents in Germany who are close to us in spirit. And this obliges all the socialist parties in Russia, and the SR party in particular, to answer the basic question openly and directly: do we accept our obligation to defend our revolution and country not only against counterrevolutionary attempts from within, but also against enemy encroachments from without? And we are profoundly convinced that the SR party can only give one answer: yes, we do.
>
> Speech by right SR Abram Gots (1917), trans. Francis King,
> in *The Narodniks of the Russian Revolution*

> The people can sense the closeness of its long-awaited freedom—a real freedom, a social freedom, the triumph of emancipated labour. The people cannot accept that once again, as so often before in history, this freedom, bought with the people's blood in our great February uprising, is just a spectre, a momentary glimpse of sunlight ... The experience of coalition with the bourgeoisie in the "coalition" Provisional Government was, and indeed should have been, a hard test for the revolutionary democracy. For day after day, step after step, we saw the revolution being diverted from its straight path, the path of social freedom. We had embarked on this path after long years of heroic struggle on our own for the emancipation of labour, for land and freedom. Instead, the revolution has gone down the winding path of compromise politics. This path leads not to the vista of free social construction, but into the blind alley of a bourgeois republic, in which freedom will once again be a mere spectre, and labour, the highest, best and only human good, will bend as before under the yoke of capitalism.
>
> Left SR Proclamation (1917), trans. Francis King,
> in *The Narodniks of the Russian Revolution*

While centrist SRs like Chernov were labeled "Hamlets" for their caution and difficulty taking decisive action, the left SRs were accused of being "Don Quixotes" for acting on their unrealizable "utopian" fantasies. There is a degree of truth to both characterizations, but the names suggest there existed some viable approach under the circumstances, and that notion is probably wrong. Russian society had been cobbled together by a state that gained its power by pitting social classes against one another. The Russian socioeconomic and political structure, in other words, had been created under the tsars for the purposes of holding together their vast, multiethnic empire on the basis of a collection of disparate "castes" without any common interest. The notion that some form of unity would now emerge ignored the fact that workers, peasants, nobles, and middle-class professionals did not in fact share many common interests. Any benefit to one group came at the expense of another. That this social problem prevented any sort of easy political compromise would grow clearer and clearer over the course of 1917. The contest of the revolution under such circumstances was always liable to turn into a struggle of us against them. The Bolsheviks, especially Lenin, accepted the stark reality of this social antagonism and turned it to their advantage.

Chernov and the leadership of the SRs also made a fateful tactical error in May when he and five other SRs accepted positions within the Provisional Government. They joined with the sole SR serving on the government as Minister of Justice, the popular but rather more liberal than socialist Kerensky. The Provisional Government appeared the central player in May, but as revolutionary sentiment, mainly among Petrograd workers and soldiers, radicalized over the course of 1917, the Soviets came more and more to represent the true seat of power, and the Provisional Government looked increasingly like it "governed" at the whim of the Soviets. When Kerensky became prime minister it did not help Chernov's case. Instead of leading the SRs and fighting for their program, Kerensky considered himself above the fray: "Parties do not exist for me at present because I am a Russian minister; the people alone exists, and one sacred law—to obey the majority will."[25] It had been the intention of SR leaders like Chernov to enter into the Provisional Government in order to endow it with more socialist and less liberal policies, but this backfired on them. When as Agriculture Minister Chernov put forward a policy to suspend all transactions on land retroactive to the day of the Tsar's resignation, liberal ministers—who considered Chernov a socialist enemy nearly impossible to work with—refused to move forward by locking the bill in committee. Being affiliated with the government made the SRs appear timid in their support of the working people they existed to support. It gave ammunition to the Bolsheviks while further alienating them from the left of their own party. Chernov had misjudged the polarization of the country.

Amidst this atmosphere of strident polarization Chernov put his hopes in elections to the Constituent Assembly, calling for its convocation by early October. The SRs positioned themselves as the party of unity that would bring the left together around their common goals. They favored the slogan "no enemies on the left," a view in sharp contrast to the Bolsheviks and left SRs. The Bolsheviks and left SRs never joined the Provisional Government, consistently supported the transfer of power to the Soviets, and actively militated for peasant land seizures, worker autonomy, and immediate peace, all of which played to the satisfaction of the working classes in the country, the city, and the military. By the fall, Lenin and the Bolshevik Party felt emboldened to embark on a plan to transfer plenary power to the Soviets, leaving themselves at the helm. On October 25, without having to put up much of a fight, they swept in to take over the reins of government and run the state on the basis of their leadership of the urban Soviets.

For their part, Chernov and the centrist SRs refused to act before they had the sanction of the elected Constituent Assembly. In the November election the SRs had received double the votes of the Bolsheviks and ten times more than each of the other parties, although since the left SRs sided with the Bolsheviks they still did not have a clear majority. The Bolsheviks delayed convocation of the Assembly until January of 1918, by which point they had done everything in their power to discredit its legitimacy. On January 5, appointed as the Assembly's opening day, the former *Duma* hall at the Tauride Palace was surrounded by Bolshevik armed forces. The SRs, at least those at the center of the party, still believed in a government policy that expressed "the will of the people," and they believed the first freely elected government in Russian history would finally bring democratic socialism to fruition. Having waited for the Constituent Assembly to meet, assuming it would be able to function, and refusing to counter Bolshevik power in any other fashion speaks to the SRs' trust in the popular will, but it also speaks to their astonishing naivety. Supporters of the Constituent Assembly held a march in the morning before the Assembly met. Bolshevik forces stationed on rooftops fired on them and killed and injured several marchers. The Bolsheviks justified such tactics by positioning themselves not as representatives of the Russian people but of the Soviets and more particularly of the urban proletariat. Although at times the Bolshevik Party revealed internal dissension about just what it meant to represent a "dictatorship of the proletariat," in practice it meant they ruled Russia with an iron fist. The left SRs who joined the Bolshevik government lasted six months, at which point Russia would be governed for the next seventy years and more by a single party.

As we have seen, populist tradition, in contrast to Marxist doctrine, had long manifested a streak of grassroots anarchism, a sense that a socialist society would not need a strong state and would do best to work out difficulties at the local level. As the SRs would soon discover, and indeed as all of Russian history served to demonstrate, vesting power in local hands can leave small, isolated, and relatively weak groups open to predation by any power that does not scruple about democratic freedoms or local autonomy. The Bolshevik willingness to rule from the top in the name of a single class, whose members could serve as their cadres, gave them the edge in any fight against a loose democratic coalition. The Bolsheviks allowed the Constituent Assembly to exist for a single day. With Chernov as Chairman, they managed over one frantic night to promulgate decrees on land reform and an armistice with Germany. They also declared Russia a republic. All of this transpired in the midst of a scene that resembled the Reichstag in 1933 when Hitler used intimidation to force representatives to grant him the enabling act. Lenin filled the assembly hall with drunken, armed pro-Bolshevik forces, who heckled the speakers to the point that some of them could not be heard. They even pointed their rifles directly at the speakers. The Bolsheviks chose to shut down the

Assembly at four in the morning, and the next day they shuttered the assembly hall forever. In effect, it was at this moment that the Civil War began. After some futile efforts to condemn the Bolsheviks and retain their elective offices, the SRs were left either to join forces with the Bolsheviks, fight against them, or return abroad into the foreign exile where so many of them had already lived much of their lives trying to unseat the Romanov Dynasty.

The SRs made their last stand in the summer and autumn of 1918 in the provincial city of Samara, where, supported by a legion of Czech troops that had been stranded in Russia by the revolutionary upheaval, they sought to recreate the Constituent Assembly. In Samara they established a "government-in-exile." It was called the Komuch, an acronym for the Committee Members of the Constituent Assembly. There they lasted four months amid rancor from the local working population, which did not appreciate their tepid support for radical reform, much less the imposition of a draft to gain soldiers for their fight against the Bolshevik Red Army. With the help of the well-trained Czech troops, they did at first manage to gather supporters from the surrounding areas and gained a sizable territory in the Volga River region, but their own actions against peasants who refused to fight for their cause ultimately resembled the authoritarian practices of the former autocratic regime. In its first big success, the Red Army swept over the Komuch territory and had it under control by early October. The Komuch fled east to Ufa, but there they were disbanded by Admiral Kolchak, leader of one of the White Armies fielded by Russia's old guard. The center position of unity and compromise from which the SRs had hoped to govern Russia had long since burned away in the heat of furious battle between the far right and the far left.

CONCLUSION

In her memoir of the Stalinist party purges and terror of the late 1930s, Evgenia Ginzburg recalls sharing a prison cell with a woman named Nadezhda Derkovskaya. Derkovskaya, it turns out, was still a proud member of the Socialist Revolutionary Party. Another inmate referred to her as a "class enemy" since by this time even many of those Bolsheviks the party imprisoned had fully internalized the conviction that the Bolshevik (now simply Communist) view was the only legitimate one. We learn that Derkovskaya has been imprisoned many times, first under the tsarist regime and later by the Bolsheviks. After the debacle of the Komuch many SR leaders, including Chernov, managed to escape abroad. Others were arrested, and in 1922 they became the target of the Bolsheviks' first show trial. The defendants attempted to use the platform of the trial in the way their predecessors had in the trials of the 1870s by denouncing the abuses of the regime that had arrested them. All of the twelve defendants who stood trial had served on the SR Central Committee, and they were all sentenced to death. Later they had their sentences commuted, but all of them wound up retried at the time of Stalin's purges, and this time they were executed. By 1937 the SRs had long since ceased to be an active revolutionary party. According to Ginzburg, who spent a good deal of time with SRs in the Gulag, they remained a tight-knit group in prison, held together by a common identity forged over so many years in prison and exile. So entrenched did this sense of commonality remain for Derkovskaya that when, tormented by nicotine withdrawal, she was offered cigarettes by the Bolshevik Ginzburg, she refused to take them on the principle that Ginzburg had never "belonged to the opposition."[1] Almost ninety years after Herzen had begun to celebrate "Russian Socialism" some people were still clinging to that dream.

Readers of this book have soaked in large amounts of information about the shifting nature of Russian populism, but are we now any closer to understanding its essential character? Can we state clearly what it was overall? In the Introduction I warned that it is a complicated topic, difficult to define according to any neat set of characteristics, and we have now seen how populism evolved through numerous permutations over the seventy, and more, years it spanned. One helpful way to take stock of the nature of Russian populism is to proceed comparatively. In the United States, toward the end of the nineteenth century there arose an entirely separate movement that dubbed itself "populist." American populism, like Russian, was agrarian. Like Russian populism it too sought to lift up common rural folk to a higher status by addressing problems of social inequality. Populism in the United States was therefore considered to be on the left of the political spectrum just as Russian populism was. But the similarities end there. Most importantly, the American version of populism was a movement that emerged from within the rural community itself, among people who had electoral power and used that power to create a new political party to advance their interests in opposition to the existing parties. The populists in the United States sought economic improvement within a framework of representative democracy. They did not favor a new economic system to replace capitalism, preferring a modification of the capitalist system that would suit their interests. The Russian populists, as we have so often stressed here, hailed from educated society; they were members of an intelligentsia that stood apart from the people, the *narod*, whom they considered to be the proper inheritors of Russia's destiny.

The reason these two populisms so differed from one another is something I hope the careful reader of this book will now be able to understand. We have seen how the tsarist autocracy ruled over its enormous empire using the help of noble servitors, parceling out allotments of land in return for service and loyalty. The system worked to hold Russia together and gradually expand its borders at the expense of surrounding peoples who were then incorporated into the population of the Russian Empire. Gentry servitors were educated, fabulously wealthy relative to their serfs (or other agricultural laborers), and spent a good deal of time in Moscow and Saint Petersburg. They were supported by the laboring masses, most of them rural, whose work sustained Imperial Russia's economy. While this system received little criticism during the seventeenth and eighteenth centuries, Russia's identity as a part of Europe, coupled with historical changes unfolding in the West from around the end of the eighteenth century, ushered in a new recognition of Russia's difference from Europe and of its apparently retarded socioeconomic and political condition.

This dawning awareness led many educated Russians to search for an exit from the dilemma of their backwardness as well as a remedy to what Chaadaev had deemed their cultural and moral exclusion from European civilization. Populism slowly emerged from around the middle of the nineteenth century as the most common and favored intelligentsia strategy to surmount that sense of backwardness and exclusion. While the various populist alternatives we have examined in the foregoing chapters generated great enthusiasm from their adherents, the problem they faced was summed up well by Orlando Figes: "The question of the peasant may have been the question of the day. But every answer was a myth."[2] It would be possible to interpret Figes's use of the word "myth" to mean simply falsehood or fairy tale, but the statement becomes richer and more evocative of the populist outlook if we understand myth as a metaphorical narrative that effectively encapsulates a world view, a vision of human aspiration, or some kernel of knowledge gathered from collective human experience. Seen this way, a myth may be illusory, but that does not mean the illusion is not a productive one.

Chaadaev himself laid down one of the cornerstones of populist myth in answer to his originally despairing assessment of Russia. He envisioned the possibility that Russians might make use of the backwardness of their society and its exclusion form European history in order to learn the lessons of that history and use them to advance beyond the present state of European civilization. Such thinking captures the spirit and creativity of the Russian intelligentsia struggling to escape from the agonizing trap, or rather series of traps, in which they found themselves. Those traps included the understanding that they belonged within the European sphere, yet stood apart from it as a result of the long separation between the two distinct histories and civilizations of West and East. More importantly, the members of *obshchestvo* combined with the peasant majority comprised most of the Russian population. Yet the lives, experiences, and mentalities of *obshchestvo* and *narod* remained almost entirely distinct and irreconcilable, even after a small amount of merging began to take place toward the end of the nineteenth century. Although European nationalism had come to posit the nation-state and national identity as natural and necessary, how would it be possible to combine two separate communities into a single national unit? Finally, control over the direction of their native land and its social, economic, and political future was out of the hands of the intelligentsia and the Russian public. Instead that control lay in the hands of an imperial dynasty for which the above problems were less crucial than was maintenance of and control over their formidable empire. Tsarist empire building and the populist visions of a *narod*-centered national community were fundamentally at odds with one another. This incompatibility is certainly one reason for the tendency of the various populisms to go to extremes in an effort to achieve their aims.

Looking back across the different forms of populism we have encountered we will find that the "myths" invented by populist thinkers were based more on hope than on an accurate assessment of real conditions. Even so, such myths asserted ideals of beneficial change and a vision of a more just and equal society, suggesting that those goals were achievable and worth striving for. The Slavophiles and their insistence on the *sobornost'* of the peasant commune obviously exaggerated the harmony, cooperation, and mutual respect among the peasantry, but what they claimed to find in peasant culture also celebrated an optimistic image of a cohesive Russian society united in peace. Herzen's Russian socialism similarly mistook the peasantry as cooperative proto-socialists; he established an ecstatic vision of a Russian socialist future that would become an essential prototype for thousands of populist socialists over the next generations. Yet today we can see much more clearly that these dreams of a socialist peasantry, or for that matter Bakunin's dream of peasant revolutionaries, were in essence little more than a projection of intelligentsia desires. So cut off and different from the intelligentsia was the *narod* that it could easily serve as the blank screen to receive those projections. Perhaps no other area of Russian culture ultimately benefited so much from populist myth-making as the world of the arts, which did not suffer from any need to reify its creativity in real-world aims. Artists drew on both the agony and idealism inherent in the populist imagination to create literature, music, and visual art that is loved and admired to the present day. Even as late as the early twentieth century, when a degree of mutual intelligibility and common interest between *narod* and intelligentsia had begun to dawn, the neo-populists developed a new vision of revolutionary change that would serve the interests of the common people. The rhetoric of the neo-populists was sufficiently persuasive to unleash a new wave of terrorism and underpin a large revolutionary movement. Here again, however, the neo-populists were hampered by their customarily excessive idealization of the Russian people. Abiding populist assumptions about the independence and revolutionary spirit of the *narod* weakened the will of the populists to take action in their fight against the proactive, domineering, and (relatively) pragmatic Bolsheviks. No happy ending would greet the generations of populist schemes and visions we have encountered here.

To return to the difference between Russian and American populism, we might also make a useful comparison between the two countries' great populist poets of the nineteenth century. The two of them were contemporaries, and both are considered by many to have captured the spirit of their respective societies: Nikolai Nekrasov (1821–78) and Walt Whitman (1819–92). Both Nekrasov and Whitman at first were accused of introducing vulgarity into the high art of poetry, both understood their work as an evocation of the entire national experience, both hoped their poetry would speak to the masses, and both were in fact read almost exclusively by intellectual elites. As with the American and Russian populist movements, however, the differences between the two poets are more evident than the similarities. Whitman, who was born into a lower-middle-class family on Long Island and had to go to work to help the family at age eleven, was very much of the people himself. He reached out to the masses with his poetry as one of them in a voice that sought both to represent the American people and to embody them in his own thoughts and feelings. Nekrasov was a member of the gentry and the intelligentsia. He deeply sympathized with the common people, and felt guilt over his estrangement from the masses, but he could only observe them and describe them from without. When, in *Leaves of Grass*, Whitman writes of himself as "Walt Whitman, an American, one of the roughs, a kosmos, disorderly, fleshly, and sensual, no sentimentalist, no stander above men or women or apart from them" he seeks both to interest readers in his uniqueness and to convince them that he and they are one and the same. Nekrasov, it will be recalled, lamented the fact that he was unable to do more for the *narod*, but he congratulated himself in his outsider capacity for having been able to serve them by finding a voice to "sing your suffering."

The essence of the Russian populist dilemma is, I think, well expressed by this comparison. Whitman has been rightly criticized for purporting to represent all of America while omitting those racial others who had already been excluded, but Nekrasov could not even be accused of such an error since he could not claim to represent the *narod* in the first place. The quandary in which the populists found themselves was the result of existing at a time of historical disjuncture. As both Russians and Europeans, they lived in a world that had raced ahead of them. They well understood that the "feudal" socioeconomic system and the autocratic political system they had inherited were a thing of the past in the modern world, and increasingly so with each passing year. On the bright side, they were acutely conscious that the disjuncture needed to be repaired, and with understandable, even laudable, desperation they fixed on the quickest methods they could find to right the social inequality they saw around them. On the dark side, however, they were tempted not merely to overcome the inequalities in Russian society but to use that struggle to bring into being a Russia they imagined as superior to anything yet in existence. While some populists—the *zemstvo* "third element" or the legal populists— managed to rest satisfied with a gradual approach to bringing about the greater good, they were not typical. More typical among the populists was the struggle to bring to fruition a utopian future and to do so as quickly as possible. That fixity on the perfect over the merely good led, among other things, to a revolutionary mindset, a worship of martyrdom, a tendency toward magical thinking, and the invention of terrorism. And when the Russian Revolution finally did take place, it is probably not going too far to say that the Bolsheviks' own urgency, utopianism, and ruthlessness lay more in Lenin's populist inheritance than in his knowledge of Marxist theory.

GLOSSARY

artel', **pl.** *arteli* non-agricultural labor collective
barin gentleman, nobleman
bogatyri heroes
Duma parliament
glasnost' open public expression
intelligentsiia intelligentsia
kulak **pl.** *kulaki* wealthy peasant, literally "fist"
liudi people, persons
mir village, commune
miroed, **pl.** *miroedy* wealthy peasant, literally "commune eater"
Molokane Milk Drinkers, a group of rural sectarians
muzhik peasant, literally "small man"
Nakaz instruction (of Catherine the Great, for the governance of Russia)
narod the people, the folk, the peasantry of Russia
Narodnaia Partia Party of the People, the Popular, or Nationalist, Party
narodnichestvo populism
narodnik, **pl.** *narodniki* populist
narodnost' nationality
obshchestvo educated society, or polite society
pochvenniki men of the soil
poltorasta 150 years, the period (at the time) since Peter the Great's reign, which the Slavophiles
    considered to have set Russia on the wrong, Europeanizing, path, separating the elites from the
    peoples
pomeshchik landowner
populizm the term for populism in present-day common usage
pravda truth, justice
prostoi simple, as in *prostoi narod,* simple people
prostonarod'e simple people
publika the public
Rus' the original Russian state
skhodka originally a peasant communal assembly, later a gathering of students to discuss the
    issues of the day
sobornost' a Slavophile term for unity within the spiritual, Orthodox, community
sochineniia compositions, essays
Trudoviki Laborites, the Labor Party
veche the old popular assembly / democratic assembly
Vpered! Forward!
zapiski notes
Zemsky Sobor Russian version of an assembly of the estates that had operated during the pre-
    Petrine era, occasionally
zemstvo a rural assembly established to manage local affairs and improve local conditions, one of
    the reforms of the 1860s

NOTES

Chapter 1: Introduction: Toward a Definition of Russian Populism

1. Cited in Boris Savinkov, *Vospominaniia terrorista* (Benson, VT: Chalidze Publications, 1986), 315.

2. Oliver Radkey, *The Agrarian Foes of Bolshevism* (New York: Columbia University Press, 1958), 3.

3. It was suggested by a perspicacious anonymous reader of this text that I acknowledge the difference between the political radicals who called themselves *Narodniki* and those others who have only been defined as "populist" by outsiders and scholars by using a capital "P" for the former and a lowercase "p" for the latter. This solution at first struck me as an excellent way to clarify the distinction, but unfortunately it did not hold up in practice. Too many socialist radicals from the era of classical populism did not refer to themselves by the name, but were closely associated with those who accepted it, while some more liberal populists, who are less at the heart of the populist story, adopted the designation for themselves. Thus I continue to employ the lowercase term throughout the text at the expense of some possible confusion.

4. On the general definition of populism see Margaret Canovan, *Populism* (Boston, MA: Houghton-Mifflin, 1981) and more recently Cas Mudde and Cristóbal Rovira Kaltwasser, *Populism: A Very Short Introduction* (New York: Oxford University Press, 2017).

5. Aleksandr Blok, "The People and the Intelligentsia," trans. Gertrude Vakar in Marc Raeff, *Russian Intellectual History: An Anthology* (Atlantic Highlands, NJ: Humanities Press, 1983), 359–60.

6. It would be misleading and unfair not to take note here that there were members of the intelligentsia who expressed their concern for the people in ways that were based more in practical activity than in idealization and dreams. On these figures, working mostly within the government, see S. Frederick Starr, *Decentralization and Self-Government in Russia, 1830–1907* (Princeton, NJ: Princeton University Press, 1972) and Susan Smith-Peter, *Imagining Russian Regions: Subnational Identity and Civil Society in Nineteenth-Century Russia* (Boston, MA: Brill, 2017). From a different angle, Richard Stites's *Serfdom, Society, and the Arts in Imperial Russia* (New Haven, CT: Yale University Press, 2005) explores the high culture of provincial Russia prior to the emancipation.

7. See N.A. Berdiaev, "*Idei i zhizn': vlast i psikologiia intelligentsia,*" *Russkaia Mysl'* 1918, I–II, 103.

8. Cited in Linda Ivanits, *Dostoevsky and the Russian People* (Cambridge: Cambridge University Press, 2008), 33.

9. Those who have written about populism as agrarian revolutionary socialism are far too numerous to mention. Two of the most influential have been Franco Venturi, *Roots of Revolution: A History of the Populist and Socialist Movements in Nineteenth Century Russia*, trans. Francis Haskell (New York: Alfred A. Knopf, 1964) and Andrzej Walicki, *The Controversy over Capitalism: Studies in the Social Philosophy of the Russian Populists* (Oxford: Clarendon Press, 1964). Ironically, the Marxist definition of populism was fully accepted by Venturi, the great champion of the populist revolutionaries and a stout opponent of Soviet Marxist interpretations. Partly as a result of his profound influence, the identification of populism with pre-Marxist socialism was normalized outside the Soviet Union.

10. For two studies in this vein see, James Billington, *The Icon and the Axe: An Interpretive History of Russian Culture* (New York: Vintage Books, 1970) and Orlando Figes, *Natasha's Dance: A Cultural History of Russia* (New York: Metropolitan Books, 2002).

11. G.P. Fedotov, "The Religious Sources of Russian Populism," *The Russian Review* 1, no. 2 (1942), 27. Fedotov also makes the following point:

> Narodnichestvo colored many sections of Russian political life. The Marxists and Westernizers remained outside this trend, but there were Narodniks among the liberals of the Kadet party as well as among the ultra-reactionary "Union of the Russian People" … Least of all is one prepared to meet Narodniks among the Russian bureaucracy, and yet there was a whole department of the government, the Ministry of Agriculture, which was infected with populist tendencies.

12. A good exponent of this view is Alexander Etkind, "Whirling with the Other: Russian Populism and Religious Sects," *The Russian Review* 62, no. 4 (2003): 565–88.

13. Ibid., 579.

14. Richard Pipes, "*Narodnichestvo*: A Semantic Inquiry," *Slavic Review* 23, no. 3 (1964), 442.

15. Nicolas Berdyaev, *The Russian Idea* (Boston, MA: Beacon Press, 1947).

16. Ibid., 101.

17. Hans Rogger, *National Consciousness in Eighteenth-Century Russia* (Cambridge, MA: Harvard University Press, 1960), 172–3.

18. Steven G. Marks, *How Russia Shaped the Modern World: From Art to Anti-Semitism, Ballet to Bolshevism* (Princeton, NJ: Princeton University Press, 2004).

19. Walicki, *Controversy*, 24.

Chapter 2: Origins

1. All quotations here are taken from Peter Yakovlevich Chaadayev, *Philosophical Letters and Apology of a Madman*, trans. Mary-Barbara Zeldin (Knoxville: University of Tennessee Press, 1969).

2. Nancy S. Kollmann, "Etiquette for Peter's Time: The Honorable Mirror for Youth," *Russian History / Histoire Russe* 35, nos. 1/2 (2008), 71. It should be noted that the guide was in part culled from Western European sources.

3. Quoted in Peter K. Christoff, *K.S. Aksakov: A Study in Ideas* (Princeton, NJ: Princeton University Press, 1982), 274.

4. Cited in James H. Billington, *The Icon and the Axe: An Interpretative History of Russian Culture* (New York: Vintage Books, 1970), 365.

5. Paul Dukes, ed. and trans., *Catherine the Great's Instruction (Nakaz) to the Legislative Commission, 1767* (Newtonville, MA: Oriental Research Partners, 1977), 77.

6. An alternate intriguing theory of what induced the nobles to rethink their conception of the peasantry involves the Pugachev Rebellion, a rebellion of the various elements among the lower classes in southern Russia (including Cossacks, Old Believers, indigenous non-Russians, and Russian peasants). The rebellion was premised on Pugachev's claim that he was the former Tsar Peter III (Catherine's murdered husband whom she had deposed); he had now reappeared in order to take back his rightful throne. The rebellion had temporary success and led to the killing of a few thousand landowners. The historian Marc Raeff has argued that this bloodshed

unleashed such fear among serf-owners that to console themselves they began to rethink the peasantry as docile and childlike. See Marc Raeff, "Pugachev's Revolt," in *Preconditions of Revolution in Early Modern Europe*, ed. Robert Forster and Jack P. Greene (Baltimore, MD: Johns Hopkins University Press, 1970), 161–202.

7. N.I. Novikov, *Izbrannye sochineniia* (Moscow: Khudozhestvennaia Literatura, 1951), 215–19.

8. On folk-collecting in this era see M.K. Azadovskii, *Istoriia russkoi fol'kloristiki, tom I* (Moskva: Gos. Uch. Ethno-Pedagog. Izdatel'stvo, 1958).

9. Malcolm Hamrick Brown, ed., *Nikolai Lvov and Ivan Prach: A Collection of Russian Folk Songs* (Ann Arbor, MI: UMI Research Press, 1987), 79.

10. Cited in David Cooper, "Narodnost' avant la Lettre? Andrei Turgenev, Aleksei Merzliakov, and the National Turn in Russian Criticism," *The Slavic and East European Journal* 52, no. 3 (2008), 356.

11. Alexander Radishchev, *A Journey from St. Petersburg to Moscow*, trans. Leo Wiener (Cambridge, MA: Harvard University Press, 1966), 143.

12. Nicolas Berdyaev, *The Russian Idea*, trans. R.M. French (Boston, MA: Beacon Press, 1947), 28.

13. See Dominic Lieven, *Russia Against Napoleon: The True Story of the Campaigns of War and Peace* (New York: Viking, 2010), 245.

14. Alexander M. Martin, *Romantics, Reformers, Reactionaries: Russian Conservative Thought and Politics in the Reign of Alexander I* (DeKalb, IL: Northern Illinois University Press, 1997), 135.

15. Sergei Nikolaevich Glinka, *Zapiski o Moskve* (Moscow: Zakharov, 2004), 256.

16. All citations found in P.I. Pestel, *Russkaia Provda* (Saint Petersburg: Kul'tura, 1906).

17. Cited in Nicholas Riasanovsky, *Nicholas I and Official Nationality in Russia 1825–1855* (Berkeley: University of California Press, 1961), 125.

18. Chaadaev, *Apology*, 163–78.

19. Ivan Kireevsky, "On the Nature of European Culture and Its Relationship to Russian Culture," in Aleksei Khomiakov and Ivan Kireevsky, *On Spiritual Unity: A Slavophile Reader*, trans. Boris Jakim and Robert Bird (Hudson, NY: Lindisfarne Books, 1998), 195.

20. Martin E. Malia, *Alexander Herzen and the Birth of Russian Socialism* (New York: Grosset and Dunlap, 1965), 296.

21. Ivan Kirievskii, "Otvet Khomiakovu," in I.V. Kireevskii, *Izbrannye stat'i* (Moscow: Sovremennik, 1984), 120–1.

22. Cited in David Saunders, *Russia in the Age of Reaction and Reform, 1801–1881* (Abingdon, UK: Routledge, 2014), 162.

23. Cited in Andrzej Walicki, *The Controversy over Capitalism: Studies in the Social Philosophy of the Russian Populists* (Oxford: Clarendon Press, 1969), 342.

24. Saunders, *Age of Reaction*, 162.

25. Kireevsky, "Nature of European Culture," 222.

26. Aleksei Khomiakov, "On Humboldt," trans. Valentine Snow, in Marc Raeff, ed., *Russian Intellectual History: An Anthology* (Atlantic Highlands, NJ: Humanities Press, 1983), 225.

27. Konstantin Aksakov in Konstantin Aksakov and Ivan Aksakov, *Izbrannye trudy* (Moscow: Rosspen, 2010), 229.

28. Ivan Aksakov in ibid., 629.

29. Kirievskii, *Izbrannye*, 122.

30. Cited in V. Bogucharskii, *Aktivnoe narodnichestvo semidesiatikh godov* (Moscow: Izdatel'stvo M.S. Sabashnykovykh, 1912), 9.

31. Cited in a speech by Yuri Samarin in Iu.F. Samarin, *Stat'i, vospominaniia, pis'ma* (Moscow: Terra, 1997), 143.

32. Cited in Nicholas Riasanovsky, *Russia and the West in the Teachings of the Slavophiles: A Study of Romantic Ideology* (Cambridge, MA: Harvard University Press, 1952), 120.

33. Cited in Christoff, *Aksakov*, 284.

34. Konstantin Aksakov in Aksakov and Aksakov, *Izbrannye trudy*, 368.

35. S.T. Aksakov, *Pis'ma S.T, K.S i I.S. Aksakovykh k I.S. Turgenevu* (Moscow: Universitet, 1894), 40.

36. Ibid., 36.

37. Cited in Edward Chmielewski, *Tribune of the Slavophiles: Konstantin Aksakov* (Gainesville: University of Florida Press, 1962), 69.

38. S.T. Aksakov, *Pis'ma*, 66.

39. K and I. Aksakov, *Izbrannye*, 324.

40. Quoted in Riasanovsky, *Russia and the West*, 135.

41. K and I. Aksakov, *Izbrannye*, 322–3.

42. Christoff, *Aksakov*, 133.

43. Ibid., 135.

44. K and I. Aksakov, *Izbrannye*, 119–20.

45. Christoff, *Aksakov*, 273.

46. K and I. Aksakov, *Izbrannye*, 282–3.

Chapter 3: Foundations

1. Geoffrey Hosking, *Russia: People and Empire, 1552–1917* (Cambridge, MA: Harvard University Press, 1997), 277.

2. Cited in Alexander Polunov, *Russia in the Nineteenth Century: Autocracy, Reform, and Social Change, 1814–1914*, ed. Thomas C. Owen and Larissa G. Zakharova (Armonk, NY: M.E. Sharpe, 2005), 68.

3. August von Haxthausen, *Studies on the Interior of Russia*, trans. Eleanore L.M. Schmidt, ed. S. Frederick Starr (Chicago: University of Chicago Press, 1972), 93.

4. Kathleen Parthé, ed. and trans., *A Herzen Reader* (Evanston, IL: Northwestern University Press, 2012), 124.

5. See Aleksandr Ivanovich Gertsen, *Sochineniia v dvukh tomakh, tom II* (Moscow: Mysl', 1986), 167; and Solomon M. Schwarz, "Populism and Early Russian Marxism on Ways of Economic Development of Russia (the 1880's and 1890's)," in *Continuity and Change in Russian and Soviet Thought*, ed. Ernest J. Simmons (Cambridge, MA: Harvard University Press, 1955), 43.

6. Cited in Aileen Kelly, *The Discovery of Chance: The Life and Thought of Alexander Herzen* (Cambridge, MA: Harvard University Press, 2016), 325.

7. Gertsen, *Sochineniia*, 163.

8. Cited in Martin E. Malia, *Alexander Herzen and the Birth of Russian Socialism* (New York: Grosset and Dunlap, 1965), 403.

9. Gertsen, *Sochineniia*, 229.

10. Parthé, *Herzen Reader*, 49.

11. See Georgi Plekhanov, *Selected Philosophical Works IV* (Moscow: Progress, 1974), 618.

12. Parthé, *Herzen Reader*, 21.

13. Cited in Plekhanov, *Selected I*, 130.

14. Anthony D. Smith, *Nationalism*, 2nd edn. (Cambridge: Polity Press, 2010), 30.

15. Gertsen, *Sochineniia*, 176.

16. Alexander Herzen, *From the Other Shore*, trans. Moura Budberg (Cleveland, OH: Meridean Books, 1956), 189.

17. Aleksandr Ivanovich Gertsen [Герцен Александр Иванович], "Крещеная собственность," предисловие ко второму изданию ["Baptized Property," preface to the second edition], 1856. Available online: http://gertsen.lit-info.ru/gertsen/public/kreschenaya-sobstvennost.htm (accessed May 27, 2021).

18. Plekhanov, *Selected I*, 130.

19. Herzen, *From the Other Shore*, 34.

20. A third, though highly inaccurate, definition would apply to states like China in which socialism refers to state control of government and capitalism is allowed to flourish. Such systems are more credibly thought of as "authoritarian."

21. Cited in V. Bogucharskii, *Aktivnoe narodnichestvo semidesiatikh godov* (Moscow: Izdatel'stvo M.S. Sabashnykovykh, 1912), 67.

22. Quoted in Franco Venturi, *Roots of Revolution: A History of the Populist and Socialist Movements in Nineteenth Century Russia*, trans. Francis Haskell (New York: Knopf, 1964), 48–9. Translated by the present author from the original French.

23. Mikhail Bakunin, *Statism and Anarchy*, trans. and ed. Marshall S. Schatz (Cambridge: Cambridge University Press, 1990), 216.

24. Ibid.

25. N.Ia. Aristov, *Afanasii Prokof'evich Shchapov (Zhizn' i sochineniia)* (Saint Petersburg: Tipografiia A.S. Suvorina, 1883), 36.

26. Ibid., 62.

27. Ibid., 43.

28. Ibid., 57.

29. Alexander Etkind, "Whirling with the Other: Russian Populism and Religious Sects," *The Russian Review* 62, no. 4 (2003), 575.

30. Cited in M. Gershenzon, "P.V. Kireevskii: biografia," in *Pesni sobranyia P.V. Kireevskim*, ed. V.F. Miller and M.N. Speranskii (Moscow: Obshchestvo Liubitelei Rossisskoi Slovestnosti, 1911), XXII.

31. S.A. Tokarev, *Istoriia russkoi etnografii* (Moscow, Nauka, 1966), 244.

32. Pavel Iakushkin, *Putevye pis'ma Novgorodskoi i Pskovskoi gubernii* (Saint Petersburg: Izdatel'stvo D.E. Kozhanchikova, 1860), 89.

33. Cited in Abbott Gleason, *Young Russia: The Genesis of Russian Radicalism in the 1860s* (Chicago: University of Chicago Press, 1980), 287.

34. Cited in V.G. Bazanov, *Sobranie narodnykh pesen P.V. Kireevskogo: zapisi P.I. Iakushkina* (Leningrad: Nauka, 1983), 35.

35. Cited in Plekhanov, *Selected I*, 135.

36. Bogucharskii, *Aktivnoe*, 30.

37. These and further quotes from the document taken from B. Bazilevskii, *Materialy dlia istorii revoliutsionnago dvizheniia v rossii v 60-x gg* (Paris: Société Nouvelle de Librairie, 1905), 2–15.

38. Ibid., 73–4.

Chapter 4: Populism in Theory

1. Donald MacKenzie Wallace, *Russia: Revised and Enlarged Edition* (London: Cassell, 1912), 120–1.

2. V.V. Bervi-Flerovskii, *Zapiski revoliutsionera-mechtatelia* (Moscow: Molodaia Gvardia, 1929), 13–14.

3. Stepniak [Sergei Kravchinsky], *The Russian Peasantry: Their Agrarian Condition, Social Life and Religion* (London: George Routledge, 1905), 240–3.

4. Petr Lavrov, *Vpered!* 1 (1873), III.

5. Andrzej Walicki, *The Controversy over Capitalism: Studies in the Social Philosophy of the Russian Populists* (Oxford: Clarendon Press, 1969), 27.

6. Cited in Vladimir Burtsev, *Za sto let: sbornik po istorii politicheskihk i obshchestvennykh dvizhenii v Rossii* (London: Russian Free Press Fund, 1897), 131.

7. Bervi-Flerovskii, *Zapiski*, 122.

8. Petr Lavrov, *Historical Letters*, trans. and ed. James P. Scanlan (Berkeley: University of California Press, 1967), 135.

9. Ibid., 137, original emphasis.

10. Ibid., 155.

11. N.S. Rusanov cited in B.S. Itenberg, *Dvizhenie revoliutsionnogo narodnichestva* (Moscow: Izdatel'stvo "Nauka," 1965), 83.

12. O.V. Aptekman, *Obshchestvo "Zemlia i Volia" 70-x gg* (Petrograd, 1924), 122.

13. Cited in Philip Pomper, *Peter Lavrov and the Russian Revolutionary Movement* (Chicago: University of Chicago Press, 1972), 148, original emphasis.

14. Cited in V. Bogucharskii, *Aktivnoe narodnichestvo semidesiatikh godov* (Moscow: Izdatel'stvo M.S. Sabashnykovykh, 1912), 111.

15. Ibid.

16. Mikhail Bakunin, *Statism and Anarchy*, trans. and ed. Marshall S. Schatz (Cambridge: Cambridge University Press, 1990), 203.

17. Ibid., 198.

18. Lavrov, *Vpered!* 1 (1873), 12–13.

19. Cited in Georgi Plekhanov, *Selected Philosophical Works* (Moscow: Progress, 1974), 125.

20. N.K. Karataev, ed. *Narodnicheskaia ekonomicheskaia literatura: izbrannye proizvedeniia* (Moscow: Izdatel'stvo Sotisal'no-ekonomicheskoi Literatury, 1958), 373.

21. Nikolai K. Mikhailovskii, *Sochineniia, tom III* (Saint Petersburg: Russkoe Bogatstvo, 1896), 775.

22. Karataev, *Narodnicheskaia ekonomicheskaia*, 463–4.

23. Isaiah Berlin, *Russian Thinkers*, ed. Henry Hardy and Aileen Kelly (London: Penguin Books, 1978), 213.

24. Richard Wortman, *The Crisis of Russian Populism* (Cambridge: Cambridge University Press, 1967), 137.

25. Cited by Plekhanov in *Selected I*, 151.

26. Cited in Daniel Field, *Rebels in the Name of the Tsar* (Boston, MA: Unwin Hyman, 1989), 164.

27. Karataev, *Narodnicheskaia ekonomichesskaia*, 338.

28. Petr Lavrov, *Narodniki-propagandisty, 1873–78 godov* (Saint Petersburg: Andersona i Loitsianskago, 1907), 112.

29. Cited in Cathy A. Frierson, *Peasant Icons: Representations of Rural People in Late Nineteenth-Century Russia* (Oxford: Oxford University Press, 1993), 112.

30. V.V. Vorontsov, *Nashi napravleniia* (Saint Petersburg: Tipografiia M. Stasiulevicha, 1893), 142–3.

31. Mikhailovskii, *Sochineniia, tom III*, 772.

32. Cited in James Billington, *Mikhailovsky and Russian Populism* (Oxford: Clarendon Press, 1958), 391.

33. Lavrov, "*Schety russkogo naroda*," *Vpered!* 1 (1873), 59.

34. Cited in Billington, *Mikhailovsky*, 90.

35. Karataev, *Narodnicheskaia ekonomicheskaia*, 322.

36. Ibid., 319.

37. Nicolas Berdyaev, *The Russian Idea*, trans. R.M. French (Boston, MA: Beacon Press, 1947), 102.

38. Mikhailovskii, *Sochineniia, tom III*, 776.

39. Cited in Wortman, *Crisis*, 19.

40. Cited in Walicki, *Controversy over Capitalism*, 67–8.

41. Cited in Martin Miller, "Ideological Conflicts in Russian Populism: The Revolutionary Manifestoes of the Chaikovsky Circle," *Slavic Review* 29, no. 1 (1970), 16.

42. Ibid., 17.

43. I.I. Iuzov [Kablits], *Osnovy narodnichestva* (Saint Petersburg: Tipografiia N.A. Lebedeva, 1888), 2.

44. Cited in Hans Kohn ed., *The Mind of Modern Russia: Historical and Political Thought of Russia's Great Age* (New York: Harper, 1955), 17.

45. Nikolai Morozov, *Povesti moei zhizni* (Moscow: Akademiia Nauk, 1947), 91.

46. Lavrov, *Vpered!* 1 (1873), 8. Italics in the original.

47. Ibid., 20.

48. Bervi-Flerovskii, *Zapiski*, 131.

49. Plekhanov, *Selected IV*, 375.

50. N.K. Mikhailovskii, *Chto takoe progress?* (Petrograd: Izdatel'stvo "Kolos," 1922), 215.

51. Karataev, *Narodnicheskaiai ekonomicheskaia*, 319.

52. Lavrov, *Vpered!* 1 (1873), 10. Italics in the original.

53. Mikhailovskii, *Sochineniia, tom III*, 791.

54. Ibid., 828.

Notes

55. Cited in Billington, *Mikhailovsky*, 174.

56. Plekhanov, *Selected I*, 49.

57. Pomper, *Lavrov*, 79.

58. Itenberg, *Dvizhenie*, 97.

59. Cited in Derek Offord, "The Contribution of V.V. Bervi-Flerovsky to Russian Populism," *The Slavonic and East European Review* 66, no. 2 (1988), 244.

Chapter 5: Populism in Action

1. Nikolai Shelgunov, *Vospominaniia* (Leningrad: Khudozhestvennaia Literatura, 1967), 133.

2. Cited in Iu.I. Gerasimova, "*Krizis pravite'stvennoi politiki v gody revoliutsionnoi situatsii i Aleksandr II*," in *Revoliutsionnaia situatsiia v Rossii 1859–1861 gg, tom 2*, ed. M.V. Nechkina (Moscow: Nauka, 1962), 103.

3. Cited in S.N. Valk (ed.), *Revoliutsionoe narodnichestvo 70-x godov XIX veka* (Moscow: Nauka, 1964), 167.

4. V.I. Neupokoev, "*Vazhneishii programmnyi document 'Zemli i voli' 60-kh XIX veka*," in *Revoliutsionnaia situatsiia v Rossii 1859–1861 gg, tom 2*, ed. M.V. Nechkina (Moscow: Nauka, 1962), 538.

5. Pavel Aksel'rod, *Perezhitoe i peredumannoe* (Berlin: Z.I. Grzhebina, 1923), 153.

6. Petr Lavrov, *Narodniki-propagandisty, 1873–78 godov* (Saint Petersburg: Andersona i Lotsianskago, 1907), 196.

7. Lavrov, *Vpered!* 1 (1873), 15–16.

8. V.K. Debagorii-Mokrievich, *Ot buntarstva k terrorizmu* (Moscow: Molodaia Gvardia, 1930), 38.

9. Nikolai Charushin, *O dalekom proshlom* (Moscow: Mysl', 1973), 214.

10. Cited in Vladimir Burtsev, *Za sto let: sbornik po istorii politicheskihk i obshchestvennykh dvizhenii v Rossii* (London: Russian Free Press Fund, 1897), 166.

11. Vera Figner, *Zapechatlennyi trud: vospominanniia* (Moscow: Mysl', 1964), 153.

12. Georgi Plekhanov, *Sochineniia, tom I* (Moscow: Gosudarstvennoe Izdatel'stvo, 1923), 128.

13. Cited in Cathy A. Frierson, *Peasant Icons: Representations of Rural People in Late Nineteenth-Century Russia* (Oxford: Oxford University Press, 1993), 44.

14. Figner, *Zapechatlennyi*, 153.

15. Lev Tikhomirov, *Zagovorshchiki i politsiia* (Moscow: 1930), 34.

16. Debagorii-Mokrievich, *Ot buntarstva*, 126.

17. Nikolai Mikhailovskii, *Otechestvennye zapiski* 10 (October, 1876), 235.

18. Paul N. Miliukov, Charles Seignobos, and L. Eisenmann, *History of Russia, Volume 3: Reforms, Reaction, Revolution*, trans. Charles Lam Markmann (New York: Funk and Wagnalls, 1969), 66.

19. Vera Zasulich, *Vospominaniia* (Moscow: Izdatel'stvo V secoiuznoe Obshchestvo Politikatorzhan, 1931), 87.

20. Lev Tikhomirov, *Vospominaniia* (Moscow: Gosudarstvennoe Izdatel'stvo, 1927), 133–4.

21. Figner, *Zapechatlennyi*, 181–2.

22. Cited in Nikolai Morozov, *Povesti moei zhizni* (Moscow: Akademiia Nauk, 1962), 362–3.

23. Cited in Richard Wortman, *The Crisis of Russian Populism* (Cambridge: Cambridge University Press, 1967), 25.

24. Cited in S.S. Volk, *Narodnaia Volia, 1879–1882* (Moscow: Nauka, 1966), 220.

25. Cited in Wortman, *Crisis*, 187.

26. V. Bazilevskii, *Gosudarstvennoe prestuplenie v Rossii v XIX veka* (Moscow, 1904), 186.

27. See S.S. Volk (ed.), *Revoliutionnoe narodnichestvo 70-kh godov XIX v* (Moscow: Nauka, 1965), 233.

Chapter 6: Populist Art

1. Vladimir Korolenko, *The History of My Contemporary*, trans. Neil Parsons (London: Oxford University Press, 1972), 218–19.

2. Cited in A. Lebedev, ed., *Peredvizhniki: al'bom* (Moscow: Izbrazitel'noe Iskusstvo, 1978), 25.

3. Frederic Jameson, *The Political Unconscious* (Ithaca, NY: Cornell University Press, 1982).

4. Nathaniel Knight, "Was the Intelligentsia Part of the Nation: Visions of Society in Post-Emancipation Russia," *Kritika: Explorations in Russian and Eurasian History* 7, no. 4 (2006), 749.

5. Geoffrey Hosking, *Russia: People and Empire, 1552–1917* (Cambridge, MA: Harvard University Press, 1997), 293.

6. Victor Terras, *A History of Russian Literature* (New Haven, CT: Yale University Press, 1991), 195.

7. Ivan Turgenev, *Sketches from a Hunter's Album*, trans. Richard Freeborn (New York: Penguin Classics, 1990), 27.

8. Nikolai Nekrasov, *Izbrannoe v dvukh tomakh, t. II* (Moscow: Gosudarstvennoe izdatel'stvo Khudozhetvennoi Literatury, 1962), 124.

9. Cited in B.S. Itenberg, *Dvizhenie revoliutsionnogo narodnichestva* (Moscow: Izdatel'stvo "Nauka," 1965), 114.

10. Cited in Sigmund S. Birkenmayer, *Nikolaj Nekrasov: His Life and Poetic Art* (The Hague: Mouton, 1968), 57.

11. Fyodor Dostoevsky, *A Writer's Diary*, 2 vols., trans. Kenneth Lantz (Evanston, IL: Northwestern University Press, 1994), 1255.

12. Cited in Rose Glickman, "An Alternative View of the Peasantry: The *Raznochintsy* Writers of the 1860s," *Slavic Review* 32, no. 4 (1973), 695.

13. Ibid., 699.

14. Linda Ivanits, *Dostoevsky and the Russian People* (Cambridge: Cambridge University Press, 2008).

15. Fyodor Dostoevsky, *Notes from a Dead House*, trans. Richard Pevear and Larissa Volokhonsky (New York: Vintage Books, 2015), 254.

16. Ibid., original emphasis.

17. Ibid., 153.

18. Ivanits, *Dostoevsky*, 33.

19. Dostoevsky, *Diary*, 168.

20. Cited in Sarah Hudspith, *Dostoevsky and the Idea of Russianness: A New Perspective on Unity and Brotherhood* (London: Routledge Curzon, 2004), 74.

21. Dostoevsky, *Diary*, 1291.

22. Charles A. Moser, *Esthetics as Nightmare: Russian Literary Theory, 1855–1870* (Princeton, NJ: Princeton University Press, 1989), 55.

23. Dostoevsky, *Diary*, 349.

24. Ibid.

25. Marc Raeff (ed.), *Russian Intellectual History: An Anthology* (Atlantic Highlands, NJ: Humanities Press, 1983), 310.

26. Dostoevsky, *Diary*, 976.

27. Ibid., 438.

28. Fyodor Dostoevsky, *The Devils*, trans. David Magarshack (London: Penguin Books, 1971), 256.

29. Olga Maiorova, *From the Shadow of Empire: Defining the Russian Nation through Cultural Mythology, 1855–1870* (Madison: University of Wisconsin Press, 2010), 5.

30. Isaiah Berlin, *Russian Thinkers*, ed. Henry Hardy and Aileen Kelly (London: Penguin Books, 1978), 53.

31. Leo Tolstoy, *A Confession*, trans. Aylmer Maude (Mineola, NY: Dover Publications, 2005), 10.

32. Cited in George Rapall Noyes, *Tolstoy* (New York: Dover Publications, 1968), 87.

33. Cited in A.N. Wilson, *Tolstoy* (New York: Fawcett Columbine, 1988), 486.

34. Ibid.

35. Leo Tolstoy, *War and Peace*, trans. Rosemary Edmonds (London: Penguin Books, 1978), 1151.

36. Ibid., 1153.

37. Leo Tolstoy, *Anna Karenina*, trans. Louise and Aylmer Maude (Oxford: Oxford University Press, 1995), 276.

38. Ibid., 790.

39. Tolstoy, *Confession*, 52.

40. Ibid., 42–3.

41. Cited in Noyes, *Tolstoy*, 258.

42. Leo Tolstoy, "The Meaning of the Russian Revolution," in Raeff, *Intellectual History*, 337.

43. Cited in Gosudarstvennyĭ russkiĭ muzeĭ, Gosudarstvennaia Tret'iakovskaia galereia, and Smithsonian Institution Traveling Exhibition Service, *Russia: The Land, the People—Russian Painting, 1850–1910: From the Collections of the State Tretyakov Gallery, Moscow and the State Russian Museum, Leningrad* (Washington, DC: Smithsonian Institution, Traveling Exhibition Service, 1986), 46.

44. Cited in Elizabeth Kridl Valkenier, *Russian Realist Art: The State and Society* (New York: Columbia University Press, 1977), 87.

45. David Jackson, *The Wanderers and Critical Realism in Nineteenth-Century Russian Painting* (Manchester: Manchester University Press, 2006), 37.

46. Cited in World Heritage Foundation Encyclopedia Edition, Night on Bald Mountain: http://self.gutenberg.org/articles/eng/Night_on_Bald_Mountain.

47. Caryl Emerson and Robert William Oldani, *Modest Musorgsky and Boris Godunov: Myths, Realities, Reconsiderations* (Cambridge: Cambridge University Press, 1994), 185.

48. Mussorgsky's dedication on the title page of the vocal score. See Richard Taruskin, *Musorgsky: Eight Essays and an Epilogue* (Princeton, NJ: Princeton University Press, 1993), 194.

49. W. Bruce. Lincoln, *Between Heaven and Hell: The Story of A Thousand Years of Artistic Life in Russia* (New York: Viking, 1998), 208.

50. James Billington, *The Icon and the Axe: An Interpretive History of Russian Culture* (New York: Vintage Books, 1970), 407.

51. My own translation from *Boris Godunov in Four Acts and a Prelude*. http://opera.stanford.edu/iu/libretti/borisrus.html#act41.

52. Emerson and Oldani, *Musorgsky*, 135.

53. Cited in Lincoln, *Heaven and Hell*, 206.

54. Emerson and Oldani, *Musorgsky*, 11.

Chapter 7: Regrets and Revisions

1. Vladimir Korolenko, *The History of My Contemporary*, trans. Neil Parsons (London: Oxford University Press, 1972), 178.

2. Petr Lavrov, *Narodniki-propagandisty, 1873–78 godov* (Saint Petersburg: Andersona i Lotsianskago, 1907), 290, 293.

3. Aleksandr Blok, "The People and the Intelligentsia," trans. Gertrude Vakar, in *Russian Intellectual History: An Anthology*, ed. Marc Raeff (Atlantic Highlands, NJ: Humanities Press, 1983), 360.

4. Aleksandr Engelgardt, *Letters from the Country, 1872–1887*, trans. and ed. Cathy A. Frierson (New York: Oxford University Press, 1993), 85.

5. Cited in Richard Wortman, *The Crisis of Russian Populism* (Cambridge: Cambridge University Press, 1967), 48. Italics in original.

6. Ibid., 50.

7. Figner cited in Nikita Prutskov, *Gleb Uspensky* (New York: Twayne, 1972), 27.

8. Cited in Cathy A. Frierson, *Peasant Icons: Representations of Rural People in Late Nineteenth-Century Russia* (Oxford: Oxford University Press, 1993), 104.

9. Gleb Uspenskii, "From a Village Diary," trans. Sylvia Fain in Thomas Riha, *Readings in Russian Civilization Volume II: Imperial Russia, 1700–1917*, 2nd edn. (Chicago: University of Chicago Press, 1969), 361.

10. Stepniak [Sergei Kravchinsky], *The Russian Peasantry: Their Agrarian Condition, Social Life and Religion* (London: George Routledge, 1905), 243.

11. See Wortman, *Crisis*, 141.

12. Theodore Dan, *The Origins of Bolshevism*, trans. Joel Carmichael (New York: Schocken Books, 1964), 70.

13. Esther Kingston-Mann, "Statistics, Social Science, and Social Justice: The *Zemstvo* Statisticians of Pre-Revolutionary Russia," in *Russia in the European Context, 1789–1914: A Member of the Family*, ed. Susan McCaffray and Michael Melancon (New York: Palgrave Macmillan, 2005), 123.

14. See Norman Naimark, *Terrorists and Social Democrats: The Russian Revolutionary Movement Under Alexander III* (Cambridge, MA: Harvard University Press, 1983), 93.

Notes

15. Lev Tikhomirov, *Pochemu ia perestal byt' revoliutsionerom* (Moscow: Vil'de, 1895).

16. Cited in Abbott Gleason, "The Emigration and Apostasy of Lev Tikhomirov," *Slavic Review* 26 no. 3 (1967), 420.

17. Ibid., 425.

18. Cited in Kyril Tidmarsh, "Lev Tikhomirov and a Crisis in Russian Radicalism," *The Russian Review* 20, no. 1 (1961), 62.

19. Cited in Arthur P. Mendel, *Dilemmas of Progress in Tsarist Russia: Legal Populism and Legal Marxism* (Cambridge, MA: Harvard University Press, 1961), 79.

20. Wortman, *Crisis*, 160.

21. G.N. Mokshin, "*K voprosu o meste i roli Ia.V. Abramova v narodnicheskom dvizhenii 1880–1890 gg.*" *Obshchetvenno-politicheskaia mysl' XIX–nachala XX BB* 63 no. 3 (2018), 14.

22. Wortman, *Crisis*, x.

23. Ibid., 19.

24. Cited in James H. Billington, *Mikhailovsky and Russian Populism* (Oxford: Clarendon Press, 1958), 186.

25. Anna Geifman, *Thou Shalt Kill: Revolutionary Terrorism in Russia, 1894–1917* (Princeton, NJ: Princeton University Press, 1993), 33.

26. I take the phrase from Martin E. Malia, *Alexander Herzen and the Birth of Russian Socialism* (New York: Grosset and Dunlap, 1965), 290–1.

27. A.P. Chekhov, *Povesti i rasskazy* (Paris: Bookking International, 1995), 283–4.

28. Mary Louise Loe, "Redefining the Intellectual's Role: Gorky and the *Sreda* Circle," in *Between Tsar and People: Educated Society and the Quest for Public Identity in Late Imperial Russia*, ed. E.W. Clowes, S.D. Kassow, and J.L. West (Princeton, NJ: Princeton University Press, 1991), 293.

Chapter 8: Neo-Populism

1. M.C. Howard and J.E. King. *A History of Marxian Economics: Volume 1, 1883–1929* (Princeton, NJ: Princeton University Press, 1992), 165.

2. Oliver Radkey, "Chernov and Agrarian Socialism Before 1918," in Ernest Simmons, ed. *Continuity and Change in Russian and Soviet Thought* (Cambridge, MA: Harvard University Press, 1955), 66.

3. Cited in Alexander Trapeznik, "V.M. Chernov, Marxism and the Agrarian Question," *New Zealand Slavonic Journal* 1997, 60.

4. Ibid., 46.

5. Cited in Michael Melancon, "The Socialist Revolutionaries from 1902 to 1907: Peasant and Workers' Party," *Russian History / Histoire Russe* 12, no. 1 (1985), 6; original emphasis.

6. See Basil Dmytryshyn, ed. *Imperial Russia: A Source Book, 1700–1917* (Hinsdale, IL: Dryden Press, 1974), 401.

7. Maureen Perrie, *The Agrarian Policy of the Russian Socialist-Revolutionary Party from Its Origins Through the Revolution of 1905–1907* (Cambridge: Cambridge University Press, 1976), 57.

8. Oliver Radkey, *The Agrarian Foes of Bolshevism* (New York: Columbia University Press, 1958), 63–4.

9. Robert Tucker, ed., *The Marx-Engels Reader*, 2nd edn. (New York: W.W. Norton, 1978), 675.

10. Cited in Manfred Hildermeier, "Neopopulism and Modernization: The Debate on Theory and Tactics in the Socialist Revolutionary Party, 1905–1914," *The Russian Review* 34, no. 4 (1975), 460.

11. Cited in Perrie, *Agrarian Policy*, 109.

12. Cited in Oliver Radkey, "An Alternative to Bolshevism: The Program of Russian Social Revolutionism," *The Journal of Modern History* 25, no. 1 (1953), 27.

13. Ibid., 29.

14. Basil Dmytryshyn, ed. *Imperial Russia: A Source Book, 1700–1917* (Hinsdale, IL: Dryden Press, 1974), 401.

15. Hildermeier, "Neopopulism," 469.

16. Sally A. Boniece, "The Spiridonova Case, 1906: Terror, Myth, and Martyrdom," *Kritika: Explorations in Russian and Eurasian History* 4, no. 3 (2003): 571–606.

17. Cited in Alexander Trapeznik, "V.M. Chernov, Terrorism and the Azef Affair," *New Zealand Slavonic Journal* 2001, 108.

18. Boris Savinkov, *Vospominaniia terrorista* (Benson, VT: Chalidze, 1986), 39.

19. Anna Geifman, *Thou Shalt Kill: Revolutionary Terrorism in Russia, 1894–1917* (Princeton, NJ: Princeton University Press, 1993).

20. Cited in Scott J. Seregny, "A Different Type of Peasant Movement: The Peasant Unions in the Russian Revolution of 1905," *Slavic Review* 47, no. 1 (1988), 61.

21. Radkey, *Agrarian*, 473.

22. Sarah Badcock, " 'We're for the Muzhiks' Party!': Peasants Support for the Socialist Revolutionary Party During 1917," *Europe-Asia Studies* 53, no. 1 (2001): 133–49.

23. Radkey, "Alternative," 34–5.

24. Cited in Badcock, "Muzhiks," 14.

25. Cited in Rex Wade, *The Russian Revolution, 1917*, 2nd edn. (Cambridge: Cambridge University Press, 2005), 78.

Conclusion

1. Eugenia Semyonovna Ginzburg, *Journey into the Whirlwind*, trans. Paul Stevenson and Max Hayward (New York: Harcourt, 1995), 113.

2. Orlando Figes, *Natasha's Dance: A Cultural History of Russia* (New York: Metropolitan Books, 2002), 224.

SELECTED FURTHER READING

Full publication details are given in the bibliography.

Chapter 2: Origins

Peter Yakovlevich Chaadayev, *Philosophical Letters and Apology of a Madman* (1969)
Edward Chmielewski, *Tribune of the Slavophiles: Konstantin Aksakov* (1962)
Peter K. Christoff, *K.S. Aksakov: A Study in Ideas* (1982)
Ben Eklof and Stephen P. Frank, *The World of the Russian Peasant* (1990)
Abbott Gleason, *European and Muscovite: Ivan Kireevsky and the Origins of Slavophilism* (1972)
Boris Gorshkov, *Peasants in Russia from Serfdom to Stalin* (2018)
Michael Hughes, "Peter Kireevskii and the Development of Moscow Slavophilism" (2008)
Aleksei Khomiakov and Ivan Kireevsky, *On Spiritual Unity: A Slavophile Reader* (1998) [A
    collection of Slavophile essays focusing on theology and philosophy]
David Marshall Lang, *The First Russian Radical: Alexander Radishchev* (1959)
David Moon, *The Russian Peasantry, 1600–1930* (1999)
Susanna Rabow-Edling, *Slavophile Thought and the Politics of Cultural Nationalism* (2006)
Aleksandr Nikolaevich Radishchev, *A Journey from St. Petersburg to Moscow* (1966) [Includes
    annotations by Catherine the Great]
Hans Rogger, *National Consciousness in Eighteenth-Century Russia* (1960)
Andrzej Walicki, *The Slavophile Controversy* (1975)

Chapter 3: Foundations

Edward Acton, *Alexander Herzen and the Role of the Intellectual Revolutionary* (1979)
Mikhail Bakunin, *The Confession of Mikhail Bakunin* (1977) [Includes perlustration by Nicholas I]
Mikhail Bakunin, *Statism and Anarchy,* trans. Marshall Schatz (1990)
Nikolai Chernyshevsky, *What Is To Be Done?*, trans. Michael Katz (1989)
Alexander Etkind, "Whirling with the Other: Russian Populism and Religious Sects" (*Russian
    Review*, 2003)
Abbott Gleason, *Young Russia* (1980) [With detailed discussions of both Shchapov and
    Iakushkin]
August von Haxthausen, *Studies on the Interior of Russia*, trans. Eleanore Schmidt (1972)
Alexander Herzen, *My Past and Thoughts*, trans. Dwight Macdonald (1982)
Aileen Kelly, *The Discovery of Chance: The Life and Thought of Alexander Herzen* (2016)
Aileen Kelly, *Mikhail Bakunin: A Study in the Psychology and Politics of Utopianism* (1982)
Martin Malia, *Alexander Herzen and the Birth of Russian Socialism* (1965)
Irina Paperno, *Chernyshevsky and the Age of Realism* (1988)
Kathleen Parthé, trans and ed. *A Herzen Reader* (2012) [Herzen's journalism in the 1850s and
    1860s]

Selected Further Reading

Franco Venturi, *Roots of Revolution* (1964)
Andrzej Walicki *A History of Russian Thought* (1979)

Chapter 4: Populism in Theory

Isaiah Berlin, "Russian Populism," in *Russian Thinkers* (1978)
James Billington, *Mikhailovsky and Russian Populism* (1958)
Nathaniel Knight, "Was the Intelligentsia Part of the Nation?" (*Kritika*, Fall, 2006)
Peter Lavrov, *Historical Letters*, trans. and ed. James P. Scanlan (1967)
Martin Miller, "Ideological Conflicts in Russian Populism" (*Slavic Review*, 1970)
Richard Pipes, "*Narodnichestvo*: A Semantic Inquiry" (*Slavic Review*, 1964)
Philip Pomper, *Peter Lavrov and the Russian Revolutionary Movement* (1972)
Franco Venturi, *Roots of Revolution* (1964)
Andrzej Walicki, *The Controversy over Capitalism* (1969)
Andrzej Walicki *A History of Russian Thought* (1979) [Includes essays on Lavrov and Mikhailovsky]

Chapter 5: Populism in Action

Ben Eklof and Tatiana Saburova, *A Generation of Revolutionaries: Nikolai Charushin and Russian Populism from the Great Reforms to Perestroika* (2017)
Christopher Ely, *Underground Petersburg* (2016)
Laura Engelstein, "Revolution and the Theater of Public Life," in *Slavophile Empire* (2009)
Daniel Field "Peasants and Propagandists in the Russian Movement to the People of 1874" (*Journal of Modern History*, 1987)
Vera Figner, *Memoirs of a Revolutionist* (1991)
Deborah Hardy, *Land and Freedom: The Origins of Russian Terrorism* (1987)
Lynne Anne Hartnett, *The Defiant Life of Vera Figner* (2014)
Martin Miller, "Ideological Conflict in Russian Populism" (*Slavic Review*, 1970)
Ana Siljak, *Angel of Vengeance* (2008)
Sergei Stepniak-Kravchinsky, *Underground Russia* (1893)
Tom Trice, "Rites of Protest" (*Slavic Review*, 2001)
Franco Venturi, *The Roots of Revolution* (1960)
Claudia Verhoeven, *The Odd Man Karakozov* (2009)
Avrahm Yarmolinsky, *The Road to Revolution* (1957)

Chapter 6: Populist Art

Many of the literary works mentioned in this chapter have been translated into English more than once. The following list suggests some useful secondary sources and a few of the more obscure primary sources that have been translated into English.

Charlotte Alston, *Tolstoy and His Disciples* (2014)
Rosamund Bartlett, *Tolstoy: A Russian Life* (2011)
James Billington, *The Icon and the Axe* (1970) [A wide-ranging cultural history with sections on populist art]

Sigmund Birkenmayer, *Nikolaj Nekrasov: His Life and Art* (1968)

Molly Brunson, "Wandering Greeks: How Repin Discovers the People" (*Ab Imperio*, 2012)

Fyodor Dostoevsky, *A Writer's Diary (I and II)*, trans. Kenneth Lantz (1994)

Wayne Dowler, *Dostoevsky, Grigor'ev and Native Soil Conservatism* (1983)

Caryl Emerson and Robert William Oldani, *Modest Musorgsky and* Boris Godunov (1994)

Orlando Figes, *Natasha's Dance: A Cultural History of Russia* (2002) [A cultural history organized around the separation between *obshchestvo* and *narod*]

Joseph Frank, *Dostoevsky: A Writer in His Time* (2012) [An abridgment of Frank's five-volume biography]

Rose Glickman, "An Alternative View of the Peasantry: *Raznochintsy* Writers of the 1860s" (*Slavic Review*, 1973)

Linda Ivanits, *Dostoevsky and the Russian People* (2008)

David Jackson, *The Wanderers and Critical Realism in Nineteenth-Century Russian Art* (2006)

Marcus C. Levitt, *Russian Literary Politics and the Pushkin Celebration of 1880* (1989)

W. Bruce Lincoln, *Between Heaven and Hell: The Story of a Thousand Years of Artistic Life in Russia* (1998)

Richard Taruskin, *Musorgsky: Eight Essays and an Epilogue* (1992)

Leo Tolstoy, *A Confession*, trans. Aylmer Maude (2005)

Elizabeth Kridl Valkenier, *Russian Realist Art* (1977)

Andrei Zorin, *Leo Tolstoy* (2020)

Chapter 7: Regrets and Revisions

Samuel H. Baron, *Plekhanov: The Father of Russian Marxism* (1963)

Aleksandr Nikolaevich Engelgardt, *Letters from the Country*, trans. Cathy Frierson (1993)

Cathy Frierson, *Peasant Icons: Representations of Rural People in Late Nineteenth-Century Russia* (1993)

Abbott Gleason, "The Emigration and Apostasy of Lev Tikhomirov" (*Slavic Review*, 1967)

Esther Kingston-Mann, "Statistics, Social Science, and Social Justice: The Zemstvo Statisticians of Pre-Revolutionary Russia," in *Russia in the European Context* (2005)

Vladimir Korolenko, *The History of My Contemporary*, trans. Neil Parsons (1972)

Arthur Mendel, *Dilemmas of Progress in Tsarist Russia* (1961)

Norman Naimark, *Terrorists and Social Democrats* (1983)

Philip Pomper, *Lenin's Brother* (2009)

Hans Rogger, *Russia in the Age of Modernization and Revolution* (1983)

Karen Snow, "The Liberal Dimension of the People's Socialist Party" (*Revolutionary Russia*, 1994)

Andrzej Walicki, *The Controversy Over Capitalism* (1969)

Richard Wortman, *The Crisis of Russian Populism* (1967)

Chapter 8: Neo-Populism

Sarah Badcock, " 'We're for the Muzhiks' Party!': Peasant Support for the Socialist Revolutionary Party During 1917" (*Europe-Asia Studies*, 2001)

Anna Geifman, *Thou Shalt Kill: Revolutionary Terrorism in Russia, 1894–1917* (1993)

Manfred Hildermeier, "Neopopulism and Modernization" (*The Russian Review*, 1975)

Hannu Immonen, "Viktor Chernov in 1917: A Reappraisal" (*Revolutionary Russia*, 2017)

Francis King, *The Narodniks in the Russian Revolution* (2007) [A documentary sourcebook]

Selected Further Reading

Michael Melancon, "The Socialist Revolutionaries from 1902-1907: Peasant and Workers' Party"
   (*Russian History / Histoire Russe*, 1985)
Michael Melancon, *The Socialist Revolutionaries and the Russia Anti-War Movement, 1914–1917*
   (1990)
Maureen Perrie, *The Agrarian Policy of the Russian Socialist-Revolutionary Party* (1976)
Oliver Radkey, *The Agrarian Foes of Bolshevism* (1958)
Oliver Radkey, *The Sickle Under the Hammer* (1963)
Alexander Trapeznik, "V.M. Chernov, Marxism and the Agrarian Question" (*New Zealand
   Slavonic Journal*, 1997)
Donald Treadgold, *Lenin and His Rivals* (1955)

BIBLIOGRAPHY

Acton, Edward. *Alexander Herzen and the Role of the Intellectual Revolutionary*. Cambridge: Cambridge University Press, 1979.

Aksakov, Konstantin and Ivan. *Izbrannye trudy*. Moscow: Rosspen, 2010.

Aksakov, S.T. *Pis'ma S.T, K.S i I.S. Aksakovykh k I.S. Turgenevu*. Moscow: Universitet, 1894.

Aksel'rod, Pavel. *Perezhitoe i peredumannoe*. Berlin: Z.I. Grzhebina, 1923.

Alston, Charlotte. *Tolstoy and His Disciples: The History of a Radical International Movement*. London: Bloomsbury Business, 2014.

Annenkov, P.V. *The Extraordinary Decade*, translated by Irwin R. Titunik, edited by Arthur P. Mendel. Ann Arbor: University of Michigan Press, 1968.

Aptekman, O.V. *Obshchestvo "Zemlia i Volia" 70-x gg*. Petrograd, 1924.

Aristov, N. Ia. *Afanasii Prokof'evich Shchapov (zhizn' i sochineniia)*. Saint Petersburg: Tipografiia A.S. Suvorina, 1883.

Azadovskii, M.K. *Istoriia russkoi folkloristika tom I*. Moscow: Gos. Uch. Ethno-Pedagog. Izdatel'stvo, 1958.

Badcock, Sarah. "'We're for the Muzhiks' Party!': Peasant Support for the Socialist Revolutionary Party During 1917." *Europe-Asia Studies* 53, no. 1 (2001): 133–49.

Bakunin, Mikhail. *The Confession of Mikhail Bakunin*, translated by Robert C. Howes. Ithaca, NY: Cornell University Press, 1977.

Bakunin, Mikhail. *Statism and Anarchy*, translated and edited by Marshall S. Schatz. Cambridge: Cambridge University Press, 1990.

Baron, Samuel H. *Plekhanov: The Father of Russian Marxism*. Stanford, CA: Stanford University Press, 1963.

Bartlett, Rosamund. *Tolstoy: A Russian Life*. London: Profile Books, 2011.

Bazanov, V.G. *Sobranie narodnykh pesen P.V. Kireevskogo: zapisi P.I. Iakushkina*. Leningrad: Nauka, 1983.

Bazilevskii, V. *Gosudarstvennoe prestuplenie v Rossii v XIX veka*. Moscow, 1904.

Bazilevskii, V. *Materialy dlia istorii revoliutsionnago dvizheniia v Rossii v 60-x gg*. Paris: Société Nouvelle de Librairie, 1905.

Berdiaev, N.A. "*Idei i zhizn': vlast i psikologiia intelligentsia*," *Russkaia Mysl'* 1918, I–II.

Berdyaev, Nicolas. *The Origin of Russian Communism*, translated by R.M. French. Ann Arbor: University of Michigan Press, 1964.

Berdyaev, Nicolas. *The Russian Idea*, translated by R.M. French. Boston, MA: Beacon Press, 1947.

Berlin, Isaiah. *Russian Thinkers*, edited by Henry Hardy and Aileen Kelly. London: Penguin Books, 1978.

Bervi-Flerovskii, V.V. *Izbrannye ekonomicheskie proizvedeniia v dvukh tomakh*. Moscow: Izdatel'stvo Sotsial'no Ekon., 1958.

Bervi-Flerovskii, V.V. *Zapiski revoliutsionera-mechtatelia*. Moscow: Molodaia Gvardia, 1929.

Billington, James H. The Icon and the Axe: An Interpretive History of Russian Culture. New York: Vintage Books, 1970.

Billington, James H. *Mikhailovsky and Russian Populism*. Oxford: Clarendon Press, 1958.

Birkenmayer, Sigmund. *Nikolaj Nekrasov: His Life and Art*. The Hague: Mouton, 1968.

Bogucharskii, V. *Aktivnoe narodnichestvo semidesiatikh godov*. Moscow: Izdatel'stvo M.S. Sabashnykovykh, 1912.

Bibliography

Boniece, Sally A. "'Don Quixotes of the Revolution?': The Left SRs as a Mass Political Movement." *Kritika: Explorations in Russian and Eurasian History* 5, no. 1 (2004): 185–94.

Boniece, Sally A. "The Spiridonova Case, 1906: Terror, Myth, and Martyrdom." *Kritika: Explorations in Russian and Eurasian History* 4, no. 3 (2003): 571–606.

Brown, Malcolm Hamrick, ed. *Nikolai Lvov and Ivan Prach: A Collection of Russian Folk Songs.* Ann Arbor, MI: UMI Research Press, 1987.

Brunson, Molly. "Wandering Greeks: How Repin Discovers the People." *Ab Imperio* 2 (2012): 83–111.

Burtsev, Vladimir. *Za sto let: sbornik po istorii politicheskihk i obshchestvennykh dvizhenii v Rossii.* London: Russian Free Press Fund, 1897.

Canovan, Margaret. *Populism.* Boston, MA: Houghton-Mifflin, 1981.

Chaadayev, Peter Yakovlevich. *Philosophical Letters and Apology of a Madman*, translated by Mary-Barbara Zeldin. Knoxville: University of Tennessee Press, 1969.

Charushin, Nikolai. *O dalekom proshlom.* Moscow: Mysl', 1973.

Chekhov, A.P. *Povesti i rasskazy.* Paris: Bookking International, 1995.

Chernyshevskii, N.G. *Izbrannye stati'.* Moscow: Sovetskaia Rossia, 1978.

Chernyshevsky, Nikolai. *What Is To Be Done?*, translated by Michael Katz. Ithaca, NY: Cornell University Press, 1989.

Chmielewski, Edward. *Tribune of the Slavophiles: Konstantin Aksakov.* Gainesville: University of Florida Press, 1962.

Christoff, Peter K. *K.S. Aksakov: A Study in Ideas.* Princeton, NJ: Princeton University Press, 1982.

Confino, Michael, ed. *Daughter of a Revolutionary: Natalie Herzen and the Bakunin/Nechayev Circle*, translated by Hilary Sternberg and Lydia Bott. LaSalle, IL: Library Press, 1974.

Cooper, David L. "Narodnost' avant la Lettre? Andrei Turgenev, Aleksei Merzliakov, and the National Turn in Russian Criticism." *The Slavic and East European Journal* 52, no. 3 (2008): 351–69.

Cross, Tuman B. "Purposes of Revolution: Chernov and 1917." *The Russian Review* 26, no. 4 (1967): 351–60.

Dan, Theodore. *The Origins of Bolshevism*, translated and edited by Joel Carmichael. New York: Schocken Books, 1964.

Debagorii-Mokrievich, V.K. *Ot buntarstva k terrorizmu.* Moscow: Molodaia Gvardiia, 1930.

Dmytryshyn, Basil, ed. *Imperial Russia: A Source Book, 1700–1917.* Hinsdale, IL: Dryden Press, 1974.

Dostoevsky, Fyodor. *The Devils*, translated by David Magarshack. London: Penguin, 1971.

Dostoevsky, Fyodor. *Notes from a Dead House*, translated by Richard Pevear and Larissa Volokhonsky. New York: Vintage Books, 2015.

Dostoevsky, Fyodor. *A Writer's Diary*, two volumes, translated by Kenneth Lantz. Evanston, IL: Northwestern University Press, 1994.

Dowler, Wayne. *Dostoevsky, Grigor'ev, and Native Soil Conservatism.* Toronto: University of Toronto Press, 1983.

Druzhinin, S.M. "A. Gakhtgausen i russkie revoliutsionnye demokraty." *Istoriia SSSR* (1967): 69–80.

Dukes, Paul, ed. and trans. *Catherine the Great's Instruction (Nakaz) to the Legislative Commission, 1767.* Newtonville, MA: Oriental Research Partners, 1977.

Eklof, Ben, and Stephen P. Frank. *The World of the Russian Peasant: Post-Emancipation Culture and Society.* Boston, MA: Unwin Hyman, 1990.

Eklof, Ben, and Tatiana Saburova. *A Generation of Revolutionaries: Nikolai Charushin and Russian Populism from the Great Reforms to Perestroika.* Bloomington: Indiana University Press, 2017.

Ely, Christopher. *Underground Petersburg: Radical Populism, Urban Space, and the Tactics of Subversion in Reform-Era Russia.* DeKalb, IL: Northern Illinois University Press, 2016.

Emerson, Caryl, and Robert William Oldani. *Modest Musorgsky and* Boris Godunov: *Myths, Realities, Reconsiderations.* Cambridge: Cambridge University Press, 1994.

Engelgardt, Aleksandr Nikolaevich. *Letters from the Country, 1872–1887*, translated by Cathy A. Frierson. New York: Oxford University Press, 1993.

Engelstein, Laura. *Slavophile Empire: Imperial Russia's Illiberal Path.* Ithaca, NY: Cornell University Press, 2009.

Etkind, Alexander. "Whirling with the Other: Russian Populism and Religious Sects." *The Russian Review* 62, no. 4 (2003): 565–88.

Fanger, Donald. "The Peasant in Literature," in *The Peasant in Nineteenth-Century Russia*, edited by Wayne S. Vucinich, 230–62. Stanford, CA: Stanford University Press, 1968.

Fedotov, G.P. "The Religious Sources of Russian Populism." *The Russian Review* 1, no. 2 (1942): 27–39.

Field, Daniel. "Peasants and Propagandists in the Russian Movement to the People of 1874." *The Journal of Modern History* 59, no. 3 (1987): 415–38.

Field, Daniel. *Rebels in the Name of the Tsar.* Boston, MA: Unwin Hyman, 1989.

Figes, Orlando. *Natasha's Dance: A Cultural History of Russia.* New York: Metropolitan Books, 2002.

Figner, Vera. *Memoirs of a Revolutionist.* DeKalb, IL: Northern Illinois University Press, 1991.

Figner, Vera. *Zapechatlennyi trud: vospominanniia.* Moscow: Mysl', 1964.

Frank, Joseph. *Dostoevsky: A Writer in His Time.* Princeton, NJ: Princeton University Press, 2012.

Frierson, Cathy A. *Peasant Icons: Representations of Rural People in Late Nineteenth-Century Russia.* Oxford: Oxford University Press, 1993.

Geifman, Anna. "Aspects of Early Twentieth-Century Russian Terrorism: The Socialist-Revolutionary Combat Organization." *Terrorism and Political Violence* 4, no. 2 (1992): 23–46.

Geifman, Anna. *Thou Shalt Kill: Revolutionary Terrorism in Russia, 1894–1917.* Princeton, NJ: Princeton University Press, 1993.

Gerasimova, Iu.I. "*Krizis pravitel'stvennoi politiki v gody revoliutsionnoi situatsii i Aleksandr II.*" In *Revoliutsionnaia situatsiia v Rossii 1859–1861 gg.* Moscow: Nauka, 1962.

Gerschenkron, Alexander. "Franco Venturi on Russian Populism." *The American Historical Review* 78, no. 4 (1973): 969–86.

Gershenzon, M. "P.V. Kireevskii: biografiia." In *Pesni sobrannyia P.V. Kireevskom*, edited by V.F. Miller and M.N. Speranskii. Moscow: Obshchestvo Liubitelei Rossisskoi Slovestnosti, 1911.

Gertsen [Herzen], Aleksandr Ivanovich. *Sochineniia v dvukh tomakh, tom II.* Moscow: Mysl', 1986.

Gertsen [Herzen], Aleksandr Ivanovich [Герцен Александр Иванович]. "Крещеная собственность," предисловие ко второму изданию ["Baptised Property," preface to the second edition], 1856. Available online: http://gertsen.lit-info.ru/gertsen/public/kreschenaya-sobstvennost.htm (accessed May 27, 2021).

Ginzburg, Eugenia Semyonovna. *Journey into the Whirlwind*, translated by Paul Stevenson and Max Hayward. New York: Harcourt, 1995.

Gleason, Abbott. "The Emigration and Apostasy of Lev Tikhomirov." *Slavic Review* 26, no. 3 (1967): 414–29.

Gleason, Abbott. *European and Muscovite: Ivan Kireevsky and the Origins of Slavophilism.* Cambridge, MA: Harvard University Press, 1972.

Gleason, Abbott. *Young Russia: The Genesis of Russian Radicalism in the 1860s.* Chicago: University of Chicago Press, 1980.

Glickman, Rose. "An Alternative View of the Peasantry: The *Raznochintsy* Writers of the 1860s." *Slavic Review* 32, no. 4 (1973): 693–704.

Glinka, Sergei Nikolaevich. *Zapiski o Moskve.* Moscow: Zakharov, 2004.

Gorshkov, Boris B. *Peasants in Russia from Serfdom to Stalin: Accommodation, Survival, Resistance.* London: Bloomsbury Academic, 2018.

Bibliography

Gosudarstvennyĭ russkiĭ muzeĭ, Gosudarstvennaia Tret'iakovskaia galereia, and Smithsonian Institution Traveling Exhibition Service. *Russia: The Land, the People—Russian Painting, 1850–1910: From the Collections of the State Tretyakov Gallery, Moscow and the State Russian Museum, Leningrad.* Washington, DC: Smithsonian Institution, Traveling Exhibition Service, 1986.

Haimson, Leopold H. *The Russian Marxists and the Origins of Bolshevism.* Cambridge, MA: Harvard University Press, 1955.

Hardy, Deborah. *Land and Freedom: The Origins of Russian Terrorism.* London: Greenwood Press, 1987.

Hartnett, Lynne Ann. *The Defiant Life of Vera Figner: Surviving the Russian Revolution.* Bloomington: Indiana University Press, 2014.

Haxthausen, August von. *Studies on the Interior of Russia,* translated by Eleanore L.M. Schmidt, edited by S. Frederick Starr. Chicago: University of Chicago Press, 1972.

Herzen, Alexander. *From the Other Shore,* translated by Moura Budberg. Cleveland, OH: Meridean Books, 1956.

Herzen, Alexander. *Letters from France and Italy, 1847–1851,* edited and translated by Judith Zimmerman. Pittsburgh, PA: University of Pittsburgh Press, 1995.

Herzen, Alexander. *My Past and Thoughts: The Memoirs of Alexander Herzen,* translated by Dwight Macdonald. Berkeley: University of California Press, 1982.

Hildermeier, Manfred. "Neopopulism and Modernization: The Debate on Theory and Tactics in the Socialist Revolutionary Party, 1905–1914." *The Russian Review* 34, no. 4 (1975): 453–75.

Hildermeier, Manfred. "The Terrorist Strategies of the Socialist-Revolutionary Party in Russia, 1900–14." In *Social Protest, Violence and Terror in Nineteenth and Twentieth-Century Europe,* edited by Gerhard Hirschfeld and Wolfgang J. Mommsen, 80–7. New York: Springer, 1982.

Hosking, Geoffrey. *Russia: People and Empire, 1552–1917.* Cambridge, MA: Harvard University Press, 1997.

Howard, M.C., and J.E. King. *A History of Marxian Economics: Volume 1, 1883–1929.* Princeton, NJ: Princeton University Press, 1992.

Hudspith, Sarah. *Dostoevsky and the Idea of Russianness: A New Perspective on Unity and Brotherhood.* London: RoutledgeCurzon, 2004.

Hughes, Michael. "Peter Kireevskii and the Development of Moscow Slavophilism." *Slavonika* 14, no. 2 (2008): 89–107.

Iakushkin, Pavel. *Putevye pis'ma Novgorodskoi i Pskovskoi gubernii.* Saint Petersburg: Izdatel'stvo D.E. Kozhanchikogo, 1860.

Immonen, Hannu. "Viktor Chernov in 1917: A Reappraisal." *Revolutionary Russia* 30, no. 1 (2017): 55–77.

Itenberg, B.S. *Dvizhenie revoliutsionnogo narodnichestva.* Moscow: Izdatel'stvo "Nauka," 1965.

Iuzov [Kablits], I.I. *Osnovy narodnichestva.* Saint Petersburg, Tipografiia N.A. Lebedeva, 1888.

Ivanits, Linda. *Dostoevsky and the Russian People.* Cambridge: Cambridge University Press, 2008.

Jackson, David. *The Wanderers and Critical Realism in Nineteenth-Century Russian Art.* Manchester: Manchester University Press, 2006.

Jameson, Frederic. *The Political Unconscious.* Ithaca, NY: Cornell University Press, 1982.

Jansen, Marc. *A Show Trial Under Lenin: The Trial of the Socialist Revolutionaries, Moscow 1922,* translated by Jean Sanders. The Hague: Mouton, 1982.

Karataev, N.K. *Narodnicheskaia ekonomicheskaia literatura: izbrannye proizvedeniia.* Moscow: Izdatel'stvo Sotsial'no-ekonomicheskoi literatury, 1958.

Kelly, Aileen. *The Discovery of Chance: The Life and Thought of Alexander Herzen.* Cambridge, MA: Harvard University Press, 2016.

Kelly, Aileen. *Mikhail Bakunin: A Study in the Psychology and Politics of Utopianism.* Oxford: Oxford University Press, 1982.

Khomiakov, Aleksei, and Ivan Kireevsky. *On Spiritual Unity: A Slavophile Reader,* translated by Boris Jakim and Robert Bird. Hudson, NY: Lindisfarne Books, 1998.

King, Francis, ed. *The Narodniks in the Russian Revolution: Russia's Socialist-Revolutionaries in 1917*. London: Socialist History Society, 2007.

Kingston-Mann, Esther. "Statistics, Social Science, and Social Justice: The *Zemstvo* Statisticians of Pre-Revolutionary Russia." In *Russia in the European Context, 1789–1914: A Member of the Family*, edited by Susan McCaffray and Michael Melancon, 113–39. New York: Palgrave Macmillan, 2005.

Kirievskii, I.V. *Izbrannye stat'i*. Moscow: Sovremennik, 1984.

Knight, Nathaniel. "Ethnicity, Nationality and the Masses: *Narodnost'* and Modernity in Imperial Russia." In *Russian Modernity: Politics, Knowledge, Practices*, edited by D.L. Hoffman and Y. Kotsonis, 41–64. Basingstoke, UK: Macmillan, 2000.

Knight, Nathaniel. "Was the Intelligentsia Part of the Nation? Visions of Society in Post-Emancipation Russia." *Kritika: Explorations in Russian and Eurasian History* 7, no. 4 (2006): 733–58.

Kohn, Hans ed. *The Mind of Modern Russia: Historical and Political Thought of Russia's Great Age*. New York: Harper, 1955.

Kolchin, Peter. *Unfree Labor: American Slavery and Russian Serfdom*. Cambridge, MA: Harvard University Press, 1987.

Kollmann, Nancy S. "Etiquette for Peter's Time: The Honorable Mirror for Youth." *Russian History / Histoire Russe* 35, nos. 1/2 (2008): 63–83.

Korolenko, Vladimir. *The History of My Contemporary*, translated by Neil Parsons. London: Oxford University Press, 1972.

Lang, David Marshall, *The First Russian Radical: Alexander Radishchev, 1749–1802*. London: George Allen and Unwin, 1959.

Lavrin, Janko. "Populists and Slavophiles." *The Russian Review* 21, no. 4 (1962): 307–17.

Lavrov, Peter. *Historical Letters*, translated and edited by James P. Scanlan. Berkeley: University of California Press, 1967.

Lavrov, Petr. *Narodniki-propagandisty, 1873–78 godov*. Saint Petersburg: Andersona i Lotsianskago, 1907.

Lavrov, Petr. *Vpered!* 1 (1873).

Lebedev, A., ed. *Peredvizhniki: al'bom*. Moscow: Izbrazitel'noe Iskusstvo, 1978.

Levitt, Marcus C. *Russian Literary Politics and the Pushkin Celebration of 1880*. Ithaca, NY: Cornell University Press, 1989.

Lieven, Dominic. *Russia Against Napoleon: The True Story of the Campaigns of War and Peace*. New York: Viking, 2010.

Lincoln, W. Bruce. *Between Heaven and Hell: The Story of a Thousand Years of Artistic Life in Russia*. New York: Viking, 1998.

Loe, Mary Louise. "Redefining the Intellectual's Role: Maksim Gorky and the *Sreda* Circle." In *Between Tsar and People: Educated Society and the Quest for Public Identity in Late Imperial Russia*, edited by E.W. Clowes, S.D. Kassow, and J.L. West, 288–307. Princeton, NJ: Princeton University Press, 1991.

Maiorova, Olga. *From the Shadow of Empire: Defining the Russian Nation through Cultural Mythology, 1855–1870*. Madison: University of Wisconsin Press, 2010.

Malia, Martin E. *Alexander Herzen and the Birth of Russian Socialism*. New York: Grosset and Dunlap, 1965.

Marks, Steven G. *How Russia Shaped the Modern World: From Art to Anti-Semitism, Ballet to Bolshevism*. Princeton, NJ: Princeton University Press, 2004.

Martin, Alexander M. *Romantics, Reformers, Reactionaries: Russian Conservative Thought and Politics in the Reign of Alexander I*. DeKalb, IL: Northern Illinois University Press, 1997.

McKinsey, Pamela Sears. "From City Workers to Peasantry: The Beginning of the Russian Movement 'To the People.'" *Slavic Review* 38, no. 4 (1979): 629–49.

Bibliography

Melancon, Michael. "Marching Together! Left Bloc Activities in the Russian Revolutionary Movement, 1900 to February 1917." *Slavic Review* 49, no. 2 (1990): 239–52.

Melancon, Michael. "The Neopopulist Experience: Default Interpretations and New Approaches." *Kritika: Explorations in Russian and Eurasian History* 5, no. 1 (2004): 195–206.

Melancon, Michael. "The Socialist Revolutionaries from 1902 to 1907: Peasant and Workers' Party." *Russian History / Histoire Russe* 12, no. 1 (1985): 2–47.

Melancon, Michael. *The Socialist Revolutionaries and the Russian Anti-War Movement, 1914–1917.* Columbus: Ohio State University Press, 1990.

Mendel, Arthur P. *Dilemmas of Progress in Tsarist Russia: Legal Populism and Legal Marxism.* Cambridge, MA: Harvard University Press, 1961.

Mikhailovskii, N.K. *Chto takoe progress?* Petrograd: Izdatel'stvo "Kolos," 1922.

Mikhailovskii, N.K. *Sochineniia.* Saint Petersburg: Russkoe Bogatstvo, 1896.

Mikhailovskii, Nikolai *Otechestvennye zapiski* 10. October, 1876.

Miliukov, Paul N., Charles Seignobos, and L. Eisenmann, *History of Russia, Volume 3: Reforms, Reaction, Revolution,* trans. Charles Lam Markmann. New York: Funk and Wagnalls, 1969.

Miller, Martin. "Ideological Conflicts in Russian Populism: The Revolutionary Manifestoes of the Chaikovsky Circle, 1869–1874." *Slavic Review* 29, no. 1 (1970): 1–21.

Mokshin, G.N. "*K voprosu o meste i roli Ia.V. Abramova v narodnicheskom dvizhenii 1880–1890 gg.*" *Obshchetvenno-politicheskaia mysl' XIX–nachala XX BB* 63 no. 3 (2018): 9–17.

Moon, David. *The Russian Peasantry, 1600–1930: The World the Peasants Made.* London: Longman, 1999.

Morozov, Nikolai. *Povesti moei zhizni.* Moscow: Akademiia Nauk, 1962.

Moser, Charles A. *Esthetics as Nightmare: Russian Literary Theory, 1855–1870.* Princeton, NJ: Princeton University Press, 1989.

Mudde, Cas, and Cristóbal Rovira Kaltwasser. *Populism: A Very Short Introduction.* New York: Oxford University Press, 2017.

Naimark, Norman M. *Terrorists and Social Democrats: The Russian Revolutionary Movement Under Alexander III.* Cambridge, MA: Harvard University Press, 1983.

Nechkina, M.V., ed. *Revoliutsionnaia situatsiia v Rossii 1859–1861 gg, tom 2.* Moscow: Nauka, 1962.

Nekrasov, Nikolai. *Izbrannoe v dvukh tomakh.* Moscow: Gosudarstvennoe izdatel'stvo Khudozhetvennoi Literatury, 1962.

Norris, Stephen. *A War of Images: Russian Popular Prints, Wartime Culture, and National Identity.* DeKalb, IL: Northern Illinois University Press, 2006.

Novikov, N.I. *Izbrannye sochineniia.* Moscow: Khudizhestvennaia literature, 1951.

Noyes, George Rapall. *Tolstoy.* New York: Dover Publications, 1968.

Offord, Derek. "The Contribution of V.V. Bervi-Flerovsky to Russian Populism." *The Slavonic and East European Review* 66, no. 2 (1988): 236–51.

Offord, Derek. *Nineteenth-Century Russia: Opposition to Autocracy.* Harlow, UK: Pearson Education, 1999.

Ogden, J. Alexander. "The Woods of Childhood: Forest and Fairy Tale in Pavel Zasodimskii's Nature Writing." *The Russian Review* 64, no. 2 (2005): 281–98.

Paperno, Irina. *Chernyshevsky and the Age of Realism: A Study in the Semiotics of Behavior.* Stanford, CA: Stanford University Press, 1988.

Parthé, Kathleen, ed. and trans. *A Herzen Reader.* Evanston, IL: Northwestern University Press, 2012.

Perrie, Maureen. *The Agrarian Policy of the Russian Socialist-Revolutionary Party from Its Origins Through the Revolution of 1905–1907.* Cambridge: Cambridge University Press, 1976.

Perrie, Maureen. "The Russian Peasant Movement of 1905–1907: Its Social Composition and Revolutionary Significance." *Past and Present,* no. 57 (1972): 123–55.

Pestel, P.I. *Russkaia pravda.* Saint Petersburg: Kul'tura, 1906.

Pipes, Richard. "*Narodnichestvo*: A Semantic Inquiry." *Slavic Review* 23, no. 3 (1964): 441–58.

Pipes, Richard. "Russian Marxism and Its Populist Background: The Late Nineteenth Century." *The Russian Review* 19, no. 4 (1960): 316–37.

Plekhanov, Georgi. *Selected Philosophical Works*. Moscow: Progress, 1974.

Plekhanov, Georgi. *Sochineniia*. Moscow: Gosudarstvennoe Izdatel'stvo, 1923.

Polunov, Alexander. *Russia in the Nineteenth Century: Autocracy, Reform, and Social Change, 1814–1914*, edited by Thomas C. Owen and Larissa G. Zakharova. Armonk, NY: M.E. Sharpe, 2005.

Pomper, Philip. *Lenin's Brother: The Origins of the October Revolution*. New York: W.W. Norton, 2010.

Pomper, Philip. *Peter Lavrov and the Russian Revolutionary Movement*. Chicago: University of Chicago Press, 1972.

Pomper, Philip. *The Russian Revolutionary Intelligentsia*. Arlington Heights, IL: AHM, 1970.

Pozefsky, Peter C. *The Nihilist Imagination: Dmitrii Pisarev and the Cultural Origins of Russian Radicalism (1860–1868)*. New York: Peter Lang, 2003.

Prutskov, Nikita. *Gleb Uspensky*. New York: Twayne, 1972.

Rabow-Edling, Susanna. *Slavophile Thought and the Politics of Cultural Nationalism*. Albany: State University of New York Press, 2006.

Radishchev, Alexander. *A Journey from St. Petersburg to Moscow*, translated by Leo Wiener. Cambridge, MA: Harvard University Press, 1966.

Radkey, Oliver. *The Agrarian Foes of Bolshevism*. New York: Columbia University Press, 1958.

Radkey, Oliver. "An Alternative to Bolshevism: The Program of Russian Social Revolutionism." *The Journal of Modern History* 25, no. 1 (1953): 25–39.

Radkey, Oliver. "Chernov and Agrarian Socialism Before 1918." In *Continuity and Change in Russian and Soviet Thought*, edited by Ernest Simmons, 63–80. Cambridge, MA: Harvard University Press, 1955.

Radkey, Oliver. *The Sickle Under the Hammer: The Russian Socialist Revolutionaries in the Early Months of Soviet Rule*. New York: Columbia University Press, 1963.

Raeff, Marc. *Origins of the Russian Intelligentsia: The Eighteenth-Century Nobility*. New York: Harcourt, Brace and World, 1966.

Raeff, Marc. "Pugachev's Rebellion." In *Preconditions of Revolution in Early Modern Europe*, edited by Robert Forster and Jack P. Greene, 161–202. Baltimore, MD: Johns Hopkins University Press, 1970.

Raeff, Marc, ed. *Russian Intellectual History: An Anthology*. Atlantic Highlands, NJ: Humanities Press, 1983.

Repin, Ilya. *Dalekoe blizkoe*. Leningrad: Khudozhnik RSFSR, 1982.

Riasanovsky, Nicholas. *Nicholas I and Official Nationality in Russia, 1825–1855*. Berkeley: University of California Press, 1961.

Riasanovsky, Nicholas. *Russia and the West in the Teachings of the Slavophiles: A Study of Romantic Ideology*. Cambridge, MA: Harvard University Press, 1952.

Riha, Thomas. *Readings in Russian Civilization, Volume II: Imperial Russia, 1700–1917*. 2nd edn. Chicago: University of Chicago Press, 1969.

Rimsky-Korsakov, Nikolai. *My Musical Life*, translated by Judah Achilles Joffe, edited by Carl Van Vechten. London: Martin Secker, 1923.

Rogger, Hans. *National Consciousness in Eighteenth-Century Russia*. Cambridge, MA: Harvard University Press, 1960.

Rogger, Hans. *Russia in the Age of Modernization and Revolution, 1881–1917*. New York: Longman, 1983.

Samarin, Iu.F. *Stat'i, vospominaniia, pis'ma*. Moscow: Terra, 1997.

Saunders, David. *Russia in the Age of Reaction and Reform, 1801–1881*. Abingdon, UK: Routledge, 2014.

Bibliography

Savinkov, Boris. *Vospominaniia terrorista*. Benson, VT: Chalidze, 1986.

Scanlan, James P. "Populism as a Philosophical Movement in Nineteenth-Century Russia: The Thought of P.L. Lavrov and N.K. Mikhajlovskij." *Studies in Soviet Thought* 27, no. 3 (1984): 209–23.

Schwarz, Solomon M. "Populism and Early Russian Marxism on Ways of Economic Development of Russia (the 1880's and 1890's)," in *Continuity and Change in Russian and Soviet Thought*, edited by Ernest J. Simmons, 40–62. Cambridge, MA: Harvard University Press, 1955.

Seregny, Scott J. "A Different Type of Peasant Movement: The Peasant Unions in the Russian Revolution of 1905." *Slavic Review* 47, no. 1 (1988): 51–67.

Shchapov, Afanasy. *Sochineniia A.P. Shchapova v 3 tomakh*. Saint Petersburg: Izdanie M.V. Pirozhkova, 1906.

Shelgunov, Nikolai. *Vospominaniia*. Leningrad: Khudozhestvennaia Literatura, 1967.

Siljak, Anna. *Angel of Vengeance: The "Girl Assassin," the Governor of St. Petersburg, and Russia's Revolutionary World*. New York: St. Martin's Press, 2008.

Simmons, Ernest ed. *Continuity and Change in Russian and Soviet Thought*. Cambridge, MA: Harvard University Press, 1955.

Smith, Anthony D. *Nationalism*. 2nd edn. Cambridge: Polity Press, 2010.

Smith-Peter, Susan. *Imagining Russian Regions: Subnational Identity and Civil Society in Nineteenth-Century Russia*. Boston, MA: Brill, 2017.

Snow, Karen. "The Liberal Dimension of the People's Socialist Party (PSP): The Evolution of Legal Populism into Duma Politics (1890–1907)." *Revolutionary Russia* 7, no. 2 (1994): 192–213.

Starr, S. Frederik. *Decentralization and Self-Government in Russia, 1830–1870*. Princeton, NJ: Princeton University Press, 1972.

Stepniak [Sergei Kravchinsky]. *The Russian Peasantry: Their Agrarian Condition, Social Life and Religion*. London: George Routledge, 1905.

Stepniak-Kravchinsky, Sergei. *Underground Russia*. London: Publishing Fund of the Russian Free Press, 1893.

Stites, Richard. *Serfdom, Society, and the Arts in Imperial Russia*. New Haven, CT: Yale University Press, 2005.

Taruskin, Richard. *Musorgsky: Eight Essays and an Epilogue*. Princeton, NJ: Princeton University Press, 1993.

Terras, Victor. *A History of Russian Literature*. New Haven, CT: Yale University Press, 1991.

Tidmarsh, Kyril. "Lev Tikhomirov and a Crisis in Russian Radicalism." *The Russian Review* 20, no. 1 (1961): 45–63.

Tikhomirov, Lev. *Pochemu ia perestal byt' revoliutsionerom*. Moscow: Vil'de, 1895.

Tikhomirov, Lev. *Vopominaniia*. Moscow: Gosudarstvennoe Izdatel'stvo, 1927.

Tikhomirov, Lev. *Zagovorshchiki i politsiia*. Moscow, 1930.

Tokarev, S.A. *Istoriia russkoi etnografii*. Moscow: Nauka, 1966.

Tolstoy, Leo. *Anna Karenina*, translated by Louise and Aylmer Maude. Oxford: Oxford University Press, 1995.

Tolstoy, Leo. *A Confession*, translated by Aylmer Maude. Mineola, NY: Dover Publications, 2005.

Tolstoy, Leo. *War and Peace*, translated by Rosemary Edmonds. London: Penguin Books, 1978.

Trapeznik, Alexander. "V.M. Chernov, Marxism and the Agrarian Question." *New Zealand Slavonic Journal* 1997: 41–65.

Trapeznik, Alexander. "V.M. Chernov, Terrorism and the Azef Affair." *New Zealand Slavonic Journal* 2001: 101–11.

Treadgold, Donald. *Lenin and His Rivals: The Struggle for Russia's Future, 1898–1906*. New York: Routledge, 1955.

Trice, Tom. "Rites of Protest: Populist Funerals in Imperial St. Petersburg, 1876–1878." *Slavic Review* 60, no. 1 (2001): 50–74.

Tucker, Robert C., ed. *The Marx-Engels Reader*. 2nd edn. New York: W.W. Norton, 1978.

Turgenev, Ivan. *Sketches from a Hunter's Album*, translated by Richard Freeborn. New York: Penguin Classics, 1990.

Uspenskii, G.I. *Vlast zemli; Ne sluchis'; Starryi Burmistr*. Leningrad: Khudozhestvennaia Literatura, 1957.

Valk, S.N., ed. *Revoliutsionnoe narodnichestvo 70-kh godov XIX*. Moscow: Nauka, 1964.

Valkenier, Elizabeth Kridl. *Russian Realist Art: The State and Society*. New York: Columbia University Press, 1977.

Venturi, Franco. *Roots of Revolution: A History of the Populist and Socialist Movements in Nineteenth Century Russia*, translated by Francis Haskell. New York: Alfred A. Knopf, 1964.

Verhoeven, Claudia. *The Odd Man Karakozov: Imperial Russia, Modernity, and the Birth of Terrorism*. Ithaca, NY: Cornell University Press, 2009.

Vlasova, Z.I. *Sobranie narodnykh pesen P.V. Kireevskogo: zapisi P.I. Iakushkina*. Leningrad: Nauka, 1983.

Volk, S.S. *Narodnaia Volia, 1879–1882*. Moscow: Nauka, 1966.

Volk, S.S., ed. *Revoliutionnoe narodnichestvo 70-kh godov XIX v*. Moscow: Nauka, 1965.

Vorontsov, V.V. *Nashi napravleniia*. Saint Petersburg: Tipografiia M. Stasiulevicha, 1893.

Wade, Rex A. *The Russian Revolution, 1917*. 2nd edn. Cambridge: Cambridge University Press, 2005.

Walicki, Andrzej. *The Controversy over Capitalism: Studies in the Social Philosophy of the Russian Populists*. Oxford: Clarendon Press, 1969.

Walicki, Andrzej. *A History of Russian Thought from the Enlightenment to Marxism*. Stanford, CA: Stanford University Press, 1979.

Walicki, Andrzej. *The Slavophile Controversy: History of a Conservative Utopia in Nineteenth-Century Russian Thought*, translated by Hilda Andrews-Rusiecka. London: Oxford Clarendon Press, 1975.

Wallace, Donald Mackenzie. *Russia on the Eve of War and Revolution*. London: Cassell, 1912.

Wilson, A.N. *Tolstoy*. New York: Fawcett Columbine, 1988.

Wortman, Richard. *The Crisis of Russian Populism*. Cambridge: Cambridge University Press, 1967.

Yarmolinsky, Avrahm. *The Road to Revolution: A Century of Russian Radicalism*. Princeton, NJ: Princeton University Press, 1957.

Zasulich, Vera. *Vospominaniia*. Moscow: Izdatel'stvo Vsecoiuznoe Obshchestvo Politikatorzhan, 1931.

Zlatovratskii, Nikolai. *Izbrannye proizvedeniia*. Moscow, 1947.

Zlatovratskii, N.N. *Sochineniia N.N. Zlatovratskogo*. Moscow: I.N. Kushnereva, 1884.

Zlatovratskii, N.N. *Ustoi: istorii odnoi derevni*. Moscow: Biblioteka Russkogo Romana, 1951.

Zorin, Andrei. *Leo Tolstoy*. London: Reaktion Books, 2020.

INDEX

Index

Index